# THE FASHION DESIGN MANUAL

## Pamela Stecker

Diploma of Secondary Teaching, Fine Arts,
Certificate of Fashion Design,
Proprietor of The Company Label

## DEDICATION

To Eric, whose golf handicap improved while I was writing this book. To my

mother, Yvonne, who is an inspiration to me, and my father, Jack, whom I'm sure

knows I've written this book.

First published 1996 by
MACMILLAN EDUCATION AUSTRALIA PTY LTD
107 Moray Street, South Melbourne 3205
Reprinted 1997

Associated companies and representatives
throughout the world.

National Library of Australia
cataloguing in publication data

Stecker, Pamela.
    The fashion design manual.

    Includes index.
    ISBN 0 7329 0716 0.

    1. Fashion — Australia — Vocational guidance.
    2. Fashion — Australia. 3. Fashion designers — Australia.
    4. Costume design — Australia. 5. Costume design —
    Australia — Vocational guidance. I. Title.
745.92

Typeset in New Baskerville and Futura by
Typeset Gallery, Malaysia

Printed in Hong Kong

Designed by Dimitrios Frangoulis
Cover design by The Incredible Sons of Hawaii Five-O
Cover photographs by Juli Balla
Index by Kathleen Gray

# FOREWORD

Celebrating my thirtieth year in fashion has provided me with the opportunity to reflect on where fashion has been, where it is heading, and how Australia fits into the global fashion scene.

Starting out as a young Australian designer in the mid–1960s was very exciting. There was a great deal of creative energy, which coincided with the emergence of the youth culture, and the mood was ripe for experimentation as the traditional rules that governed the way young people should look and behave were broken down.

The economy was booming, jobs were plentiful and the post–war baby boomers spent a large portion of their income on the new fashions — much to my appreciation!

Fashion and society have changed dramatically since those times. The economy is less predictable, unemployment is higher and technology is changing the way we do things so rapidly that it is difficult to keep pace. Fashion also becomes more varied by the day. It draws on so many influences that numerous trends exist concurrently, and it often becomes confusing for the designer and consumer alike. And yet, I must say that for the designer and the dedicated wearer of fashion, times have never been better.

Technology constantly tempts us with the most wonderful new fabrics which encourage the manipulation of fit, form and comfort as never before. Telecommunications permit the relaying of fashion ideas around the world simultaneously. And computerisation relieves the designer of some of the more laborious aspects of garment production.

Very few industries enable a young designer to start with little except ideas, talent and ambition, and to build a successful business the way the fashion industry does (although today it is more difficult to succeed without some business training).

Very few creative fields permit the freedom of expression and individual personal style that fashion does. Or the opportunity to market skills internationally and to use them as a passport to worldwide travel. And few careers offer as much fun, and glamour, financial success and yes, risk, hard work and long hours, as fashion does!

For those whose enjoyment comes from wearing, exploring and playing with other people's designs and ideas, fashion has never before permitted so much flexibility and freedom to choose. Personal style is now much more important than slavishly following trends — how you wear it is what it's all about.

My own philosophy on quality and style is simplicity and versatility. I aspire to provide the basic framework on which my customer can build her own individual look. Therefore, one of the most gratifying things about being a designer is observing the personal statements that individuals make when they are wearing something I have designed. At that point the garment ceases to be my creation and becomes part of another individual, who is making a comment about her likes and dislikes and the way she wants to present to the world.

Understanding how fashion works, the trends and cycles, the history, the influences and influencers, and the components of colour and fabric, line and shape, can be very helpful in developing one's personal style.

Pamela Stecker's *The Fashion Design Manual* is the first book of its kind for the Australian fashion industry. It addresses the behind the scenes workings of the fashion world, and presents it from several viewpoints — that of the designer, the retailer and the consumer, and also brings Australian fashion into perspective with the international scene.

The depth of Pamela's personal experience and knowledge of the industry, combined with her extensive research and detailed illustrations and photographs, make this book an inspiring and informative read for all fashion enthusiasts.

Carla Zampatti

# CONTENTS

# INTRODUCTION

This book is a comprehensive guide to the creative process of fashion designing, written with particular reference to the Australian fashion industry.

For those who are planning a career in the fashion industry, or who want to fill a gap in their fashion knowledge, or for those who enjoy fashion as a hobby and are interested in how it all works, *The Fashion Design Manual* covers the many facets of fashion design. The more technical aspects of patternmaking, grading and garment construction are not included here because they are more than adequately discussed in existing publications.

*The Fashion Design Manual* is intended to be used as a resource book, and to be referred to frequently for ideas and inspiration. It provides a concise fashion design course in itself and is ideally suited as a text for all fashion courses. The focus is on womenswear, rather than menswear or childrenswear, because fashion for females is more complex and varied, and changes more dramatically and more directly in response to social and other influences. However, many of the concepts and information covered can be applied equally well to those other areas of fashion.

Information in this book is divided into three parts.

Part 1 explores the international world of fashion. The history of Western fashion is discussed in some depth because it is the historical source to which the Australian industry looks for direction, inspiration and guidance, and is the model upon which our industry is based.

Influential overseas designers, and the ways in which they have left their mark on our culture by changing our style of dress, are also covered in some depth.

The design process itself is dealt with — what it is and how a designer comes up with new ideas.

The tools of fashion design — the design elements and principles — and the ways in which they are used in clothing design are very important. So too is the equally important process of evaluation. A designer must not only be able to create, but needs to be able to analyse a design, to differentiate between good and bad design, and to recognise marketable garments.

Part 2 deals with the process of creating fashion designs. Instruction is given in fashion sketching, identifying and selecting the fabrics and trims which are the raw materials of fashion, and putting together garment components.

Garments are intended to fit the human form, so information is included on body types and fitting. From the creation of a single garment, the next step is to coordinate a range of garments. The designer should know what garments to include in a range, and how to coordinate them. This is discussed in detail.

For fashion retailers, the information on trends, design details, fitting and fabrics is valuable. Product knowledge is a great selling tool. Workroom operating procedures are outlined for designers who may want to set themselves up, or for retailers who would like to put their own ideas into production.

Part 3 concentrates on the opportunities which exist within the Australian Fashion Industry.

Firstly, an overview is given of Australia's influential designers, past and present, and the contribution each has made to our unique Australian style.

The fashion industry offers many and varied careers. The discussion of these careers, and suggestions on how to open doors into these fields, will help both the novice and the fashion worker wanting to make a career move.

In addition, there is a review of the fashion resources existing in Australia — fashion courses, organisations, awards and events and publications for both the student and the professional.

In conclusion, a word about the way this book is intended to be used. *The Fashion Design Manual* provides an overview of the extremely complex and creative process of designing fashion. Although some of the information may be stated as fact, rules about how to design fashion have been carefully avoided because there is no right or wrong. The information presented here is a guide as to what is generally accepted in our society as the design principles which apply to creations we consider to be beautiful. But the greatest designers have always been those who followed their own view of what constitutes beauty, and have created new trends by breaking traditionally accepted approaches to fashion.


Go for it.

# ACKNOWLEDGMENTS

My acknowledgements and thanks go to all of those people in the fashion industry who have expressed their enthusiasm for and interest in this project. Those individuals or companies who have provided information, photographs and documents used in the book have been acknowledged in the text, and I thank them for their valuable contributions.

To the literally hundreds of people who were obliging enough to take a phone call, answer a question or otherwise be of assistance, please excuse the omission of every individual name, and rest assured that your expertise has been invaluable.

There are also others I would like to thank for the assistance they willingly gave and which was most appreciated:

Sue McGuinn, Peter Debus, Jo Gill, Elizabeth Gibson, Dimitrios Frangoulis and Adrian Saunders of Macmillan for their patience and encouragement. Juli Balla for the cover photographs. Diana Slasor for photographs. For extra illustrations, Esmeralda Aponte, Lucy Greig and Gillian Diamond.

Also Harriet Ayre-Smith, Chanel (Australia), Nicole Bonython, Vianney Ovens, Diana Marsh, Annie Nichols, John Godley, Hanna Wegner, Julia Raath, Australian Buckles and Trims, Lincraft Fabrics, The Bead Company of Australia, The Australian Museum, Colvin Communications International Pty Ltd, David Jones (Australia) Pty Ltd, Designer Trim, Dita Feather Fashion Accessories, Grace Bros, Vivian Humphry Fashion Marketing, John Kaldor Fabricmaker Pty Ltd, and Oxford Art Supplies.

## TEN COMMANDMENTS FOR DESIGNERS

Thou shalt not imitate.

Thou shalt not cater.

Thou shalt not seek effectiveness for its own sake.

Thou shalt not employ expedients.

Thou shalt not exploit thyself nor suffer thyself to be exploited by others.

Thou shalt not concern thyself with the opinions of any but the sensitive and the informed.

Thou shalt not give to anyone the thing that he wants, unless for thyself the thing that he wants is right.

Thou shalt not compromise with popular taste nor with fashion nor with machinery nor with the desire of gain.

Thou shalt not be satisfied.

*Porter Garnett, 1871–1951.*

THE FASHION DESIGNER

# INTRODUCTION

This chapter explores the costume changes in western dress which have taken place from the earliest recorded times to the end of the 20th century.

As designers, a knowledge of where fashion has come from helps us to understand how it is progressing in our own time, and to anticipate where it may lead in the future.

Historical costumes provide a wealth of inspiration and ideas which can be adapted to our modern lifestyle. However, care should be taken not to use these too literally in case they look like actual costume rather than new trends inspired by the past.

The garments discussed in this chapter were mostly worn by the wealthy classes. Due to wealth and positions of influence, this class was generally the first to establish and spread new trends. Some trends did filter down to achieve mass acceptance, but they were usually simplified to suit the practical requirements of working people, and so did not reach the extremes of the more fashion-conscious.

# MESOPOTAMIA: 3500–330 BC

Costumes worn by the early civilizations of Mesopotamia — the Babylonians, Assyrians, Cretans and even the early Egyptians — were much alike. Most information about them comes from art and architecture — temples, tombs, sculpture, vases and coins.

The usual dress for both men and women was an ankle-length rectangle of woolly fur or fur-like fabric, wrapped and knotted around the waist. The torso was left bare, or covered with a rectangular mantle.

Despite their almost primitive style of dress, the Sumerians appear to have been very particular about their personal grooming, with emphasis on elaborate hairstyles. Wigs and false beards are known to have been worn (Fig. 1.2).

The Assyrians became the ruling empire around 880 BC and introduced a new style of garment. This was a woven ankle-length tunic with sleeves, worn with an embroidered and tasselled mantle, usually thrown over one shoulder, and a narrow fringed scarf. Fringing indicated rank, with higher officials wearing thicker and longer fringes, king's attendants wearing shorter fringes, and lesser officials wearing no fringing at all. Fabrics were usually richly decorated, often pleated and worn with sashes, neck ornaments and jewellery such as armlets, bracelets, large heavy earrings and rings. Fabrics included coarse wools, leather, fine cottons and silks. Brilliant purples, blues and whites were popular colours.

The most important development in clothing in Mesopotamia occurred when the Persians overran the Babylonians in the late 7th century BC Traditionally, the Persians wore garments cut from tanned hides which were sewn to fit the contours of the body, and were in fact the earliest form of tailoring (Fig. 1.3). When combined with the softer, woven fabrics used by the tribes they conquered, we see the first development of fitted clothing, especially trousers and jackets with set-in sleeves.

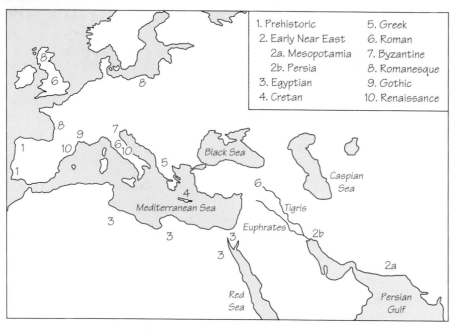

1. Prehistoric
2. Early Near East
   2a. Mesopotamia
   2b. Persia
3. Egyptian
4. Cretan
5. Greek
6. Roman
7. Byzantine
8. Romanesque
9. Gothic
10. Renaissance

*1.1 (top)  Location of pre-Renaissance cultures around the Mediterranean Sea.*

*1.2 (bottom left)  Sumerian dress as shown in early mosaics, circa 3000 BC.*

*1.3  Around 7th century BC, the Persians were wearing fitted trousers and jackets.*

# EGYPT: 4000–332 BC

Egyptian dress was extremely formalised and sophisticated, and changed very little over the millennia. It served an important role as a form of class distinction.

The basic garment for men was the *shenti*, a loincloth wrapped around the hips and fastened with a belt (Fig. 1.4). Several transparent skirts could be worn over the shenti and were knee-length or short and stiffened into a triangular shape similar to a pyramid.

Egyptian women wore a transparent, close-fitting sheath of very fine linen. Over this was worn the *kalasiris*, a semi-transparent robe which was knotted on the chest and adorned with the traditional broad jewel-encrusted collar (Fig. 1.5). Female nudity or near nudity while dancing or working was not uncommon.

Fabrics were made of woven plant fibres such as linen. Although leather was popular, sheep were considered unclean and so wool was never used. Sandals were made from gold, leather and woven straw, but Egyptians frequently went barefoot. Gold was used in all forms of jewellery, including hair accessories, necklaces, belts, earrings, chains, bracelets, rings and medals.

The Egyptians used an extensive range of colours. Dazzling white was very popular. Blue was favoured by pharaohs going to war, as it reflected the colour of

*1.4 The shenti as worn by Egyptian men.*

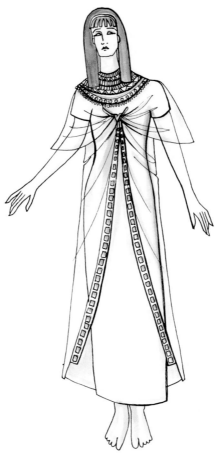

*1.5 The kalasiris, a semi-transparent Egyptian robe, was knotted to form a cape.*

Although the men were nearly always naked, they were every bit as vain and fashion conscious as the women. On their slim, smooth and hairless bodies they wore a simple loincloth of patterned fabric, often decorated with beads. Colours favoured by the Minoans were lively — yellow-green, red, blue, purple, brown, grey and white, sometimes checked.

Hairstyles were varied, but the typical Minoan style was the spiral curl which fell from above the ear and past the side of the face, as commonly seen in frescoes (Fig. 1.7).

When not barefoot, men and women wore knee-high boots with a moderately high heel, or richly embroidered shoes. Accessories included gold buttons, belts, beret-style hats, turbans and caps, and elaborate headdresses. Earrings, long

the sky god, Amon. Green symbolised youth and life, and yellow represented the gold flesh of the sun and the gods. Triads of colours were popular — red, blue and white; red, yellow and blue, or cream, blue and black.

Apart from royalty, who wore artificial beards, men were clean-shaven. Hair was worn short to accommodate the real hair or woollen wigs worn by all well-dressed Egyptians. Wigs were dyed black, blue or red. Women's hair was often decorated with forehead bands, clips, gold ornaments, ribbons and flowers.

Heavy eye make-up was used for protection against the sun, as well as decoration. The face was painted with a white lead-based cream. The lips, cheeks, and temples were tinted orange-red, the eyes outlined with black kohl, and the lids were coloured green or blue with malachite powder. Eyebrows were elongated and curved down around the eye in an arabesque which symbolised clairvoyance.

# THE MINOANS: 2700–1100 BC

The Minoans can be credited with the development of several clothing forms still in use today. The bell-shaped silhouette was worn by women to emphasise their wasp waists. They wore a bodice, sometimes with puffed or cap sleeves, which left the breasts exposed, and an ankle-length, flounced skirt (Fig. 1.6). A metal framework similar to the much later crinoline was created to support the brightly coloured, light-weight skirts. From an early age, both males and females were encased in corsets stiffened with light metal bones to create the narrow waists of which they were very proud.

*1.6 Cretan snake goddess with tightly fitted bodice and flounced skirt.*

1.7 Fresco taken from the Minoan palace at Knossos.

himation included bright saffron, red, emerald green, red-purple, dark green and white. Accessories included hats, walking sticks, gloves and leather sandals.

Women's hairstyles were varied and complicated — chignons, braids, ringlets, top-knots — and hair was sometimes bleached because fair hair was a valued rarity. Men wore their hair curled to frame the face, or long and tied back, and were often bearded. Unrestrained use of jewellery was common. Both men and women wore numerous gold chains and pendants, rings, bracelets and jewelled pins.

strings of beads and pearls, rings, bracelets and gold bejewelled ornamental pins were popular jewellery.

# GREECE: 700–53 BC

Classical Greek dress was influenced by Minoan styling. Its most easily recognisable form for both men and women was the *chiton* (Fig. 1.8). This garment consisted of a draped rectangle of fabric, about 180 centimetres wide and longer than the height of the wearer, fastened on the shoulders with pins and brooches known as *fibulae*. When worn in its simplest form, the chiton was left open at the side and wrapped around the body, with the end of the fabric draped over the shoulder and falling free.

The wearing of the chiton developed into sophisicated forms of folding, twisting and wrapping, enhanced with stitching and pressed pleats. Belts and girdles worn under the bust and on the waist or hips, created the effect of two separate garments, such as a skirt and blouson top.

The *peplos* was a similar garment worn over the chiton and was like a small cape draped over the shoulders. It often featured brightly coloured woven patterns of wavy lines, oval shapes, animals and scenes (Fig. 1.9).

The outermost garment worn by both men and women was the *himation*. Another rectangle of fabric initially worn as a cloak around the shoulders, it later developed into an elaborately draped garment often worn over the head. The himation was floor-length, nearly four metres wide, and could be worn behind the back and draped over the forearms, like a shawl, or twisted and wrapped around the body and over the shoulder in a similar way to the chiton. Lead weights were sometimes sewn into the ends, to sway with the body's movements. Instead of the himation, warriors and travellers sometimes wore a shorter garment known as a *chlamys*, over the chiton.

At first wool was a favoured fabric but this later changed to lighter textiles such as linen, occasionally silk, cotton, and a flax fibre known as *byssus*.

For the poorer and lower classes, garments were plain coloured, white or reddish-brown. The upper classes used dyes and decorated clothing with simple borders or all-over patterns painted and embroidered in multiple colours. The choice of colours for the chiton and

1.8 Greek costume showing the draped chiton and himation (3rd–2nd century BC).

1.9 The construction of the Doric peplos (left) and the later Ionic chiton (right).

# ROME: 750 BC–AD 476

Roman dress lacked innovation and styles were borrowed from other cultures, particularly Greek. Dress for men and women was similar. The *tunic* was a fitted undergarment. It had a hole for the head and two for the arms, and was drawn over the head. Sometimes tube shaped sleeves were added. In cold weather, as many as four tunics might be worn at one time.

The *toga* went over the tunic and was a similar shape to the tunic. It first appeared in the 6th century BC as a simple, short garment, becoming longer and more elaborate until, by the 1st and 2nd centuries, it was extremely impractical to wear (Fig. 1.11). Although capable of great beauty and elegance, the drapery became so complex that it required constant re-adjustment and the wearer often required assistance when dressing. The toga was a semi-circular, rectangular or oval shaped piece of woollen fabric, approximately six metres wide and two metres long. It was draped and arranged about the body, without the asistance of fastenings, and covered the left arm while leaving the right arm free.

Roman women gradually changed from the toga to the *stola*. Undyed, long and draped and usually in silk or cotton, this robe had sewn instead of fastened shoulder seams, and was worn with a girdle below the bust, and one around the hips. Undergarments in the form of a girdle, which provided support by crossing between the breasts, and a type of underpants were worn by Roman women.

The *pallium* was an overcoat, and the *palla* a cloak worn by both men and women. They were rectangles of unbleached wool which enfolded the body and arms and fastened with a fibula under the chin or on the left shoulder, similar to the Greek himation.

Women wore different colours from men, and usually preferred finer and lighter silk, linen and cotton fabrics. The lower classes wore unbleached, grey or white woollen garments. For special occasions, the women favoured embroidery, fabrics threaded with gold,

1.10 Ornate hairstyles were favoured by Roman women (Roman bust, 1st century AD).

*1.11 The Roman toga of the 3rd–4th century AD.*

and brightly coloured ribbons and fabrics in red, yellow and blue.

Jewellery worn by the Romans included pins, fibulae, and rings for every occasion. Heavy gold snake bracelets and necklaces were popular, as were garments and shoes studded with emeralds, pearls, opals and aquamarines. Wreaths and garlands of flowers, gloves, fans, mirrors, and umbrellas were worn as accessories. Boots and open sandals were worn by the men, and women wore a slipper type of shoe.

Women wore eye make-up, face paint, rouge, and dyed their hair. Their hairstyles were extremely varied, ranging from a simple knot to elaborate coiffures with waves, plaits and curls (Fig. 1.10). Men wore their hair short and well-groomed with short, stiff curls on the forehead and back of neck, or brushed forward to frame the face.

# BYZANTIUM: 315–1453

Costume made great advancements in terms of colour and ornament with the emergence of the Byzantine Empire and the rise in popularity of Christianity. Because the Christian religion required the body to be covered and that the shape of the body, particularly the female form, be obscured by clothing, nudity was no longer acceptable.

The fusion of the comparatively simple line of Greek and Roman dress with the brilliant ornamentation of the East produced clothing and fabrics of dazzling richness and variety, and it is for the lavish silk taffetas, velvets, damasks, brocades and tapestries that Byzantine costume is admired (Fig. 1.12).

*Samite* was the fabric commonly used, although cotton, wool and linen were also available. Samite was a thick, strong silk, well able to support the heavy ornamentation, the jewels and pearls sewn onto it and the gold thread woven into it. Christian symbols were used as decorative motifs.

Roman influence can be seen in the basic garments of both men and women. The undergarment was a slim-fitting long-sleeved tunica worn at varying lengths and often embroidered. Over this was worn the *dalmatica*, a long, loose-sleeved robe with close fitting bodice and fuller skirt which was worn either unbelted or belted above the waist (Fig. 1.13). Instead of a toga, a sumptuously decorated, rectangular outer cloak was worn around the shoulders. The cloak fastened on the right shoulder with a rectangular embroidered ornament called a *tablion*.

In the later centuries of Byzantium, men wore shorter tunics to allow more freedom of movement. Their legs were covered by ankle-length trousers known as *bracae*, or hose, which followed the shape of the leg and foot and were sometimes cross-gartered, that is, tied with leg bandages.

Although all colours were used, the preferred combination for the Imperial court was that also used by the Roman emperors — purple with gold embroidery. Other colours used included red, green, blue, plum, violet, brown, black, grey and white.

The open sandal was now replaced with a fabric or leather shoe which followed the shape of the foot and was painted and embroidered for both men and women.

Byzantine jewellery was also rich and ornate. Precious jewels, pearls and, in particular, cloisonné enamelling were used to great effect in heavy collars of Egyptian influence, earrings, finger rings and brooches.

*1.12 5th and 6th century Byzantine costume was remarkable for its richness in colour and decoration.*

garments have been salvaged from peat bogs in northern Europe, and other information has come from burial sites.

The barbarian man's costume consisted of two main items. Trousers were secured with cross-garters. The *singlet* was worn over the trousers and was a knee-length fitted tunic of coarsely woven fabric (Fig. 1.14). The singlet had decorative wristbands and hem and was belted. Over this was the *sagum*, a long cloak with embroidered edges.

Women wore a simple long-sleeved tunic gathered at the waist with a girdle, and over this a short, bloused tunic with elbow-length sleeves. A mantle similar to the Roman palla, or a fur cloak was also worn.

Both sexes wore long flowing hair. The men were moustached and often wore *Phrygian caps* which were like a helmet of leather or wool, and featured an embroidered border.

The Saxon males in England favoured the belted tunic with an embroidered border which could be worn either long or short. Nobility also wore the *surcote*, an outer tunic made from fine linen or silk which was heavily embroidered. It had elbow-length sleeves so the tunic sleeves underneath could be seen.

The Anglo-Saxon *gunna*, from which our word 'gown' is derived, was the robe worn by Saxon women. It was often hooded or worn with a veil, and a matching sash was tied at the waist.

Colours were bright and often symbolic — white for purity, red for Divine love, gold for virtue, green for youth, blue for holiness, violet for humility and purple for dignity.

Fabrics varied according to the climate, and the wealth and social standing of the wearer. They ranged from leather and fur, wool, coarse felt, and cloth from camel hair, to soft linens and silks. Shoes were soft and cut to the shape of the foot (Fig. 1.15).

Gold jewellery was worn by the wealthy classes, bronze by the ordinary

*1.14 This gold statuette found in France and dated circa AD 500 wears a fitted tunic featuring geometric decoration.*

*1.13 The ornate tunic and dalmatica fastened with an embroidered tablion.*

Men's hair was worn similar to the Roman style, medium to short and brushed forward to frame the face, while women wore theirs long in braids, rolls, frizzed, or wrapped in a turban. From all accounts, Byzantine men and women wore no make-up.

# EARLY MIDDLE AGES: 5TH–9TH CENTURY

Our knowledge of the costume and lifestyles of these times is limited because of the restless, nomadic nature of the tribes and because they left few written records or images of themselves. A few

*1.15 Costume of the early Middle Ages as shown in a 5th century breviary.*

person. Bracelets, necklaces, earrings, crowns, and brooches set with precious stones, glass beads, chased and inlaid metal buckles, and metal plaques as ornaments on hide jackets were popular. Precious metals or stones were used as buttons for the first time. Make-up was not generally worn, although the Anglo-Saxon women used blue powder in their hair and painted their cheeks.

# MIDDLE AGES, ROMANESQUE: 10TH–12TH CENTURY

Although design and decoration changed during these years, basic garments changed very little. The richly embroidered Dalmatic tunic worn by the Byzantines was still common. Men wore the *gunna*, a tunic with fitted sleeves and a fuller thigh-length skirt, bloused and belted at the waist (Figs. 1.16 & 1.17). The *sherte* was a new style, a straight knee-length garment with back, front and side slits, similar to the modern shirt, and sometimes worn as an undergarment.

Women also wore the gunna as a full-length dress. It fitted close to the body, with a low neckline, wide sleeves and belt. The *stola* was also floor-length, but full-skirted, sleeveless, and pinned at the shoulder like the Greek chiton. As an undergarment, the corset was worn to lift women's breasts, and to narrow the waistline.

From 1095 to 1228, inspired by the Crusades to the East, embroidery and weaving flourished amongst the upper classes. The results were fabrics beautifully decorated with squares and circles, flowers and animals, and smocking. Knitted hose were common for men and women, worn with garters to hold them up. Footwear included knee-length boots for men, and pointed

*1.16 A gunna from the 12th century Romanesque period showing decorative Eastern influence.*

*1.17 The sherte and gunna of the Romanesque period were worn with cross-gartered knitted hose.*

shoes. Typical colours were white, blue, green, vermillion, grey and black.

Accessories during this time included gloves with fingers, pouches dangling from belts, ornaments in gold or silver, metallic plaques, rings, bracelets and brooches.

Various forms of headdress were popular for women. The *wimple* was a rectangle of fabric draped under the chin and fastened at the temple. *Chin-straps* were strips of cloth fitted under the chin and pinned at the temple, worn with snoods and coronets. *Headrails* were colourful pieces of fabric worn across the forehead and fastened at the back of the head.

Women's hair was worn with a centre part and coiled. The ramshorn was often created from false hair. At home, hair

was worn loose and flowing or in long tresses. Men's hair was usually bobbed to ear level.

# EARLY GOTHIC: 12TH–14TH CENTURY

Costume was now worn either loose in the classical style or, for the first time, taking on a slightly fitted line. Lacing was used at the side of the tunic to draw the fabric in against the body and curved seams were used for shaping.

In the 12th and 13th centuries, men wore a *cyclas* over their tunics. The cyclas was a tunic-like garment with side seams and deep armholes, a little shorter at the hem and sleeves so the tunic could be seen underneath.

The *surcote*, originating in the East, was also widely worn in the mid-13th century. Similar to the cyclas, it was open at the sides and sleeveless with a scooped neck, often lined with fur.

As an undergarment, men wore loose-fitting *braies* which were held at the waist by a cord threaded through a casing. These were made from linen and were a forerunner of modern briefs. Hose, cut on the bias to give the fabric a slight stretch, were drawn over the top, and tied to the braies.

Gradually, long flowing dress for men was replaced with shorter tunics and hose and, by the 14th century, for the first time in many centuries, there was an obvious difference between costume for men and women (Figs. 1.18 & 1.19).

In the 12th and 13th centuries, women wore the *bliaud*, also of eastern influence. It was a two-piece dress with a closely fitting bodice, long hanging sleeves and low curved waistline attached to a long, full skirt. This was the first fitted garment with armholes. Women also wore the one-piece *cotehardie* which fitted smoothly over the bodice and hips, had a gently flared skirt and long tight sleeves. The sleeves of the close-fitting *doublet* worn underneath were laced or buttoned on the lower arm and could be seen. The sideless *surcote* was a clever-

ly cut gown reduced to a shoulder yoke, centre panel and skirt and was worn over the cotehardie. Women's hose were worn only to knee height and were held up with garters.

Italy and England adopted the French fashion for *parti-colouring*. This was originally used as a means of identification in battle, but in civilian life lost its significance and merely added liveliness to an otherwise fairly simple form of dress.

Women still tended to wear their hair covered, but occasionally it was coiled and plaited. Men's hair was bobbed and curled.

# LATE MIDDLE AGES: 15TH CENTURY

The new wealth of this period fostered an active interest in fashion. The *doublet* was the basic garment for men at the turn of the century. It had a chin-high collar, was roundly padded and tightly laced below the waist. This provided the fashionable male silhouette of a broad, deep chest and narrow hips, and was further exaggerated by the *houppelande* worn over the top. The houppelande was a full gown of floor- or thigh-length, with full ballooning sleeves, high collar, and *dagged* hemline. It was fur-lined and belted at hip level (Fig. 1.20).

There was a ladies' version of the houppelande, exactly the same in all details, except it was worn belted high under the breasts and open to a deep 'V' at the neck to give a longer silhouette. The basic garment for women was the close-fitting *kirtle*, worn under the houppelande. The square-necked bodice was laced or buttoned down the front or sides, and the gored skirt flared into floor length folds and sometimes a train. Interchangeable sleeves, pinned or tied on, enabled the kirtle to be worn in different ways. Aprons were sometimes worn (Fig. 1.21).

*1.18 14th century clothing was fitted as shown by the bliaud worn under this sleeveless surcote.*

*1.19 Parti-coloured hose and dagging created interest in a simple dress style.*

In the early 15th century, the popular hairstyle for men was the bowl-crop shaved at the side and back with a thatch of hair on the crown. Women's hair was dressed in metal or silk casings, and covered with veils. Ladies wove gloves, mirrors, keys attached to a belt, gold chains and a rosary. Male accessories included a dagger, walking stick and gloves.

The second half of the 15th century saw the extremes of dress which often occur as part of the decline of an era. As dress became more ostentatious and extravagant, laws were passed to limit extreme and absurd fashions. For example, a law was passed to limit the length of a long pointed shoe known as the *poulaine*, which attained lengths of up to 60 centimetres, and had to be tied

1.21 *The hennin of the 15th century.*

to the leg with a cord to enable the wearer to walk!

Although make-up was still not worn, women removed their eyebrows and shaved their hairlines up to the *hennin* for a hairless look, and leeches were applied to the skin to whiten the complexion.

Amongst women the maternal look became popular, so they wore padded pillows tied under their gowns and walked with their backs arched and stomaches thrust forward to appear pregnant. The male silhouette was exaggerated through the use of large shoulder pads and heavily padded fullness in the outer gown, which was stitched into stiff regular folds.

Hosiery for men became even more

1.20 *The houppeland of the late Middle Ages was fur-trimmed and heavily padded.*

important with the introduction of the *codpiece*, a triangular gusset which joined the legs at the groin. The codpiece itself became ornamental and exaggerated, and was padded or used as a coin purse.

# THE RENAISSANCE: 16TH CENTURY

With Renaissance costume for men, we see for the first time a style of dress which bears a similarity to modern day menswear. The silhouette of the first half of the century was characterised by wide horizontal shoulders, puffed sleeves, fitted jackets and padded hose.

The *pourpoint* was a new development. In linen or silk, with stand collar, set-in sleeves and front fastening, it eventually became the shirt of today. Over this went the richly decorated *doublet*, the equivalent of today's waistcoat. The doublet had detachable sleeves and the waistline was V-shaped from the hips to the crotch, ending with a short peplum. Towards the end of the century, with the emergence of the wasp waist for both males and females, a pinched waist and padded front created a pot-bellied shape known as the peascod belly. Over the doublet went *jerkin*, a knee-length gown worn open with or without sleeves, fur trimmed, with revers and a large square collar (Fig. 1.24).

Hoisery worn by men had developed into upper and lower hose. The lower hose were knitted to fit close to the leg shape. The upper hose were roundly padded and slashed, and were appropriately called pumpkin breeches. Bulging codpieces were still popular.

Women also adopted the horizontal silhouette with large padded sleeves, over which the sleeves of the overtunic were folded back to reveal a luxurious fur lining. Skirts were long with a train, and from 1530 were split down the front to reveal the underskirt. The gown was

1.22 *Renaissance costume worn by Queen Elizabeth 1, circa 1593.*

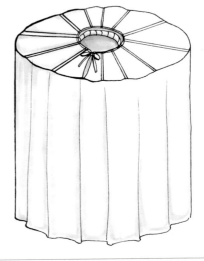

1.23 *The wheel farthingale supported the skirt at right angles for a horizontal silhouette.*

1.24 *The pumpkin breeches and doublets of the late Renaissance were padded and slashed.*

belted or tied with a sash. The low square neckline known as *décolletage* appeared for the first time.

The wasp waist for women emerged around 1550, and was made possible by two extremely uncomfortable devices. The first was the *vasquine*, a metal cage-like corset, bolted onto the body to create a flat-chested look. Below this the richly decorated *stomacher* was worn, as the name suggests, to flatten the stomach (Fig. 1.22). The second device was the *farthingale*. First invented in Spain in the late 1400s, the farthingale was an extremely unwieldy and uncomfortable metal, cane or whalebone frame placed under the skirt to hold it out into a bell-shaped silhouette. The French or wheel farthingale was the most extreme version, causing the fabric of the skirt to sit at right angles to the body before dropping to the floor (Fig. 1.23).

The ruff was popular neckwear in the latter part of the 16th century. Made of starched and crimped cotton, linen or lace, it was held up by a metal frame-work, extended higher than 20 centimetres, and sometimes had to be supported from underneath by a wooden or cardboard frame. The limited movement allowed by the ruff was a status symbol, implying that the wearer was not required to perform demanding tasks, hence our term 'white collar worker'. At times, the décolletage and ruff were worn together, for maximum effect.

Fabrics were dramatically stiff and drapeless. Rich shades of colour were used, often in contrasts. Plenty of gold was used, along with red, green, purple, yellow, blue, and black.

Accessories for men and women included gloves, spectacles, lace-edged handkerchiefs and purses. Pearls and all types of precious stones were common in brooches, rings and necklaces. Footwear for both men and women consisted of high cut shoes trimmed with bows, rosettes or ribbons.

# BAROQUE: 17TH CENTURY

In menswear, the doublet was still the basic upper garment. It had a skirt attached to a high waist, tied or buttoned at the front or sides, and was still slashed on the bodice and sleeves to allow ease of movement and to show the fine shirt underneath. The shirts featured turned back cuffs, up to 15 centimetres wide and edged with lace, which were worn over detachable sleeves. The *whisk* was a flat, wide lace-edged collar which fell over the shoulders.

Fitted knee breeches replaced the stuffed melon hose. They tied at the knee with garters, lace or ribbon. Around mid-century, men's breeches developed into a divided skirt known as petticoat breeches. These were decorated with hundreds of metres of ribbon, and achieved a very feminine appearance in keeping with the lace trims and long wavy hairstyles popular at the time. The loose hose worn underneath petticoat breeches showed below the hem, and separate flounces could also be worn on the lower leg (Fig. 1.25).

Low, broad-brimmed hats sporting plumes of exotic feathers were the order of the day and capes flung flamboyantly around the body were worn with swords and spurs.

The return to a rounder silhouette was also reflected in women's dress. The décolletage returned as a deep, rounded neckline on short-waisted bodices with large full sleeves. Skirts were cut separately from the bodice and were still very heavy and bulky but fell naturally or tucked up for a casual appearance. Sleeves were shortened to three-quarter length.

As the century progressed, the woman's bodice began to evolve into the boned corset. Whalebone ribs elongated the torso and pushed the bosom upwards, and a broad collar fell over the shoulders. Bodices were fastened by rows of lacing, ribbon or brooches down the front or back, and were sometimes sewn to the matching skirt (Fig. 1.26).

Because female dress had always been constructed by male tailors, the shaping and cut had always been very similar to men's. With the development of the *mantua* (a pleated outer robe), women took to making their own clothing. This marks the start of a gradual break away from male domination in dress, and the foundations of the distinction between men's and women's fashion.

The colours of the heavy satins, velvets and fine wools used in the French court were light and subdued, and several colours could be used together in one outfit. They were often given meaningless names such as 'laughing monkey', 'dead leaf', 'ham', or 'smoked beef'.

1.25 Baroque male fashion became very effeminate with metres of lace and ribbon.

1.26 The Fontanges was popular headwear for 17th century women, and was worn with boned bodices and back-swept skirts.

# ROCOCO: 18TH CENTURY

Hooped petticoats for women quickly became popular and, by 1720, had become so enormous that doorways and carriages had to be widened to allow them through. Bell-shaped skirts gradually became more horizontal, flat across the front and back, and up to 1.5 metres wide. *Panniers* were basket-type props tied to the hips to support the skirts instead of hoops.

As skirts became wider, necklines also widened. Long-waisted corsets were still worn, and stomachers were decorated with row upon row of bows. Sleeves were elbow-length with the frills of the chemise hanging below (Fig. 1.27).

A new femininity was expressed in fabrics and decoration. Fabrics were now crisp taffetas, luminous satins in pearly colours, and gold and silver metal cloths and brocades. They were decorated with floral embroidery, artificial and real flowers, beads, fur, feathers, ruching, tulle, ribbon and lace, often used all together.

Men continued to wear the jacket, waistcoat, breeches and stockings and, throughout the 18th century, their dress became increasingly simplified. The collarless jacket for men, known as the *justaucorps* or *redingote* was the precursor to the suit coat of today. It fitted to the body and the knee-length skirt was pleated and padded at the side. Trims were reduced, leaving only an edge of lace or braid at the front, cuffs and pockets, and buttons and buttonholes extended the full length.

Shoes for men had buckles, low heels and round toes, and differed from women's shoes which had high heels

*1.27 The mantua was supported by panniers (circa 1729).*

and pointed toes. Men still wore wigs, although now much smaller and generally short in front with long ringlets or plaits at the back.

Around 1780, there were further changes in women's costume. Panniers became obsolete because of their sheer impracticality, and the *Polonaise* look took their place. The main feature of the Polonaise was the petticoats worn five to ten centimetres above the ground, and the skirt pulled to the back to resemble a bustle.

Male fashion at this time derived from the all-men's clubs of London. The members of many of these clubs were based in grand country estates, and provided a strong rural English influence on male costume.

# THE FRENCH REVOLUTION AND NEO-CLASSICISM: 1789

French Revolutionaries were called Incroyables, their female counterparts were the Marveilleuses. They adopted an unkempt appearance to mock the court, with creased clothing, general untidiness and shaggy hairstyles. The Incroyables wore *culottes*, which were long loose trousers, with dandy style striped stockings and double-breasted jackets featuring tails and exaggerated lapels (Fig. 1.28).

*1.28 The Incroyables and Marveilleuses of the French Revolution were noted for their untidy and careless dress.*

The Marveilleuses wore a Grecian style high-waisted dress known as the chemise gown. This was cut in muslin, often worn with flesh coloured tights or completely without undergarments, and was dampened to cling closely to the body until frequent occurrences of pneumonia, tuberculosis, and influenza resulted in its being outlawed.

Women's hairstyles copied the short curls of the early Greeks. A touch of gruesome humour was the red ribbon à la guillotine, worn around the necks of the Marveilleuses. Slippers without heels were worn. The spencer jacket, or *bolero*, became popular and, along with the paisley shawl, was often the only source of warmth for the fashionable lady.

After the Revolution, men's costume still showed the influence of the relatively simple country style of the English aristocracy. In place of lace and embroidery, powdered wigs and fitted breeches, men wore woollen cloths, loose-flowing hair and baggy trousers. The tail-coat was similar to modern day tails, being cut straight across at the front waist, with the tails behind falling to knee level. The cut-away frock coat had tails which tapered from the front waist. The double- or single-breasted waistcoats worn under the coat were also similar to those worn today. The shirt collar was worn standing up, and white cravats were tied with a soft bow on the outside of the collar.

# ROMANTIC, THE INDUSTRIAL REVOLUTION: 19TH CENTURY

Changes which altered the world of fashion forever took place during this time. Women's dress was now mostly produced by female dressmakers. 1800 saw the arrival of ready to wear shops in the United States, a development which threatened the existence of custom tailoring. In 1846 the sewing machine was invented and paper patterns became available. All of this made fashion ideas more accessible to larger numbers of people, and helped foster the expression of individuality through dress.

In response to the femininity of female fashion, men emphasised their masculinity. Tight-fitting, full-length trousers or pantaloons cut in elastic fabrics such as stockinet, buckskin, or nankeen — a dull yellow cotton brought from China — were worn. Other male paraphernalia included gloves, fob watches, knee-length boots and sideburns. The trousers gradually became looser over the hips and the fly or front closure was introduced. Worn with the trousers were dark coloured double-breasted coats, with tails and high-cut collars, embroidered waistcoats and frilled

1.29 *The male dandy of the Romantic Age (circa 1820) and the crinoline of the Victorian Age (circa 1850).*

shirts with standing collars and cravats. Voluminous caped great-coats and top hats completed the outfit (Fig. 1.29).

Dull colours for men's business wear were introduced around 1820 when the soot and smog resulting from the Industrial Revolution made it impractical to wear brightly coloured silks and satins. This tradition of dark blues, blacks and greys still applies to the business uniform of today.

After 1820, the movement of the female waistline to its natural position was accompanied by the revival of the corset. Corset stays were curved to alter the shape of the hips, waist and bust, resulting in the hour-glass figure. Wide bonnets, bodices, leg-of-mutton sleeves, bustles and gored skirts created a fuller

effect and further emphasised the small-ness of the waist. Use of the *crinoline*, a series of steel hoops suspended by tapes, and layers of petticoats created the bell silhouette.

Late in the 19th century the look was much sterner and more angular, and reflected the emergence of women into the new world of sports and employment.

Changes in menswear were extremely subtle, but nonetheless continuous. A new informality was now preferred, and the looser fitting lounge suit known as the *sack suit* became common. The *ditto suit* also made its appearance. It was a business suit usually cut in plaid or check, and worn with a bowler hat. Trousers now appeared with a front crease, an innovation attributed to Edward VII. Shirts were printed for the first time, often with spots and stripes, and the standing collar was turned down at the front. Accessories for men included hats

of many styles, neckties, monocles, gloves, spats and walking canes.

# 20TH CENTURY

Technological and social changes have been powerful forces influencing costume in the 20th century. Improvements in communication, the advent of cinema and television, the space programme, synthetic fibres, the two World Wars, and the youth and women's movements are but some of the developments which have contributed to major advances in our style of dress.

Men's fashion in the early years followed the general trend set in the preceding century — sober English-inspired suits, starched shirt collars and cuffs, and straw hats and fedoras. Formal and business dress consisted of the frock coat, striped trousers, top hat and spats. During World War I, many men wore military uniform.

Flannel trousers known as Oxford Bags were fashionable around 1925, and there was an increasing trend towards the lounge suit for informal day wear. Other than these subtle changes, men's costume relied mainly on fabric, cut, width and single- or double-breasted jackets for variation.

Women's fashion, on the other hand, reflected new ideas and new-found free-dom. Costumes for different activities had been popular since the previous century, when cycling, tennis, golf and boating became fashionable. The early century saw the continuation of tailored ladies wear. The S shaped sway-back and monobosom of the Gibson girl epitomis-ed the look of the time, and was created by the corset and a forward stance, which made the bust appear as a single curve, without a cleavage (Fig. 1.30). The ideal measurements were a 36 inch (91 cm) bust, and 18 inch (46 cm) waist.

With the outbreak of World War I, many women participating in the war

1.30 The umbrella or walking stick helped maintain the forward bosom and backward hip movement of the early 20th century Gibson Girl look.

1.31 Monkey fur and handkerchief hemlines were popular in the late 1930s.

1.32 Women's skirts became shorter and shoulders broader during World War II.

effort required more practical clothing allowing freedom of movement. Because of this, skirts rose quite quickly and silk stockings and tango shoes came into focus. For the first time, simple working clothes for women, along the lines of what men had been wearing for the past 100 years, became commonplace.

By the jazz age of the 1920s, skirts were quite skimpy and knee-length, drop-waisted tubular flapper dresses were worn to dance the charleston. The 'garçonne' flat-chested effect was achieved by a slouched stance and underwear — brassieres, teddies and camisoles — which flattened the bust. The collections of Coco Chanel now led the fashion scene and, because of their simplicity, her styles were eagerly copied by mass

manufacturers.

The waistline again rose in the 1930s with all detail reduced to a minimum. Tight-fitting dresses relied on good cut, often on the bias, for impact. Accessories were Art Deco jewellery, brooches, hatpins, wrist-watches and gloves. Popular colours were beige and grège (Fig. 1.31).

During World War II, the military look for both men and women dominated. The general silhouette was broad shoulders, nipped-in waists and flared skirts which were easy to walk in (Fig. 1.32). In 1947, the New Look collection created by Christian Dior took women back to a new age of luxury and elegance, and in doing so created headlines.

The return to the natural shoulder

line, tiny waistline, full hips and bust, and longer, extravagantly full skirts changed fashion literally overnight. After a decade of austerity, this was exactly what women were looking for in fashion.

The 1950s saw for the first time several fashion directions occurring at once. Paris-inspired fashions were sophisticated (Fig. 1.33). Dior had produced his A-line trapeze dress, and the low-waisted H-line. Jayne Mansfield and Marilyn Monroe promoted the 'sweater girl' look, full-busted and small waisted. Padded bras were popular.

Audrey Hepburn captured the alternative, art student look with black tights, flat shoes and youthful ponytail. For the boys, fashion influence was through the likes of James Dean, Marlon Brando and

Elvis Presley, with black leather jackets, white T-shirts, winkle-picker boots and slick-back hairstyles. Jeans, formally used for work, became acceptable for both boys and girls as casual dress.

The 1960s saw the beginning of an era of British influence in young fashion. It began when Mary Quant opened her shop 'Bazaar' in King's Road, London in the early sixties. She, and others like Barbara Hulanicki of Biba, represented the many new young designers making clothes for their affluent friends. They devised their own fashions, using the new stretch and synthetic fabrics enthusiastically, with no regard for classic fashion rules. They wore mini-skirts with panty-hose, clashing colours, op and pop

*1.33 Full skirts, puff sleeves, floral prints and short gloves were part of the luxurious look of the 1950s.*

*1.34 The Jackie Kennedy look worn in 1961 was copied worldwide.*

art patterns, and novelty plastic outfits with cutout shapes. The Swinging Sixties saw fashion trends invented by the masses instead of by the fashion elite, and marked the emergence of street fashion as a powerful fashion force.

Pierre Cardin, Courrèges and Ungaro were the first of the French designers to respond to this modern wave. Their fashions were space age, clean, sculptured and experimental. The trouser suit, introduced by Yves Saint Laurent, became acceptable wear for women. So did mid-thigh hemlines, flat shoes, boots, gleaming white and primary colours. The clean-cut simplicity of the early 1960s was epitomised by Jackie Kennedy. Her two piece suits, short jackets with three-quarter sleeves, pillbox hat on bouffant

hairdo and flat shoes were copied worldwide (Fig. 1.34).

In the late sixties, styles became very mixed. Unisex ethnic and the hippie look became popular, with both men and women wearing peasant clothing. Although the mini prevailed, maxis and midis appeared and disappeared quickly. Men's suits also became more casual, and heralded the arrival in the 1970s of the new dandy. Long hair, coloured and frilled shirts, shiny fabrics, wide collars and cuffs, large bow ties and loud neck ties symbolised the ideal for the new man — sensitive, slightly flamboyant and no longer dowdy.

For women in the 1970s, hiphugger jeans, pantsuits and hot-pants were worn with chunky platform shoes. T-shirts

*1.35 Peasant costume and all styles of ethnic dress typified the early 1970s.*

became a political tool, with slogans printed on the front. Variety in style, an endowment from the strong individualism of the previous decade, also carried over into the 1970s. Early in the decade, a romantic revival had started and long dresses by the likes of Laura Ashley became popular for day and evening wear (Fig. 1.35).

Gradually the trend turned back to a more tailored style. Investment dressing became a catchword and natural fibres, neutral colours and classic styling became increasingly popular and remained a strong trend in the 1980s.

The fashion of the 1980s was diverse and changing very quickly, with no one style really dominating. The decade started with Punk, a youth movement originating in England in the late 1970s (Fig. 1.36). The kids wore green and orange spiked hair, black plastic garbage bags, ripped clothing held together with safety pins, chains and heavy black make-up. Punk was picked up by Zandra Rhodes and incorporated into her 1978 collection. This provided it with an air of respectability and commercial appeal and, by the 1980s, punk had filtered into mainstream fashion through black studded belts, black stockings, coloured hair and a popularity for black clothing.

Around the same time, the multi-layered look of the Japanese started to emerge as a new force. Japanese fabric technology, simple styling and neutral colouring, when combined with the talents of designers such as Issey Miyake and Yohji Yamamoto, strongly influenced world fashion into the mid-1980s. Another strong influence which carried on into the 1990s was the understated style of the Italians. The relaxed tailoring of designers such as Giorgio Armani at times challenged the fashion supremacy of Paris. The business suit for women became firmly established and more varied in styling and colour as the decade progressed.

Numerous personalities created new styles of dressing which were picked up by different socio-economic groups. Lady Diana Spencer wore ruffled collars, short hair, flat shoes and delicate clean lines. Jane Fonda promoted physical fitness with her aerobics videos and exercise fashions. Rock videos were a new force. Cyndi Lauper's op shop dressing, Madonna's provocative Gaultier designs, Boy George's layered dressing, Michael Jackson's leather coat, studs and black glove, and black American rap music and dress provided an endless source of fashion inspiration for alternative lifestyles, values and ideas (Fig. 1.37).

As we approach the 21st century, the phenomenon of 'fin de siècle' is apparent. This nervousness about the end of the century, combined with the

*1.36 Punk as a fashion trend began on the streets of England.*

worldwide economic recession of the early 1990s, has resulted in a new conservatism. Rapid social and technological change and environmental concerns have created angst and uncertainty about what the future holds, so rather than looking forward to new lifestyles and an exciting new world, we are looking backwards with nostalgia to a seemingly innocent and simpler past.

The fashion of the early 1990s was quite eclectic, with much influence drawn from past decades. We saw bold sixties floral designs in prints and accessories and short, simple tubular silhouettes. Pucci-inspired prints were given a new lease of life as leggings and body-suits in stretch fabrics. There was also the return of the Brigitte Bardot sex-kitten as seen in the A-line silhouette, bee-hive hairdo, eye-liner, up-lift bras and sling-back shoes. Flared pants re-emerged for a short time, and platform shoes made a strong comeback. Grunge and deconstructionism introduced long slim silhouettes, flowing fabrics and a multi-layered, mix-and-unmatched look. This softness has filtered through to previously rigid and structured career dressing, particularly with improved manufactured fibres such as microfibre, viscose/rayons and elastomerics which combine performance with comfort (Fig. 1.38).

Brand awareness amongst the youth culture is greater than ever before, and while the street-wear and surf fashions are designed to separate 'Generation X' from older generations, the pressure to conform to a set dress code within each sub-group is as powerful as it has ever been. Labels such as 'Mambo', 'Stussy' and 'Hot Tuna' are either the only thing to wear, or not to be seen dead in.

There is an apparent contradiction here. While technology, the increasing range of products available, the emergence of cultural minorities, and the loosening up of traditional cultural structures are providing a wider range of choices as far as style of dress is concerned, our level of exposure to marketing and stereotyping via television, film, videos and other media means that we are increasingly conditioned to 'fit the legends'. This concern over conforming to image will increase as our societies become more anonymous, as we retreat to the safety of our chosen group, and as technologies such as virtual reality further condition our experiences and perception of the world.

The beginning of the next millenium should herald a new enthusiasm and direction for world fashion. The changes the future brings will create new attitudes and new requirements for the way we dress, and the ever-innovative human mind will provide new ways of dealing with our human needs for protection, modesty and display.

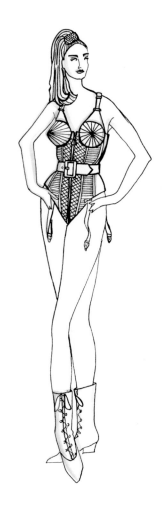 

*1.37 (left) Street fashion was synthesised into high fashion chic in the late 80s and early 90s, and was eagerly promoted by movie and pop stars, supermodels and other celebrities.*

*1.38 (right) New dress codes for fashionable youth, inspired by surfwear, streetwear and sports-wear, are constantly and rapidly changing.*

CHAPTER 2

# INTRODUCTION

Understanding the role played by leading designers in the development of fashion as we know it today serves several purposes.

It can inspire us and serve as a source of ideas for themes, materials, decorative treatments and approaches to garment construction. It can

also provide us with an understanding of how past and present designers create clothing which expresses the times in which they and their

clientele live.

As designers, the more we know about the influences in our lives and how we are affected by them, the more we are able to provide our

customers with the clothing they want to wear. We can also learn much about design from the masters of fashion, about the infinite variety of

colour, line, shape and texture, and how to apply these elements to express our own creative impulses.

It is useful to note how these designers got started, what gave them their break into their chosen field, how they were successful in their

businesses. It is also interesting to compare the different styles which were successful at any time, and for what length of time each designer

maintained his or her fashion leadership. It is necessary, but sometimes difficult, for a designer to change with the times and the rise, fall and

sometimes rise again of the fashion greats reflects the constantly changing nature of the entire industry, and of society.

## CHARLES FREDERICK WORTH (1825–1895)
born: bourne, lincolnshire, england

Charles Frederick Worth started his career at the age of twelve, working in a London draper's shop, and a year later commenced a long apprenticeship with the firm of haberdashers, Swan and Edgar's.

Moving to Paris in 1845, Worth found a job at Maison Gagelin, selling fabrics, mantles and shawls. He married Marie Vernet, the young lady who modelled shawls for clients, and moved quickly from designing dresses for her to his own department in the store where he designed and made up dresses for clients in Gagelin's fabrics.

In 1858, in partnership with a wealthy Swede named Otto Bobergh, Worth opened his own house. Patronage by Empress Eugénie of France ensured his success and, for the following decade, Worth designed for the members of her court as well as for many of the crowned heads of Europe.

The 50 years of Worth's reign, from mid-19th century to the beginning of the 20th century, saw quite significant developments in fashion. The crinoline was at its height (or width) of popularity in the 1850s but, in 1864, Worth introduced a new silhouette which flattened the front of the skirt, and swept the volumes of fabric back into a train. This back fullness gradually progressed to the raised waistline and bustle. In the later years of the 19th century, when the silhouette became simpler and perfect fit was more important, Worth created the princess line.

Worth's designs displayed an expert understanding of the use of fabrics. He worked closely with French silk manufacturers who made up special designs and widths to suit his requirements. He was most famous for his evening gowns, often created in white, and lavishly trimmed with embroidery and lace.

Worth was responsible for the

23

founding of many of the traditions of couture. He was the first person to open a boutique which sold his own creations, a couture house on which all subsequent houses were modelled. He was the first designer to establish a style which was recognisable as his own, and used his influence to set new trends, an honour which had previously been reserved for powerful members of society.

Worth was the first to sew his name on a label inside a garment. His collections of clothing for a single event or for individual clients, based on a theme, set the tradition for today's designer collections. So too did the annual showing of these collections.

Worth was responsible for fusing the art of British tailoring with Parisian chic, to create a style which lasted for nearly a century. After his death, the business was carried on by succeeding Worth generations, until it was finally sold in 1954. The name of Worth is now only available as perfume.

## PAUL POIRET (1879–1944)
### born: paris, france

Paul Poiret's parents were cloth merchants, and Paul started his career by selling some fashion sketches to the Raudnitz Soeurs. In 1896 he became apprenticed to Doucet and in 1900 moved to the House of Worth.

Four years later, in 1904, Poiret opened his own house and, with the patronage of the famous actress Réjane, was soon a success. In 1905, Poiret married Denise, a slim, dark-haired woman who served as Poiret's muse and whom he set about to make into the woman of the future. Amongst the fashionable set, the two became the last word in style.

Poiret's first great achievement was to persuade women that the brassière was a much more desirable undergarment than the corset. He created gowns of elegant line, much simpler than those of the Belle Epoque they replaced, and

revived the use of brilliant reds, royal blues, yellows and greens.

His inspiration ranged from the harem pants, tunics and turbans of Russia, to ancient Greek and Neoclassical costume, to the Oriental kimono shape and the coloured saris of India.

In 1911 Poiret developed perfume and cosmetic products, established the Ecole Martine, an art school for young girls, and commenced production of hand-made fabrics and furnishings, pottery and household items.

With the outbreak of World War I, Poiret closed his house and joined the French army. On his return, with fashion becoming more understated and designers like Chanel, Vionnet and Molyneux starting to emerge, his theatrical clothing seemed loud and gaudy. Not able to regain his former prominence, Poiret sold out to backers in 1925, and died in 1944, a virtual unknown.

◀ 2.1 The bustle designed by Charles Worth was popular during the 1860s.

▶ 2.2 The 1912 Lampshade tunic by Poiret was called 'Sorbet' after the glass bead embroidery in sherbet colours of pink, mauve and green.

## MADELAINE VIONNET (1876–1975)
born: aubervilliers, france

Leaving school at the age of 12 to work for a dressmaker, Vionnet got an early start in fashion. She worked in London for a while before returning to Paris in 1901 to join Callot Soeurs as an assistant, making up toiles.

Vionnet moved to Doucet in 1907 and, in 1912, left to open her own business. She put her ideas into action by draping and cutting her fabrics on miniature dummies. This provided her with tremendous freedom, and allowed her to innovate as she worked.

The bias cut, the development for which she is most famous, allowed her garments to cling and drape over the body as if they were part of it. Using fluid fabrics like crepe and satin, joined with diagonal seams and faggoting, she moulded her garments to the uncorseted natural shape of her clients. Some garments were cut from one piece of fabric woven wider especially for her, and made without fastenings. They appeared to be quite shapeless until slipped over the head, when they hugged the body like a second skin.

Vionnet usually worked with plains, in the subtlest of colours — rose, flesh, pink, mauve, yellows and greens, as well as black used in a most dramatic way. Beading and embroidery were occasionally used for decoration, as were stripes and tiny florals.

Vionnet liked to use bias cut triangles and squares in her cowls, halter necks, and handkerchief skirts, geometric shapes for appliqués, cut-outs and tucks, and decorated fabrics with intricate designs created by pin-tucking.

Madame Vionnet's contribution in the realm of cut and drape was very important in bringing haute couture into the 20th century. She closed her couture house and retired in 1939.

*2.3 Vionnet mastered the bias cut and produced softly draped, body-hugging gowns.*

## GABRIELLE 'COCO' CHANEL (1883–1971)
born: saumur, france

From the age of 12, Chanel lived in a convent where she was left by her father after her mother's death. At age 18 she worked for a short time in a tailoring shop, before moving on to become a night-club performer. She was nicknamed 'Coco', a name which stayed with her for the rest of her life, after two of the songs she sang.

Chanel started her business in 1910 by opening a small hat shop which sold her own hats and dresses to accompany them. She opened two more shops in Deauville and Biarritz, specialising in clothing which suited the casual sea-side life of these French resort towns. Her styles were simply cut, loose fitting, and worn without corsets.

Chanel herself claimed to be the 'first to live the life of this century'. Her clothes appealed to women who had become accustomed to the practical, easy and comfortable clothing they wore during World War I.

Chanel is renowned for her suits, 'the little black dress', the use of grey, navy and beige, the twin set, chemise dresses, flat Chanel pumps and slingbacks, and particularly her use of costume jewellery. Like her dresses, the perfume Chanel No. 5, so named because of her belief that it was her lucky number, is considered a classic.

*2.4 Chanel's easy and comfortable clothing made sportswear internationally fashionable (1933).*

In 1939 Chanel closed her couture house. She emerged from retirement in 1954, at the age of seventy-one, and successfully relaunched the tweed suits and little dresses which had made her famous in pre-war years.

The Chanel tradition is now carried on by Karl Lagerfeld, who has updated the classic styles to create a look appropriate for the 1980s and 90s, while retaining the features which make them easily identifiable as idiomatic of Coco Chanel.

## ELSA SCHIAPARELLI (1890–1973)
### born: rome, italy

Unconventional, imaginative and sometimes shocking, Schiaparelli was an entertainer in the realm of haute couture. She was the great rival to Chanel, partly because they both had such strong personalities. Elsa grew up in Italy, was sent to convent school, studied philosophy, and ended up in Paris in 1920, with a young child to support after her husband left her.

Her big break in the fashion world came in 1928 when a sweater she designed attracted the attention of a store buyer, who ordered forty. That was the now famous black sweater with the white trompe l'oeil bow at the neck.

Schiaparelli didn't waste the opportunity. She immediately started a business called 'Pour le Sport', selling knitwear and sportswear, and opened a salon in 1929 which added evening wear, day wear and accessories.

Although her designs were witty and frivolous, they were also practical. She dyed zippers to match fabric, and left them exposed for decoration as well as function. She was famous for her buttons, which were created to suit a current theme — circus clowns, acrobats, cupids, drums, zodiac signs. Her clothing featured broad shoulder pads, nipped-in waists, dyed furs and peplums.

In collaboration with many artists of her day, Schiaparelli produced fanciful and creative designs, hats in the shape of lamb chops and icecream cones, fabric prints with newspaper designs, and novelty handbags and jewellery.

Her last show was held in 1954. She died 19 years later, and was buried in an oriental robe of a colour made famous by her, Shocking Pink, also the name of her perfume.

## EDWARD MOLYNEUX (1891–1974)
### born: london, england

Molyneux was born and raised in London and studied art with the aim of becoming a painter. He sold sketches for magazines and advertisements, and won a competition sponsored by the designer, Lucile, for his sketch of an evening gown. He subsequently worked with Lucile as she travelled to her salons in America, and then as a designer in her Paris store.

Molyneux suffered the loss of an eye while fighting in World War I, but this did not prevent him establishing his

2.5 Schiaparelli was noted for her witty trompe l'oeil motifs, the first of which was this 1928 hand-knitted jumper.

2.6 Molyneux complemented the sleek lines of his eveningwear with exotic trims (1933).

own couture house on his return to Paris in 1919. His success was rapid and, between 1925 and 1932, his business expanded to Monte Carlo, Cannes, Biarritz and his home town London.

The beauty of Molyneux's style was its simplicity, although his garments were not unknown for their extravagance. In a typically British way, he understood how to use understatement to emphasise a point. Mixing with the society ladies he dressed gave him insight into their exact requirements so that his designs were always extremely appropriate, the height of elegance, and in excellent taste.

The look of the 1930s was epitomised by Molyneux's style. The tall, streamlined figure in a slim pleated skirt, or backless, slip dress for evening is typical. He frequently used navy and black in his tailored suits and, although his garments were conservative in cut and detail, he sometimes experimented with unusual decorative effects in feathers, leathers and beading.

In 1945, Molyneux returned to Paris, but times had changed and his health was poor. He retired in 1950, handing over most of his clientele to Jacques Griffe.

In 1965 Molyneux worked with John Tullis, his nephew, on a ready-to-wear range under the name of Studio Molyneux. He retired after this, and died in 1974.

## CHRISTIAN DIOR (1905–1957)
born: granville, normandy, france

The son of a wealthy manufacturer, Dior enjoyed Parisian artistic life, studied political science, ran an art gallery, undertook military service, sold fashion sketches, and worked briefly as a designer for the couturier Robert Piguet.

After time spent in the army during World War II, he returned to Paris where he settled into his career in fashion with a job as designer for Lucien Lelong,

2.7 Paris was restored to fashion leadership after World War II when Dior introduced the 'New Look' in 1947.

working alongside Pierre Balmain. The cotton entrepreneur Marcel Boussac offered Dior a position as designer with his existing couture house Gaston et Philippe. Dior accepted provided that Boussac let him create an entirely new couture house.

Thus, the House of Dior opened in 1946 and the first collection, in 1947, was an immediate success. Initially called the 'Corolla Line', after the petals of an upturned flower, it was soon known as the 'New Look' and featured skirts which used up to 70 metres of fabric, and bodices that were boned and stiffened.

Every new Dior collection was built around a strong theme, named after the predominant mood of the garments.

The 'Envol' (Flight) in 1948, the 'Zig Zag', the 'Trompe l'Oeil', the 'Vertical', the 'Oblique', and the 'Oval' in 1951, the 'A-line', and the inverted 'Y-line' of autumn 1955, all described the gradual evolution of his ideas.

Christian Dior died suddenly of a heart attack in October 1957, at the height of his career. In just over ten years, the house of Dior had grown enormously, with separate divisions for perfumes, hats, jewellery and shoes.

In his short time, Dior had succeeded in capturing the mood of women of the day. He was able to recreate the celebration of fashion and dressing that the war had destroyed, and influenced women's fashions throughout the world.

He is well remembered for the sculptured silhouettes of his afternoon dresses, which created a world of fantasy in rich taffetas or velvets, worn with long gloves, hats, high heels, and brooches pinned to the bodice or ropes of pearls.

Yves Saint Laurent was Dior's immediate successor. In 1960, Marc Bohan took over as head designer. The house is now headed by Gianfranco Ferre.

## CRISTOBAL BALENCIAGA (1895–1972)
born: guetaria, spain

Balenciaga learned about making clothes from his dressmaker mother. His talent was discovered and fostered by the Marquesa de Casa Torres, who allowed the young Cristóbal to copy a Drécoll suit she owned. She became his patron, financing his training and later his three shops in Spain.

He emigrated to Paris in 1937 and, by the 1950s, was head of one of fashion's foremost couture houses.

Balenciaga had an architectural approach to his clothes. They often framed the body, standing away in severely stiff fabrics like faille, shantung, gazar or thick wool. The chemise dress,

THE FASHION DESIGN MANUAL

the large flat bow, semi-fitted and loose jackets, the pillbox hat and scarves and shawls were features of his work.

He is remembered for his creations in black, be it little black dresses, suits or ballgowns, for his use of brilliant colours, and for his ability to interpret and respond to the times well before many others.

Among the men Balenciaga trained in his perfectionist ways were Givenchy, Courrèges and Ungaro, who regarded him as a mentor.

## PIERRE CARDIN (1922–)
### born: san biagio di callalta, italy

Pierre Cardin was born to French parents, and grew up in the French region of Loire. He first worked for a tailor in Vichy, Italy, then moved to Paris in 1944 where he worked for Schiaparelli and Paquin before joining Dior in 1946. He opened a small boutique for men's and women's wear, and produced his first collection in 1957, followed by ready-to-wear in 1963.

Although his early designs were simply but boldly tailored, Cardin's reputation as an innovator grew in the 1960s with his forward thinking, space-age designs. He popularised the use of everyday materials for fashion items, like vinyl and metal rings for dresses, carpentry nails for brooches, and common decorative effects including geometric cut-outs, appliqués, large pockets, helmets and oversized buttons. His body-stockings, catsuits, leggings and tubular dresses made from knitted fabrics were worn with tabards, tiny skirts and plunging necklines.

Like Balenciaga, Cardin's work was architectural in its simplicity, with the body often a secondary consideration to the form and line of the garment.

In the 1980s Cardin's name became a worldwide phenomenon through his licensing agreements which number over 500 in 93 countries. He was the first designer to license the production of items ranging from accessories, to furniture and food, communications and aeroplanes, under his name.

## ANDRÉ COURRÈGES (1923–)
### born: pau, france

Fashion in the 1960s was dominated by Courrèges. He started out as a civil engineer, dabbling at the same time in textile design and architecture, until he joined the French Air Force during World War II. He moved to Paris in 1945 where he filled in time working with a fashion company until he joined Balenciaga in 1949. Courrèges stayed with Balenciaga for 11 years, then left to open his own house in 1961.

His short period of fashion domination commenced in 1964 with his introduction of mini-skirts, short shorts, pantsuits and white boots. It swept in a new era dominated by a stark futuristic simplicity, often referred to as the space-age look. The body, especially legs, arms and the midriff, was important.

Pants were featured in Courrèges's work. They were hip height, slim-fitting stove-pipes, worn with boxy tops which exposed the midriff. He used simplified

2.8 The influence of Balenciaga's Spanish heritage is apparent in this black taffeta late-day dress (1951).

2.9 Cardin's space-age designs reflected the emphasis on youth which prevailed in the 1960s.

beige, and ice pinks and blues. Plain colours, grids, stripes and stylised flower shapes predominated. Fabrics were always those with body to hold his strong architectural silhouettes.

Courrèges still operates from his Paris headquarters, working in such diverse fields as menswear, active sportswear, uniforms and accessories.

## MARY QUANT (1934–)
### born: london, england

After studying at Goldsmith's College of Art from 1950 to 1953, Mary Quant spent a short time working for the milliner, Erik. In 1958 she opened her shop 'Bazaar', in the centre of London's growing boutique fashion scene on King's Road. In the 1960s, the young, with more freedom and money to spend than ever before, became a dominant force in fashion, and Quant succeeded in expressing this mood in her clothing.

Her designs were bright and simple, mix and match, and often unisex. The 'look' consisted of mini skirts, skinny rib pullovers, tights and hipster belts and 'wet-look' garments in PVC worn together in clashing colours. Pinafores were also popular.

Mary Quant still designs, mainly for the Japanese market, but is mostly noted for her work in the 1960s.

## BILL BLASS (1922–)
### born: fort wayne, indiana, usa

Bill Blass studied art in New York then worked as an artist for a sportswear manufacturer. After time in the army

2.10 Courrèges's futuristic look was widely copied during the 1960s (mini jumpsuit with shoulder and hip yoke, circa 1968).

flower shapes for decoration, and cute accessories like Mary Jane shoes, fitted bonnets, sunglasses, short socks and gloves.

In 1965, Courrèges reorganised his clothing into three levels — Prototypes, which showed couture, Couture Future, featuring ready-to-wear, and Hyperbole, a cheaper range aimed at the young ready-to-wear market.

In 1967 he experimented with transparent fabrics and cut-outs which further exposed the body. He used knitted bodystockings and pastel colours, and all-white garments trimmed with topstitching, piping and binds in contrasting navy, flouro orange, lime green,

2.11 A 1966 Mary Quant mini dress.

2.12 Blass had great success with his green and white lace baby-doll dress of 1968.

during World War II, he worked as a designer for Anne Klein, then for Anna Miller and Co and stayed with that company when it merged with Maurice Rentner Ltd in 1959.

Bill Blass ended up buying the company, renaming it after himself in 1970. He proceeded to become well known as a designer of sportswear and evening wear, and through the licensing of numerous products.

His style of sportswear is traditional and clean-cut, borrowing fabrics and detailing from menswear. At the same time his garments manage to be soft and fluid, with a consciousness of female curves. He favours natural fibres — pure wools, cottons, linens and silks. Strong colours and clean bold patterns also characterise his work. He had great success with his use of lace, frills and ruffles in the 1960s.

Blass's evening wear is often tailored, as can be seen in his tailored jacket combined with bold flounces, a combination which worked well for him in the 1980s.

## YVES SAINT LAURENT (1936–)
### born: oran, algeria

At the age of 16, Yves Saint Laurent won a competition run by the International Wool Secretariat, for his design of a black draped cocktail dress. After completing his university studies in Oran, he moved to Paris where he found a sketching job with Vogue. The editor, upon seeing some of his designs, introduced him to Christian Dior who promptly hired him as an assistant.

Dior died suddenly in 1957, and Saint Laurent, at the age of twenty-one, was thrust into the position of head designer at the House of Dior. His first collections carried on the tradition of Dior, and he was hailed as the saviour of France since half of France's fashion exports came from the House of Dior, and the French economy relied heavily

2.13 This 1970 safari suit by Yves Saint Laurent adapted traditionally male garments to suit the needs of contemporary women.

on his success.

By 1960 his designs were showing the influence of youthful street fashions, and included turtle neck sweaters, black leather jackets, and knitted caps. These collections were met with outrage by the press and were considered unsuitable for Dior's clientele. That year, Saint Laurent was called up for military service, but was discharged soon after because of a nervous breakdown. On his return, finding that he had been replaced by Marc Bohan, he successfully sued Dior and, with business partner

Pierre Bergé and American backing, set up his own couture house in 1962. This was followed in 1966 by the opening of the Rive Gauche ready-to-wear shop.

Yves Saint Laurent's achievements and innovations are numerous. His first collection showed the pea jacket and smocks, two garments he continually returns to in endless variations. 1965 showed the influence of Mondrian; 1966 was pop art dresses and the smoking jacket; 1968 was the safari look and the shirt dress, and the following year the pantsuit.

In the 1970s Saint Laurent created the look that was perfect for the new business woman, a well tailored elegance featuring the blazer as the mainstay.

He is noted for his brilliant use of bright colour often offset with black, his reference to past couturiers and his skilful use of appliqué and beading.

Yves Saint Laurent is heralded as being the designer who restored couture to its position of status after the emergence of ready-to-wear and street fashion in the sixties, and at the same time elevated ready-to-wear to a level of respectability.

## OSCAR DE LA RENTA (1932–)
### born: santo domingo, dominican republic

De la Renta studied art in Santo Domingo and Madrid, but got his break in fashion after he designed a gown for the daughter of a US ambassador. Upon seeing the gown on the cover of *Life* magazine, Balenciaga offered de la Renta a job in Paris, where he stayed for a couple of years. He moved on to Lanvin, then to Elizabeth Arden in New York, and finally to Jane Derby. Upon the death of Mrs Derby, de la Renta opened his own business. By 1968, his label was established, and he was producing a boutique line.

De la Renta's work is characterised by simple silhouettes, extravagant deco-

*2.14 De la Renta showed dramatic frills and bows in 1984.*

He joined Beau Brummel Neckwear as a sales representative in 1967, and the following year designed a range of top quality ties under the name Polo. He soon expanded this into an entire menswear range, which featured wide collars and lapels to match his wide ties and traditional Ivy League styling.

1971 saw the launch of his women's range and the establishment of the Ralph Lauren label. This was followed by boys' and girls' wear, fragrances, cosmetics and home furnishings.

Lauren's clothes are often the same from year to year because he designs to suit an ideal, the elegant lifestyle of a bygone era. His women's wear was initially copied from men's clothing, and his evening wear also has the understated elegance characteristic of men's evening wear.

Lauren's inspiration derives from a mixture of American and English past. The prairie look and frontier fashions, denim skirts, petticoats and fringed jackets, Fair Isle sweaters, hacking jackets, pleated skirts, fly-front shirts and tartans are typical. Cotton, linen, denim, tweed, flannel, velvet, lace and cashmere are his choice of fabrics.

## ISSEY MIYAKE (1938–)
### born: hiroshima, japan

Issey Miyake graduated from the Tama Art University in 1964, then moved to Paris to study fashion at the Chambre Syndicale de la Couture Parisienne. In 1966 he went to work for Guy Laroche in Paris, then moved over to Givenchy in 1968. He travelled to New York in 1969, where he joined Geoffrey Beene as a ready-to-wear designer.

Back in Tokyo in 1970, he established the Issey Miyake Design Studio. His first collection was shown in New York in 1971, and his next show was in Paris.

Miyake draws upon all forms of Japanese culture and costume, from origami to samurai armour to peasant dress. Although influenced by Western style, he often prefers Japanese garment construction techniques and has developed a genre which combines both East and West.

Layer over layer of wrapped and tied clothing typifies his style. Miyake leaves much of the creative process of dressing to the wearer, with loose, often formless garments that can be draped and worn in many ways. His colours also relate to his cultural heritage. Neutral black, grey, cream and indigo, textured fabrics, and Oriental inspired prints are his trademarks.

Miyake is well known for his wire,

ration, and usually bright, often contrasting colours. His clothes are always opulent, showing the influence of his home country. His evening gowns and cocktail dresses, for which he is most famous, are ruffled, frilled, embroidered or jewel-encrusted bodices, generally close-fitting, and skirts are wide and full.

## RALPH LAUREN (1939–)
### born: the bronx, new york, usa

In New York, Ralph Lauren worked as a salesman at Brooks Brothers and Allied Stores while studying business at night.

*2.15 Ralph Lauren's 1981 'Santa Fè' collection drew inspiration from American Indian blankets.*

2.16 *The shape of the clothing is determined by the body of the wearer in Issey Miyake's designs.*

ready-to-wear designer for both men's and women's wear.

Armani's women's jackets are constructed along men's lines, with styling always finely tailored, understated and uncluttered.

Armani's notable contributions to fashion are soft, generous blazers for women, tailored trousers and shorts, culottes, and the use of linen and leather.

2.17 *Armani's couture sportswear designs have been compared to Chanel's because of their masculine inspiration and easy, uncontrived shapes (Spring 1993).*

2.18 *Lagerfeld's simple, modern femininity is apparent in this crêpe de chine blouse and pleated skirt.*

## KARL OTTO LAGERFELD (1938–)
### born: hamburg, germany

As a 16 year old, Lagerfeld won first prize in a competition sponsored by the International Wool Secretariat for a coat design (another first prize winner in the dress category was Yves Saint Laurent, also 16 years old), and was hired to work as design assistant for Pierre Balmain, who put his design into production. Three and a half years after joining Balmain, Lagerfeld went to Patou, where he stayed for only a year before moving on to Italy in 1964 to study art history.

Back in Paris the following year,

cane and plastic sculptured bodices, draped skirts, unusually textured fabrics, and theatrical spectacles such as the Bodyworks show held in 1984.

## GIORGIO ARMANI (1934–)
### born: piacenza, italy

In 1961 Armani landed his first fashion job as design assistant with the menswear manufacturer Nino Cerruti, and after that worked for several designers, including Emanuel Ungaro. In 1975 he established himself as a fashion consultant, and rose quickly to success as a

Lagerfeld worked freelance as a designer for Chloé, Krizia and Charles Jourdan shoes. In 1967, still working freelance, he did some innovative work with fur and leather for Fendi of Rome, using unusual furs and dyeing them to bright colours.

In 1983, he took on the House of Chanel as designer for both the couture and the ready-to-wear. His creative energy and ability to interpret and play with the classic look propelled Chanel to a position of prominence in the 1980s.

1984 saw Lagerfeld's first collection under his own name. His genius lies in his ability to mix and match, to draw inspiration from a vast range of sources, and to combine them in a way that is totally original, and totally contemporary.

## DONNA KARAN (1948–)
### born: forest hills, new york, usa

Donna Karan was born into the fashion business, with a father who was a haberdasher and a mother who was a model and saleswoman. After attending Parson's School of Design, Karan worked for the Anne Klein label for a year, then moved on to Addenda. She returned to Anne Klein in 1968, and worked with Louis Dell'Olio as designer after Klein's death in 1974.

In 1984 Donna Karan started her own company and was very successful with her coordinated range of garments aimed at the working woman of the 1980s. The staple garment was the body suit, and the main feature of her garments was their flexibility and ease of care.

Fabrics were body hugging and reflected the increased importance of fitness and a well maintained physique which characterised the decade.

◀ *2.19 Simple, sensuous luxury combined with comfort and practicality is Donna Karan's hallmark.*

▶ *2.20 Indian inspiration mixed with body piercing is typical of Gaultier's eclectic style (Spring 1994).*

## JEAN-PAUL GAULTIER (1952–)
### born: paris, france

Gaultier started his fashion career at 17, working with Pierre Cardin as assistant designer. He then worked for Jacques Esterel, Jean Patou and again for Cardin in 1974 in a manufacturing plant in the Philippines. He started his own company in 1977, and became popular during the 1980s with his witty ready-to-wear collections which had their roots in the London street fashions.

Gaultier's work is identifiable by the clever blending of fabrics and finishes, mixing old with new, and a playful challenging of traditional ideas. Sweatshirting combined with fabrics such as lace and satin, wrap skirts for men, bold use of tartans, and pointed cone-shaped bra cups are some of his innovations.

CHAPTER 3

# INTRODUCTION

We wear clothing for three basic reasons. First, it provides a protective covering for our vulnerable bodies against the elements, the environment and other physical dangers. Second, it conceals our private parts for the purposes of modesty and decency. Third, it serves as a status symbol, a means of identification and method of display for sexual and social attraction.

'Clothing' defines what we wear, 'fashion' is how we wear it. Fashion is a style of clothing that many people choose to wear at a given time; and fashion really has little to do with the practical reality of why we wear clothing at all.

## THE FUNCTIONS OF CLOTHING

Some clothing performs a protective role in our modern society. Fire fighters wear heat- and flame-proof overalls, medical staff wear sterilised gowns in operating theatres, and most people will put on a raincoat to keep dry, a T-shirt to prevent sunburn or a pullover to keep warm. But the need to feel comfortable, warm and dry often takes second place to the demands of fashion (Fig. 3.1).

As humans we are preoccupied with body image and, more often than not, are dissatisfied with the body's natural form. So we use fashion to alter, conceal, distort and sometimes mutilate our bodies in an effort to 'improve' our appearance and to conform to society's standards of physical beauty. Social convention, politics, economics, industry, scientific invention, international trade and influential personalities have more of an effect on contemporary taste than do considerations of comfort, warmth and suitability.

As we have seen in our study of the history of costume, there have been times when a society's interest in personal appearance has reached ridiculous extremes. Unattractive and absurd fashions which distort natural body proportions, and extreme costumes which inconvenience the wearer or restrict and deform the body to the point of causing health problems, have all made their appearance on the fashion scene. The codpiece, the hennin, the corset, the crinoline, the bustle, shrink-to-fit skin tight jeans and platform shoes have all been quite willingly worn at some stage or other.

Even more extreme than these are the physical mutilations practised by some societies (Fig. 3.2).

Take, for example, the ancient Chinese practice of foot-binding for women whose worth was determined by the smallness of their feet; or the bound, pointed heads of the Mangbetu in Africa. Many African and Pacific Island cultures practise tattooing and cicatrisation. During cicatrisation, ash is rubbed into an open wound so that it heals as a raised welted scar. The Surma women in Ethiopia stretch their lips to accommodate lip plates or labrets. The African Toposa often remove their lower teeth to make their top jaw and teeth protrude to resemble the cattle they prize highly.

In our own society, body piercing and tattooing are not uncommon, and technology is providing a whole new range of possibilities, with silicon implants permitting body sculpture to take place from the inside instead of through external mechanical methods.

Human standards of decency and modesty are subject to changes in fashion. These standards vary dramatically from one culture to another according to social practices, religion and tradition. What is considered to be the 'proper' way to cover the body changes with fashion as social conditions change.

For example, nudity or near-nudity was quite acceptable amongst the great ancient civilisations of Egypt and Greece. It was the spread of Christianity, and the church's ideology that the body be covered, which totally changed these

3.1 The R.M. Williams Classic Oilskin Raincoat is laden with features to protect the wearer in the outdoors. (Photograph courtesy of R.M. Williams Pty Ltd.)

3.2 An Australian Aborigine (early 20th century) showing scarification.

# WHY DO FASHIONS CHANGE?

## SOCIAL CHANGES

A fashion trend is the direction in which fashion is moving. Ties getting narrower or wider, skirts getting shorter or longer, waistlines moving higher or lower, blue becoming more popular than yellow, and bikinis worn more than one-piece swimsuits, are examples of the changes fashion might make from one season to the next.

Fashions change because people and society are constantly changing. People change physically and mentally with age and their personal tastes and requirements in clothing reflect their past experiences, present state and expectations for the future.

The way we dress is a very obvious expression of our total lifestyle, reflecting our individuality, personality and attitudes as well as those of the society in which we live. Even those of us who rebel against convention by dressing in an unorthodox way are responding to the mood of the time, and to our role in society as we see it. For instance, the dress of the French revolutionaries, the Incroyables and the Marveilleuses, symbolised their rejection of everything associated with the decadent French court.

Similarly too, the emergence of the Punk movement in London in the late

attitudes throughout Europe — attitudes which are still prevalent today.

Even so, what is considered appropriate today is far from the rigid standards of Victorian times, when even table legs were covered!

Our standards also change according to situation, location and time of day. What is considered suitable for one situation may be quite unacceptable in another. Whereas a skimpily clad, even topless, swimmer at the beach on the weekend is quite acceptable to most people in that setting, a person dressed in the same way travelling to work on a peak-hour bus would shock most people and be considered most inappropriate.

Display is the third function of clothing and forms the root from which fashion stems. Whether consciously or unconsciously, dressing-up and adornment are used for personal satisfaction and for sexual attraction. They are also a means of identifying our place in society or as a member of a group of people by signifying status, position, power and wealth (Fig. 3.3). Part of our social con-

ditioning involves learning to recognise the symbolism attached to various forms of dress. We recognise the white 'dog-collar' as representing a member of a religious order and a white gown and veil as belonging to a bride. The uniform of a police officer conveys the authority society accords the role of law enforcer. A fur coat or expensive-looking jewellery implies wealth and high status; and studded leather jackets and tattoos represent a rebellious attitude to society.

We use the non-verbal messages of our clothing to convey certain impressions to other members of society and, depending on the individual, these messages may be subtle or overt. They also change according to our moods and environment and the people we are seeking to impress.

3.3 The Qantas uniform is immediately recognisable as belonging to Australia's internationally respected airline and represents the high standards of aviation and service we associate with Qantas. (Photo courtesy Qantas Airways Ltd.)

1970s expressed the younger generation's rejection of the morals and values held by mainstream society. They violated standard perceptions of beauty by dyeing their hair bright colours or shaving it off, wearing razor blades and chains, slashing clothing and stockings, and by adopting black as their theme colour.

Many of our attitudes to fashion and clothing are culturally based. From the day we are born our ideas about beauty and taste in everything, including clothing, are guided and conditioned as to what is acceptable and appropriate. Because we are products of our society, our attitudes change with changes in society so that what was considered to be the height of fashion and the perfectly proportioned figure in the 1950s differs from what we consider to be perfect today, and will differ again from our view of perfection in future decades.

This process of change evolves steadily along with changes in music, art, philosophy, religion, morals, attitudes and lifestyles, from one generation of ideas to the next.

## THE DESIRE FOR CHANGE

Fashion also changes because we like change. Our senses require constant stimulation so as to remain alert, being easily dulled and bored by unvarying repetition, and attracted and excited by change and novelty. Although we constantly seek the new, it is only a few who have the ability or desire to initiate, explore and develop these changes.

# WHO CHANGES FASHION?

The public often misinterprets changing fashion as being dictated by the whims of influential designers. The evolution of fashion is a far more subtle process

than that, and is very responsive to the mood of the times in which we live.

Until the mid-19th century, we did not have 'designers' to create new trends. Trends were set by the wealthy and powerful, namely royalty and the noble classes. These were then copied by the fashion conscious members of the lower classes from newspaper or magazine illustrations.

This system started to change in 1858, when Charles Frederick Worth opened a boutique to sell his own creations. It was to become the first couture house. He was the first designer with his own recognisable style and he used his influence with the rich, powerful and famous to set new trends.

Since then, fashion has turned full circle. Prior to 1858, the fashionable member of society selected the design, fabric and trims and had garments made up by a dressmaker. Then in the first half of the 20th century, dictatorial designers specified everything — skirt lengths, colours, accessories, hairstyles — and no self-respecting woman would dare be seen without the correct accessories or wearing the wrong length skirt.

The latter half of the 20th century sees a collaboration between designers and the public, where Haute Couture fashion is inspired by street fashion and individuals have the freedom to choose from the varied styles of many designers to find a way of dressing to suit personal tastes and lifestyles.

Each new era brings with it a new way of dressing. Fashion in this century differs from fashion of any other time because we now have access to technology which has transformed cloth and clothing production. Prior to the Industrial Revolution, fashion was a cottage industry. Inventions such as the sewing machine in 1840 initiated the development of the ready-to-wear industry. Computer technology has sped up the process of textile and garment production and greatly increased the variety and

number of styles, fabrics and trims which can be produced.

Fashion trends which used to take years to travel from one part of the world to another can now be transmitted instantly via satellite communications, and success in the industry often relies on the ability to interpret and reproduce new trends as quickly as possible.

The designer's role is to interpret the mood of the time, and to create styles which express that mood. He or she must be able to respond to and guide the tastes, needs and desires of the consumer — sometimes before they are conscious of being ready for it. However, a new fashion works only when it is willingly adopted by the people. A new mode created in Paris or London can never be forced onto a person in Australia who doesn't want to wear it.

# FASHION CYCLES AND THE 'TRICKLE DOWN' THEORY

Fashion involves leaders and followers. There are those who dress to suit their own lifestyle, philosophies and attitudes, and those who slavishly follow trends established by others.

The term 'fashion cycle' refers to that process which starts with the first introduction of a new style to the consumer, develops into mass popularity and declines into démodé, finally to be superseded by the next trend. In short, it is the life span of a fashion trend.

New fashion trends are introduced by fashion leaders, those groups or individuals with social power, wealth, status or influence. They want to be different, to stand apart from others. They do not feel obliged to follow convention and they seek leadership by being the first to establish new trends. These trends are then copied by the followers of the group who are less assertive.

3.4 *Internationally acclaimed Australian bands like INXS reflect and influence fashion trends. Clothing worn here is by Morrissey Edmiston. (Photo courtesy of MMA International.)*

Today's fashion leaders may be designers who themselves have reached 'superstar' status, or celebrities who have temporarily captured public interest. Film stars, rock stars, cultural and political leaders, sporting personalities, international models, and television and media personalities exert more influence over what the general public wears in the late 20th century than the royalty or aristocracy, who had led in previous eras (Fig. 3.4).

As the fashion followers observe the leaders, they gradually become accustomed to new colours, shapes, and details of design and start to imagine themselves in a similar version of the new style. They see the new style appearing in advertisements, in store windows, in magazines, and worn by their friends. The style will most likely have been modified through numerous variations since its first appearance, to accommodate the more conservative tastes and figures of the general public, and thus it becomes a well-established, quite acceptable and widespread fashion trend. This process is also known as the 'trickle down' theory because the trend starts at the top and trickles down through the various levels of society until is worn by nearly everyone.

It is at this point of saturation that the trend begins its downward run on the popularity curve, because the consumer starts to tire of it and decides that it is no longer novel or exciting. Through overuse, the look becomes tedious, and the public starts to search for something fresh. Enter the fashion leaders with another new trend, and the cycle starts over again (Figs. 3.5 & 3.6).

Fashion cycles vary in duration. A fad may last only a matter of months or one season, while classic styling may endure for twenty years or more. The average length of a fashion cycle is seven to nine years although, with the rapid rate of social and technological change occurring in the late 20th century, this period appears to be shortening.

In recent decades we have seen the new phenomenon of past trends being repeated in shorter and shorter cycles, as well as past styles which refuse to die carrying over from one fashion cycle into the next. Add to this international influences on our style of dress, and we have a selection of clothing styles that, for the individual and for Western

3.5 *The evolution of a fashion trend. Depending on their socio-economic position, consumers buy at different stages of the fashion cycle.*

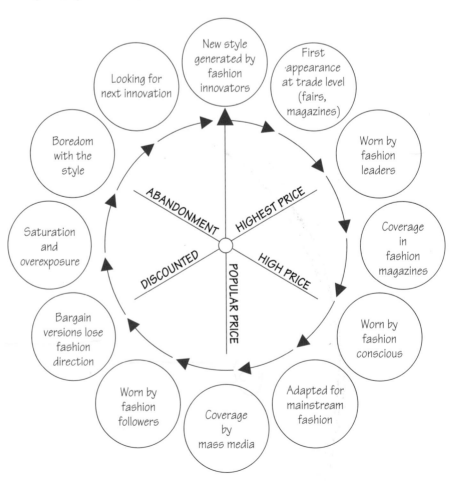

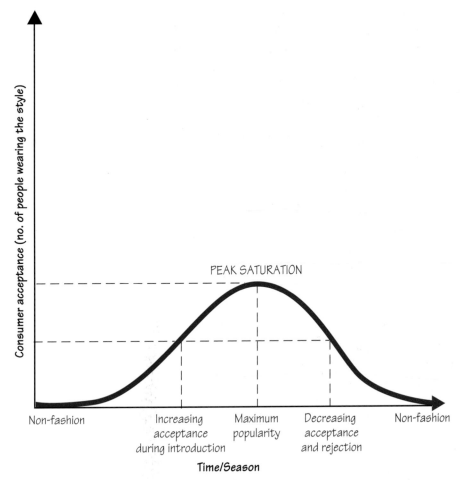

societies in general, is probably more flexible and versatile than at any other time in history.

Why is it that styles which were considered attractive and flattering at the height of their popularity now look strange and unattractive? Figure 3.7 shows the pattern our tastes follow in our acceptance and rejection of passing fashion trends.

When a trend is new, it is considered daring, even outrageous, because we are not used to it. Once we have accepted a trend, we think of it as smart and stylish. The same trend will eventually pass because we see it constantly and it no longer excites or stimulates us. We start to think of it as boring, dull, even dowdy.

As time passes, and we are no longer exposed to styles of past eras, we start to reappraise their 'differentness', and think

◀ 3.6 Popularity curve of the fashion cycle. An average fashion style goes through levels of acceptance and rejection in its lifetime.

▼ 3.7 Changes in fashionable taste. Our appreciation of a fashion trend is directly affected by its place in time.

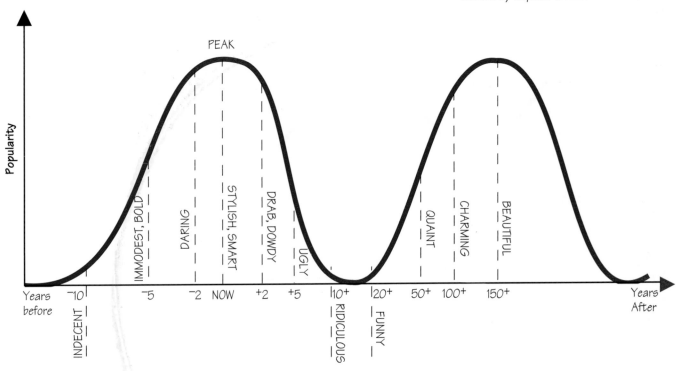

of them as being ugly, then quaint, then perhaps charming and possibly beautiful. It is often at this stage that the styling makes its reappearance on the fashion scene. This long term cycle can be seen very clearly in the history of the silhouette.

# CLASSICS AND FADS

Different fashion items have different life cycles (Fig. 3.8). A fad is the shortest lived of all the trends. It reaches its peak of popularity quickly and stays there for a very short time, perhaps not even a full season, and then dies out just as quickly.

The temporary nature of a fad is usually due to its extreme design. Ex-treme silhouettes, strong colours, bright bold prints, new emblems and exag-gerated accessories are typically faddish, and usually have great appeal for younger sections of the market.

A classic style is one originally intro-duced as a fashion item but, because of its superior design features and broad appeal, stays popular over a long period of time. Conservative, generally simple styling means it can be worn year after year and appeals to most age groups and tastes. A true classic does not alter at all, while others adjust slightly to accommodate changes in fashion with the basic components staying the same.

True classics include Levis 501 jeans, the Chanel suit, Bonds T-shirts, the American Ivy League look, pleated skirts, navy blazers, shirtmaker dresses, and the 'little black dress'.

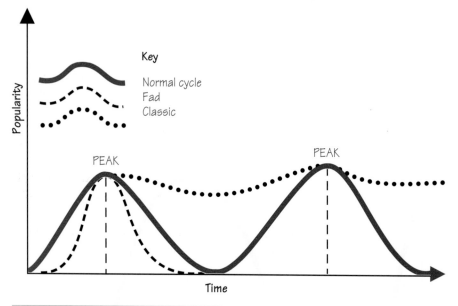

3.8 Fashion cycles of fads and classics. Fashion fads have rapid increase in popularity and equally rapid decline. Fashion classics have ongoing popularity over a sustained period of time.

## CHAPTER 4

# INTRODUCTION

Designing is the process of combining known components in different ways to create new products or effects.

The elements and principles of design are the components designers employ in all forms of art and design, including fashion, architecture,

graphic design, painting and sculpture, even music and poetry.

An understanding of how the elements and principles work, and how to manipulate them, enables the designer to create different visual

effects, and to analyse and appreciate all art forms.

This chapter deals with line, shape and texture. Value and colour are dealt with in Chapter 5 because of their separate importance.

# ELEMENTS AND PRINCIPLES

Every visual design can be broken down into five basic components, known as the *Elements of Design*. These are:

1. Line    4. Colour
2. Shape   5. Texture
3. Value

Design elements can be compared to the letters of the alphabet in that as the 26 letters form the basis of our written language, and can be rearranged and used in different combinations to create hundreds of words with many different meanings, so too can the elements of design be arranged and organised in many ways to create an infinite variety of designs.

*The Principles of Design* are the ways in which design elements may be used. These principles are:

1. Repetition    6. Contrast
2. Gradation     7. Dominance
3. Rhythm        8. Proportion
4. Radiation     9. Balance
5. Harmony       10. Unity

Different design theorists may group the elements and principles differently and may also use slightly different terminology. However, once the basic concepts have been grasped, you will find that such differences are merely matters of personal preference, and that the underlying design theory remains the same.

Visual designs affect us emotionally and psychologically because our senses and instincts react to every design we see. Depending on how the elements and principles have been used, each variation in arrangement and use causes us to respond differently. Understanding how and why a viewer responds to the various elements and principles of design, and knowing how to control and use them to create specific effects, are essential to good designing.

A knowledge of design also assists in recognising well-designed, marketable garments and in analysing why they work. The elements and principles may be used on a garment in one of two ways. *Structural use* refers to those methods which are used in the actual making of the garment, such as seams, darts, panels, openings, pleats, tucks, hemlines and so on. Structural details are more noticeable on garments with plain fabrics and minimal trims.

The other use of elements and principles is through *decorative application*. A detail is decorative if it can be removed without interfering with the underlying garment structure. These treatments include piping, beading, embroidery, textile design, braids, lace trims, buttons and other trims which tend to be used as a decorative finish only.

In a successful design, the structure and decoration of a garment are in harmony with each other and with the function of the garment.

THE FASHION DESIGN MANUAL

4.1 Line types.

| TYPE OF LINE | PSYCHOLOGICAL ASSOCIATION | VISUAL EFFECT | STRUCTURAL USE | DECORATIVE USE |
|---|---|---|---|---|
| Straight | Powerful, stable, masculine, dignified, sure, can look stiff | Opposes natural curves, counters roundness, slims | Seams, yokes, fabric pattern, garment edges, stiff fabrics, darts, pleats, panels | Rows of buttons, zippers, tucks, braids |
| Vertical | Bold, sophisticated, strong, alert, elegant | Slims, adds height | Shirt fronts, back & side seams, darts, pleats, tucks, fabric pattern, sleeveless garments | Any trims |
| Horizontal | Relaxed, calm, gentle, serene | Shortens, broadens, widens, masculine | Shoulder pads, yokes, waistlines, hemlines, wide necklines, wide sleeves, wide collars, darts, panels, fabric pattern, wide brimmed hats, midriffs, belts | Welt pockets, epaulettes, tabs, any trims |
| Diagonal | Interesting, dramatic, restless, indecisive, may unite contrasting directions, active | Slims if more vertical, widens if more horizontal | Panels, seams, fabric patterns, darts, 'V' necklines, collar & lapels, flared trousers, 'A' line skirts, bias cut stripes, raglan sleeves | Pockets, chevrons, any trims |
| Zigzag | A series of connected diagonals — erratic, intense, abrupt, fun, not serious, busy | Angular, counters roundness, enlarges, eye-catching | Pleats, garment edges, fabric pattern, notched collar & lapel, herringbone | Rick-rack, any trims |
| Perpendicular | Conflicting, disturbing | Attracts attention | Seams, yokes, darts, bands, tabs | Any trims |
| Alternating | Sharp, moving, speedy, jumpy, confused, excited | Eyecatching, dominant, may be too violent | Seams, fabric pattern, houndstooth check | Any trims |
| Cross-over | Conflicting, contrasting | Creates a focal point at the point of intersection | Wrap-over skirts & bodies, seams with stripes or checks, fabric pattern, shoulder straps | Lacing, any trims |
| Converging | a. Weight, older  b. Youthful | a. Dragging, descending  b. Uplifting, light.  Emphasises direction | Décolletage neckline, yokes, pleats, darts, seams, panels, collars, handkerchief hemlines, fabric pattern, godets. | Pockets, quilting, any trims |
| Full curve | Active, rounded, forceful, feminine, exuberant | Emphasises body curves, counters thinness and sharp angles, better on thin bodies | Scalloped edges, seams, gathers, soft fabrics, fabric pattern | Pockets, collars, any trims |
| Soft curve | Passive, gentle, feminine, smooth, youthful | Gently emphasises body curves, flattering | Princess lines, drapes, scoop necklines, soft fabrics, seams, yokes, garment edges | Pockets, collars, any trims |

| TYPE OF LINE | PSYCHOLOGICAL ASSOCIATION | VISUAL EFFECT | STRUCTURAL USE | DECORATIVE USE |
|---|---|---|---|---|
| *Undulating* | Feminine, sensuous, gentle, fluid, graceful | Roundness, softens angles | Fluted edges, fabric pattern, frills & ruffles | Any trims |
| *Ogee* | Sinuous, feminine, seductive, graceful | Softens angles, flattering | Panel lines, fabric pattern | Any trims |
| *Opposing curves* | Feminine | Harmonious movement, focal point, emphasises direction | Panel lines, drapes, fabric pattern, wrap garments, garment edges | Any trims |
| *Spiral* | Natural, continuous, feminine | Focal point, eye catching | Floral fabric patterns | Stitching, embroidery beading, flowers, any trims |
| *Thin* | Delicate, calm, fragile, subtle, may be weak | Light-weight, recedes | Seams, garment edges, darts | Embroidery, piping, fringing |
| *Thick* | Forceful, assertive, masculine, confident | Heavy, adds weight, moves forward, attracts attention | Borders, inserts, binds, bands, fabric patterns | Belts, cuffs, collars |
| *Even* | Smooth, firm, certain, steady, regular | Smooths, flatters | Seams, edges, pleats, fabric pattern | Piping, any trims |
| *Uneven* | Wobbly, unstable, indecisive | Emphasises bulges, adds interest | Fabric pattern, seams, garment edges | Any trims |
| *Long* | Continuous, graceful, flowing, smooth | Emphasises direction, length or width | Garment edges, seams, garment openings, hemlines, gathers | Zippers, stitching |
| *Short* | Staccato, efficient, abrupt, busy | Divides spaces, adds interest | Tucks, darts, fabric pattern | Smocking, faggotting, button holes, stitching, any trims, lacing |
| *Broken* | Interrupted, uncertain, casual, sporty | Rhythmic, attracts attention | Fabric pattern, tucks, unpressed pleats | Stitching, button holes, belt loops, interwoven trims |
| *Textured* | Decorative, busy | Attracts attention, adds weight | Fabric pattern | Lace, embroidery, braids |

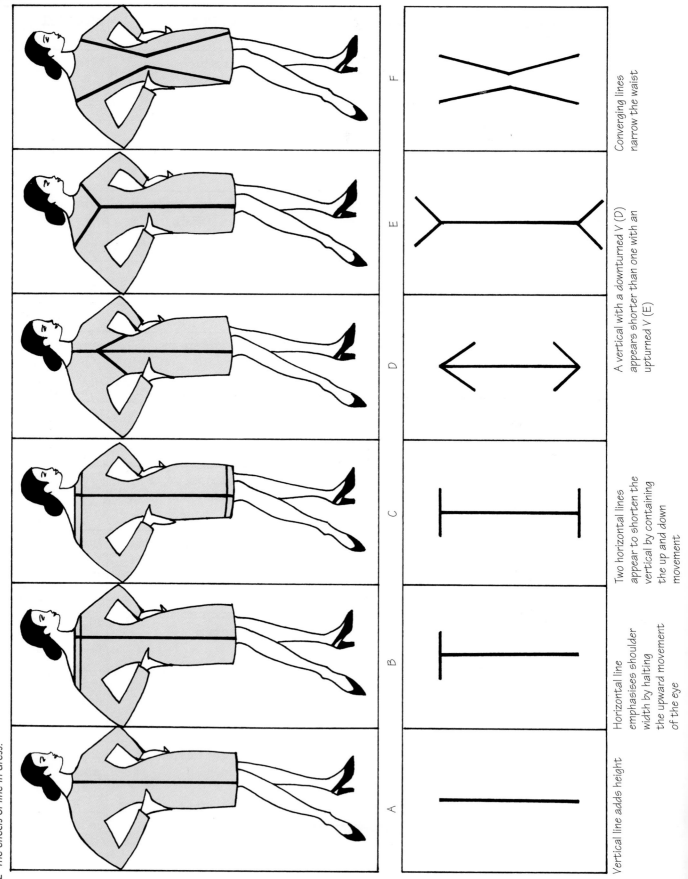

4.2 The effects of line in dress.

| A | B | C | D | E | F |
|---|---|---|---|---|---|
| Vertical line adds height | Horizontal line emphasises shoulder width by halting the upward movement of the eye | Two horizontal lines appear to shorten the vertical by containing the up and down movement | A vertical with a downturned V (D) appears shorter than one with an upturned V (E) | | Converging lines narrow the waist |

4.2 The effects of line in dress (continued).

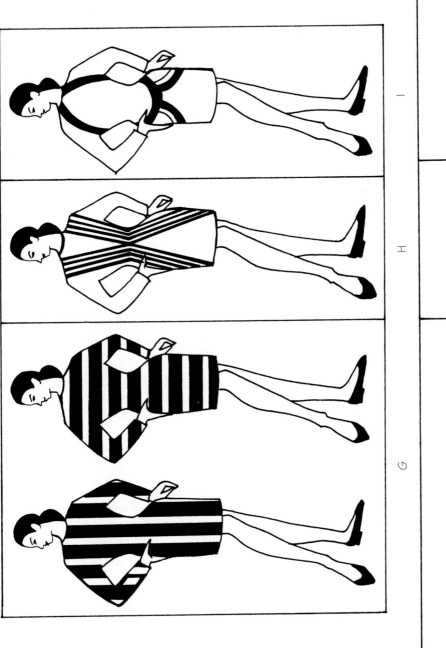

G

H

I

An area appears taller when divided by vertical lines, and wider when divided by horizontal lines. (Boxes are all the same size)

Diagonal lines appear to bend the straight horizontals

Full curves appear larger and emphasise body curves more than straight lines. (Circles are the same width and height as the squares)

# THE ELEMENTS OF DESIGN

## 1. LINE

A line is a series of connected points. It is the simplest of the design elements and is incorporated into the other four elements. All lines have direction, width and length. Line works in a design in the following ways:

### (a) Directing

Line creates movement by leading the eye up and down, side to side or around the garment. Line may be straight, curved or bent, horizontal, diagonal or vertical; or it may be a combination of all these directions.

### (b) Dividing

Line acts as an edge between parts of a garment by dividing the area it passes through. It defines shape and can divide or connect shapes and garment parts.

### (c) Psychological effect

We respond to the quality and character of a line by associating different types of line with certain emotional and psychological states.

Repeated sharp zigzags are disturbing, like lightning, and their movement is often too violent for heavy use in clothing. A designer may use curves to soften their impact to create a forceful but not overwhelming design.

A thick line seems to convey strength and alertness, while a thin line implies weakness or delicacy. An uneven line conveys uncertainty, while a straight line implies firmness and sureness.

The type of line used should suit all the other aspects of the garment. For instance, a wide band on a neck and sleeve edge may be suitable for a strong simple fabric like linen, but may look too severe and heavy on a delicate chiffon. For chiffon, a narrow band on the sleeves and neckline would be more suitable. Similarly, a bold zig-zag print may be too aggressive on a casual summer dress, but would look more appropriate on a dramatic evening gown.

### (d) Optical illusion

Lines may cause visual distortions which affect the way a garment appears when being worn. Depending on the skill of the designer, these effects may conceal figure problems or exaggerate them (Figs. 4.1, 4.2 & 4.3).

For example, vertical lines create the illusion of height, elegance and slimness because they lead the eye up and down, while horizontal lines emphasise shortness and width because of their side to side movement. A vertical line also appears longer than the same line used horizontally, so vertical stripes are usually more flattering than horizontal stripes. Sometimes, however, evenly spaced horizontal lines can add height, because the eye follows them up and down like a ladder.

Curved lines can also create illusions. Because a very curved line makes the figure look rounder and fuller than a slightly curved line, full curves should be avoided. Slightly flatter curves are more flattering.

Two lines angling together create strong directional effects. A narrow angle draws the eye down into the narrow point, whereas a wider angle draws the eye out and emphasises width.

These optical effects are particularly important when dressing certain figure types, and are discussed in more detail in Chapter 15.

## 2. SHAPE

*Shape* is the outer edge or contour of an area surrounded by a closed line. *Silhouette* is the shape of a garment when being worn. *Space* is the area within a shape, or the unenclosed area surrounding a shape. *Form* is a three dimensional shape. We speak of the human form when discussing body shapes. Interest in clothing is created through the interaction of shapes and forms and the play of two-dimensional and three-dimensional areas as the body turns, bends and moves. The bodily contours inside a garment give the garment shape, and, in turn, the garment alters the apparent shape of the body by concealing or revealing its forms.

Garments have three-dimensional form in that they are viewed from the back, front and sides. Shape and space feature in the structural and decorative features of the garment — the pockets, buttons, collars and panel lines.

There are three basic types of shape (Fig. 4.4):

### (a) Geometric

These shapes include the circle, square, rectangle and oval. They are regular, easily measured, and able to be constructed mathematically.

### (b) Natural

These shapes are found in nature and living things. They are usually curved and organic and may have a random appearance.

### (c) Non-objective

These are neither geometric nor natural, and generally refer to human-made shapes and accidental shapes.

As with line, different types of shape cause different sensory responses.

The regular, strong angles and straight lines of cubes, rectangles and squares appear stable, confident and powerful, while the sharper angles and diagonal lines of triangles, diamonds and pyramids seem unstable but more exciting.

Geometric shapes of unequal proportions, such as rectangles, cones, pyramids and diamonds, are more interesting to the eye than are the per-

4.3 Optical illusions in dress.

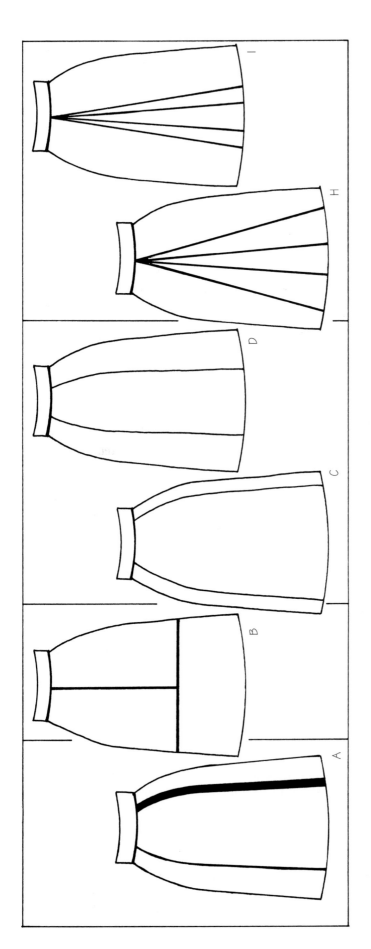

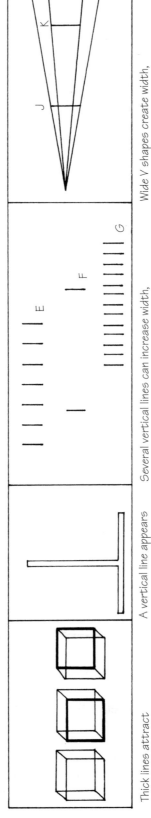

Thick lines attract attention

A vertical line appears longer than a horizontal line of the same length

Several vertical lines can increase width, depending on how they are spaced. Skirt C appears wider than D. G appears wider than E, which in turn looks wider than F

Wide V shapes create width, narrow V shapes slim. The inside angles of H and I are the same. The vertical lines J and K are the same length

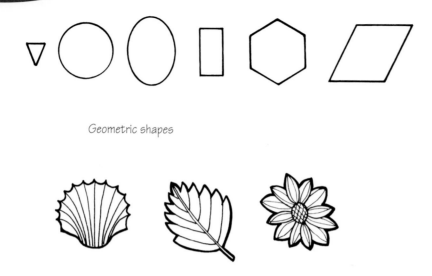

Geometric shapes

Natural shapes

Non-objective shapes

4.4 Types of shape.

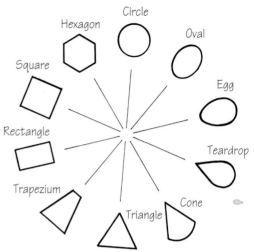

4.5 The shape wheel. All shapes can be created from these basic shapes. Shapes next to each other are harmonious. Those opposite on the wheel are contrasting.

fect regularities of the square, cube, circle and sphere. Their slight unevenness holds the attention of the viewer as he or she compares and considers the differences. The firm sharp edges of geometric shapes seem more aggressive than natural or non-objective shapes.

Curved shapes suggest femininity and confidence, and are subtly intriguing with their gentle changes in direction.

## Visual effects of shape

A designer alters an area by creating, dividing, pushing, pulling and rearranging lines, shapes and spaces. In this way new designs are created.

Shape and space create visual illusions in the same way line does. The nature of a shape affects the appearance of the wearer in terms of height, weight and size, and also influences our psychological impressions of and responses to the wearer (Fig. 4.6).

As with line, a shape or space which is divided vertically appears longer and narrower than one which is divided horizontally. Horizontal divisions make the figure appear shorter and wider. A shape which angles away from the body implies width and bulk, while a shape which tapers appears to slim and narrow the body.

Curves also emphasise well-rounded body forms and are put to good use in producing a voluptuous, feminine look. The fuller the curve, the stronger the effect.

The position of an item on a garment, overlapping shapes, type of outline, size and boldness all affect the apparent nearness or distance of shapes to the viewer. For example, large bold patterns seem to advance, appear larger and make the wearer seem bigger in size, while small delicate patterns blend into the distance and do not jump out at the viewer. Smaller shapes are more flattering on larger figures.

Thick outlines such as a wide band around a neckline or pocket also bring shapes forward, whereas fine or broken outlines cause shapes to recede.

## Space

Space is not as passive in design as we may think. It plays an important role in defining relationships within a design because it forms the background onto which a designer arranges other shapes and spaces.

As a background, the functions of space are:

1. To provide a visual rest as the eye moves over the other details of the design.

2. To accentuate or quieten the shapes arranged on it.

3. To unite foreground shapes by introducing common features, or define shapes by separating and isolating them.

4.6 Visual effects of shape and space.

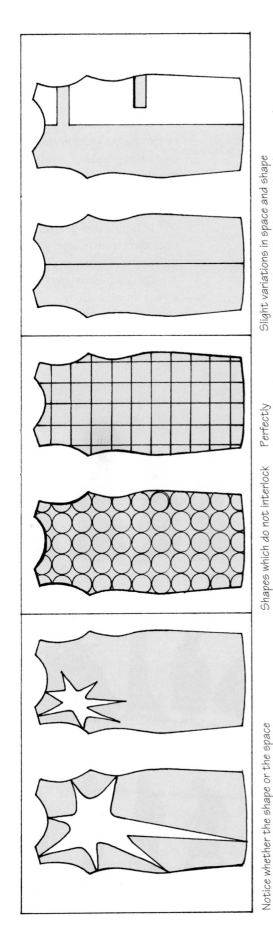

Notice whether the shape or the space around it is more noticeable

Shapes with sharp, thick outlines advance

Shapes with light or broken outlines recede

Shapes which do not interlock perfectly create new shapes

Perfectly interlocking shapes

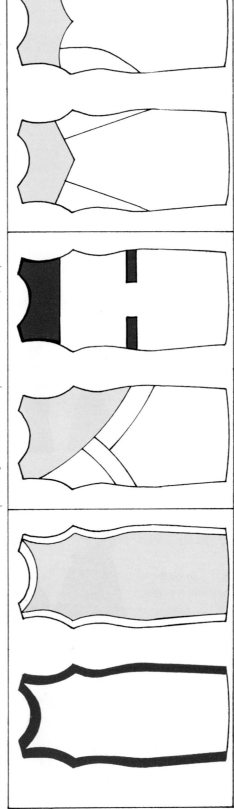

Slight variations in space and shape are more interesting than regular shapes and spaces

The right shoulder appears to advance because it overlaps the other shapes

Filled spaces appear to advance

Curved shapes appear larger and emphasise feminine curves more than straight lines

Spaces introduce variety into a design. Arrangements of space and shape which are slightly varied or irregular hold the interest of the viewer longer than those which are perfectly even and regular.

Large, simple areas of space suggest calmness and confidence but may lack excitement. Small, complex shapes and spaces are busy and interesting, but may cause confusion and tension. If a space is too crowded, the eye becomes tired and distracted.

Some shapes fit together perfectly with no space between them. Other shapes form spaces where edges do not interlock, and create new interesting patterns which enhance the original design. Further shapes are also created when outlines intersect.

Shape and space are created structurally in garments through the use of seams and garment edges, panel lines, darts, yokes and inserts. They mould the shape of the garment by tapering or adding fullness to the silhouette. Further interest can be added to shape and space with the introduction of the other elements — line, value, colour and texture.

## Silhouette

The silhouette is fundamental to the style of a garment. The size, shape and proportions of the silhouette are easily seen from a distance and are therefore noticed before all other details, excluding colour.

Because the eye is drawn to garment edges, the side seams, shoulder line, waistline and hemline of the silhouette all need to work well together to create a strong shape and a well proportioned garment. The human form is three-dimensional, so the designer must consider every angle of the silhouette as it moves and turns. Back and side views are as important as the front view, and there should be a sense of flow and continuity from one view to another.

Enrichment of the silhouette takes place through the addition of line, shape

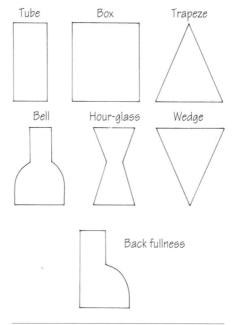

▲ 4.7 Basic fashion silhouettes. These seven silhouettes have recurred regularly in fashion.

▼ 4.8 Historical changes in silhouette.

and space, colour and texture. While adding variety and interest, all elements should work in harmony with the silhouette to enhance the overall concept of the design.

A basic silhouette can be changed by moving the waistline, raising or lowering sleeve, jacket, trouser and skirt lengths, or by widening or narrowing shoulders, sleeves, trouser legs and skirts. Techniques such as padding on shoulders and hips, draping, gathers and contour lines also create exaggerated versions of the basic silhouette.

Fashion trends can be clearly observed from a study of the cyclical changes in silhouette over the centuries. In past centuries, the silhouette changed very slowly and a new style could take decades or even centuries to evolve.

Improvements in garment production techniques, which occurred with the onset of the Industrial

2700BC    400BC    1200    1300    1400    1500    1600

1670    1730    1780    1800    1850    1900

1920    1940    1950    1960    1970    1980    1990

Revolution and our improved world-wide communications, has sped up the process to such a degree that each new season shows changes in silhouette, colour, fabrics and details.

There are seven main silhouettes which rise, peak and fall in popularity (Fig. 4.7). They are the tube (rectangle), the box (square), the A-line (trapeze), the wedge, the hour-glass, the bell, and the back fullness. Within these seven categories, there are endless variations of length, waistline position, fullness and proportion. Although the silhouettes recur regularly, each cycle brings with it new interpretations and new fashion features (Fig. 4.8).

Men's fashion silhouettes also change, but in recent years the garments have remained fundamentally the same, with only subtle changes in fit and detailing. Fit for men's garments range from body hugging to baggy, while changes in detail include width of neckties, lapels, cuffs and trouser legs.

## 3.  TEXTURE

Texture describes the nature of a surface. In fashion design, texture refers to the nature of the surface of fabrics and trimmings used in a garment. It is important because consumers are first attracted by the colour of a garment, then automatically reach out to determine whether they like the feel of the fabric. Texture is considered a design element because all fabrics have a surface texture which plays a major role in every garment design. Texture is:

### (a)  Visual

Light falling onto a surface can be seen as shadows, highlights, sheen, etc. Light and shade play across knitted or rough woven surfaces such as hessian, whereas smooth surfaces such as satin have no shadows and reflect light. A cloth appears transparent when light passes through its surface, whereas no light passes through an opaque cloth. Visual texture may also be applied to fabrics through surface treatments such as printing, embroidery, smocking, quilting and appliqué.

### (b)  Tactile

Changes in fabric surface due to the arrangement of the individual threads in weaving or knitting can be felt on the skin. 'Hand' refers to the feel of a fabric, its coarseness, softness, drape or stiffness.

### (c)  Audible

The friction created by fabric surfaces rubbing over each other can be heard. The crisp rustle of silk is known as 'scroop'.

Textures suggest things about the wearer which we respond to on a psychological level (Fig. 4.9). We make assumptions about age, personality, degree of sophistication, wealth, lifestyle and occupation according to certain fabrics and textures. We would assume that a man commonly wearing a silk shirt and linen trousers would not be a gardener, because, if for no other reason, those fabrics are totally unsuited to dirty, heavy work.

*4.9  Texture suggests lifestyle. The rough textures of these cotton knits look casual and cosy. (Cotton Knits by Thorobred Crucci. Photo courtesy Australian Cotton Foundation Ltd.)*

Textures fall into four basic categories which create different moods (Fig. 4.10). The categories are:

## (a) Rough/Matt

These textures are sporty, casual, 'outdoorsy' and comforting. Soft fluffy textures such as fleecy knits and lambswool seem to offer cosiness and comfort, while the coarser textures of tweeds, hand-knits and corduroys suggest warmth and protection in casual, outdoor environments.

## (b) Rough/Glossy

Rich, luxurious and glamorous, such fabrics as shimmering lamés, brocades, sequins and dupion silks seem to reflect the night lights and life of wealthy sophisticates.

## (c) Smooth/Matt

Business-like, official and mature, these textures are often found in suiting fabrics, are generally crisp and tightly woven and they look good quality. Such fabrics wear well, do not crease and are very practical for the no-nonsense business person. Denim and garberdine are examples of smooth or matt texture.

## (d) Smooth/Glossy

These textures are associated with young, fancy, slinky, evening wear. The rustle of taffeta, or the smooth swish of satin are sounds we associate with luxury and glamour.

The mood created by fabric texture must suit all other details of the garment, including the colour, proportion, shape, decoration and the function of the garment.

For example, a soft, delicate and loosely woven fabric such as cheesecloth is not suitable for a garment in everyday use and subjected to continuous wear and tear. A smooth, tightly woven, heavy weight fabric, such as poly-cotton drill would be much more comfortable and serviceable in this instance.

Texture also determines how a fabric will perform, and a successful design respects the fabric's textural characteristics. The designer plays with a cloth to determine the hand and to see how it responds when pleated, folded, gathered and so on. In this way, the fabric shows how it should best be used and guides the designer's styling decisions.

As with the other design elements, textures come and go in fashion. Moderately textured fabrics such as gaberdine, drill, light-weight flannel, light-weight linen and polyester crêpe de chine are classic textures which have remained popular over a long time. Their plain surfaces mean that people do not easily tire of them, and they are suitable for a wide variety of styles.

## Physical aspects of texture

Texture affects wearer comfort. Because fabrics are worn against the skin, rough, coarse textures can be quite irritating, and some skin types have allergic reactions to certain fibres, particularly wool. Better quality garments are lined with smooth, lightweight, slippery fabrics, which do not add bulk but slide easily over the skin, protect against irritation, and help retain the shape and prolong the life of the outer fabric. Undergarments are made from smooth, soft fabrics for this reason (Fig. 4.11).

Because textures absorb and/or reflect light and heat, we experience temperature differences when we wear different fabrics. Dull surfaces absorb heat, while shiny surfaces reflect heat and are cooler to wear.

4.10 *The texture wheel. Textures directly opposite on the wheel have contrasting qualities.*

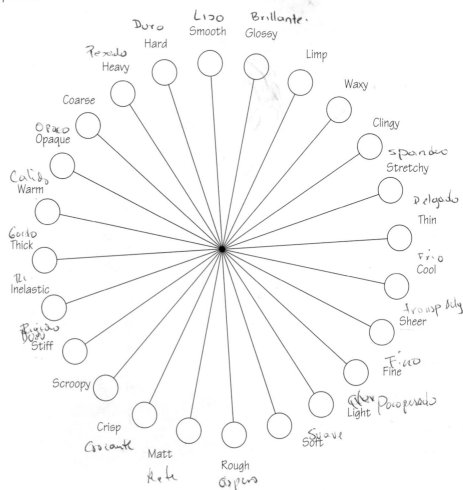

▲ 4.11 *Texture and comfort. Fabrics used in underwear must be soft and non-irritating to the skin. (Photo courtesy Berlei.)*

Light-weight, drapey fabrics such as jersey or satin are very revealing because they cling to the body. Light, stiff fabrics such as taffeta or linen take on their own form because they stand away from the body, and are good for creating dramatic silhouettes.

Smooth, plain surfaces tend to require more construction and trimming detail to add interest to the design. The more complex the texture, the simpler the design should be because any detailing tends to become lost in the pattern.

Reflective surfaces have certain qualities the designer should be aware of. Dull textures are slimming because they absorb light. Smooth, shiny surfaces like satin seem to advance and enlarge the figure. They also make colours seem brighter than do matt surfaces. Red satin is brighter and more noticeable than red flannel.

The colour of velvets and corduroys is determined by the reflection of light on the pile of the fabric (Fig. 4.12). Colour changes according to the direction of the nap, so it should always be cut one-way. This also applies to shot fabrics and lamé, leather and some satins.

Sheer fabrics soften colours because the skin tone of the wearer is seen beneath the fabric. From a distance, some textures have a directional movement,

## Visual effects of texture

Texture creates visual illusions that affect the appearance of the figure. Coarse and bulky textures have an enlarging effect. Bold checks, wide wales on corduroy, thick pile on furs, and fluffy surfaces conceal body contours and make the figure look larger than do smooth fine textures.

Large, bold textures can also overpower small garments or small figures, so a texture must be in correct proportion to the garment or trim for which it is to be used.

▼ 4.12 *Nap and pile fabrics.*

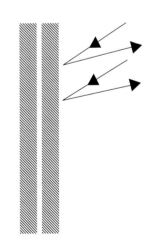

Light reflects off the surface of downward facing fibres, making the fabric look lighter and shinier

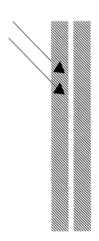

Light is absorbed into the upward facing pile fibres, making the fabric look dark and rich

that is, they seem to lead the eye horizontally, vertically, or diagonally. This frequently occurs with all-over prints and, while the effect may not be noticed at close range or from small fabric swatches, it could cause some visual distortion once the garment is made up.

Texture is introduced into a design in one or more ways. Firstly, every fabric has *self-texture*, which is the surface created when the fibres are woven or knitted together. Secondly, texture may be applied through various *finishes* to the fabric. These are numerous and range from polishing surfaces and crinkle effects to flocking, embossing, moiréing and napping. Thirdly, texture may be applied *decoratively*, through fabric combinations, accessories, trims and surface treatments such as printing, appliqué, smocking, embroidery and beading (Fig. 4.13).

To avoid visual confusion, it is advisable to limit the number of textures to no more than three per design. This works especially well if one texture is used as the dominant texture, and colour and tonal variations are kept very simple.

*4.13 Texture and decoration. The smooth, slinky quality of Lycra® is enhanced by the application of richly textured trimmings. (Designed by Manon Youdale. Photo courtesy of Du Pont, Australia, Ltd.)*

# CHAPTER 5

# INTRODUCTION

Colours are the children of light, and light is their mother.

Johannes Itten

Daylight is the source of colour, and colour is a vital part of our total human experience. Like all living things, we respond physically, emotionally and psychologically to variations in the quality of light. We are alert and stimulated by sunlight and ill at ease when deprived of light. The colours we wear affect our appearance, our moods and the attitudes of other people towards us.

## THE EXPERIENCE OF COLOUR

Colour is one of the more important elements of fashion design because it is the first thing we notice about a garment. When shopping, we look for colour first, then fabric, silhouette, and finally detailing. Colour is a major deciding factor in everything we purchase and choose to surround ourselves with, from cars and furniture to shampoo, washing powder and even food. It is not surprising that we are so sensitive to colour when we consider that a person with normal vision can distinguish over 10 000 colours, 160 pure hues, 200 greys, and 20 degrees of brightness.

To experience colour, three factors must exist. These are *light*, which is the source of colour, a *surface* which reflects colour, and the *eye* which perceives colour. White light is composed of a spectrum

of seven colours — red, orange, yellow, green, blue, indigo and violet (Fig. 5.1). The colours of the spectrum can be seen when light passes through a prism, or in a rainbow when daylight is refracted by water droplets in the air. They appear different because they are of varying wavelengths. Warm colours such as red have longer wavelengths and seem to advance towards the eye. Cool colours such as blue and violet have shorter wavelengths, and seem to recede from the eye.

Objects appear coloured because their surfaces absorb certain parts of the spectrum and reflect other parts back to our eyes. Our eyes see this reflected light as colour, but the absorbed light is not visible. For example, we see the colour red when an object reflects red light rays back to our eyes, and absorbs all the other colours of the spectrum. A blue object reflects blue and absorbs red and all other light rays. A white surface reflects all light rays back to our eyes, while a black surface absorbs all light,

reflecting no colour back to our eyes (Fig. 5.2).

Johannes Itten (1888–1967) was a German colourist who developed the theory of seasonal colours. From studies conducted with his students, he discovered that individuals are most comfortable using colours which suit their personal colouring and personality. His theories form the basis from which many colour and image consultants work today.

All colours have three characteristics:

### 1. Hue
This is the name of a colour, such as red, yellow, blue or green. The term 'hue' should not be interchanged with the term 'colour', because hue refers to only one dimension of colour. Technically speaking, 'colour' describes the effect achieved when hue, value and chroma are used together.

### 2. Value
Also called 'tone', value is the lightness

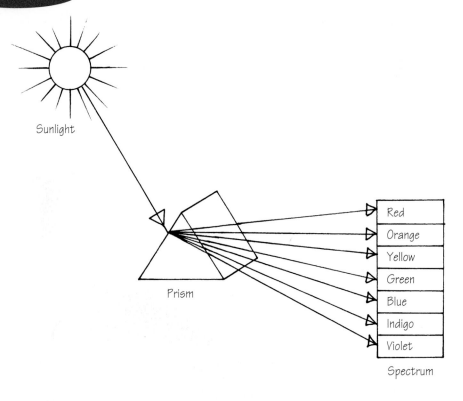

Sunlight

Prism

Spectrum

Red
Orange
Yellow
Green
Blue
Indigo
Violet

◀ 5.1 *Refracting white light. Sunlight passing through a prism is split into a continuous band showing the seven colours of the spectrum.*

▼ 5.2 *The way we see colour. All light is reflected from a white surface, a blue surface reflects only blue light, a red surface reflects only red light, and all light is absorbed by a black surface.*

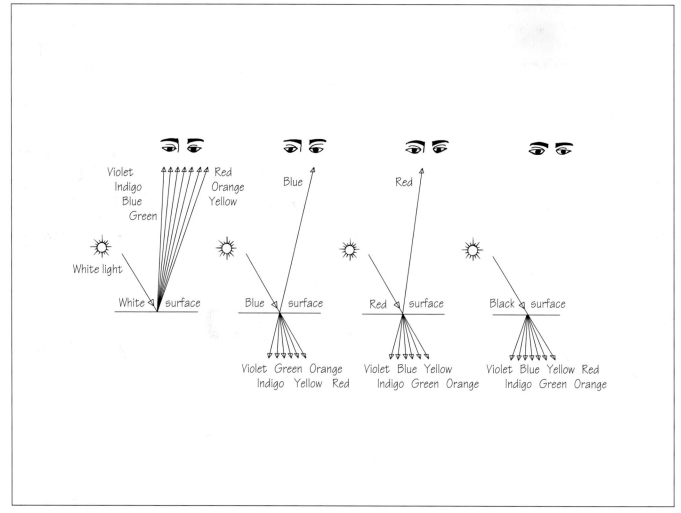

Violet Indigo Blue Green — Red Orange Yellow

White light

White surface

Violet Green Orange
Indigo Yellow Red

Blue

Blue surface

Violet Blue Yellow
Indigo Green Orange

Red

Red surface

Violet Blue Yellow
Indigo Green Orange

Black surface

Violet Blue Yellow Red
Indigo Green Orange

or darkness of a colour. It is the quality which makes light blue different from dark blue.

### 3. Chroma

Chroma is the purity of a colour. It is the clarity, intensity, brightness or dullness of a hue. It is the quality which makes yellow different from ochre, or from lemon. The colours of the spectrum are pure in chroma.

# VALUE

Value deals with black, white and grey — true neutrals because they do not convey any colour. Because value can be used without considering colour, it stands on its own as a separate element of design. The use of colour, however, must include a consideration of value.

Value is the most important of the three dimensions of colour. The eye responds immediately to patterns created by the interplay of light and dark, and to the moods this interplay creates. Variations in value can emphasise, conceal, produce movement, and evoke emotional and psychological responses.

Value is measured in two ways. The *value scale* measures degrees of lightness and darkness, and the *value key* measures the degree of harmony or contrast created by combinations of light and dark.

## THE VALUE SCALE

The value scale is a gradated scale of nine tones ranging from white at the top to black at the bottom (Fig. 5.3). The scale is divided as follows:

| | |
|---|---|
| 1–3 (white to light grey) | High value |
| 4–6 (mid greys) | Intermediate value |
| 7–9 (dark grey to black) | Low value |

High value

Intermediate value

Low value

1
2
3
4
5
6
7
8
9

(a)  (b)

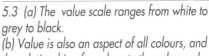

5.3 (a) The value scale ranges from white to grey to black.
(b) Value is also an aspect of all colours, and the relationship of a colour to the value scale can be seen here.

Values are said to be *contrasting* when far apart on the scale, and *harmonious* when close together on the scale. For example, 2 and 9 are contrasting tones, and 4 and 6 are harmonious. Emotional response to a colour scheme is determined largely by the degree of harmony and contrast in the tonal relationships.

## THE VALUE KEY

Tonal combinations are known as value keys, and may be major or minor, depending on whether they contrast or harmonise (Fig. 5.4).

Minor keys are harmonious and use combinations which are close together on the value scale, for example 7, 8 and 9. They are quiet and restrained. Major keys have strong contrasts and are bold and striking, for example 1, 5 and 8 on the value scale.

Value keys can be further defined according to their use of High, Intermediate or Low tones, and can be classified as follows:

### 1. High major key

This is predominantly light with dark contrasts, and is confident, stimulating and up-beat.

### 2. Intermediate major key

This key has mainly mid-tones, with small areas of strong contrast, and is powerful, rich and masculine.

### 3. Low major key

This is predominantly dark with light contrasts, and is dramatic, dignified and formal.

### 4. High minor key

This key has very light tones which are delicate, feminine and peaceful.

### 5. Intermediate minor key

This has closely related mid-tones and is restrained, passive and dreamy.

### 6. Low minor key

Very dark tones which may be depressing and sinister or rich and formal are characteristic of this key.

Value keys work best when one tone dominates the design, and the others work to support and add interest. When several or all tones are equally dominant, strong competition between them results in visual confusion and disunity.

5.4 Value keys. By varying tonal combinations the designer can change the appearance of a garment. Major value keys are contrasting, minor value keys are harmonious.

## VISUAL EFFECTS OF VALUE

Lightness or darkness in value creates visual illusions which affect the appearance of garments. Light tones make forms advance and appear larger, while darker values appear to recede and reduce in size (Figs. 5.5 & 5.6).

Knowledge of this effect can be used to visually alter garment and body proportions. A dark skirt teamed with a light bodice creates quite a different effect to a light skirt with dark bodice, and can be used to help correct 'bottom-heavy' or 'top-heavy' figures (Fig. 5.7).

The asymmetrical use of strong contrasts can distort proportions and make

High major       Intermediate major       Low major

High minor       Intermediate minor       Low minor

one side of a garment or figure look quite lopsided in relation to the other side. To correct this imbalance, the stronger tone may be used in smaller quantities as an accent only.

Strong contrasts can be used to draw the eye away from an undesirable feature, and create a new focal point (Fig. 5.8). For example, a white collar on a dark dress attracts the eye to and pleasantly frames the wearer's face.

When used together, light tones make dark tones appear darker, and dark tones make light tones appear lighter. A light grey looks lighter when used with black, and a dark grey looks darker when used with white (Fig. 5.9). Because contrasts in value are powerful, a designer should ensure that they do not distort or overwhelm a garment, but provide interest and variety by supporting the initial design concept.

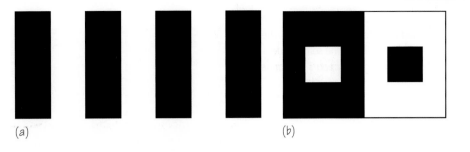

(a)                                    (b)

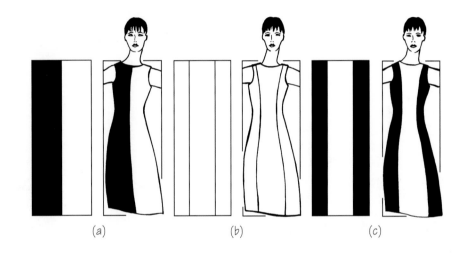

(a)                (b)                (c)

5.5 (top)  Visual effects of value. (a) The black and white widths appear different, although they are actually the same. (b) Although the white areas are the same size as the corresponding black areas, the illusion is that the white areas are bigger.

5.6 (centre)  Size effects of value. Figure problems can be disguised by the illusions created through light and dark contrasts. Garment (c) is the most slimming because the eye sees mainly the centre white panel. Garment (a) is more slimming than garment (b).

5.7 (left)  Altering proportions with value. Physical proportions can be altered through the distribution of light and dark values.

5.8 (right)  Strong contrasts used asymmetrically can upset the balance of the figure, or correct an unbalanced figure. Contrasting values used as an accent draw the eye away from figure problems.

▶ *5.9 Identical values can appear different when used on different backgrounds. The 'I' panel in this diagram is the same value throughout although it appears to change.*

▼ *5.10 Chroma, the brightness of a colour, is lowered when a colour is mixed with black, white, grey or through the addition of its complement.*

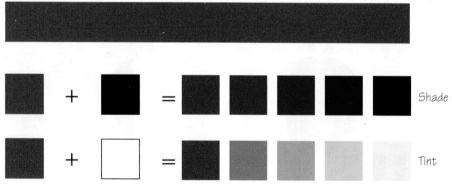

Shade

Tint

# CHROMA

*Chroma* refers to the purity of a colour. It is the strength or weakness, brightness or dullness of a colour. It is also known as *saturation* (or *intensity*). Chroma ranges from neutral grey, which has the lowest level of chroma, through to the pure chroma of the colour spectrum which has the maximum intensity.

Chroma can be altered by mixing a colour with black, white, grey or its complement (Fig. 5.10). A *tint* is a pure hue with white added and is high on the value scale. A *shade* is a pure hue with black added and is low on the value scale.

Two colours of the same hue (e.g. red), and the same value (e.g. intermediate), may still be quite different colours due to their differences in chroma (e.g. hot pink, scarlet, terracotta).

# CHARACTERISTICS AND USAGE OF COLOUR

## THE COLOUR WHEEL

The colour wheel was devised by Isaac Newton for the study of colour. It explains colour relationships and promotes our understanding of colour mixing and colour schemes.

Newton's colour wheel is only one of many colour relationship theories used to organise colour. At the turn of the century Albert H Munsell developed a system of colour identification in an attempt to standardise colour terminology. His colour notation system identifies and numbers various hues and is used by governments, industry and colour organisations worldwide.

The basic colour wheel is a continuous circle of pure colour, with the colours occuring in the same sequence as in a rainbow and the natural colour spectrum. We augment the original seven colours of the spectrum with purple which is placed between red and violet.

Pure hues are used for the colour wheel. They are free from the addition of black, white, grey or any other colour, and are at their most brilliant. Colours on the colour wheel are evenly spaced, and grouped into primary, secondary and tertiary colours.

*Primary* colours are those which cannot be mixed from other colours, but can themselves be mixed in different combinations to create other hues. The primary colours are red, blue and yellow.

*Secondary* colours are created when equal quantities of any two primaries are mixed. The secondary colours are green, purple and orange.

*Tertiary* colours are mixed from a primary and a neighbouring secondary colour, or from two secondary colours. The tertiary colours are red-orange, yellow-orange, yellow-green, blue-green, blue-violet and red-violet. (See Fig. 5.11, on the inside cover of this book.)

## COLOUR TEMPERATURES

Colours are associated with temperature. *Warm* colours are red, red-orange, orange, yellow-orange, yellow and red-violet. Warm colours suggest heat, and are often the colour of things we think of as warm — the sun, fire, earth tones, summer fruits and flowers. Warm colours appear to advance because of the predominance of yellow, so they attract attention and have an enlarging effect.

*Cool* colours are violet, blue-violet, blue, blue-green, green and yellow-green. Cool colours suggest cold sensations and are associated with things like ice, water, the sea, the sky, winter days and grass. Cool colours recede because of the predominance of blue, so they make objects, shapes and areas appear smaller and more distant.

The phenomenon of warm and cool colour has a physical as well as psychological basis. Scientific experiments have shown that different parts of the spectrum record different temperatures when measured with a thermometer, and that people feel warmer in a room painted with red than they do in a room painted green.

Colour consultants analyse skin undertones as either warm or cool and advise that the most flattering colours are those which are the same as the wearer's skin tone. An individual's personal colouring is usually overlooked by fashion colour cycles and designers, but if both warm and cool colours are included in the range, a designer can be sure that there is something suitable for all complexions.

## NAMING COLOURS

Although we need to be familiar with the technical language of colour to be able discuss it in a design context, descriptive terms are used to denote colours in everyday use. Terms such as apricot, avocado, lavender, rust, bronze, sand, marine and camel are subjective and open to misinterpretation because a person who has never seen an apricot or avocado would have no idea of the colour implied by such terms. However, these names are far more scintillating and likely to excite our imaginations than 'the dress, orange in hue with high value and low intensity'.

## HARMONIOUS COLOURS

Harmonies occur frequently in nature and can be seen in the green and blue of the sea, the yellow and green of plants and grasses and the reds, oranges and yellows of a sunset.

Harmonious (also called *analogous*) colours are adjacent on the colour wheel and are related because they have been mixed from a common hue. Yellow and orange are harmonious because both contain yellow. Colours are more harmonious when chromas are weak, and more contrasting when chromas are strong.

*Simple harmony* refers to the use of related colours which occur next to each other on the colour wheel.

*Extended harmony* refers to the use of related colours which occur alternately on the wheel. This is a broader use of colour and therefore more interesting than simple harmony (Fig. 5.12).

## COMPLEMENTARY COLOURS

Complementary colours are opposite each other on the colour wheel, meaning they have no hue in common. Red and green, yellow and purple, and blue and orange are complementaries.

Complementary colours intensify each other. When green and red are

*5.12 Simple harmony (left) and extended harmony (right).*

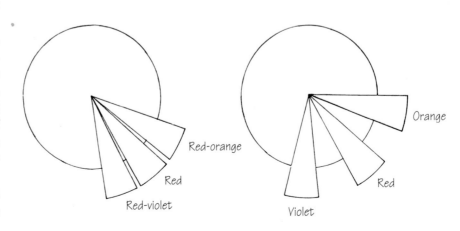

THE FASHION DESIGN MANUAL

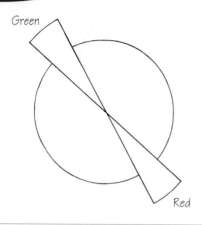

Green

Red

*5.13 Complementaries.*

Yellow : Violet = $\frac{1}{4}$ : $\frac{3}{4}$

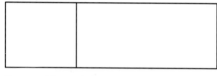

Orange : Blue = $\frac{1}{3}$ : $\frac{2}{3}$

Red : Green = $\frac{1}{2}$ : $\frac{1}{2}$

*5.14 Goethe's ratios show how to vary the proportions of complementary colours to achieve balance; that is, so that one does not overpower the other.*

used together, the red appears redder and more warm, and the green appears greener and more cold. They both appear stronger and more vivid (Fig. 5.13).

To harmoniously balance proportions in a complementary colour scheme, it may help to refer to Goethe's ratios (Fig. 5.14). These are:

$$\text{Yellow } \tfrac{1}{4} \text{ to Violet } \tfrac{3}{4}$$

$$\text{Orange } \tfrac{1}{3} \text{ to Blue } \tfrac{2}{3}$$

$$\text{Red } \tfrac{1}{2} \text{ to Green } \tfrac{1}{2}$$

Reduced contrasts produce subtle complementary schemes through the addition of white, black or the complementary hue to reduce the chromatic intensity of a colour.

## DISCORDS

A *discord* occurs when the natural tonal order of the colour wheel is reversed.

For example, red is normally darker than orange but a discord is created when white is added to the red so that it becomes pink, which is lighter in value than the orange.

Discords add excitement to a colour scheme, but must be used carefully so as not to overpower the design.

*Reverse discord* can be created by darkening a naturally light colour, but the impact is not as strong as normal discord. An example of a reverse discord is orange reduced to brown, and used with blue.

Orange and pink together is a harmonious discord, and red and pale green is a contrasting discord.

## COLOUR SCHEMES

Colour schemes are the relationships between the different colours in a design in terms of hue, tone and chroma. A successful colour scheme is pleasing to the eye, suits the mood of the fabric or garment it is to be used on, and is interesting, varied and united. A colour scheme may be:

### 1. Achromatic
This uses only black, white and grey tones. Depending on the value key, the effect may be soft or bold, but it is always smart.

### 2. Monochromatic
Composed of colours created from one hue, with the addition of black, white, grey or other colours, the effect is harmonious and safe.

### 3. Harmonious
Colour schemes which are harmonious have one or more hues in common. The effect is more varied than a monochromatic scheme.

### 4. Complementary
Using colours opposite each other on the colour wheel results in a bold, strong and contrasting effect.

### 5. Combined harmonious/complementary
These are mainly harmonious colour combinations, livened up with complementary accents. The overall effect is still harmonious, with exciting highlights.

An *accent* is a colour used in small quantities as a highlight. An accent colour is often complementary to the main colour, and usually has high chroma.

Colour schemes may also include unrestricted combinations of the above. The overall mood of the scheme is established by the Value Key, and is modified through the use of hue, chroma and accent colours. (See Fig. 5.15 on inside the cover of this book.)

## COLOUR PSYCHOLOGY

All colours are imbued with psychological and symbolic significance, and colour preferences reflect our past experiences, personalities and personal colouration. Certain character traits and emotions are identified in terms of colour — green for envy, red for passion, yellow for cowardice or ill-health, blue for peace and tranquility, white for purity and innocence, black for death, mystery or evil.

Broadly speaking, light, bright colours are more popular than dark, dull colours. Blue is the most popular colour overall and is favoured by men, followed by red, which is favoured by women.

Traditionally, colour has been associated with gender. Warmer, lighter colours such as pinks, yellows and pastel shades are usually considered to be feminine, while cooler, darker colours like blue and grey suggest masculinity. Colour also suggests age. Young people tend to prefer light, bright, warm colours, which seem to suit the happy, carefree days of childhood. Primary and secondary colours appeal to this age group.

The colours we consider to be sophisticated are dark and cool, and are often worn by older people who prefer more mellow colours. Brown, navy and neutrals are common choices.

## PHYSICAL EFFECTS OF COLOUR

### Temperature

The designer's colour palette usually changes with the seasons. Cool, light colours are preferred in summer because they reflect light and heat, and are therefore cooler to wear. Warm, dark colours are worn in winter. Not only do the earth and autumn tones suggest warmth and cosiness, they also physically absorb light and heat. While white objects may absorb as little as 10 per cent of light rays hitting their surface, black objects may absorb over 95 per cent of light rays.

## VISUAL EFFECTS OF COLOUR

Colours deceive the eye. They change continually according to different lighting, surfaces, backgrounds, position, even geographic location. Colours react with each other and to each other. These reactions can create sometimes subtle, sometimes very strong, visual illusions. Proportions in a garment can be dramatically affected by the following aspects of colour.

### 1. Size

As with value, objects, shapes and areas of the same size can actually appear different in size if they are coloured differently. Dark, cool and dull colours make objects appear smaller than the same objects in warm, light or bright colours. For example, if a dress is cut in black, and also cut in bright red or purple the black version would be more slimming than the red or purple versions (Fig. 5.16).

### 2. Density

Colours can convey a sense of visual weight. Warm, dark and bright colours tend to look dense or heavy, and cool, light and dull colours are visually lighter in weight.

A designer should consider visual weight in the case of a two colour dress, where the bodice is one colour and the skirt another colour. If the colours were, for example, purple and white, the skirt would be better in purple and the top in white, because the garment has better balance with the 'heavier' purple on the the bottom half and the 'lighter' white on the top (Fig. 5.18).

*5.16 The purple dress appears larger than the black dress because warm, bright colours appear larger.*

*5.17 (bottom) Figure faults can be camouflaged by using value, hue and chroma to alter apparent sizes.*

| SIZE | VALUE | HUE | CHROMA |
|---|---|---|---|
| To enlarge an area | High values<br>Light tones<br>Tints<br>Strong contrasts | Warm hues<br>Red, oranges and yellows | Pure chroma<br>Brights<br>Strong colours<br>High intensity |
| To reduce an area | Low values<br>Dark tones<br>Shades<br>Soft or no contrasts | Cool hues<br>Blues, greens and purples | Weak chroma<br>Dull<br>Greyed<br>Low intensity |

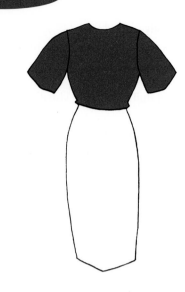

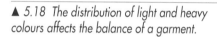

▲ 5.18 The distribution of light and heavy colours affects the balance of a garment.

▶ 5.19 The mottled mixture of values and hues in this uniform make it perfect for camouflage because they blend in with many backgrounds. (Photograph courtesy of Australian Defence Industries Ltd.)

## 3. Value

Visual impressions created by value are stronger than those created by hue. Because strongly contrasting values are very dramatic and demand attention, the first thing a viewer becomes aware of is dark against light. However, when values are similar, the hue becomes more noticeable (Fig. 5.19).

When two hues of identical tone are used together, they cause visual 'flashing'. This means the colours appear to jump around, glow and pulsate, because they are both competing equally for attention. This effect is usually undesirable, and can be lessened by changing the tone of one or both of the colours.

White unites and draws colours together, black separates colours. The effect black has is similar to that of a stained glass window, where the colours are contained and isolated by the dark outline (Fig. 5.20).

## 4. Visual mixing

This occurs when small areas of colour used close together appear to take on some of the neighbouring colour, and can be compared to the effect created by the Impressionists and Pointillists in their dot paintings. It often happens with stripes, florals and prints and is particularly noticeable from a distance when the colours seem to blend to create a new colour. For example, with red and white stripes, the white appears redder, and the red appears whiter, so that from a distance the stripes merge to look pink. Similarly, yellow and blue used together often merge to create green.

When matching plains with printed, striped or multi-coloured fabrics in the one garment or coordinating accessories, the effects of visual mixing must be taken into consideration and care taken to match the colours from a distance as well as close up. With the above red and white example, the choice of a pink belt and buttons may actually look better on the garment than either red or white accessories.

## 5. Simultaneous contrast

Some colour combinations have the effect of exaggerating the differences between them. This effect is known as

▼ 5.20 Black borders act as a barrier and isolate colours, while white draws them together.

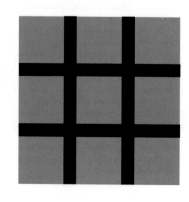

simultaneous contrast and can greatly affect the appearance of colour.

For example, identical hues can appear different with different coloured backgrounds because hues used together cast their complement onto each other. Red placed on a blue background will look more orange, and red placed on a yellow background will appear more purple.

Simultaneous contrast is also evident when a strong chroma is used with a neutral. The neutral takes on the complementary colour of its neighbour, so a grey used with a strong purple will appear slightly yellow (Fig. 5.21). The way to cancel the yellow and achieve the look of a neutral grey would be to use a purplish-grey with the purple. So, when using orange with grey, the grey may need to be warmer or more orange to appear neutral.

## 6. Motion

Warm and cool colours with very bright chromas tend to clash and vibrate in front of the eyes when used together. This occurs because the eye continually tries to focus on both the short wavelengths of the receding cool colours and the long wavelengths of the advancing warm colours. The effect can be very disturbing and uncomfortable to look at, and can be relieved by reducing the brilliance of one or more of the colours.

## 7. Colour and texture

Because the surface characteristics of fabric affect the action of light and the degree of absorption or reflection, they also affect colour.

Shiny, smooth surfaces enhance colours and make them appear much brighter, livelier and larger than do rough, dull surfaces.

Colours may also be opaque or transparent. Because some light passes through transparent fabric and is neither reflected nor absorbed, some colour intensity is lost, so that transparent fabrics have a much softer appearance than opaque fabrics.

This colour difference may become apparent when different textures are used on the same garment, and the colours do not match. It can also be a problem when trying to coordinate garments or match accessories with different textures.

## COLOUR MATCHING SYSTEMS

A useful tool for designers to match fabric and trim colours is the professional colour selector. There are several international colour selection systems available.

The Pantone® Professional Colour System is an American system commonly used in Australia and overseas. (Pantone is a registered trademark.) It is a selector with approximately 1700 printed colour strips, each with its own code number which identifies the value, hue and chroma of the colour.

More specifically for the designer working with textiles, Pantone's Textile Colour Selector and Swatch Cards provide cotton fabric swatches and the appropriate colour and colour codes, which give a clearer idea of how the final colour will appear in fabric.

The advantage of using these systems is that the colours are classified, so as to leave no room for misinterpretation. The number of a required colour can be quoted to any dyer, printer, embroiderer or manufacturer worldwide, and provided they are using the same system, colours can be accurately matched.

See Chapter 7 for more discussion on colour as it relates to fashion.

*5.21 A neutral takes on the complementary colour of its neighbour — the grey surrounded by the purple appears slightly yellower than the same grey used alone.*

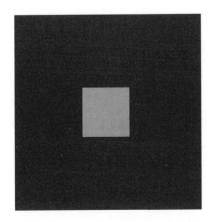

# INTRODUCTION

As discussed in Chapter 4, the Principles of Design are the techniques designers use to organise the Elements of Design (Fig. 6.1). Principles work in three ways. They may be:

1.   Directional

Principles with movement, which lead the eye over the design, are said to be directional. These include repetition, gradation, radiation and rhythm.

2.   Highlighting

Highlighting principles draw attention to a part of a design, and create a focal point. They include radiation, dominance and contrast.

3.   Synthesising

The effect here is unity, with design details pulled together by repetition, gradation, harmony, balance, unity and proportion. These principles draw the viewer's attention to the common aspects of the design, thereby integrating and uniting them.

# 1. REPETITION

Repetition occurs when a line, shape, space, value, colour or texture is used more than once. It emphasises the psychological, physical and visual qualities of the element being repeated (Fig. 6.2).

*Regular repetition* is the same in all aspects of the repeat, and can be tedious if overused because of the lack of variety.

*Irregular repetition* occurs when there are slight variations in the spacing between the repeated features. This introduces a degree of uncertainty into a design, reduces the repetitive impact and is more interesting because the eye is able to make comparisons between slight variations.

Repetition may be used in a design with vertical, horizontal, diagonal or random arrangement. The repeated motifs may also be parallel, inverted, reversed, alternate, dropped or sequential.

Repetition is directional because the eye travels over the repeated features, from one to the next then on to the next and so on. This movement emphasises and links common features in a design, thereby uniting the design. It can also emphasise width if used horizontally, and height if used vertically. Repetition is also a synthesising principle because the same feature used in different parts of a design helps bring those parts together.

The symmetry of the human body ensures that repetition occurs to a certain degree in every garment design. Left and right sides of collars, lapels, sleeves, sometimes pockets, and garment halves in trousers, skirts and dresses are usually repeated, unless the garment is asymmetrical. Necklines, waistlines and hemlines also create vertical repetition.

Structural use of repetition in a garment includes pleats, gathers, darts, pockets, skirt tiers, yokes and panel lines. As for decorative application, repetition is used in all printed, woven and knitted fabric designs, and is often evident in fabric colours. Trims are easily repeated — buttons, beading, braids and applied motifs are a few examples.

THE FASHION DESIGN MANUAL

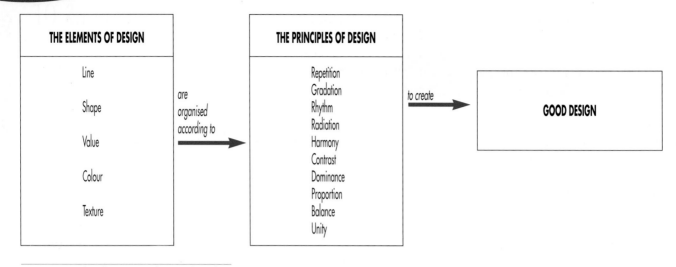

| THE ELEMENTS OF DESIGN | | THE PRINCIPLES OF DESIGN | | |
|---|---|---|---|---|
| Line | | Repetition | | |
| Shape | | Gradation | | |
| | are | Rhythm | | |
| Value | organised | Radiation | to create | **GOOD DESIGN** |
| | according to | Harmony | | |
| Colour | | Contrast | | |
| | | Dominance | | |
| Texture | | Proportion | | |
| | | Balance | | |
| | | Unity | | |

▲ 6.1  How the Elements and Principles of Design are used to achieve desired results.

Regular  Parallel  Reversed  Dropped

Irregular  Alternate  Inverted  Sequential

▲ 6.2  Types of repetition. The movement of repetition emphasises and links common features in a design.

# 2. GRADATION

Gradation occurs when a series of two or more parts, identical but for one detail, change with each repetition in consecutive increasing or decreasing steps (Fig. 6.3). Line, shape, space, value and colour use gradation frequently, but textural gradation is difficult to achieve in fabrics and not commonly used.

Because gradation is a variation of repetition, it is also directional and synthesising. The eye follows the gradually increasing or decreasing changes as they move through the design. Two otherwise unrelated or contrasting components

*6.3 Gradation applied to the Elements. Gradation, a variation of repetition, is also directional and synthesising.*

can be united as one gradually changes to become the other. For example, red can gradually change to brown, then to olive and finally to green, with quite an harmonious effect.

As with repetition, gradation emphasises the qualities of the gradually changing element. In the example above, we would be made aware through gradation of the relationship between the two colours — the relative warmth of the red, coolness of the green, and the muddied combinations of the two.

When working with different sizes, gradation makes large shapes appear larger and heavier, and small shapes appear smaller and lighter by comparison. This visual weight affects their placement on garments. Large shapes are best used near the shoulders or the lower half of the garment where they

look as if they are being supported.

Gradation may be introduced into a garment design in the same way as repetition.

# 3. RHYTHM

Rhythm is organised motion. It arranges the features of a design so the eye moves easily over the garment. Rhythm occurs when a number of components are arranged into an ordered, predictable pattern which the eye can follow. Rhythm has a visual beat. The beat may be fluid if curves or gradual changes are harmonious, or staccato if the movement is sudden and opposite (Fig. 6.4).

Rhythmic effect becomes stronger when a pattern is repeated, but repetition

Line — movement

Line — length and thickness

Line — direction

Shape — size and direction

Shape — contour

Space

Tone and colour

Tone — light to dark
Texture — opaque to transparent

is not essential for this effect.

The drapery of ancient Greek and Roman costume, Japanese kimonos and Indian saris demonstrate a use of rhythm so skillful and flattering that variations of these styles regularly recur in the fashion cycle.

There are different types of rhythm. *Regular rhythm* follows an identical repetitive pattern. *Graduated rhythm* follows a regular but increasing or decreasing pattern similar to the widening ripples caused by a stone thrown into a pond. This effect is also known as *concentrism* and can be seen in the gradually increasing layers of a tiered skirt. *Random rhythm* occurs at irregular intervals throughout a design.

Rhythm is used most effectively with line, shape and space, but can also be observed when colour changes hue, value or chroma in recognisable waves.

With any movement there is direction, and rhythm invites our eye to anticipate and follow its pattern. Any pause or interruption brought about by a sudden change from the established pattern destroys rhythm. For this reason, functional, structural and decorative aspects must reinforce the rhythm of a garment, or the effect will be lost.

When line, shape, space or colour is used rhythmically, its psychological, physical and visual nature becomes part of the rhythm. A rhythm created by smooth, undulating lines reminds us of gently lapping waves, and is peaceful and calming. Sharp, jagged lines may create a forceful and exciting rhythm, suitable for dramatic evening wear. Conversely, such an aggressive rhythm may disturb and overpower a garment.

Flowing hemlines, gathers, frills, drapes and curved seam lines which break a garment into rhythmic panels are structural uses which create soft, fluid rhythms. Pleats, stitching, tucks and sharp folds create abrupt, staccato rhythms.

Trims and applied decorative effects such as beading, ric-rac and other braids,

*6.4 Rhythm invites the eye to anticipate and follow its pattern.*

Regular     Graduated     Random

Rhythm can be created with individual motifs or continuous design details.

The visual beat of rhythmic lines can be fluid or staccato

Shapes also have rhythm, which is strengthened when repeated.

Similar directions

Opposing directions

Several directions

All directions

Radiation creates the feeling of movement in different directions

The spreading silhouette and panel lines show radiation in shape and line

A supporting yoke softens the central focus of radiating lines by acting as a dividing space

Radiating shapes

---

scalloped lace edges and prints, also create an infinite variety of rhythmic effects.

# 4. RADIATION

Outward movement in all directions from a central point, such as the spokes in a wheel, is known as *radiation*. This powerful movement spreading from the centre focuses interest on the hub as well as on the outer edges, creating a pull in both directions (Fig. 6.5).

Therefore, the placement of these inner and outer parts should be carefully considered. The outer edges of radiating lines can create a strong en-

larging effect and, if placed on the wrong part of the body, may be very unflattering. For example, if a peplum finishes at the widest point of the hips, they may appear much larger than they really are because of the wide outer edge of the peplum hem. At the same time, the narrowness of the waist is highlighted because the tapering lines draw the eye to that focal point. A supporting yoke or space between the radiating lines may be introduced into the centre point to soften the focus, reduce the visual pull and provide interest through variety. Depending on the combinations of lines used, the eye-leading quality of radiation makes it a directional principle. The gaze follows the length of the spreading lines as well as hopping in a

6.5 *Radiation works best when used with restraint.*

circular movement from one line to the next.

Lines used at a similar angle or direction to each other and to the body lead the eye in that direction, but radiating lines moving in opposing directions pull the eye first one way, then the other. Radiating lines fanning out in several directions emphasise the difference between the smallness at the centre and the width at the outer edge, while a full radiating circle focuses the eye at the centre and spreads outwards.

Radiation is limited in use to line, shape and space. It is evident in drapes, folds, darts, gathers, sunray pleats, flares, peplums and capes. Applied trims of all sorts may be arranged in radiating lines. Bows radiate from a centre knot and many fabrics exhibit partial or fully radiating motifs and patterns, for example florals.

Radiation works best when used with restraint and against a simple background. It is often used in drapery and clinging designs because the folds drawn into a cluster mould well to the shape of the body. When used like this, radiation should be the dominant feature of the design, with little other distracting detailing.

# 5. HARMONY

Harmony occurs when one or more qualities of a design are alike. These similar features are repeated throughout a design to create a feeling of agreement and consistency. It is therefore a synthesising principle (Fig. 6.6).

When two or more colours are related to each other because they have one colour in common — for example red and orange both have the colour red in common — harmony is said to exist. The same concept can also be applied to all the other principles and elements of design.

Tastes vary as to what is harmonious in a design according to fashion, culture and attitudes of different eras. For example, the strong optical prints considered fashionably harmonious in the 1960s seemed loud, garish and overpowering in the 1980s.

All of the design elements can be used harmoniously by linking them with the mood of the garment. The sharp, crisp linear pleats of a tailored skirt reflect the efficient nature of the business suit. A fluid, undulating hemline reinforces the sensuous, body clinging nature of a chiffon evening gown.

Shapes and spaces created by pockets, collars and cuffs will harmonise if they are soft and curved, or straight and angular, in accordance with the major forms of the garment.

Harmony can be achieved by combining monochromatic and harmonious colour schemes, and complementary colours can harmonise if used with intermediate colours which link the two otherwise unrelated colours. Red and green may be used together successfully if linked with colours which combine both, such as red-brown or green-brown. This linking process is known as *transition* and can be used with

*6.6 All of the design elements can be used harmoniously by linking them with the mood of the garment.*

The tonal extremes of white and black can be made harmonious through the linking effects of the mid-tones of white-grey, grey and black-grey

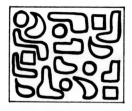

Transition helps opposing shapes harmonise within a pattern

TRANSITION

Tailored jacket and skirt for office wear shows harmony of design and function

Tailored jacket and lace skirt for office wear is disharmonious

Repeated rounded forms create harmony

The pointed collar fights the other design details

73

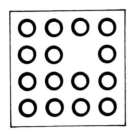

No contrast, total sameness, is monotonous

A little contrast creates variety and interest

Too much contrast creates confusion

Line

Shape and space

Texture

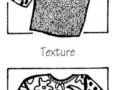

Tone

Line, shape and tone

Pattern

The contrasting shapes of the peplum on this dress draw attention to the hip area

opposing lines, shapes, textures, tones or colours. Tones which fade from light to dark, shapes which slide smoothly from square to, say, circular, or textures which gently move from clinging to fluid folds subtly introduce harmony into a design.

For a garment or outfit to achieve harmony, the three aspects of function, structure and decoration must be in accordance with each other. This means that occasion, climate, size, gender, age, personal colouring, lifestyle and personality all need to be considered. No matter how good a design may be, if it is unsuitable for its intended purpose it cannot be considered successful.

The garment and the accessories worn with it should harmonise with the physical characteristics of the wearer. Tall

or large people are able to wear bold designs, prints and accessories which would look oversized on a more petite figure. Fabric design and texture also need to be in harmony with the gender and age of the wearer.

However, complete sameness can be extremely boring since it is mostly repetition and becomes predictable and stale quite easily. A degree of variety is essential to prevent such tedium, and the best way to introduce variety is through an unexpected contrasting detail which will make the viewer sit up and take notice.

Simple effects such as a small splash of contrasting colour, a shoulder yoke cut in gleaming satin used on a pure cotton jumpsuit, or the normally casual parka cut in luxurious padded silk, will

*6.7 The different uses of contrast.*

often add the element of surprise and variety we are constantly seeking.

# 6. CONTRAST

Contrast is opposition, conflict, tension. Pure contrast exists when two or more features are totally unrelated, having absolutely nothing in common (Fig. 6.7).

When used with restraint, contrast enhances a design by overcoming tedium. Tedium can occur in an harmonious design because there is complete sameness — no beginning, no end, no focus or movement, no plan. However, a design with too much contrast loses all cohesion, all sense of belonging together. Because of the intense competition between the parts of the design, it is unsettling and unsatisfying, incomplete.

A small amount of well placed contrast overcomes tedium without distracting too much from the rest of the design. It creates a satisfying sense of completeness.

Contrast occurs in varying degrees, ranging from totally unrelated opposites to subtle differences, with an endless selection between the two. A line may be straight, slightly bent, or circular. A colour may be red, red-green, grey, green-red or green. A shape may be filled, partly filled or empty.

Contrast works with all the elements of design individually or in combination. We have contrast when a red square and green square are used together, further contrast with a shiny red square and a matt green square, and even further contrast with a shiny red circle and a matt green square.

Contrast is a highlighting principle because the extreme differences magnify and draw attention to the opposing qualities of the elements concerned. It can be bold and exciting, or aggressive and disturbing. For this reason, placement of contrasting features is important. Contrast on those parts of the garment which are not meant to be the focus of attention should be avoided because an area or feature will appear larger as a result of the attention drawn to it.

All garments have inbuilt contrast in the form of horizontal and vertical edges, seams, yokes, darts, waistlines, and hemlines.

# 7. DOMINANCE

Every design should have a focal point, a centre of interest with a design message supported by the other features in the design.

When a garment is well designed, one strong feature sets the theme or mood, and the other details follow to reinforce that mood. For example, a dress with a bold animal print needs very little design detailing other than a

*6.8 Dominance and the Elements of Design.*

Line

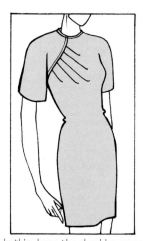

In this dress the shoulder seam and tucks are dominant. The silhouette or colour is secondary

The shoulder details of the same dress are lost, and the print is dominant. The silhouette is secondary

Pattern

Space

Shape

Texture

Tone/Colour

simple, clean silhouette because the pattern of the print is dominant, and any further additions would clutter the garment and detract from the effect.

When there is no dominant feature, the eye becomes bored and restless, and wanders over the design looking for organisation, something to explore and hold the attention.

When there are several features of equal visual strength, the eye is distract-ed by the various demands for atten-tion, and jumps from point to point in an attempt to find the most important feature on which to concentrate.

The structure, function and decora-tion of a garment should send the same design message to the viewer as the dominant feature. For example, if the dominant feature on a delicate pale pink evening dress was a heavy black leather belt, the two styles would be in conflict, and destroy the unity of the design.

Any design element or principle may be used as a dominant feature (Fig. 6.8). Because dominance is a highlighting principle, the qualities of that feature are emphasised. In this way a large green spot on a bright yellow dress seems larger and greener than if there were twenty large green spots, because it is the only centre of attention. This highlighting quality can be used to lead the eye away from a problem area. For example, an elaborate border on a skirt hem may draw attention away from a large bust.

Elements and principles which have strong, advancing qualities dominate most successfully because they are more noticeable. Sharp, thick lines are more dominant than delicate thin lines, shiny textures more dominant than matt textures, and bright, warm colours more dominant than cool dull colours.

Qualities which are quiet and rece-ding work best in the role of supporting and enhancing the theme of the design and the dominant feature. At the same time, however, they should not be insig-nificant. Any feature which does not make a positive and interesting contri-bution to the design should be omitted.

Structural use of dominance includes silhouette, fabric colour and texture, internal shape through the use of panel lines and seams, draping and inserted features like pockets, binds, belts, ties and collars. Decorative uses are as varied as trims themselves, and can be as simple as buttons down the front of a dress, or as elaborate as an all-over beaded gown.

# 8. PROPORTION

Proportion is the way all the parts in a design relate to each other individually and to the design as a whole. Pro-portion is determined by distances, sizes, amounts, degrees or parts.

We initially judge a design as a whole, but then find it interesting to compare the parts of the design, to analyse the differences and similarities. This makes proportion a synthesising principle, because the process of comparison unites the separate garment parts.

The *Golden Mean* is accepted through-out the western world as being the ratio of perfect proportion. It is useful because it provides a mathematical means of dividing a design into balanced segments. The Golden Mean works on the principle that proportion is most pleasing when all areas of a design are not exactly the same, but when there is an eye-satisfying relationship between the unequal parts.

The Golden Mean is based on the proportions of 3:5:8 or 5:8:13. That is, the smaller part has the same relation-ship to the larger part, as the larger part has to the whole. This ratio relates well to the female form. The ideal figure is approximately 8 heads tall, with the natural division of the waistline falling at the 3/8 level from the top of the head, and the remaining 5/8 section extend-ing from the waist to the soles of the feet. When the natural waistline is raised or lowered, or other divisions are intro-duced, the Golden Mean is a helpful guide to creating satisfying proportions (Fig. 6.9).

A figure problem is one which deviates from the 'ideal' proportions our society sets as its standard. Garment proportions can be altered to visually

*6.9 The Golden Mean.*

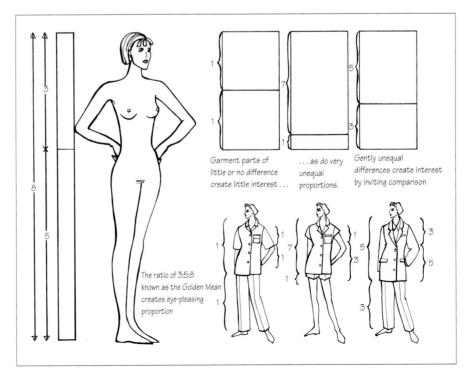

The ratio of 3:5:8 known as the Golden Mean creates eye-pleasing proportion

Garment parts of little or no difference create little interest . . .

. . . as do very unequal proportions.

Gently unequal differences create interest by inviting comparison

Different effects and styles can be created from one design idea by
changing the proportions

The figure looks taller, slimmer
and more youthful with high
waist and longer skirt

Even proportions
emphasise squareness,
and make the figure look
shorter

The elongated torso creates
the illusion of height, but
draws attention to the thighs

correct figure problems, especially when reinforced with the visual illusions created by line, tone and the other design elements and principles.

Therefore, a person who has a short body and long legs can adjust those imperfect proportions by wearing belts and waistlines on the lower hip level, thereby creating the illusion of more evenly, more 'perfectly', proportioned body and legs. Of course, this can also exaggerate imperfect proportions. The above example of long legs and short body would appear worse if belts and waistlines were raised, so that the wearer appeared to have no body at all, but legs which extended to the bustline (Fig. 6.10).

Generally, classic proportions are

those which follow, or vary only slightly from, natural body divisions. These divisions occur at joints and points where there is a change in direction. Horizontal divisions occur at the neck, shoulder, bust, waist, hip, knee, ankle, elbow and wrist. Vertical divisions occur through centre front, centre back and sideways between front and back. A garment should provide the wearer with comfort of fit and movement in order to be functional, and garments which are designed to follow these natural proportions fit better, are more comfortable and usually more flattering.

As with all other elements and principles, proportion conveys psychological associations. Even proportions imply reliability and stability, while very uneven

*6.10 How proportion can determine effect and style.*

proportions seem weak and unstable because the larger area overwhelms the smaller area.

Visual illusions also come into play because the scale and proportion of design features and details are affected by all the other parts of the design (Fig. 6.11).

Proportion works with all the design elements. The relative amounts of thick and thin, short and long, broken and solid line can be varied. The size of individual shapes, their position on the garment, and background spaces must be considered separately, and as part of the whole design.

Colour proportions can be varied according to the amounts of hue, chroma and value used together. Different effects are created according to the amount of green used with red, bright used with dull, or light used with dark. Colour changes within a garment also affect proportions because visual divisions are created between the colours. Bulky textures must be considered in relation to the size of the space they occupy. They can appear heavy and clumsy when used in very small amounts.

Elements with advancing qualities have greater visual power and need to be used in relatively smaller quantities than elements with receding qualities. For example, a bright red used with pale grey will overpower the grey if used in equal quantities, so the proportions should be adjusted so that there is less red and more grey.

Proportion is determined structurally by the placement of every seam, dart, panel line or collar. In fact, every part of a design, whether functional or decorative, alters the proportions of the garment parts separately, and therefore of the garment as a whole.

Understanding proportion does not limit the designer, but rather opens up a realm of possibilities, because numerous variations of one basic idea can be created by manipulating these relationships.

## SCALE

Scale is an aspect of proportion which deals only with size. It relates the size of parts of a garment to the garment as a whole and to the wearer (Fig. 6.12).

The scale of garment details is more effective when consistent. For example, men's shirts during the 1970s had large cuffs and collars, and were worn with wide belts, wide ties and flared pants. Conversely, small details, such as dainty pin tucks, are usually teamed with narrow cuffs and collars and small buttons.

Harmony, unity and balance are only achieved in a design when the scale is correct. A child dressing up in her mother's clothes is an exaggerated example of how absurd incorrect scale

*6.11 Visual illusions affect scale and proportion.*

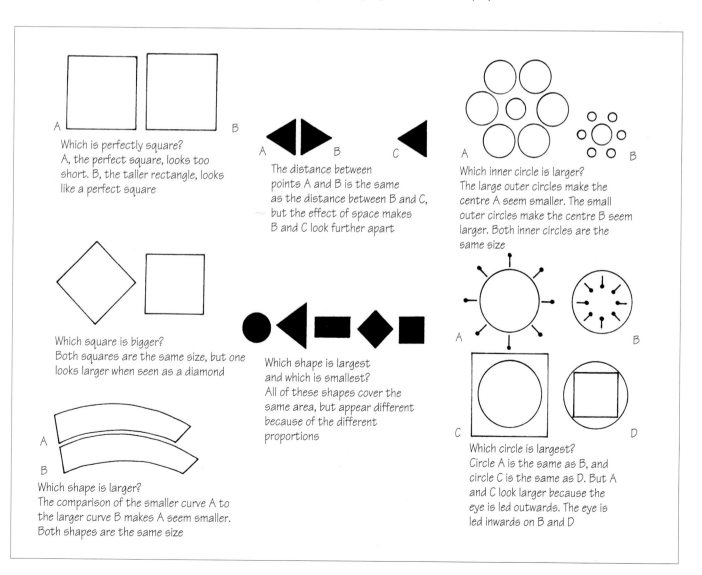

Which is perfectly square?
A, the perfect square, looks too short. B, the taller rectangle, looks like a perfect square

The distance between points A and B is the same as the distance between B and C, but the effect of space makes B and C look further apart

Which inner circle is larger?
The large outer circles make the centre A seem smaller. The small outer circles make the centre B seem larger. Both inner circles are the same size

Which square is bigger?
Both squares are the same size, but one looks larger when seen as a diamond

Which shape is largest and which is smallest?
All of these shapes cover the same area, but appear different because of the different proportions

Which shape is larger?
The comparison of the smaller curve A to the larger curve B makes A seem smaller. Both shapes are the same size

Which circle is largest?
Circle A is the same as B, and circle C is the same as D. But A and C look larger because the eye is led outwards. The eye is led inwards on B and D

Differences in scale exaggerate size

Small accessories emphasise
the wearer's largeness . . .

. . . but so do
very large accessories

Medium size
accessories suit
most people

Large accessories
overwhelm a tiny person

Small and average sized
textures are suitable for
most garments. Large textures
can overpower a garment

Moderately sized trims, neither
too large nor too small, work
best for most garments

can appear. The differences in scale exaggerates the smallness of the child and the largeness of the clothes.

Shape and space are most directly concerned with scale, but scale also applies to line, colour and texture in the same way that proportion does. Colours, textures, values, lines, shapes or spaces with advancing qualities have to be scaled down in size, that is, made smaller than if they had receding qualities. For example, a bow on the shoulder of a dress may have to be made smaller if it is cut in bright red, because of the advancing nature of that colour, than if it is cut in black.

Scale also applies to fashion accessories. A huge handbag on a petite woman looks oversized, while a dainty handbag on a large woman looks ridiculously small and makes the wearer seem larger by comparison. However, a large handbag worn by a large women may, through repetition, also emphasise her size.

The relative sizes of pockets, collars, sleeves, cuffs, peplums, belts, buttons, fabric prints or textures, and trims of all descriptions play an important role in determining the success or failure of a garment. A garment which looks awkward or clumsy may simply need a slight adjustment in the scale of its component parts to achieve perfection.

# 9. BALANCE

Balance occurs when the visual weights of the parts of a design are equally dis-

*6.12 Harmony, unity and balance are only achieved in a design when the scale is correct.*

tributed so as to create equilibrium. A sense of steadiness and stability prevails when a design is perfectly balanced.

The concept of visual balance is similar to that of physical balance, where stability is achieved when the parts of a design are evenly distributed around a balance line or point. It really works just like a pair of scales (Fig. 6.13).

Every part of a design has a visual weight which contributes to the balance of the overall design. The balance may be altered by adjusting the size, strength (weight or density) and distance of the component parts from the central axis.

Balance may be formal or informal.

*Formal balance* is symmetrical and occurs when one side is repeated exactly on the other side of the axis, or is reversed to become a mirror image. It is predictable, stable and serene. Formal balance draws attention to the features it repeats, and may emphasise body irregularities because it encourages comparison of one side to the other.

*Informal balance* is asymmetrical and occurs when the objects on both sides of the axis are equal in visual weight but not identical. These differences may be simple variations or strongly contrasting, but each side should compensate for what the other side lacks to create a

6.13 *Types of balance. Every part of a design has visual weight.*

feeling of equality and unity. The variety of informal balance is more exciting and dramatic than formal balance because it allows the eye to examine the differences between the features. This process of comparison means that balance is a synthesising principle. As the eye moves over the design, it unites the different components to create a co-ordinated, well planned garment.

Balance may also be horizontal, vertical or radial. *Horizontal balance* occurs when the left and right sides of the central balance line are equal. A garment with horizontal balance will never look lop-sided. *Vertical balance* occurs when the upper and lower parts of a design are equal, avoiding a top-heavy or bottom-heavy appearance. *Radial balance* is the

combination of horizontal and vertical balance, so that all sides of the central point are equal.

A well designed dress, for example, should balance horizontally through the left and right sides of the garment, and vertically between the bodice and the skirt. The sense of balance should also continue as the figure moves and turns, and should flow from front to back, and side to side when the body is front on, back on or in profile to the viewer.

As with proportion and scale, those features with advancing properties appear heavier than those with receding properties. To achieve balance, they should either be used in smaller quantities or with larger quantities of the receding features. So light, bright colours, shiny

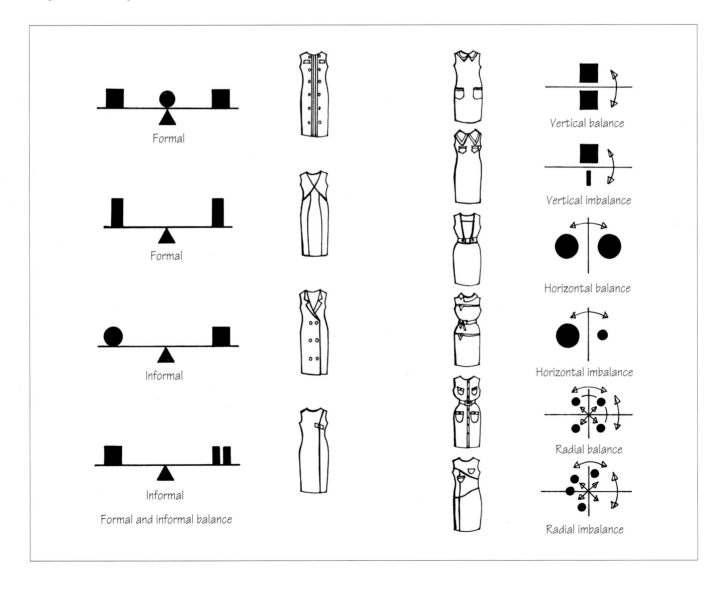

Formal

Formal

Informal

Informal

Formal and informal balance

Vertical balance

Vertical imbalance

Horizontal balance

Horizontal imbalance

Radial balance

Radial imbalance

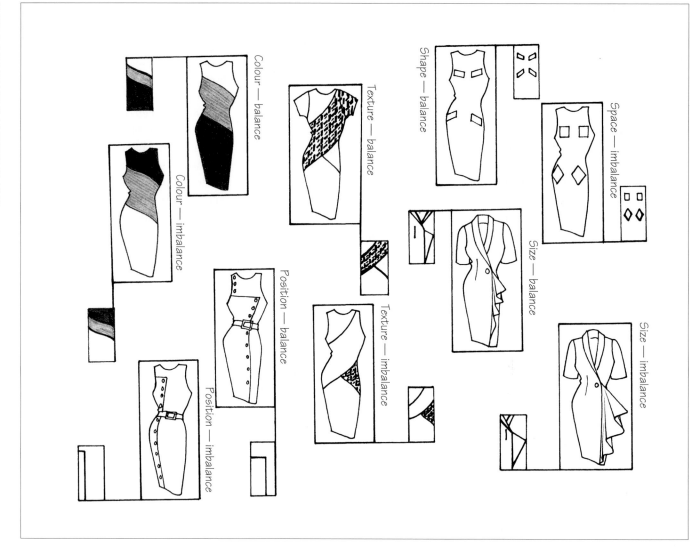

6.14 *Balance is affected by the Elements and Principles of Design.*

textures and bold prints may need to be used in smaller quantities than dull, dark colours, matt textures and fine prints. Simple, open areas have less weight than cluttered areas, so may be used in greater proportion (Fig. 6.14).

Contrast is effective when used to balance the strong impact of a feature. For example, a design with hard, sharp lines may be balanced through the addition of a slightly curved section, or a solid line may be balanced with a broken line.

The position of a feature affects its visual weight. The further a detail is from the central axis, the heavier it seems. So a design with a wide border at the hem could be balanced by a greater number of smaller 'lighter' tiers near the waist or on the bodice. Because of our experience with gravity, we feel most comfortable when heavier things are lower, and lighter things higher. Therefore, in fashion terms, we often prefer things which are closest to the face to be lighter, and feel that larger, heavier things can be supported better when they are used lower on the figure.

Consider the classic tiered skirt. Notice that the tiers always start off narrower and shorter near the waist, and gradually widen and deepen down the length of the skirt. Reverse the order of the tiers, with the wider ones at the top and narrower at the hem, and see how unbalanced and top-heavy the skirt looks.

Heavier textures may also look better on the lower half of the figure. Trousers and skirts are usually in heavier fabric than blouses. When a light-weight fabric like chiffon is used in a skirt, it is often used in enormous quantities, thereby creating the visual weight necessary to balance the top.

Structurally, balance in a garment can be adjusted by moving darts, seams, yokes and panel lines, by adding or subtracting fullness through pleats, gathers and ruffles, or by arranging openings symmetrically or asymmetrically.

All decorative treatments convey different weights and densities, and their use must be considered in the context of all the other garment parts.

# 10. UNITY

Although the most important principle of design is unity, it is considered last because it is the culmination of the design process, the final step which can only be completed when all the other principles and elements have been dealt with.

All design strives to achieve unity. Unity exists in a design when every component supports the central concept and there is a sense of cohesion and oneness.

The combined effect of the elements and principles used in a design should be to create a garment which is neither boring nor confused, neither insipid nor overwhelming. Any tension or conflict must be integrated into the design, instead of fighting against it. Because strong competition between the elements destroys unity, it should be balanced by equally strong non-competing forces.

The problem a designer faces in achieving unity is two-fold. The eye demands variety, movement, excitement, surprise and novelty to keep it amused, or else it loses interest and moves to the next interesting thing it spies. In other words, the eye needs contrast. At the same time, however, in order to understand and feel comfortable with the visual concept being presented the eye needs to see a connection between the individual parts of a design, to see that they are all heading towards the same conclusion. This is harmony.

Opposing principles can be used together to create this balance between the two unrelated concepts of harmony and contrast. For example, a colour may be used repeatedly to add consistency and continuity to a design but, to alleviate boredom and inject interest and excitement, a contrasting or discordant colour could be added.

Harmony and unity are not the same. A design may be beautifully harmonised but lack the sense of completion, of perfect finish, that a united design displays. The best test for a completely united garment is the sense that not one tiny detail, not one line, shape, or trim could be added, removed or altered without spoiling the overall effect.

The mood of a design is determined by its position between harmony and contrast. If it is predominantly bold and contrasting, the design may be described as exciting or innovative. If it tends towards calmer, more conservative and harmonious effects, it would be described as classic.

Unity is the most synthesising of the design principles. It *is* synthesis.

Function, structure and decoration follow the same purpose in a united design. Every single aspect, no matter how seemingly insignificant, interacts with every other aspect. Individual garment parts work separately and together. Several garments worn as an outfit work separately and together. Garments and accessories work separately and together. And, finally, garments, accessories and the wearer work separately and together to complete a successful outfit.

Unity is *static* when based on regular, harmonious features. It feels solid and passive. *Dynamic* unity works using fluid, lively features and irregular shapes, and is active and constantly moving.

Unity is achievable in as many ways as there are variations in design.

# IN CONCLUSION ...

The *Elements of Design* are the tools a designer works with. The elements are arranged according to the *Principles of Design* to create a garment which is suitable for its intended use.

Although each element and principle has been dealt with separately, they all work together to create the final effect. The success of a garment relies on the combination of all of the parts of the design, and they are all of equal importance.

## CHAPTER 7

# THE ROLE OF THE DESIGNER

# INTRODUCTION

As a background to discussing the role of the designer, it is helpful to understand how each season's fashion emerges onto the world scene. The new fashion ranges which appear in our stores each season are the result of a process which starts as much as two and a half years prior to the public appearance of the garments. This process involves the careful study of the basic components of fashion, and the analysis and prediction of which colours, textures, lines and shapes are most likely to be popular with consumers in the future, and therefore successful at retail level.

The three main areas which set the scene for fashion trends world wide are colour analysis and prediction, textile development, and the international collections.

# SETTING A TREND

## COLOUR ANALYSIS AND PREDICTION

Twice yearly, international colour experts who work in fashion and related industries, such as cosmetics and interior design, meet in Paris to pool information and clarify and define future colour trends. They bring with them a wide range of opinions gathered from textile producers, designers, marketing experts, manufacturers and others with whom they have already consulted. This broad base of information is used to provide the fashion industry with a clear direction for coming seasons.

The conclusions arrived at by these colour professionals filter down through all levels of the fashion industry, generally by means of colour forecast reports. These reports are issued well in advance of the season and cover all aspects of the emerging colour 'moods' (Fig. 7.1).

## TEXTILE DEVELOPMENT

Fabric trends also precede fashion trends. Textile technologists and designers work with the most recent colour information when they are developing new yarns, fabrics, textures, weights of fabric, patterns and prints. Manufacturers of threads, trims and accessories also work with the textile producers, so there is consistency in direction throughout the industry.

Without this general agreement there would be chaos if every textile manufacturer produced colours and textures different from what the trimmings manufacturers were working with, which could again be different from what the designers would be looking for, which may be nothing like what the consumer wants to wear! Early research and collaboration is essential to the smooth functioning of the fashion industry.

At the European yarn and fabric fairs which are held about 18 months ahead of the season (in the northern hemisphere), the fabric houses present their new ranges. These fairs enable designers, clothing manufacturers, buyers and fashion reporters to get their first directions, collect samples and discuss requirements and ideas with suppliers.

*Interstoff,* held in Frankfurt, Germany, *Premier-Vision* in Paris, France and *Idea-Como* in Como, Italy, are three major European fabric shows.

## INTERNATIONAL COLLECTIONS

The third important influence on our fashion directions are the twice-yearly international collections shown in Paris, Milan, New York and London. These are attended by fashion buyers and designers as well as fashion analysts, commentators, journalists, wealthy private clients, and fashion enthusiasts who are lucky enough to gain admission.

## SUMMER

### SYNTHETICS

UNnatural, slick and shiny brights that spring from the shades so often associated with pure synthetic fibres. Colours that out-distance anything in nature. Strong! Saturated! . . . Searing!

### APPLICATION:

- Any one colour may stand alone
- Important for all plain fabrics
- As accents for 'Naturals'
- Obvious for synthetic fabrics, finishes and coatings

- For iridescents, shine, gloss effects
- Add black-and-white helpmates
- Mix with each other for bold contrast

### COLOURS:

| | | |
|---|---|---|
| YEL-LON | TANGAMIDE | VINYL VIOLET |
| GRASS-A-TATE | SHRIMP-LENE | BLUE NYLON |
| TURQ-LON | PVC PINK | POLY-GREEN |
| RED-LON | TRI-ORANGEADE | JADEX |

*7.1 Colour forecast reports summarise emerging colour trends. (Forecast courtesy of The Fashion Service (TFS), supplied by Ragtrade Resources.)*

The main aim of these showings is to promote the reputations of the couturiers and their fashion houses, and to sell new ideas to the fashion-buying public. They are a means of testing the re-actions of the fashion world's who's who to a new skirt length, a new silhouette, or a totally new fashion statement.

Fashion reporters observe, record, analyse, interpret and photograph what they see. The information they gather and distribute is used in forecast reports and newspaper and magazine articles, and as an inspirational guide for the design of new garments and ranges which will be selling in Australia about 12 months later (Fig. 7.2).

## THE ROLE OF THE FASHION DESIGNER

There are many ways in which a designer may work, and many different categories of fashion design which require specialised knowledge. The broad apparel categories are womenswear, menswear and childrenswear. These can be broken down into more specialised areas such as outerwear, sportswear, evening wear, lingerie, swimwear and knitwear.

Australian fashion houses 'borrow' heavily from international trends, and companies here tend to place more emphasis on successfully interpreting these trends for the Australian market place than on developing original ideas. Our small population and conservative, casual style of dress reinforce this tendency towards adaptation rather than innovation.

Australian couture or designer labels are often small operations with the owner as designer. So it is usually the owner/designer of the company who benefits from the publicity and prestige associated with high quality, exclusive garments because they have their name on the label inside the garment. Some larger up-market companies use designers who usually work anonymously as employees under the company label, and receive no public recognition for their work.

A desire for recognition of their talents and the freedom to design in their own style inspires many designers to venture out on their own and start up their own businesses. Occasionally a designer is talented enough or fortunate enough to have an employer who is willing to allow them to develop a range under their own name within the company structure and with the financial backing necessary to get such a venture off the ground.

The mass-produced, middle to cheaper end of the fashion industry employs the largest number of designers. This work tends not to be as creative as the more elite 'designer' or couture end of the business because the garments are often just copies, adaptations or cheaper versions of overseas designs. So the designer's role here is more a matter of coordinating and producing than developing new trends. However, the sheer size of some of these companies in Australia means that the work they offer may be more financially rewarding for a designer than working for a smaller, higher prestige label. A large company can provide a wider range of career opportunities and bonuses such as overseas travel.

How a designer works and what a designer actually does depends on his or her past experience, the fashion house, the type of garments being produced, cost restrictions and so on. Because the designer is involved in every stage of range production, the best way to understand the process is to follow it through step by step, and to examine the designer's role along the way (Fig. 7.3).

The designer's first task is to research his or her market, and to research and forecast the trends most likely to be successful. The research process also includes sourcing materials, trims and services. The second step is to design a coordinated range of garments. The

▶ *7.2\* These international fair dates are correct at the time of printing, but may change from year to year. Those fairs which extend over two months, for example from end August to beginning September, are mentioned in the first of those months. (Information courtesy of Ragtrade Resources.)*

# INTERNATIONAL FAIR DATES*

**Key:** M/W: Menswear, W/W: Womenswear, C/W: Childrenswear, RTW: Ready to Wear, Acc: Accessories

## January

| | |
|---|---|
| Heimtex | Frankfurt |
| Pitti Immagine Uomo | Florence |
| Pitti Immagine Oltre | Florence |
|    Avantegarde M/W | |
| NAMBS | New York |
| Hong Kong Fashion Week | Hong Kong |
| It's Cologne, M/W | Cologne |
| Swimwear Fabrics | Monte Carlo |
| Pitti Immagine Bimbo, C/W | Florence |
| New Delhi Garment Fair | New Delhi |
| Pielespana (Leather) | Barcelona |
| Gaudi Hombre, M/W | Barcelona |
| Nordic Fashion Fair | Helsinki |
| Textima, (Fabric/apparel) | Amsterdam |
| Haute Couture | Paris |
| Design in Knitwear, | London |
| Pitti Immagine Filati (Yarn) | Florence |
| Pret a Porter, W/W | Paris |

## February

| | |
|---|---|
| Action Sports, | San Diego |
| SEHM, European M/W | Paris |
| Mode Enfantine, C/W | Paris |
| Sisel Hiver (Sport/Leisure) | Paris |
| Salon International Lingerie | Paris |
| Collection Premiere | Düsseldorf |
| Designer Collections, M/W | Paris |
| Intermoda RTW | Lisbon |
| Cologne Mens Herren Mode | Cologne |
|    Interjeans | |
| RTW, W/W | Milan |
| RTW Berlin | |
| International Collections | London |
|    London Show, W/W | |
| International Men's & Boy's Wear, IMBEX | London |
| British Yarn Show | Leicester |
| International Spring Clothing | Belgrade |
|    Tokyo Pretex (Fabrics) | |
| Mens | Munich |
| Imagenmode RTW | Madrid |
| Childrenswear | Cologne |
| Menswear | Montreal |
| Modam, W/W, M/W and Acc. | Amsterdam |
| ISPO | Munich |

## March

| | |
|---|---|
| Harrogate Fashion Fair | Harrogate |
| World Fashion Trade Fair, RTW | Osaka |
| Contemporary RTW | Milan |
| Prato Expo | Florence |
| Igedo, Idego Dessous, W/W RTW | Düsseldorf |
| Milano Collections Donna | Milan |
| Fabrex | London |
| Moda in Tessuto | Milan |
| Designer RTW | Paris |
| Magic | Las Vegas |
| Premier Vision (Fabrics) | Paris |
| Canadian International W/W Show | Montreal |
| SIG, Sport & Leisure | Grenoble |
| Deutsche Tuchschau, M/W Fabrics | Neuss |
| Portuguese Offer (Fabrics) | Lisbon |
| Mipel (Leather) | Milan |
| Ideacomo (Fabrics) | Cernobbio |
| Modaberlin, M/W, W/W, C/W & Acc. | Berlin |
| Bobbin | Miami Beach |
| Mostra Internacional | Barcelona |
|    De Tecidos (Fabric) | |

## April

| | |
|---|---|
| Interstoff (Fabric) | Frankfurt |
| Bangkok RTW | Bangkok |

## May

| | |
|---|---|
| International Hosiery Expo | Charlotte |
| Tokyo Fashion Week | Tokyo |
| Techlextil | Frankfurt |
| Kortex | Seoul |
| Euromode Textilia RTW | Thessaloniki |
| Kyotoscope (Fabrics) | Kyoto |
| Fashion Promotions | Düsseldorf |

## June

| | |
|---|---|
| ESMA, Knitwear | Milan |
| Expofil (Yarn) | Paris |
| Pitti Immagine Uomo, | Florence |
|    M/W Designer RTW | |
| NAMBS | New York |

## July

| | |
|---|---|
| Pitti Immagine Bimbo | Florence |
| Pitti Immagine Teenager | Florence |
| Apparel Fair | Hong Kong |
| Pitti Immagine Filati | Florence |
| It's Cologne | Cologne |
| Collections Premieren | Düsseldorf |

## August

| | |
|---|---|
| MAB, M/W | London |
| Herren Mode Woche, M/W | Cologne |
| RTW | Berlin |
| India Garment Fair | New Delhi |
| ISPO | Munich |
| International Fashion | New York |
|    Boutique Show | |
| International Kids Fashion Show | New York |

## September

| | |
|---|---|
| Pret a Porter | Paris/ |
| SEHM (European M/W) | Paris |
| Igedo, W/W, RTW | Düsseldorf |
| Igedo Beach, Igedo Dessous, | Düsseldorf |
|    W/W RTW | |
| Action Sports | San Diego |
| Magic | Las Vegas |
| Bobbin | Atlanta City |
| Action Sports Retail | Atlanta City |
| British Yarn Show | Leicester |
| Fabrex | London |
| Texprint | London |
| Premiere Vision (Fabrics) | Paris |
| Modit — Milanovendemoda | Milan |
| Fashion Week (Spring/Summer) | Hong Kong |
| International Fashion Week | Madrid |
| Harrogate Fashion Exhibition | Harrogate |
| Moda In | Milan |
| Prato Expo | Florence |

## October

| | |
|---|---|
| Milano Collezioni Donna | Milan |
| NAMBS | New York |
| Interstoff (Fabric) | Frankfurt |
| Asian High Fashion Fair | Kobe, Japan |

## November

| | |
|---|---|
| Interstoff, Asia | |
| Hong Kong Apparel Fair | Hong Kong |
| International | Cologne |
|    Leisure/Sports/Swimwear | |

## December

| | |
|---|---|
| Fashion Promotions | Düsseldorf |
| ESMA, Knitwear | Milan |
| Expofil | Paris |

third stage is sampling and evaluation, and the fourth and final stage is production and sales. Although not directly responsible for production and sales, the designer must understand these processes and be on hand should advice be needed.

# 1. RESEARCHING THE MARKET

Fashion research involves looking back to where we have already been, looking at the era in which we currently live and looking forward to future trends. As we have seen in our study of fashion trends,

designing to suit the times is all important in the development of new styles. A design that is too early or too late will be unsuccessful because customers are either not yet ready for it or have already tired of it.

Therefore, the first stage of creating a new line is to thoroughly investigate all fashion and consumer trends operating in the market place. This enables the designer to be in tune with the evolution of fashion cycles, and to more accurately understand the tastes and requirements of the person who is likely to buy the garments. The information a designer needs is shown in Figure 7.4.

Ongoing research into trends and influences should be second nature to a designer and undertaken throughout the year. However, research is particularly important at the beginning of a range because it sets the direction for the development of the new styles.

*The customer* — age, size range, taste, lifestyles, budget, colour preferences, habits, social and economic standing.

*The location* — where the garments are to be sold and worn, i.e. city, country, local, interstate, international, local preferences.

*The environment* — season, climate, time (day, evening) and occasion (formal, informal, casual).

*The company image* — upmarket, mass market, made-to-measure, price range, type and location of sales outlets (boutiques, department stores, markets, mail order).

▼ *7.3 From designer to consumer — the steps in producing a garment.*

▲ *7.4 The designer needs to have a clear understanding of the market he or she is designing for.*

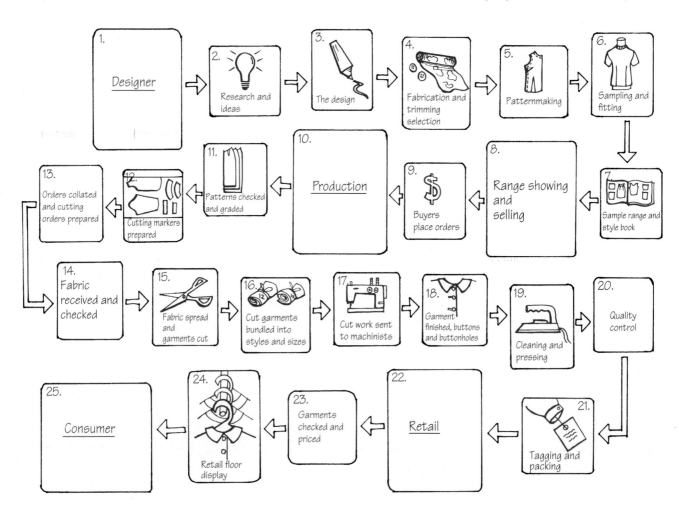

*7.5 An image board of trends, ideas taken from current magazines and sources of inspiration, is a good way to collect and organise ideas. (Photograph courtesy of Table Eight.)*

The designer should constantly investigate and seek out new fabrics, trims and techniques. Trend spotting, going to fashion shows, films and exhibitions, watching music videos, reading magazines, travelling overseas to review the designer collections and investigate the shops, and anything else which will provide ideas and information about the life and times in which we live is essential for the designer who wants to be successful (Fig. 7.5).

Once this information has been collected, it is reviewed and assessed and forms the basis from which the new range will develop. When sifting through the many fashions which co-exist at any one time (due to the varied preferences of different consumer groups), the designer must be able to select exactly those which will most suit his or her customers and will result in maximum sales.

## FORECASTING THE TRENDS

Anticipating future trends is known as *fashion forecasting*, and is an extension of the research process.

Forecasting is vital since the designer works at least six months ahead of the selling season and so must have a fairly good idea of what styles customers will be looking for. Predicting consumer demand is also an important part of the financial and market planning of any company, and is necessary when ordering fabrics and trims which are purchased well in advance of the season.

The forecast report is a popular way of obtaining advance information on fashion trends. Forecast reports can be subscribed to and offer a service similar to magazines in a variety of formats. They use slides, photographs, videos or illustrations, and include analyses of best sellers, style adaptations, shop front displays and street fashions, often with fabric swatches. Some even provide measurements for accurate 'knock-offs', and details on accessorising. Others specialise in fabric and colour forecasting. They may provide colour cards and news on parades, exhibitions and trade fairs.

These reports are usually expensive because their production involves considerable research. Information is gathered from a network of researchers in cities around the world who frequent the stores, cover shows, see ranges and talk to designers. They research, analyse and interpret the areas of colour, fabric, silhouette, detailing, trims and accessories. This information is then sent out to clients up to two years in advance of the season, via publications and audio-visuals.

The cost of purchasing forecast reports needs to be weighed against the costs and time involved in undertaking private research every season. Although an average price of $A2000–$3000 for several reports each year seems expensive, it is much cheaper than frequent trips overseas.

One other disadvantage of reports compiled in Europe and the USA is that they are not adapted to Australian tastes, figure types, climate and lifestyle. Therefore, to follow them too closely could be a mistake in the Australian market place, and careful interpretation and adaptation on the part of the designer is necessary.

Predictive 'bureaux de style' are now numerous and themselves exert a considerable trend-setting influence on the fashion industry. Regular conferences by members of the forecasting fraternity to discuss differences in perceived fashion directions avoid the problem of a multiplicity of trends, and ensure a cohesive approach to trend analysis.

Categories covered by trend reports for both men and women include colour, advanced collections (career fashions), sportswear, knitwear, tailoring, directions in tops and bottoms, T-shirts, jeans, sportswear coordinates, activewear (aerobics, swimwear), graphic design (logos and labels), childrenswear, age groupings (25–35, young boutique) and so on.

## SOURCING

As part of the initial research undertaken at the commencement of a season, the designer previews fabric and trim ranges in order to have a general idea of what

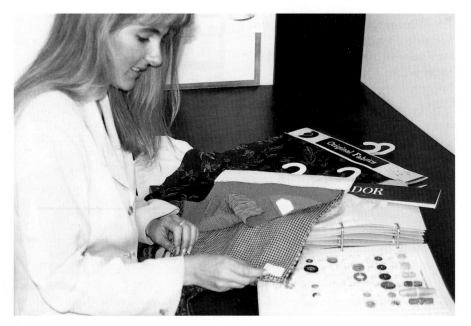

7.6 Reviewing a fabric range. The designer previews the fabrics and trims from various suppliers before starting to design the range. (Photograph courtesy Table Eight.)

will be available for the new range.

Establishing competitive sources for all goods and services required for the production of a range is an important part of range planning. Sources need to be updated regularly because the very nature of the fashion industry means that suppliers and products change frequently (Fig. 7.6).

Sources need to offer good response times, reliability, flexibility, quality and competitive prices. In Australia such requirements are often hard to satisfy because the majority of our fashion materials are imported. This places the supplier and manufacturer at the mercy of shipping schedules, industrial disputes and fluctuating currency values. Alternative means of obtaining materials are essential to safeguard against shortages beyond the control of the designer.

## SOURCING FABRICS

The designer may deal with the following people when looking for suitable fabrics.

### 1. Textile producers

Textile mills weave or knit fabrics which may be sold direct to garment manufacturers or wholesalers or sold through a textile agent. Only 5 per cent of all fabrics used in Australia are manufactured locally.

The Australian textile industry has difficulty competing with overseas manufacturers because the cost of labour here is much higher and the small domestic market limits the benefits gained from large-scale manufacturing plants. The lead time for the production of locally manufactured fabric is around eight weeks. There are two categories of textile producer.

(a) Specialised

By completing one particular process in the production of fashion fabrics, for example spinning, weaving, knitting, printing or finishing, a textile producer is said to be specialised. This is also the case if the producer produces a particular product line, for example luxury fabrics (linens, silks, brocades), industrial or daywear fabrics (cottons, drill, homespun, poplin) or prints or knits.

(b) Vertically integrated

A vertically integrated operation undertakes all the processes (spinning and weaving or knitting) necessary to produce the unfinished greige goods, then finishes and distributes its own range of fabrics.

### 2. Converters

Converters use fabric mills and printing plants to convert unfinished or greige goods into finished fabrics. The converter specifies the design, colour and finish required and uses a contractor to carry out the dyeing, printing, waterproofing, mercerising and other processes.

The converter usually works closely with apparel manufacturers and retailers who are unable to do their own large minimums, or with the large manufacturers who require short lead times to respond to fashion trends.

### 3. Importers

Australia imports fabrics from all over the world. Our major sources are the Asian countries — Japan, Taiwan, Korea and China — but we also import smaller quantities from the USA and Europe. Lead times from Europe and Asia are 12–16 weeks, and up to six months from China.

Imported fabrics are often ordered on *indent*; that is, they must be ordered in advance to suit the overseas manufacturing cycle, and paid for when the order is placed.

### 4. Agents

Agents represent manufacturers and wholesalers, sell on commission and do not carry any stock.

### 5. Stockist wholesalers

These suppliers purchase finished goods from manufacturers and carry the fabric stocks which are then sold to apparel manufacturers and fabric retailers. Stockist wholesalers are a convenient source of fabrics because their lead times are short and further supplies for recuts and good sellers may be readily available.

The designer should become familiar with a wide range of wholesalers since they usually cater for specific sectors of the market. Some firms specialise in basic fabrics, for example wools, daywear cottons, knits and so on, while others carry novelties such as brocades, metallics or plastics. Some firms specialise in evening or luxury fabrics, which include linens, silks, laces and velvets. There are also those who specialise in printed fabrics.

## 6. Jobbers

When ordering fabric, the aim is to purchase enough to fill all orders without accumulating a surplus. Because fabrics are often ordered before exact requirements are known, some excess is inevitable; however, some fabrics can be carried over to the next season, thereby minimising wastage. Excess fabrics with a short life cycle and suitable for one season only should be disposed of in-season.

Disposal agents known as 'jobbers' purchase excess fabrics at well below the market price then resell them to other manufacturers or fabric retailers at a discounted price of approximately 75 per cent of the original wholesale price. The vendor can expect to get 30–50 per cent of the original purchase price. The value depends on the demand for the fabric, quantities for sale and the range and balance of colours.

FORECAST SUMMER  FABRICS

FLOWER PRINTS

18 SILK JACQUARD WITH RICH ORNAMENTAL FLOWER DESIGN

19 FLAT BI-COLOURED CUT-OUT FLOWERS ON COTTON GROUND

20 LINED UP SMALL FLOWERS ON VOILE GROUND

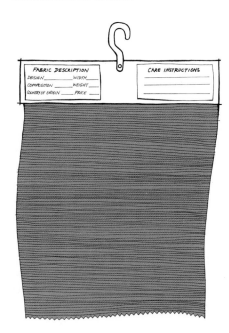

▲ 7.8 Textile forecast reports are available to help the designer keep up with new fabrics on the market. (Reproduced from The Fashion Service (TFS) Womenswear Forecast, courtesy of Ragtrade Resources.)

◄ 7.7 Fabric samples are shown on headers and the large swatch of fabric is known as a feeler.

## PURCHASING FABRICS

A designer may spend several weeks selecting and ordering fabrics for a new range. Fabrics from each supplier are considered for quality, performance, fibre content, construction, colour, price, exclusivity, availability and date of delivery (Figs. 7.7 & 7.8).

Once the fabric has been chosen, sampling is ordered for the sample range. Some basic fabrics may also be ordered in bulk at this time; but, where possible, bulk orders are made after the range has been shown and customers have placed orders. Fabrics are supplied on bolts or rolls. A bolt is a length of fabric, usually 30–40 metres in length, wrapped around a flat cardboard core. A roll is wrapped around a cardboard cylinder and may be of any length, usually up to 50 metres.

As each order is confirmed, all details — style name or number, supplier, price, content, care instructions, colourways and delivery dates — are recorded with a swatch of the fabric for later inclusion on the fabric storyboard.

## SOURCING TRIMS

Trims add the finishing touch to a garment and their careful selection is important if they are not to overpower a design or look like an afterthought.

The sourcing of trims is a similar process to that of sourcing fabrics. Once again, suppliers specialise in different products, — sewing threads, appliques, beading, braids, buttons, belts, buckles and so on.

Trims are generally ordered once fabrics have been selected. If individual items, such as shoulder pads, belts or appliqués, have to be made to particular specifications, they are usually sampled while the garment pattern is being developed. Allowances must be made for the longer lead times involved in developing such items.

Colour matching to the fabric is important. Zippers and threads are available in a wide range of colours, but trims such as buttons are usually dyed to achieve perfect colour match. Minimum quantities often apply with certain treatments such as dyeing, or the dyer may charge a set dye fee regardless of the quantity dyed.

Standardised printed labels for fibre content, size and care can be purchased from stock. Personalised printed or woven labels, swing tickets, badges and such can be made to order with usual minimums of 5000–10 000 units.

Lead times for trims depend on the availability of stock. Standard items permanently in stock may be delivered immediately, while non-standard items which have to be ordered, imported or made up may have lead times of 12–16 weeks.

## SOURCING SERVICES

As well as sourcing materials, the designer may call on a variety of specialist services from outside sources. These services are generally used on a freelance or random basis. They include:

- designers, patternmakers and graders, to help with styling, sampling and pattern production.

- textile and print designers who may be employed full-time by fabric mills, printing companies or design studios, or may design to order on a freelance basis. They may specialise in the construction of woven or knitted fabrics and develop new fabrics according to particular specifications, for example, uniforms. Or these designers may create designs to be printed onto greige or finished goods. A painted sample of the print, known as a *croquis*, is approved and a sample of the design is printed. This is called a *strike-off*, and must also be approved before the production run commences.

- dyers, who set a minimum metreage for dyeing or charge a set fee for very small quantities.
    *Piece-dyed* fabrics are dyed after weaving and have smaller minimums, usually 200–300 metres, because the greige goods are held in stock and dyed to order. Yarn- and solution-dyed fabrics have larger dyeing minimums. With *yarn-dyed* fabrics, the yarn is dyed and then woven. *Solution-dyed* fabrics are synthetic fabrics which are dyed while in the liquid state, before being made into thread and woven.
    *Lab-dips* are initial dye tests performed on fabric swatches to test colours. *Crocking* is caused by faulty dyeing, when the excess dye-stuff rubs off.
    *Garment dyeing* involves dyeing garments after they have been made up. Problems may arise with garment dyeing when fabrics or threads of differing composition dye different shades in the one garment.

- printers, for placement prints on cut garment pieces or metreage printing on lengths of fabric. The designer may provide the print design, or purchase a design from a print studio. The printer charges a fee for the art work and for each screen. A screen is required for each colour used. Because of the setting-up costs involved in having any printing done, the printer usually establishes minimum quantities which must be printed to cover these costs. These minimums vary from 50–1000 metres, depending on the printer. Before the production run commences, the printer will produce several strike-offs to test the colours and print quality.

- laundries, for washing treatments, especially for denim and sportswear. Made-up garments as well as fabrics by the metre can be washed to achieve a faded or stonewash effect.

- knitters, to provide knitted fabrics by the metre, fully-fashioned knitted garments, and knit trims, such as collars, cuffs and basques.

- cut, make and trim (CMT) manufacturers, who are supplied with patterns, trimmings and fabrics, and return the completed garment.

- pressers, who press the garment after it is fully made up.

- pleaters.

- embroiderers, to apply numerous types of surface treatment to fabric, for example appliqué, edging, studding and beading.

- covered button and belt makers.

- testing laboratories. If a manufacturer is unsure of the performance of a fabric, or the fibre content or care requirements for labelling purposes, the fabric or garment can be sent to a laboratory for analysis and testing. Some large manufacturers and retailers have their own testing laboratories and routinely test their own products as part of their quality control programme. Commonly performed tests include colourfastness, washability, shrinkage and abrasion (e.g. pilling).

With most of these services, new styles or designs involve considerable initial outlays of time and money to develop, test and sample. These costs can be spread over the final production run but, with very small quantities, the costs may be deemed too high. In such cases, the designer has to weigh up the costs involved against the value of the finished garment.

## FABRIC AND TRIM STORYBOARDS

Once ordering is completed, a fabric and trim storyboard is compiled. Storyboards are created to record information about all fabrics and trims used in each range. Swatches of each fabric and trim in the colourways chosen are taped to the board and grouped according to the combinations to be used together (Fig. 7.9).

The information to be noted next to each fabric swatch may include:

- fabric style and article number
- colours chosen
- fibre content and care instructions
- width
- price per metre

- sampling and bulk delivery dates
- quantity ordered
- supplier's name and telephone number.

For trims, the information includes:

- article name and number
- width/size
- colours chosen
- supplier's name and telephone number
- price per unit or per metre.

Croquis and lab-dips may be included on the board if swatches are not available.

Designer, fabric and trim storyboards are useful records of a range if kept from season to season.

7.9 The fabric story board organises the fabrics into stories and records all appropriate information.

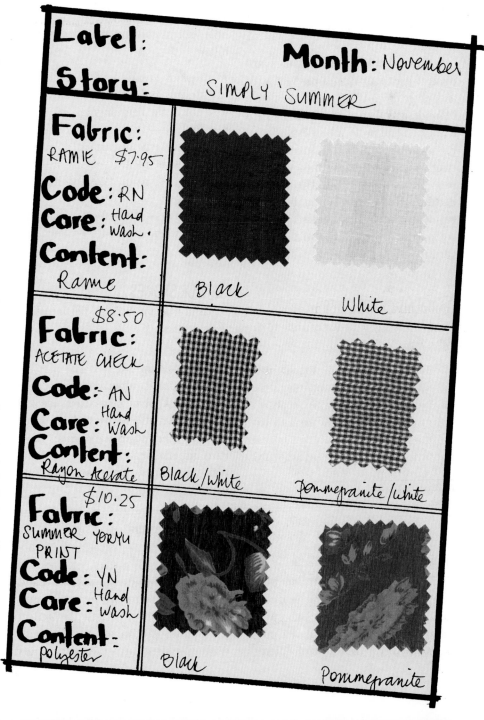

# 2. THE DESIGN PROCESS

## RANGE PLANNING

A designer's success is measured by his or her ability to create fashionable garments featuring new ideas which customers want to buy. The fashions must be different from what every other manufacturer is producing whilst at the same time in keeping with the current look and latest trends. Range planning is the second step in designing a new range.

Most Australian fashion houses produce at least four ranges per year, with an average of 70–100 garments per range. More designs than are really needed are developed and prototype styles made up. From the prototypes, the smaller, final range is selected during the evaluation process (see Chapter 9). The designer decides on the number and type of garments, the themes, fabrics, trims and colours, before the design of individual garments can proceed.

## GARMENT CATEGORIES

Garments are grouped according to the following.

- Type of garment, for example separates (skirts, pants, shirts, blouses, jackets), dresses, coats.
- Occasion, for example evening wear, day wear, sportswear.
- Style, for example classic, innovative.
- Age group.
- Price range.
- Colours.

## STORIES

Stories are the themes around which groups of garments in the range are built. Stories help to unite the diverse styles, fabrics and colours, and a range of garments will have several different stories which may or may not relate to each other.

A story may be drawn from any source — historical or folk costume, a famous personality, a new film or video, a work of art — the list is endless. Alternatively, it may be based on any of the elements and principles of design using fabric, colour, trim or detailing as the common uniting factor.

## FABRIC AND TRIM SELECTION

The major influences in the designer's final selection of fabrics and trims are as follow.

- Fashion trends — do the colours, designs and textures suit the direction of the new range?
- End use — does each fabric and trim suit the type of garment for which it is to be used?
- Cost — is the cost within the budget?
- Delivery — is the fabric or trim available when needed for production?

## COLOUR STORIES

In fashion terms, colours fall into four main groups.

### 1. Staple colours

These are classic colours used every year, such as black, white, beige, navy blue and grey, and combinations such as black and white, and red, navy and white. These have universal appeal because they traverse age groups, market segments and seasons.

### 2. Seasonal colours

Because of their physical and psychological qualities, certain colours are associated with different seasons. Light and bright colours are generally associated with summer because they reflect heat and suggest coolness and freshness. Winter requires warmer, darker colours because of the desire for warmth and cosiness.

### 3. Fashion colours

Fashion colours vary from year to year according to the dominant themes of the season. One year the emphasis may be on earthy, natural colours, while the next year may see pastels favoured.

### 4. Accent colours

These colours are used in small amounts as trims or accessories to accentuate the appearance of a garment.

When coordinating colour, the designer aims to achieve interest, a sense of balance and unity in every garment and in the range. In planning the colour stories, the designer is actually creating colour schemes based on the four colour categories.

Firstly the staple and seasonal colours are chosen, colours which have proven successful over past seasons. Very often these colours will be cut in classic styles which don't alter much from year to year, and appeal to a large section of the market, therefore ensuring a certain level of sales. These form the 'bread-and-butter' part of the range.

Having established the conservative, staple colours, the designer selects the fashion colours. Fashion colours are less reliable because they change from year to year and are often only accepted by the more fashion-conscious consumers. Fashion colours have a life cycle which extends over a period of several years. Initially they are introduced in small quantities to test the market. If consumer acceptance is high, the colour is used in greater quantities the following season. When a colour becomes too popular, sales begin to wane as customers seek new colours, and the colour is dropped from the range.

Accent colours are generally fashion colours used in small quantities with staple colours, or with other fashion colours. They are often less commercial colours which are acceptable only when used as a highlight to update old styles and colours, or to enhance otherwise unexciting colours. Accent colours are often restricted to trims or small details placed on the garment, for example pockets, collars, buttons or belts, and have quite a short life cycle.

Fabrics, trims and colours usually tie in with the themes chosen for the range. For example, a designer using a military theme may use camouflage prints in khaki, green, brown and beige, or may update the traditional look by using an unusual theme, colour or fabric combination.

When working with colour, Australian designers need to be aware that most of our trends emerge from the European and American fashion scene. Because the light, lifestyle, climate, geography and racial colouring of these international fashion centres differ from Australia's, what works in those places does not necessarily work here.

Even within Australia, there are considerable climatic and lifestyle variations from state to state. The designer needs to know his or her market, and to interpret the overseas colour trends to suit regional requirements. This may even mean putting together different colour stories for different states.

## GARMENT DESIGN

When it comes to planning and designing individual garments in a range, there are many factors the designer must keep in mind. The original idea for a garment may have to be modified to suit:

- the needs of the consumer
- the image and market requirements of the fashion house
- fashion trends
- the 'rules' of design
- the aesthetic and visual appeal of a garment
- hanger appeal

- its relationship to the human body in terms of comfort, fit and size
- the intended function, for example workwear must be durable and easy to clean
- the characteristics of the fabric used in terms of weave, drape, elasticity, thermoplasticity
- budget and resource limitations
- availability of materials, for example fabrics and trims
- sales targets.

Because designing clothing is a creative process, it is inevitable that the designer will at times be pulled in different directions by opposing influences. Fashion is a form of communication and an expression of personal taste through the variables of texture, colour, line and form, but there are always the requirements of the market place to be taken into consideration.

Mass production allows a variety of fashion 'looks' to be available at one time. There are usually several dominant styles, with rapidly changing minor trends co-existing at any one time. This suits our varied life-styles, and permits individual freedom of expression through dress.

How then, can a designer, who is working up to 12 months ahead of the current season and is constantly exposed to latest influences (new trends, fibres, colours and technological developments), satisfy the needs and tastes of consumers while retaining personal integrity, creativity and style?

The answer is that a designer must be decisive, and believe firmly in his or her own creativity, instincts and understanding of fashion. Some of this fashion awareness, or flair, is natural aptitude while the rest is gained through education and experience.

The designer needs to have a focus, a constant image to draw on to maintain a clear vision and consistency in style. This vision usually acts as both a stabilising factor and source of inspiration. By

focusing on a particular source of inspiration, the designer is able to express his or her own style and adapt it to satisfy the needs of the consumer and sales figures. (Chapter 8 discusses inspiration in more detail.)

The starting point for the new range may be variations of good sellers from recent past ranges. Next come the new looks for the season. Each garment begins with a concept which the designer feels is important to present to the consumer. Sometimes the idea is already complete in the designer's mind and can be sketched and sampled immediately. Sometimes it evolves through a series of sketches, or develops as the designer drapes fabric on a model or mannequin (Fig. 7.10).

Draping is a three-dimensional, sculptural approach to fashion designing that permits the free and experimental development of ideas. The designer cuts out the basic idea in a

7.10 The designer starts to clarify design ideas on paper once all sources of inspiration have been explored. (Photograph courtesy of Table Eight.)

cheap fabric, such as muslin or calico, and pins it onto the dress form or model. From time to time, as the designer works, allowing the fabric to fall, fold and drape, he or she will step back to check how the idea looks on the form, how it moulds to the curves of the human body. In this way, ideas develop by accident, or existing ideas can be reworked and perfected from every angle (Fig. 7.11).

For those designers who sketch their ideas, the rough sketch is known as a *croquis*. When the designer is happy with the way the garment looks on paper, it is redrawn accurately by the designer or an assistant. Design and construction details, back views, measurements, fabric swatches, trims, colours and anything else that may be required for sample production are included on the accurately drawn production sketch.

## DESIGNER STORYBOARD

As the sketches are completed, they are added to the designer storyboard. This board is similar to the fabric and trim

7.12 *This patternmaker is using the flat pattern method, an efficient way of making a pattern from a sketch instead of from draped fabric. (Photograph courtesy of Table Eight.)*

storyboards, and is a compilation of all the styles grouped into stories with fabric swatches. It is the designer's means of keeping track of new styles, and everyone in the design room should have access to the board so they all know how the range is proceeding.

# 3. SAMPLE PRODUCTION

Once the designs have been created, the designer's next job is to oversee and direct the production of the new styles from beginning to end. This is the third process in the design and development of the range, and involves the making of prototypes to test the design.

The first step is for the designer, designer's assistant or patternmaker to make a paper or cardboard pattern (Fig. 7.12). This is where the designer's

technical skills become very important. A knowledge of fabrics, trims, fit, pattern-making, draping and sewing techniques is essential to enable the designer to create or guide his or her design assistants in the creation of a specific look.

From the first pattern a *sample garment* is cut, very often in a cheap fabric such as calico, and is made up by the sample machinist.

This completed first sample (known as the *toile*) is fitted onto a dress form or model to check the styling details, proportions, fit and sizing (Fig. 7.13). With middle-to higher-priced garments, fittings, alterations and resampling are repeated (usually in the correct fabric) until the designer is satisfied that the garment is perfect. If several different fabrics are to be cut in the same style, the garment is usually also sampled in each of those fabrics to prevent any unexpected problems with differences in fabric performance.

7.13 *Fitting. Alterations are made on the dress stand or house model, and the patterns are adjusted accordingly. (Photograph courtesy of Table Eight.)*

7.11 *Draping has advantages over designing on paper because the proportion and fit of the garment can be related directly to the human form, and the flow and drape of the fabric is immediately apparent. (Photograph courtesy of Table Eight.)*

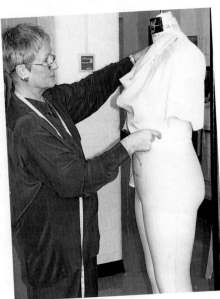

Once the sample is satisfactorily completed, the pattern is graded to the necessary size range. *Grading* is the process of increasing or decreasing a sample size pattern according to standard body measurements. The grader decides where to apply the measurements so as to produce a set of patterns in the required size range while maintaining the proportion of the original design. The

number of sizes will depend both on the requirements of the market sector being supplied and the fit of the garment.

After grading, a design specification is prepared (Fig. 7.14). This summarises the design details, including fabrics, trims, special treatments and making notes and is kept on file in the design room.

A detailed make specification and production sheet is also prepared. The make specification describes how the garment is to be made (Fig. 7.15). The production sheet records cutting quan-

tities, delivery dates and terms and conditions (Fig. 7.16). These forms are done in multiple copies and forwarded to the various design, accounts, and production departments while the top copies are pinned to the garments for issue to the makers.

Garment *costings* are also prepared at this stage. Every metre of fabric, trim, label, miscellaneous item and process used in the production of a garment must be measured and recorded on a costing sheet. From the sample garment costing, the final production cost of the garment can be calculated, as well as the selling price and profit margin. (See Chapter 18 for more information on costing and production procedures.)

## RANGE EVALUATION — THE WEEDING PROCESS

When a sample garment has been completed, it must be evaluated to assess its suitability for inclusion in the range. This is an important process in which all key people involved in the sampling, selling and production of the garment should participate since they each have their own considerations and viewpoints to offer. The aim of the evaluation process is to ensure that the garment styling suits the habits, needs and wants of the consumer — that the right garment in the right quantities at the right price is produced. The evaluation must be made from the customer's point of view, and with an understanding of how the buyer thinks when purchasing a garment.

Every aspect of each garment — from colour, fabric and trim choice, to style details, production costs and final selling price — is discussed.

When evaluating individual garments, the designer considers the following criteria:

### 1. Marketing factors
Does the customer need it? Does it suit the image of the label in the market place? Does it suit the consumer in terms of age, price, occasion?

*7.14 Design specifications sheet.*

## MAKE SPECIFICATIONS

*Copy*

STYLE _8747_     DATE _15th July_

SHOULDER PADS _____     RANGE _Simply Summer_

SEAMS _1.5 cm_     FABRIC _Paste Floral Bemburg Print._

STITCHES _3.5 per cm._

TOP STITCHING _Pinstitch armholes, neckline & front panel._

FUSING _Front panel._

BUTTONS _11_    SIZE _20 L_    TYPE _Flat, 2 hole_

         SIZE _____    TYPE _____

BELT _____    ZIP _____

PLEATING _____

HEM _1 cm o'locked._

OVERLOCKING MUST BE SAME COLOUR AS FABRIC _____

LABEL MUST BE SEWN WITH THREAD THE SAME COLOUR AS LABEL _____

| ELASTIC WIDTH | 16 _____ | WAISTBAND FINISHED | 16 _____ |
| | 18 _____ | | 18 _____ |
| | 20 _____ | | 20 _____ |
| | 22 _____ | | 22 _____ |
| | 24 _____ | | 24 _____ |

SPECIAL INSTRUCTIONS _____

_Front panel self-faced & overlocked._

GENERAL _____

MAKERS SIGNATURE _Y. Theodoros_

T8-06

*7.15 Make specifications sheet.*

## 2. Appearance factors

Does the garment look good? Does it have consumer appeal? Do the colours suit Australian complexions and environments? Will it generate demand in the market place? Is it new (colours, fabric and styling)? Does it have hanger appeal; will it encourage potential customers to try it on? Does it fit well? Is it flattering? Is the proportion and balance pleasing? Does it look expensive or cheap?

## 3. Performance factors

Do the designs and fabrics suit the end-use? Will the garment wear well? Is it comfortable? Does the fabric clean easily? Will the garment still look good after normal wash and wear? Is there room for movement? Are fit and fabric suitable for the climate? Does the fabric irritate the skin (should it be lined)? Is it warm enough (should it be lined)?

## 4. Costing factors

Is the selling price right? Can it be mixed and matched with other garments? Is it too cheap or too expensive for the consumer? Does the price suit the quality of the garment? Is the cost of maintaining the garment (e.g. dry cleaning) appropriate for the price and quality of the garment? Can it be made more cheaply and still look as good? Will enough sell at this price? Is the profit margin sufficient?

## 5. Social factors

Does it suit the wearer's image? Does it enhance the wearer's self image? Does it suit the wearer's age, lifestyle, peer group identity and roles? Is it appropriate for the occasion? Where and when can it be worn? Is it versatile (can it be worn for different occasions)? Does it enhance the wearer's social acceptability?

The next step is to use the designer storyboard as an overview to analyse the range as a whole. A successful range should present interesting individual garments as well as a coordinated, total look. It should have variety in:

- types of garment (separates, dresses, suits)
- types of occasion (formal, casual, day, evening)
- classics and innovations.

The successful range will:

- appeal to various needs within the target market in terms of colouring, figure type, taste
- have strong, clear and new themes
- coordinate, show unity and strong direction
- mix and match
- have garments which can be sold both separately and as sets
- cater to different budgets.

*Copy*

| | | | PRODUCTION SHEET No. | 14006 |
|---|---|---|---|---|

EST. YDG. **3·2 M**

ACTUAL YDG. **3·1 M**

EST. YDG.

ACTUAL YDG. — STYLE **87147**

FABRIC WIDTH **115 cm** — DESCRIPTION **A-LINE DRESS, BUTTON FRONT.**

DATE TO CUTTER **15th JULY**

CUTTER **MORAN**

DATE TO MAKER **22nd JULY**

MAKER **G.THEODOROS**

MAKER PRICE: —

DUE DATE **22ND AUGUST**

FABRIC **PASTE FLORAL BEMBURG PRINT**

LINING — AV.

INTERLINING **1·3 "·,** AV. **1·3m** x **2**

| COLOUR | 8 | 10 | 12 | 14 | 16 | TOTAL | METERAGE NEEDED |
|---|---|---|---|---|---|---|---|
| BLUE | 40 | 80 | 80 | 80 | 40 | 320 | 992M |
| ECRU | 25 | 50 | 50 | 50 | 25 | 200 | 620M |
| BLACK | 20 | 40 | 40 | 40 | 20 | 160 | 496M |

SPECIALS

| COLOUR | 8 | 10 | 12 | 14 | 16 | TOTAL |
|---|---|---|---|---|---|---|

| BUTTONS | **11 × 20L** | LABEL | |
|---|---|---|---|
| BUTTONS | | SWINGTAGS | |
| ZIPS | — | SIZE LABEL | |
| ELASTIC | — | CONTENT | **POLY/VISCOSE** |
| SHOULDER PAD | — | BARCODE | |
| OTHER | | | |

CONDITIONS

1. Late delivery of garments will incur a 10% penalty on invoice total.
2. For complete delivery made on or before a Wednesday, payment will be made on the following Friday.
3. Invoices/Delivery Dockets must state style, price and quantity per size and colour.
4. Any discrepancy between cutters total and makers total must be brought to our attention within 48 hours of receipt of cut work.
5. Production samples for each size must be approved within 48 hours of receiving the cut work and before production commences. The expense of any production that does not meet with approval will be incurred at the makers expense.

MAKER'S SIGNATURE: *G.Theodoros*

*7.16 A production sheet.*

# CUSTOMER APPEAL

Obviously, the most important factor to be considered when evaluating the range is the customer who will buy the garments. Every possible aspect which will influence the customer's choice of garment should be considered, and garments which do not satisfy these requirement should be weeded out.

Many consumers feel that fashion is dictated by fashion designers and manufacturers. In reality, it is consumers who determine fashion trends by their acceptance or rejection of styles presented to them at retail level.

Designers or fashion houses should be consistent in the types of garment they show. Changes in image are confusing to regular customers who come to expect a certain type of fashion from a particular supplier. Established designers know who their customers are and how to cater to their tastes, whether it be young and trendy, high fashion or middle of the road.

Variety and balance are the most desirable aspects of any range. To appeal to the widest range of customers possible within a particular market, the garments should offer choice in cost and styling. More innovative, fashionable garments may be balanced by a selection of classics. There should be glamorous as well as practical garments, large and small, tall and short girl garments, more expensive and cheaper garments, and a balance between the garments themselves — separates, skirts and pants, dresses, long and short sleeves, jumpsuits and so on. There should also be a balance in the fabrics used — prints and plains, brights and not-so-brights, neutrals or pastels.

The range usually incorporates a series of themes, or stories. The number of garments in each story, and the number of stories in the range, varies from one company to another. Each story should be easily identifiable and include a variety of styles which would appeal to various tastes, figure types and budgets. The styles should coordinate and work together to support the main theme of the story, without overlapping or repeating ideas.

Sometimes there are a couple of good garments which do not fit into a group or theme. These are known as *items*, and are shown with the range because they are proven good sellers.

Because fashion evolves from one season to the next, each range should be developed on four levels:

- safe, classic styles which can be carried from season to season with minor, if any changes
- best sellers from the previous range, perhaps simply refabricated or done in new colours and trims
- current trends which are the latest looks for the season
- innovative ideas leading into the next range. A few garments which are high fashion, and therefore not likely to be good sellers, may be included in the range. Although they may not be profitable in terms of quantities sold, they add flair to a range and, since they reflect the leading edge of fashion, are useful for publicity in terms of parades, magazine editorial and promotional campaigns.

This cross-section of trends works well because it allows customers to buy garments to complement their existing wardrobe and accessories, as well as move gradually into a new look. The product mix will depend on the company image. Older, more conservative labels will have more of the safe classics and best-sellers, while young contemporary labels will have more new trends and innovations.

Invariably, some styles are dropped from the range before it reaches the showroom. However, careful planning in the initial stages of the range should avoid the elimination of too may styles, because time is too short between ranges to be spent on styles which cannot be used.

## CHAPTER 8

# SOURCES OF INSPIRATION

# INTRODUCTION

Many people hold an image of the fashion designer feverishly creating at the drawing board, with ideas for the new collection stumbling over each other in their haste to get onto the paper. Or there is the image of the designer working in his or her studio, surrounded by a team of assistants, pinning and draping fabrics onto a glamorous model.

While there is an element of truth about these situations, they do tend to be rather romanticised versions of the way most designers work.

It is true that all designing is a creative process. It involves the translation of an idea into a solid form, whether it be a dress, a building or a piece of furniture. But, more than a purely spontaneous bursting forth of ideas, designing tends to be a logical process of problem solving resulting in a creation which provides answers to a set of questions or requirements.

## WHERE DO IDEAS COME FROM?

Put simply, it is the designer's job to conceive of new products which customers will want to buy. The designer achieves this by ensuring that he or she has an in-depth understanding of the requirements of the market, and is able to satisfy those needs by offering a continual supply of new ideas which will appeal, excite, and motivate purchase.

So, how do these ideas come about? Generally they don't just happen. Sometimes the proverbial flash of inspiration will occur, but the designer more often works to a routine which continually feeds and stimulates his or her imagination to ensure that there is a supply of ideas ready to be tapped as the need arises.

The brain is like any other organ of the body — the more it is exercised and the better it is nourished, the more efficiently it will perform when it is needed. Everybody goes through flat spots, when they feel uninspired and lack enthusiasm or direction. Listed below are some ideas which may help in avoiding these blanks or restarting inspiration if they do occur.

### KEEPING A JOURNAL

This is probably the most useful exercise you can undertake as a designer. A journal is used to record your ideas, things you have seen, small sketches, cuttings from magazines, scraps of fabric, ribbons and braid, photographs of paintings, costumes and architecture, paint swatches, favourite designs. Over the years this will build into your own personal resource book, a vast supply of ideas and a valuable monitor of your own evolving style (Fig. 8.1).

### ARTS AND CRAFTS

Because fashion reflects changes in society, the designer must always be alert in recognising new trends. He or she should keep in touch with social influences such as music, architecture, art, film, books, theatre and the cult movements which develop in these fields and filter through the various levels of our society. Take, for example, Jean Paul Gaultier's designs for Madonna's world tour in 1990 which set a strong 'underwear as outerwear' trend worldwide. Fashion designers are sometimes involved in costume design, as seen in Ralph Lauren's costumes for *The Great Gatsby* and *Annie Hall*, and Jean Paul Gaultier's costumes for *The Cook, The Thief, His Wife and Her Lover*.

Fashionable crafts and hobbies also influence design. In the 1960s and 1970s, tie-dyed T-shirts, embroidered jeans and crocheted dresses were popular, with

*8.1 You can create fashion storyboards by collecting inspirational material for your journal. (Reproduced from The Fashion Service Forecast. Courtesy of Ragtrader Resources.)*

some of these treatments re-emerging in the early 1990s.

## THE MEDIA

Local and overseas magazines as well as newspapers and trade publications exist to keep you up-to-date with local and world events, influential identities and technological developments. They also present new ideas in commercial graphics, layout and colour use. Therefore, the print media is especially invaluable in promoting design techniques.

## MUSEUMS, GALLERIES AND LIBRARIES

These institutions carry a vast range of objects and ideas, from costume and textile collections to paintings and sculp-tures, birds and insects, skeletons and industrial inventions. Sources of inspiration in such places are limitless.

## NATURE

Nature is the ultimate source of inspiration to many artists and designers and provides endless variety in colour, pattern and form.

## FOLK AND HISTORICAL COSTUME

Costumes are regularly rediscovered as themes for new collections. Each new interpretation is created from the contemporary viewpoint, so is always different from the previous viewing. As contemporary viewpoints change, so too do the inspirations drawn from history.

## STREET FASHION

Street fashions are particularly important indicators of new directions. Night clubs, progressive boutiques, local magazines and newspapers are rich sources of ideas.

## SHOPPING

From opportunity shops, second-hand book shops and flea markets to department stores and up-market boutiques, ideas are always there waiting to be discovered.

Designers should also constantly shop the stores which stock their own garments, and those of their competitors, to compare their styling, fit, prices, stock turnover, good sellers, markdowns and customer responses.

## TRAVEL

Especially overseas, travelling to trade fairs, collections and to see the locals in 'fashion forward' cities can be very rewarding. Interstate travel can also present a different viewpoint on clothing needs with regard to climate and lifestyle.

## DOODLING

Being able to express yourself visually is a tremendous asset to design. A myriad of latent ideas can come to the surface when you draw and doodle. Doodling is a great way of experimenting before you put scissors to fabric. The Dadaists used doodling to tap into their subconscious — you could try a similar approach.

## THE MUSE

A designer may draw inspiration from a specific ideal of beauty, a personal view of the needs of a particular woman or man, or by the changing needs of women or men in general. Many successful designers have a *muse*, an ideal person who serves as a tangible source of inspiration and keeps their vision constant.

From 1956, when Givenchy created Audrey Hepburn's wardrobe for *Funny Face*, she served as his muse. In the 1980s the model Ines de la Fressnage was used by Karl Lagerfeld at Chanel to represent the house and to epitomise and bring fresh life to the Chanel look. He now works closely with Claudia Schiffer. Actress Anouk Aimeé served as muse for Emanuel Ungaro, who now works with Swedish model Jutta Grappengeisser. Princess Caroline of Monaco has inspired Marc Bohan at Dior, and Yves St Laurent works with Catherine Deneuve and Loulou de la Falaise. Christian Lacroix favours the grey-haired Marie Seznec.

Your muse may be yourself, a friend or mentor, or someone famous who epitomises the person you would like to see wearing your designs (Figs. 8.2 & 8.3).

8.2 Designer Adele Palmer is her own muse. Her needs and wants reflect those of her buying public. (Photograph by Glenn Gibson. Reproduced courtesy of Elle magazine.)

## THE CONCEPT

Donna Karan is a conceptual designer who successfully uses her own lifestyle and that of women like herself as a guide for the clothing she creates.

Ralph Lauren is a also conceptual designer who holds an image of the way people live and what their needs are. He presents a romantic vision of America, of comfort and simplicity which is secure and dependable, and his success is proof that it is the same vision to which many others aspire.

## CAD

The use of Computer Aided Design (CAD) helps designers visualise their ideas on computer. They are able to use a variety of 'tools' to create different qualities of line and texture, and have a choice of literally millions of colours to work with (Fig. 8.4).

The designer can interchange garment parts, raise or lower hemlines, add pleats or fullness, vary colours and

textures and try out various trims. Photographs of models can be scanned in to determine how the designs would look when worn, and the final designs can be stored in the computer's memory to recall for immediate reuse or later modification. Full colour, finished drawings or photographs can be printed. Having such a range of options to manipulate can be an inspiration in itself.

◄ *8.3 Designer George Gross works with his sister, Kathy Gross. 'She keeps me in touch with the outside world.' (Photograph by Glenn Gibson. Reproduced courtesy of Elle magazine.)*

▼ *8.4 The vast range of images, colours and textures available with modern computer technology helps the designer create accurate sketches of new ideas. (Photograph courtesy of Lectra Systems Pty Ltd.)*

## CHAPTER 9

# DESIGN ANALYSIS

# INTRODUCTION

For the fledgling designer the problem of evaluating a design can be quite confusing. The question of good design and good taste is difficult to explain because it is intangible, often easier to sense than to logically analyse.

Good taste may be defined as the know-how to recognise 'what goes with what'. When applied to fashion, it is the ability to discern which fabrics, colours and styling work well together and will appeal to many people.

There are no constant criteria by which a designer may judge right and wrong, or good and bad design. Some trends deliberately ignore accepted standards of beauty, thereby challenging social convention and creating controversy.

However, we need to evaluate design to determine the ultimate worth of a garment. When evaluating clothing we use a combination of two methods. The first is analytical, or *objective*; that is, what looks good according to a set of aesthetic criteria. The second is *subjective*, what is liked according to personal taste.

# AESTHETIC CRITERIA

The fundamentals of the design elements and principles, as discussed in previous chapters, are used as a constant guide in the judgement of all design, including fashion. These fundamentals make use of certain universal responses to beauty which appear to be grounded in our psychological makeup.

That is not to say that the elements and principles are rigid rules, but rather that designers with a well developed sense of design find that they have a preference for things which are in harmony with design theory.

Visually educated people analyse the arrangement of line, shape, texture, value and colour in a design in terms of visual pleasure and satisfaction. Each design can be dissected and analysed methodically by looking critically at each aspect and asking questions about why it does or does not work.

When analysed in this way, a good design should create a sense of order. The human mind is disturbed by discord and confusion, and seeks stability and organisation. However, total order is boring, so a design needs to be tempered by our requirement for variety and excitement. A good design must be satisfying, comfortable, interesting and stimulating at the same time. This is achieved through the organising principles of unity, balance, harmony, contrast and dominance, amongst others.

As the eye views a design, it wanders back and forth examining every aspect and fixes on points of interest more frequently and for longer periods of time than on areas of less interest (Fig. 9.1). When the eye has examined all details, it moves on to whichever feature next catches its attention. A good design holds the viewer's interest because it is pleasurable to examine every aspect in detail.

Designers sharpen their critical powers by practising observation and analysis. When looking through magazines, note your own eye movements as you examine a design which interests and pleases you, compared to one which you consider to be badly designed. Don't make quick decisions based on what you like or don't like, but rather concentrate on why the design succeeds or fails in your opinion.

By studying the designs of famous couturiers and successful designers, you can learn the subtleties of high quality design, and compare their work with

THE FASHION DESIGN MANUAL

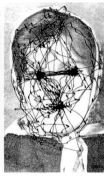

*9.1 The eye wanders over a design and continually returns to explore those points of interest.*

your own and that of less successful designers.

## MATERIALS CAN MAKE A DIFFERENCE

The quality of workmanship and materials used in fashion has a bearing on whether a garment is well or badly designed. The appearance of a garment can be spoiled or improved by the way it is made and the fabrics and trims used in its production.

Part of the design process involves selecting materials appropriate to the task, and a particular silhouette or sleeve or skirt shape can take on a totally different appearance if cut in an inappropriate fabric. Likewise, a good line can be ruined if it pulls or strains on the body, or if the seams are stretched or puckered. Also, a garment which is not well finished or pressed properly will look amateurish and clumsy.

## FIT AND FINISH

The best way to learn about fit and finish is to examine the garments of top designers. Try them on to see if they feel comfortable, if the sleeves are too short or if the waist is too tight. Turn them inside out to see how they are constructed, the type of lining used, the type of seaming, and examine the outside for finishing details — top stitching, buttonholes, pockets and so forth.

## PERSONAL TASTE

Despite the importance of the elements and principles of design, there are still no hard and fast rules about what makes good fashion at any particular time. This is where the skill, sensitivity and experience of the designer comes to the fore. Many design decisions are determined more by taste or feel than by design rules.

Within the subjective viewpoint, we are dealing with the concepts of taste, style and personal preference because the creation and wearing of clothing is inseparable from the expression of personality, moods and ideas.

Clothing can be used to create moods, emotions and personalities. It also creates impressions about the wearer's values, level of education and social and political status. A person's taste is formed by their attitudes, likes and dislikes, which are in turn formed through their background and past experiences. People tend to like the things they are used to.

Personal style is the way individuals express themselves through their dress. It is their solution to the problem of what clothes to wear and how to wear them. A distinctive style communicates information about the wearer, and becomes a summary or symbol of their personality.

People with good fashion taste are generally known to have the ability to recognise which styles suit the personality and physical attributes of the wearer.

Good taste is an intangible quality, partly instinctive and partly learned. It is the ability to recognise or create excellence and beauty through a heightened sensitivity to combinations of fabric, colour and design. Our own taste, or 'what we like', may or may not be based on aesthetic criteria. Sensitivity to beauty depends on the individual's perceptual abilities, and people vary in the way they perceive and are affected by things such as colour, balance and rhythm. Some people, for example, are sensitive to certain colours, while others may be blind to them. Some people are more sensitive to good composition or textures, or shapes than others.

Part of a fashion designer's role is to use his or her well-developed sense of style and understanding of fashion design, to guide those with less fashion awareness. A designer must also be able to recognise what is attractive and satisfying to many people. However, mass acceptance of a style should not be interpreted as an indication of beauty or good taste. It may only mean that the appearance of a style was perfectly timed to satisfy the needs of the buyers at that time. There are many examples of fashions in the past which, in retrospect, turn out to be in very bad taste. The judgement of a style of dress must always be made in light of the culture, time and place in which the clothing was worn. Time is the truest test of good design and good taste.

Styles which carry on as classics over a long period of time, are usually considered to have survived the fickle and less trustworthy whims of short-term fashionable taste, and are proven to be of enduring quality and therefore in the best of taste.

# PART

# 2

CHAPTER 10

# INTRODUCTION

Drawing is a necessary fashion skill because it is the most effective way of communicating ideas. A well-executed drawing can add a sophisticated and professional finish to your presentation and is a valuable selling tool for your designs. The viewer is immediately able to see what you are talking about, rather than having to create the image in their mind.

In the same way that everyone can learn to play a basic game of tennis, or a few tunes on the piano, this chapter demonstrates certain techniques which, with practice and experimentation, will enable the beginner to develop adequate sketching skills. It is not necessary to become a professional artist — a designer rarely has the time to spend on detailed illustrations — but you need to be able to draw fashion figures and designs reasonably accurately and quickly.

# LEARNING TO DRAW

In the early stages of sketching, be more concerned with clarity and accuracy than developing a recognisable individual style. Style comes with time and practice and evolves as drawing skills and confidence grow. While learning it is better to experiment with different styles and to be adaptable to new trends and influences.

Learning to draw is mostly about learning to see the way things really are, instead of the way we think things are. Most people draw from memory rather than from accurate observation. To overcome this, some quick exercises are explained at the end of the chapter which will develop your powers of observation

and assist with a more accurate representation of the figure and clothing.

## REFERENCE FOLDER

Start collecting fashion illustrations now so that over time you build up a comprehensive collection of work by artists in different media and styles. These will give you ideas for experimenting with new techniques. When you are trying something new, it is helpful to see how other artists have handled similar problems. It is also a good idea to include different fashion poses in your reference folder and to keep updating them because poses go in and out of style like everything else in fashion.

A simple way to learn to draw is to copy another artist's work. This has been

done for centuries by art students who benefit from the experience of the masters while honing their own skills. However, make sure you don't sign your name to another artist's work! You can later apply the things you have learned through imitation to new illustrations, with different poses and garments.

If you practise regularly, and experiment continually, you will improve. Rather than be discouraged by drawings which don't turn out as you had hoped, analyse them as you would a fashion design. Were the colours right, or did they get muddy? Is the proportion right? Is the figure positioned well on the page? What don't you like about it, and why? Even more importantly, what *do* you like about it (there is always something good) and why?

If you just throw a drawing away, without conducting a critique, you have wasted a learning experience. If nothing else, at least you know what *not* to do again!

## SKETCHING FROM FASHION PHOTOGRAPHS

This is mostly done for convenience since not many people have the luxury of working with live models. Photographs are simpler to work from in some ways because the three-dimensional human figure is already translated to a two-dimensional shape on the page, so the pose, shadows, light source, drapery and

*10.1 To the left is a production sketch and to the right is a fashion illustration — two different approaches to the same garment. (Fashion illustration courtesy of Jayson Brunsdon.)*

clothing can be more easily identified and analysed.

The major body masses, proportions and angles can be drawn onto the photograph if this helps the initial analysis, but do not trace the figure as it will be too short for a fashion drawing.

There are two types of fashion drawing which are useful to the fashion designer. These are the *production sketch* and the *fashion illustration*. A designer should be able to do both (Fig. 10.1).

## THE PRODUCTION SKETCH

The production sketch is a technical drawing of a garment and is used for catalogues and specification sheets and by patternmakers and machinists when making a new garment. It is a clear and accurate drawing, correct in proportion and detail, and provides all the information needed to construct the garment, including technical notes and measure-

ments if necessary. Artistic style is unimportant in a production sketch, because its function is to inform, not to impress. Production sketches are often drawn flat, as if the garment is laid out on a table.

A production sketch should provide the following information.

1. Title with season and theme; for example, 'Floral Follies, Summer 2001'.
2. Front and back garment views, showing
   (a) silhouette and garment proportions, and
   (b) measurements if necessary.
3. Design details, including trims, pockets, buttons, belt, collar, topstitching.
4. Construction details, such as types of seams, hems, fastenings, width of pleats.
5. Fabric swatches.
6. A brief description of the garment.

## THE FASHION ILLUSTRATION

The fashion illustration is an artistic style of drawing. It is used for displays and promotions and should create a fashion image which will excite and induce the viewer to purchase. Fashion illustrations are used in fashion magazines and may be quite distorted or difficult to interpret (or may only show half the figure) but they always convey a sense of glamour, excitement or innovation. Textures and details may be very stylised, and silhouettes exaggerated to make a strong fashion statement.

A drawing may fall anywhere between the two extremes of production sketch and fashion illustration, depending on its specific purpose. For example, a drawing which is to be shown to a department store buyer needs to inform as well as inspire. So the illustrator may use an artistic style which is fairly accurate, with the silhouette and details clearly visible.

# DRAWING THE FIGURE

The body is measured by head lengths; that is, by the distance from the top of the skull to the bottom of the chin. The classically proportioned body measures seven and a half head lengths from head to toe. The ideal fashion figure is taller and slimmer than the average person, so the illustrated figure is elongated to nine or ten head heights. This extra length goes into the legs and neck, and creates an elegant image (Fig. 10.2).

To draw a correctly proportioned fashion figure, these four steps should be followed (Fig. 10.3):

### 1. Plan the page

Place a mark on your page where you want the top of the head to be, and another mark where you want the toes to finish. Leave some space above and below these lines so that the figure is

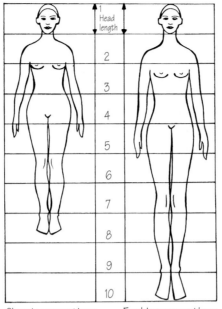

Classic proportions     Fashion proportions

*10.2 Classic proportions versus fashion proportions. The body is measured by head lengths. The classically proportioned body measures seven and a half heads, and the fashion figure measures up to 10 head lengths.*

*10.3 Drawing the figure.*

away from the edges of the page, and is centred vertically.

### 2. Plan proportions

Divide the space between these lines into ten equal sections, numbered one to ten. Each one of these sections equals one head length, and the body is broken up as shown below.

| Section | | |
|---|---|---|
| 1 | } | Head |
| | | Shoulders |
| 2 | } | Chest |
| 3 | | Waist/Elbows |
| 4 | | Hips/Crotch |
| 5 | | Fingers |
| 6 | } | Knees |
| 7 | } | |
| 8 | | Calves |
| 9 | | Ankles |
| 10 | | Toes |

### 3. Geometric body shapes

Draw in the masses of the body using simplified geometric shapes.

The head is egg shaped; the shoulders are wedges; the neck is a cylinder; upper

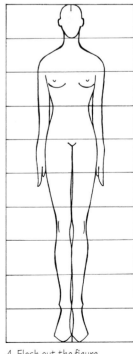

1. Plan the page
2. Plan proportions

3. Geometric body shapes

4. Flesh out the figure

| Top of head 1. Chin | |
|---|---|
| 1.5 Shoulder: 1½ head lengths wide 2. Chest | |
| 3. Waist/Elbow | |
| 4. Hip: 1½ head lengths wide | |
| 5. Fingers | |
| 6. | |
| 6.5 Knees 7. | |
| 8. | |
| 9. Ankles | |
| 10. Toes | |

and lower torsos are tapered rectangles; arms and legs are cylinders; hands and feet are wedge shaped, and the joints are represented by circles.

Correct proportions for the width of female hips and shoulders is approximately two times the length of the head.

### 4. Flesh out the figure

Flesh out the figure by adding bone and muscle details. Because of the slimness of fashion models, the muscle and bone structure is often noticeable, so some anatomical knowledge is helpful and life drawing classes using a nude model will greatly help your figure drawing.

## THE MOVING FIGURE

There are four basic steps to drawing the moving figure (Fig. 10.4).

1. Proportion your page.
2. Draw in the head, then the curve of the spine from neck to crotch.
3. Mark in the position of the feet.
4. Draw the angle of the shoulders, hips and knees.

10.4 The moving figure.

The centre of balance of the moving figure is in the pit of the neck and this should always lie directly in line with the foot or feet supporting the weight. If the weight is balanced with 50 per cent over each leg, the balance point is centred evenly between the two. If the weight is balanced 100 per cent over one leg, the balance point is directly over that leg. If the weight is 25 per cent over one leg, and 75 per cent over the other, the balance point moves 75 per cent towards the weight-bearing leg. A horizontal line drawn across the iliac crest (the front bone) of the hip is a useful check-point. When a person is standing with the weight balanced evenly on both feet, the line of the hips is horizontal. When the weight is on one foot, the line tilts up on the side supported by the leg and drops on the unsupported side.

To get the correct length for an arm resting on the hip, draw a line from the shoulder to the waist, and swing an arc outwards. Mark in the elbow joint just below the arc and connect to shoulder and to wrist.

Look at the negative space as well as the positive shapes. In other words, draw the triangular shape inside the bent arm instead of the arm itself, or the space formed by the parted legs instead of the legs themselves. This will improve your observation.

## CHOOSING THE POSE

The pose you use should show off the garment to its best advantage. Some movement in the figure is desirable, but running, jumping, or sitting figures tend to detract from the garments. The S-shaped pose is always good for front views, as is the figure with one arm raised or resting on the hip. Three-quarter views are good for showing front and back at the same time. Back views are acceptable if the back of the garment is the feature and if the front view is shown in a smaller accompanying sketch. Two figures used as a pair showing front and back views at the same time provide an opportunity to experiment with new arrangements. Standing figures with one leg propped up are good for showing full skirts, trousers and culottes.

# FACES, HANDS AND FEET

Faces, hands and feet are not the most important part of a fashion drawing, but can spoil the overall effect if badly drawn. If you have trouble with these features, the only way to get better is to practise. You may develop shorthand ways of representing faces, feet and hands which you can draw quickly and efficiently, and keep them very light and understated so they don't attract attention.

# FRONT FACIAL VIEW

The face gives us important fashion information because it is usually the first part of a drawing we look at (Figs. 10.5

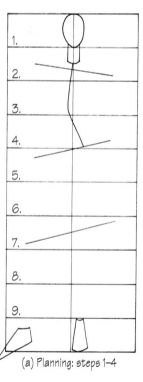

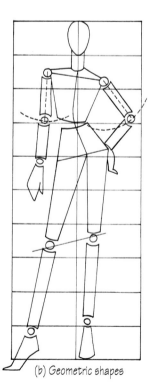

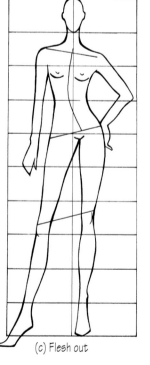

(a) Planning: steps 1–4     (b) Geometric shapes     (c) Flesh out

& 10.6). It indicates age, style and image. The face should suit the clothing. A natural hairstyle and soft features with little make-up suits a casual look, while an elegant hairstyle and more defined, made-up features are suited to sophisticated evening-wear.

The hairline is on level one. It curves around the face and behind the ears. The eyes are on level three. They are almond shaped, with one eye's width between them. The eyebrow curves from the inner corner of the eye to the outer corner. Draw eyebrows with an upward flicking motion to indicate the individual hairs. If eyebrow pencil is used, brows may be shown as a smooth line. Shading in the eye socket and highlighting on the brow bone gives depth to the eyes.

The nose is just below level four. It is usually best understated, often just a hint of nostrils is enough. The nostrils are just wider than the space between the eyes. The small indentation below the nose, and laughter lines either side of the mouth, do not need to be shown as they can age the face.

Ears sit between the eyes and the nose. Make them flat from the front view. The mouth sits just above level five. The outer corners are roughly in line with the centres of the pupils. Indicate teeth by drawing one simple shape instead of individual teeth.

The chin and neck should be firm outlines. Heavy, saggy jawlines make the face look older. Contour the face by shaping the cheekbones and shading lightly in the cheek hollows. Harsh outlines on the face are unflattering and ageing. Our faces do not actually have lines drawn around the features. We see edges of shapes and forms by tonal changes and shadows cast onto the surface of the skin. So, save outlines for emphasis and indicate facial features through soft shading.

When shading, a flat layer of colour over the entire face can look plastic, so use skin tone only on facial contours, and use white as a highlight for the brow, eyes and cheekbones.

*10.5 (top)  Drawing the face.*

*10.6 (bottom)  Facial features, front view — eyes, nose and mouth.*

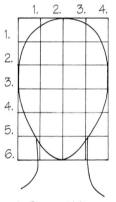
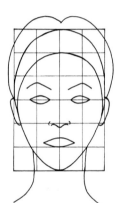

1. Draw guidelines and head shape

2. Position the basic geometric features

3. Flesh out the face

4. Finishing details and shading

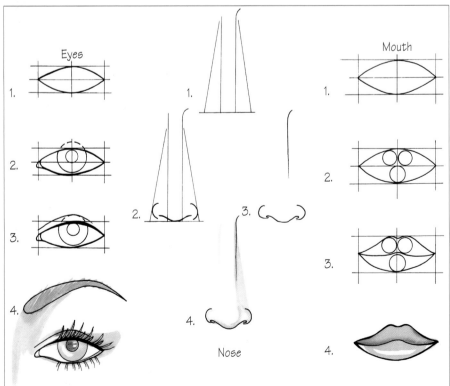

Eyes

Nose

Mouth

## PROFILE FACIAL VIEW

The true profile is when only one side of the face can be seen. Turned side-on, the head is still egg-shaped but tilts to fit diagonally into a square. The features are aligned horizontally as in the front view, but in profile they are drawn quite differently from the front view (Fig. 10.7).

Eyes are in the middle of the head. The eye is wedge-shaped, the pupil faces forward and the eyebrow arches up from the inside edge of the brow bone.

The ear is positioned below the centre line and slightly to the back. Keep the internal ear structure simple to avoid attracting too much attention to it.

The nose begins below the centre line and finishes in line with the ear.

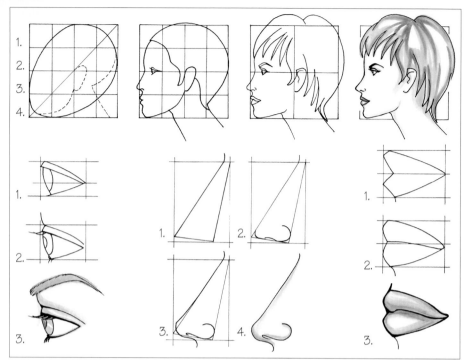

The neck curves up behind the ear. The back skull is usually fuller than expected, so don't flatten this part of the head. The profile hairline curves from the hairline at level one, down the side of the face, behind the ear and onto the neck.

# THREE-QUARTER FACIAL VIEW

These facial views are somewhere between the full front view and the profile (Fig. 10.8).

The head follows contour lines as it tilts up and down. As the head tilts up, the facial features move up the face, exposing their underneath surfaces and the lower chin and neck areas. As the face moves down, the features move down the face, showing their upper surfaces and more of the forehead and head.

## HAIR

Hair is drawn in three stages, starting, as always, with basic shapes (Figs. 10.5 & 10.7). Begin with the egg-shaped head, and draw the hair over that shape. The steps for drawing hair are:

1. Draw in a basic silhouette of the hair shape.
2. Draw in the large clusters or locks of hair as they grow out and away from the scalp. With shading and light and dark line work, show partings, curls, waves, braiding, ties etc. Hair is usually darker near the hair line and highlighted on top.
3. Fill in the fine, wispy hair around the face, ears, back of neck and over the head to soften the finished look.

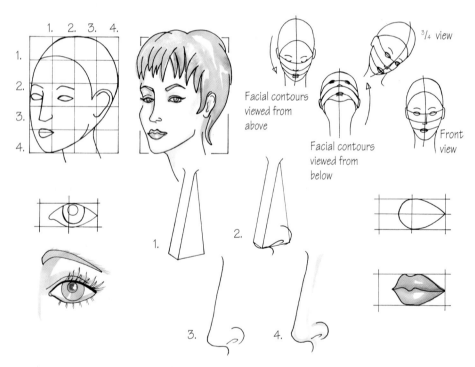

*10.7 (top) The face in profile.*

*10.8 (bottom) The face and features in three-quarter view.*

Minimise nostrils and keep outlines light and delicate. The nose and chin shape well away from the forehead and should be clear and firm. Heavy jawlines look masculine or old.

Lips protrude from below the nose. In profile, they are simple wedge shapes, with the top lip usually more prominent than the lower lip.

Hair is thicker at the root and finer at the tip, so use your pencil in a flicking motion to achieve this effect. A rounded, feathery line captures the growth and movement of hair far more than heavy, flat shading.

Hair and make-up are part of the overall fashion look and should tie in with clothing and accessory details. Keep up to date with changing trends and use them in your drawings to greatly contribute to your fashion statement.

## HANDS

The hand is basically diamond-shaped and approximately two-thirds of a head length from wrist to fingertips. Divide the diamond into halves for the first joint. Then divide the remaining half into thirds for the finger joints. Add the thumb and divide the hand into four fingers (Fig. 10.9).

Make hands simple, long and slim with a hint of bone to prevent rubbery fingers, keeping linework smooth and avoiding heavy outlines. Fingers are flat on top with a curved pad underneath. Fingernails are best when very understated, if indicated at all (Fig. 10.10).

## FEET

The foot is basically wedge-shaped, tapering from the ankle and over the arch of the instep to the toes which sit flat on the ground. From behind, the back calf muscle tapers down in a long tendon to the heel, and the foot forms a triangle with the ankle bones jutting out each side. Think of the wedge in different angles and positions as it turns and the foot will become simpler to draw (Fig. 10.11).

Fashion figures are often drawn with high-heels because they add extra height. In heels, the toes are flat on the ground and the arch of the instep becomes more pronounced, appearing shortened as it curves up to the ankle. Shoes are easier if the foot is drawn first and the shoe drawn onto it (Fig. 10.12).

Make sure the feet are big enough, about one head height in length, because they are a visual support for your stand-

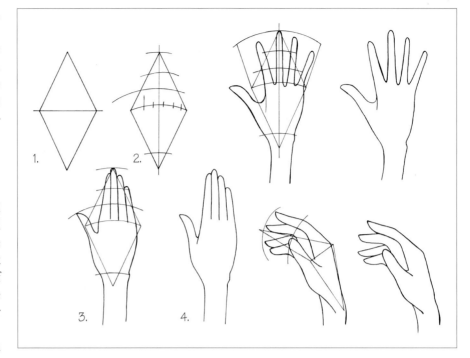

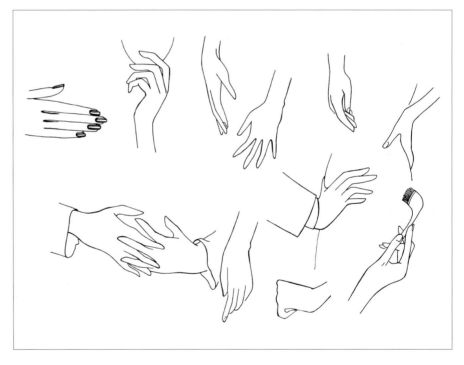

10.9 (top)  The structure of hands.

10.10 (bottom)  Female hand poses.

ing figure, like the base of a statue. Keep lines smooth, flowing and simple and, if you have trouble with feet, use light linework to make them less noticeable.

# PENCIL TECHNIQUES AND SHADING

Your pencil is a tool you must master if your drawing is to reach its full potential. Your linework needs to convey a sense of authority; short, scratchy lines look hesitant and unsure. Practise making

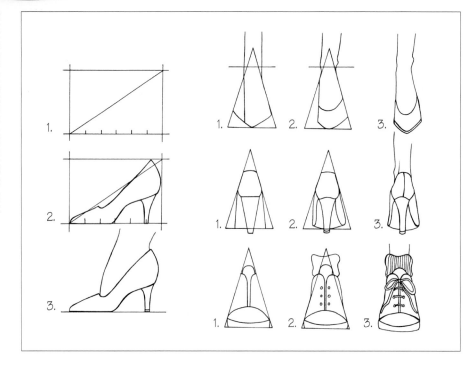

10.11 (top)  *The structure of feet.*

10.12 (bottom)  *Female feet poses.*

to create the illusion of three dimensions and are suitable for pencil or other media.

*Shading* represents the fall of light and shadow on the figure and clothing, so it is necessary to establish a light source. Fashion photography often uses several light sources, but for fashion drawing it is better to work from only one source. For figures in outdoor settings, the sun shining from above is the only source of light. Interiors or night-time scenes have artificial light, so it may emanate from different directions or be of stronger or softer intensity than occurs naturally.

*Highlights* occur where light falls directly onto a surface and can be shown in your drawings by leaving a small patch of the white page showing through, or can be coloured white with paint or a soft waxy pencil.

*Shadows* fall where light is prevented from hitting the surface. This occurs on the side or sides of an object furthest from the light source, or when one form is behind another, as with under garment edges, hems and fabric folds.

*Light* bright and warm colours advance, *dull* dark and cool colours recede. On a walking figure, the back leg and foot should be shaded, and the front foot should be light. A spot of highlight can be placed on the front knee to bring it forward. The further back the form, the darker the shading can be.

*Outlines* work the opposite way. Sharp, clear outlines define forms and bring them forward. Soft, light outlines, or no outline, allows a form to recede into the distance. Light/dark contrasts are also stronger in the foreground, and softer as objects move into the distance.

When using *colour*, try using complementaries for shadows instead of blacks and greys. They still look like shadows, but add a lot of vitality to your work.

Shading can be created by *cross-hatching* which builds up a texture of

smooth flowing lines, sharp aggressive lines, fine delicate lines, or any type of line which will allow you to expand your drawing vocabulary with confidence. The type of line you use always conveys a message or mood (Fig. 10.13).

Shading is not essential in a drawing, but adds depth and movement to a design. The following techniques help

The fall of light and shade
on a three-dimensional object

Shading can be built up using
cross-hatching or tonal chiaroscuro

Bold outlines and light tones bring forms forward,
soft outlines and dark tones push forms back.

10.13 Pencil techniques, shading & light
source. Texture, character and mood are
expressed by the type of line used in a
drawing.

parallel or criss-crossed lines, or by *chiaroscuro*, a flat, tonal shading. Chiaroscuro uses the flat edge of a pencil to create varying degrees of lightness or darkness which follow the form of an object. Use a *tortillon*, a pencil-shaped roll of paper, to blend and smooth areas of shading.

## STYLISATION

Every person has a unique style of drawing which is their trade mark on a piece of work. Stylisation makes a work identifiable as belonging to a particular designer or illustrator.

Stylisation is also used to emphasise a fashion image by exaggerating and distorting forms and details to make a stronger statement (Figs. 10.14 & 10.15).

Whatever style you use, keep up-to-date with changing trends in illustration and perceptions of beauty so that your

10.15 *Exaggeration of style is used to emphasise the mood of an image. (Fashion illustration courtesy of Bernard Touzell.)*

10.14 *Simplification of style. This illustration has been reduced to the simplest of form and line. (Fashion illustration courtesy of Jayson Brunsdon.)*

style suits the fashion. A drawing can look old-fashioned in the same way that a garment can. Keep abreast of fashion, art and lifestyle trends through magazines, books, films, videos, exhibitions and music, even architecture and interior decoration, so that you are able to make informed interpretations of designers' ideas.

Drawing stylisation tends to fall into two basic categories — *simplification* of forms and *exaggeration* of forms. Simplification involves reducing the figure and garments to their most concise, even abstract, form. Exaggeration uses distortion to enhance and emphasise an image, somewhat like caricature. Stylisation is not judged according to accuracy, but by the power of the illustration to convey its message.

Art galleries are full of style ideas, so look to other artists for inspiration. Artists such as Matisse, Degas, Picasso

and Warhol will present you with numerous techniques you can experiment with.

## MATERIALS

### PENCILS

Graphite pencils (which used to be lead) range from 6H to 9B, then to BB and EE, with 6H being the hardest and producing the lightest, finest line, and EE being the softest and blackest.

For fashion drawing, the 2B pencil, or softer, is ideal. Hard H pencils leave indentations on the page when erased and these marks are difficult to cover with further pencil lines or shading.

With practice, using a 2B or softer pencil, enough control can be exerted to achieve the lightness of line required with the advantage of a wider range of dark and thick lines being available from the same pencil.

Pencils vary in quality, softness and smoothness, often according to price. Cheap pencils can be scratchy and gritty, so try several different brands until you find one you like to use.

There are two ways to hold a pencil, resulting in different types of line (Fig. 10.16). Holding it upright like writing with a pen uses the point of the pencil, and makes a thin line which can be lightened or darkened by varying the pressure of the index finger.

Holding the pencil under the hand, like a knife, uses the flat edge of the pencil lead and is most effective for shading. It can also be tilted up on end to use the point for thick or thin lines, and lightness or darkness is again controlled by index finger pressure.

Holding the pencil further from the tip allows you to achieve very light line work with a free, sketchy quality. Holding further down towards the tip gives firmer control, and a stronger, more purposeful line.

Sharpen pencils with a knife blade instead of a standard pencil sharpener

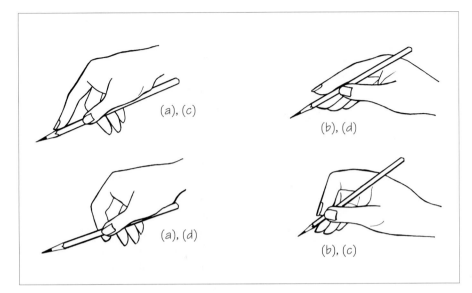

10.16 Holding the pencil under the hand (a) gives a broad, soft line, whereas an upright pencil (b) gives a sharper, clearer line. Hold the pencil close to the tip for a firm line (c), or further back for a lighter line (d).

to expose a long lead which can then be shaped to a point or flat edge for a wide or narrow line.

## FELT PENS

These are usually transparent, water-soluble pens with a variety of tips ranging from those suitable for fine line work to those with flat chisel-shaped tips suitable for broad areas of colour. Some are also available with rubbery or paint-brush shaped tips, which give a more 'painted' finish.

Felt pens are quick and easy to use, and work best with a bold approach. Work from light to dark colours. Because they are transparent, overlapping colours blend to create new colours (Fig. 10.17).

Felt pens tend to leave streaky lines which blend a little if used quickly. They are not as suitable for large flat areas, but are great for quick rendering of florals, stripes, checks and plaids, or for textured fabrics like tweed. Fine black writing pens with a 0.4 millimetre felt tip are useful for defining outlines.

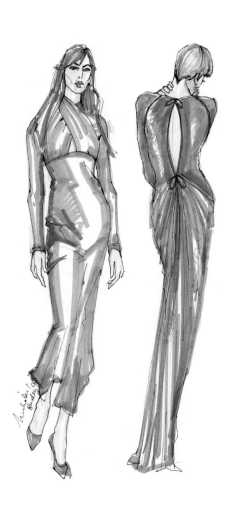

10.17 Felt pens are ideal for quick rendering in colour. (Fashion illustration courtesy of Nicholas Huxley.)

## GOUACHE

Paints are composed of pigments suspended in a binder. Water-colours and gouache are both water-based paints which are easy to apply and give a smooth, even coverage. Water-colours are transparent while gouache paints are opaque. Paints become more transparent when used with water as a wash, and more opaque when mixed with white.

Gouache works well when applied in flat, even layers of colour with clear outlines, or precisely rendered prints. It looks good in large or small areas, and is ideal for a hard-edge style.

Use enough water to help the paint go on smoothly, but not so much that the white page shows through. Keep colours clear by using clean water, and by waiting until colours dry between applications.

Lightly sketch in pencil the outlines, highlights and areas to be left unpainted. Highlights can be added afterwards with white paint, but the white page itself tends to be clearer and brighter. Mix the colours well to avoid streaks and outline each area before filling in. Although layers of gouache do not cover each other very well, dark colours may be applied over light colours.

Finishing details and outlines can be introduced with a fine brush, pens or soft crayons and pencils.

## TRANSPARENT WASH USING PAINT OR INK

Washes are transparent layers of water-colour paint or ink which overlap to create drawings of great subtlety, beauty and simplicity (Fig. 10.18).

Inks are made from concentrated pigments dissolved in a water-based medium. They are transparent and may be diluted further with water for extremely subtle overlapping and mixing of tones and colours. Inks may be used with a pen for linework or with a brush for wash effects.

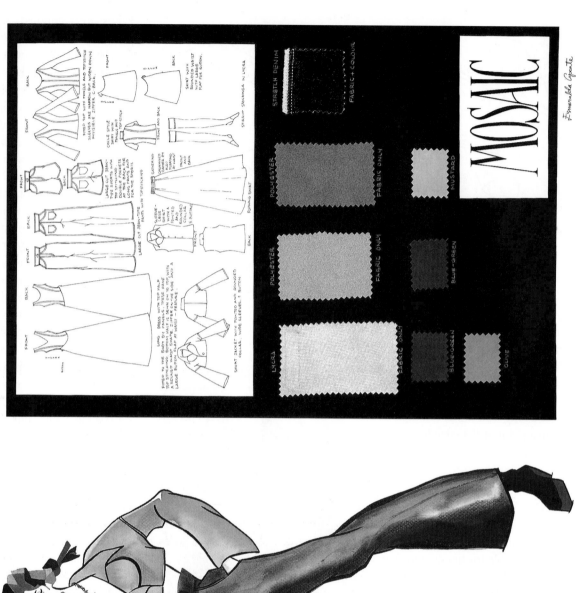

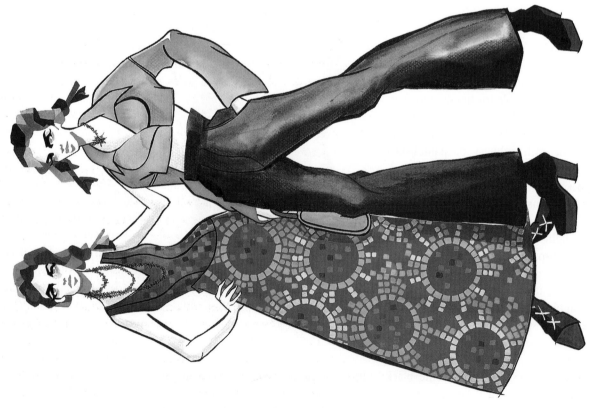

10.18 A good fashion layout includes all the information required to present the concept to the viewer. Read about presentation and layout on p. 128. (Designs and illustration courtesy of Esmeralda Aponte.)

10.19 Wash is most effective when used simply, to allow the subtlety of the medium to show through. (Fashion illustration courtesy of Luci Torres.)

Sketch in the fashion figure in pencil, keeping in mind that all linework will show through the transparent colour, and may not erase once it is painted over.

Apply skin tone to the face and figure, leaving eyes and highlights white. Working quickly, apply the colour in layers, starting with the lightest wash, and gradually building up to the darkest colour for the shadows. Test the colour first on scrap paper to be sure that it is not too dark or too watery. Unless you want the colours to run together on the page, allow each wash to dry before

applying the next layer. Work with a clean cloth handy to mop up excess water and drips.

Avoid muddying the page, concentrating instead on creating subtle tonal variety by restricting the number of colours, and by limiting the number of shades to around three per colour.

Once the wash is dry, you may work over it, adding details like hair, facial and garment details with pen, pencil or other media.

## COLOURED PENCILS, CHARCOAL, CHALK, CRAYONS AND PASTELS

These media are soft-textured and may be dry like chalk and charcoal, waxy like crayons or greasy like pastels. They are ideal for soft, shadowy effects, can be used flat for broad swathes of strong colour, or with a sharpened tip for clearer outlines (Fig. 10.19).

Very soft effects can be achieved by smudging and blending the colours on the paper. Use a tortillon, or use a cotton ball to apply the pigment to paper already dusted with talcum powder, for a smooth finish. This works much better than rubbing with your finger.

Always use a spray fixative with these media to prevent spoiling your finished work through smudging.

These media work best on large drawings which do not require a lot of fine detail. Keep your work bold and simple, showing mainly the silhouette, shadows and colours. Keep facial features simple. Thick fabrics and bold textures work well, as do large floaty volumes of fabric such as chiffon or organza evening gowns.

Coloured pencils and wax pencils are good for quick sketches or detailed drawings and give soft, delicate effects with subtle blends of colour, tone and shading.

Aquarelles are water-based pencils or crayons which can be applied as a wash, or washed over once the colour has been laid down.

## COLLAGE

Interesting effects can be achieved with mixed media. Paper and fabric pieces may be cut or torn, stuck down and drawn or painted over. Adhesive or pressure sensitive texture sheets like Letratone® may also be used in this way. They achieve a professional finish and are a quick way of representing textures (Fig. 10.20).

## PAPER

Choice of paper depends on the media being used. A3 is usually the best size. Cartridge is the most versatile paper and, although best used with dry media, can be used with watercolours. However, unless it is primed for use with water, cartridge will swell and buckle. For this reason, more expensive watercolour paper such as Arsches is the best paper to use with paints and inks.

Litho or bond paper is suitable for practice sketches because it is cheaper

10.20 An endless variety of textures and effects can be created through the use of collage and mixed media. (Illustration by Evert Ploeg. Reproduced courtesy of Ragtrader magazine.)

and, being semi-transparent, is useful for reworking sketches.

Coloured and textured papers provide background and textural interest which enhance the quality of a drawing. White wax pencil works well as a highlight on coloured papers. Try Canson, Ingres or Miteintes papers.

## BRUSHES

Brushes come in a variety of sizes, shapes and qualities. For use with inks and paints, sable is the best quality and most expensive. For learning purposes, squirrel, camel, hair or nylon are acceptable. Bristle brushes tend to leave a streaky finish, and may be too harsh for some papers.

You will need a selection of brush sizes and types. Use the appropriately sized brush for each job — large brushes for large areas, and the smallest for fine details and outlines. Different shaped brushes give you different types of line and texture. Round, pointed brushes are most commonly used but try also the Japanese calligraphy brushes, flat lettering brushes or blunt-ended brushes.

Don't splay the hairs when mixing paints or cleaning because this bends and eventually breaks them. Leaving the brushes standing in water also makes the hairs brittle and dissolves the glue which holds them together. After use, wash brushes in warm soapy water to thoroughly clean the hairs, rinse and dry lightly. Smooth the hairs to a point and store with the hairs standing up so they are in good shape for reuse.

## MISCELLANEOUS EQUIPMENT

Spray fixative prevents smudging and fading and is essential to protect your work. Painted work should be covered with glassine or tissue paper.

Examples of erasers are gum, plastic or soft putty. Soft putty can be moulded into shape and is used for pastels.

A palette is necessary for mixing colours. Keep some scrap paper handy for getting rid of excess water and for testing colours before you apply them.

# TEXTURES AND PATTERNS

These may be rendered in a controlled, accurate way to depict the fabric as realistically as possible, or may be done with a looser, more impressionistic approach which creates the 'feel' of the fabric rather than showing every detail.

The second of these options is more suited to the fashion industry because it is quicker and because simple drawings look better and are clearer and easier to interpret than cluttered, overworked drawings.

It is not necessary to show a texture over the whole surface of a garment. Try fading it in areas of highlight and darkening it in shadows, or render only the dark side of the figure, leaving the light side plain. This allows you to show details which would otherwise be covered by the texture and introduces variety into your technique.

A white space down the highlighted side of the body between the colour and the outline adds interest and creates the effect of a highlight.

Keep the size of the texture in correct proportion to the size of the figure. Very small textures cannot be rendered accurately, so sometimes an impression of the overall effect is all that can be shown. Also be aware of the way that body contours, design lines and fabric folds interrupt the flow and direction of a texture or pattern, a stripe or a check.

## SHINY SURFACES

Satins and taffetas are smooth and reflective. They have many highlights which contrast with rich, deep shadows.

1. Draw the outline of the garment and lightly indicate areas of shadow and highlights

2. Apply light tone to all shaded areas, leaving highlights white. When dry, add layer of mid-tone. Erase guide-lines

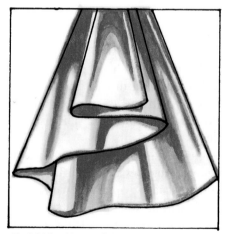

3. Add final layer of dark tone in deep shadows. Strengthen outlines to bring up major forms. Add more highlights with white pencil or opaque paint

*10.21 Satin and taffeta (lustrous).*

Colour application should be smooth and follow the folds of the fabric (Fig. 10.21). Restrict yourself to three tonal layers to keep the texture simple. Highlights may be emphasised with white paint or pencil. Details and outlines should be smooth and even to reflect the smooth nature of the fabric. Satin is heavy and drapey and requires undulating, fluid lines which cling close to the body, whereas taffeta is crisp and light and should be drawn with more angular, sharper lines and a silhouette which sits away from the body.

Velvet is like satin with its sheen but is thicker, heavier and has a rougher finish because of the pile. Rendering treatment can be similar to satin, but round off hemlines to indicate the thickness of the fabric, and shade over the highlights with a pencil to give a more textured finish resembling the nap.

## SHEERS

Fabrics such as chiffon, organza, lace and tulle are semi-transparent, therefore the skin and underlying fabrics can be seen. Tonal variations of the same colour result from the build up of fabric layers so, the more layers there are, the darker the final wash.

Start by sketching the outergarment and the lining shape beneath. Lay down areas of mid-tone (usually the lining or undergarment) and skin tones, leaving white spaces for highlights. Apply shadows and accents where underlying fabric folds and drapes occur. When dry, apply the lightest, most transparent tone for the sheer outergarment. Add soft shadows where the fabric folds and drapes, keeping brush strokes smooth and simple (Fig. 10.22).

Even darker tones may be added where lining and outergarment overlap and fold. To finish, lightly outline the hemline, garment parts and major folds and creases with a fine pen or pencil.

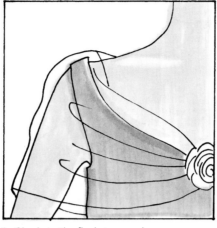

1. Shade in the flesh tone and undergarment, showing highlights and darker tone for shadows

2. Place a layer of light tone over the skin and undergarment for the sheer

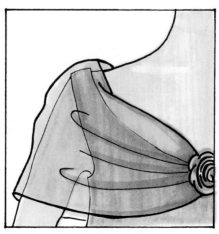

3. Use a second layer of colour where the fabric is doubled, or for folds and shadows. Strengthen outlines

10.22 Chiffon and organza (sheer).

## BROCADE AND SEQUINS

These fabrics have the shine, highlights and dark shadows of satins and taffetas, but their surfaces are rough with a pattern which needs to be shown (Figs. 10.23 & 10.24).

Apply the flat base colour to the garment, leaving plenty of highlighted areas. When dry, add a darker tone of the same colour for shadows then start the pattern with the same darker tone. Add a third darker, patterned tone to shaded areas and, if necessary, pick up outlines and shapes such as sequins or brocaded motifs with a darker but fine line. Finish with flecks of white highlights for a bit of glitter.

## PATTERNS AND PRINTS

Sketch in the main features of the pattern and fill in the areas with the lightest colour, loosely following the pattern and leaving the remaining patterned area white. Build up the pattern by repeating this with the next darkest colour and so on. Leave highlighted areas white or lighter than the rest of the pattern. Bring up fine details by outlining with a fine black or coloured pen or pencil (Fig. 10.25).

## CHECKS AND STRIPES

Folds, tucks, pleats, darts, body contours, design lines and panel lines distort the direction of the stripe or check, so this needs to be shown. Horizontal stripes follow the flow of a hemline, so start from the bottom and work up (Fig. 10.26).

Build up a check or plaid by starting with the lightest coloured stripe and adding darker colours either horizontally or vertically (Fig. 10.27).

## LACE

The open texture of lace is best represented with linework over a base colour. Sketch in the silhouette of the garment and, if the garment is lined, the shape of the lining within that. Colour the

1. Lightly sketch in the design of the brocade

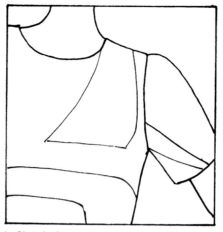

1. Sketch the garment design, pencilling in highlights to be left white, and shadows

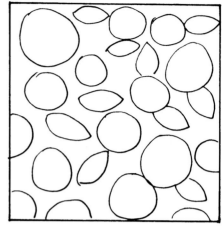

1. Lightly sketch in main shapes of pattern

2. Apply the light tone first, leaving highlights for the sheen of the fabric

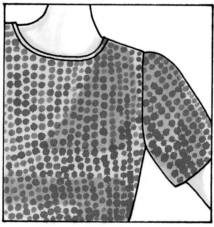

2. Fill in the lightest tone, leaving strong highlights. Add shadows with darker tones. Add sequins as spots or circles

2. Apply light, then medium tones, leaving white areas uncoloured. Outline print shapes

3. Add darker tones and outlines on bolder forms. Use white paint or pencil to show the shiny metal threads

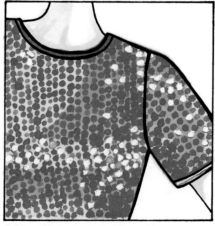

3. Use white paint to add sparkle in highlighted areas

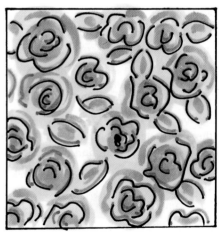

3. Use a pencil or marker to define print details and areas using darkest tone

10.23 Brocade.

10.24 Sequins and beading.

10.25 Prints and patterns.

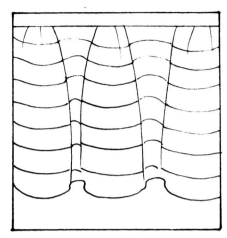

1. Draw in guidelines, showing stripes following hemline, and broken by fabric folds and body contours

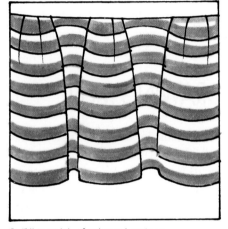

2. Fill in width of coloured stripes

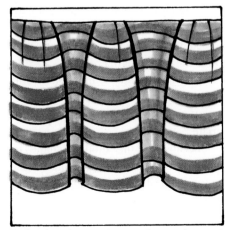

3. Finish outlines with a pencil or marker, and add shadows

*10.26 Stripes.*

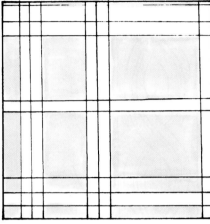

1. Draw in guidelines. Lay down a light wash in the ground colour, leaving white areas uncovered

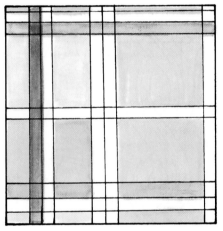

2. Lay down all horizontal and vertical bands in mid-tones. When dry, lay down bands in dark tones

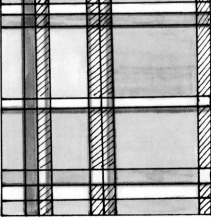

3. With a soft pencil or paint, draw in fine accent lines and diagonal lines to represent weave

*10.27 Checks and plaids.*

lining with a mid-tone, adding shadows in a darker tone. Apply skin tone where necessary. For dark lace, the motif is best drawn loosely, almost as a squiggle, over large areas of the garment. White lace can be shown by using opaque white linework over the base colour and is very effective when done on a dark coloured paper. The edge of lace is important, so show delicate scalloped or shaped edges on hems and necklines (Fig. 10.28).

## KNITWEAR

Depending on the yarn and the gauge, knitted garments can be fine and clingy, thick and bulky, or anything in between. The body contours beneath may be quite revealed or totally concealed. Showing knitted stitches over the entire garment can be too much, so pick up the texture in selected areas such as shadows and highlights, as well as on basques on cuffs, hems and necklines. Also show decorative details, such as cable stitch, which are unique to knitwear. A looped or zig-zag line usually shows the knit quite well (Fig. 10.29).

## FUR

Furs are bulky, so round off edges, cuffs and collars and make the garment thick and luxurious on the figure. The treatment depends on the type of pelt. Some, such as lynx, are long and fluffy, while others, such as mink, are smooth and sleek. Fur is treated somewhat like hair. The mass is built up by background shading, and the effect of individual hairs is added last. Keep the direction of your shading and lines controlled so that the fur looks sleek and well groomed, not tangled and matted.

Most furs show where the edges of the pelts are joined, so lightly shade these broad lines. Apply distinguishing markings like stripes, spots or coloured flecks as flat loose shading, and indicate darker shadows in the few plush folds a fur has. Leave plenty of white space to

1. Lightly sketch in the arrangement of lace motifs, paying attention to edge finish

2. Draw the motifs in more detail. Lay down a light tone over the denser areas

3. Pick up textural and design details with a fine marker or pencil

*10.28 Lace.*

1. Sketch the basic cable shapes

2. Apply a medium tone to recessed areas, leaving raised areas light

3. Use a darker tone on deep shadows, and indicate stitches and outlines with a pencil or marker

*10.29 Knitwear.*

create a light airy feeling. Soften all edges so they look fuzzy, and then indicate the hairs with short flicking lines. A dry paint brush with gouache is effective for fur (Fig. 10.30).

## HERRINGBONE AND TWEED

To indicate the different coloured yarns used in these weaves, first apply the ground colour and darker tones for shadows and creases, leaving white spaces for highlights. Over this, indicate the zig-zag of the herringbone with a fine pen or pencil, keeping the linear pattern fairly straight and evenly spaced (Fig. 10.31).

Tweed also has extra coloured slubs and textures which can be added afterwards with pen or pencil, along with final details and outlines.

# DRAWING MEN

The formula for the female figure works well for the male figure, with a few adjustments (Fig. 10.33). We use an eight and a half to nine head figure, with the waist positioned at level four. Generally, all features are broader and more angular — jaw-line, neck, shoulders, hands and feet (Fig. 10.35). The body is also straighter, tapering a little to the hips. The muscles are more clearly defined, but there are no feminine curves. Masculine shoulders are approximately twice the head length.

The male stance is more static and conservative than the female although action poses for sportswear are appropriate.

Because of the subtle changes in men's fashion, a drawing should show attention to silhouette, detailing, fit and texture. The width of the collar and lapel, the shoulder line, tie shape, and trouser leg are important.

Men's faces follow the same basic structure as women's (Fig. 10.34). The features have the same positioning but they are heavier and squarer. The fore-

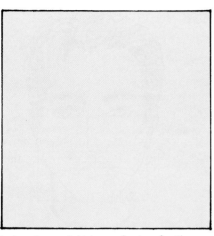

1. Lay down a light layer of colour for the background

1. Lay down a light layer of colour for the background

1. Lightly pencil in the stitching pattern

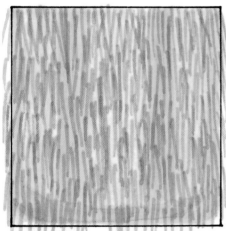

2. Show shadows on edges and where pelts are joined together with medium tone. Add first layer of hairs using darker tone

2. Use a pencil or marker to sketch in the vertical and diagonal lines of the herringbone pattern

2. Place a crescent-shaped highlight towards the light source. Use a middle tone to colour the fabric and darker tone as shadow

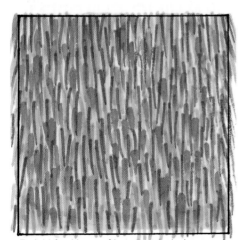

3. Add final layer of hairs using darker tone

3. Use a pencil, marker or white paint to add random speckles

3. Finish by emphasising stitching lines with a pencil or marker, especially in shadows

*10.30 Fur.*

*10.31 Herringbone.*

*10.32 Quilting.*

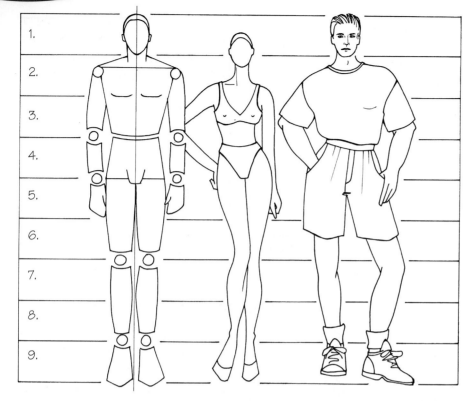

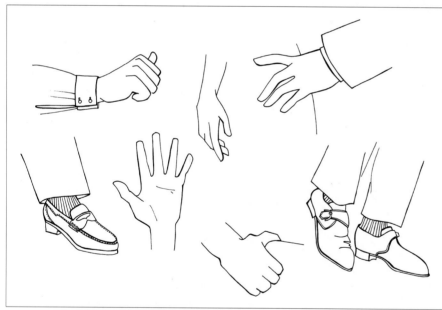

*10.33 (top left)  A comparison of male and female proportions.*

*10.34 (top right)  The male face.*

*10.35 (bottom)  Male hands and feet.*

head, brow, jaw and chin are strong and clear, but the eyes, lashes, cheekbones and top lip are less emphasised than a woman's because they are not defined by make-up. Expressive features such as a well-defined nose, furrowed brow or laughter lines give the face character and ruggedness.

Young men have a fairly low hair-line, similar to women, but older men have a slightly higher hairline which recedes at the sides.

# DRAWING CHILDREN

Because children change so much, they need to be analysed in three stages — toddlers, children and teenagers.

After drawing adults, children's proportions take a little getting used to because the head seems so large compared to their overall height (Fig. 10.36).

## TODDLERS

Up to about two or three years of age, boy and girl toddlers are indistinguishable. The facial features, hair and clothes are often unisex, and the child may wear a nappy and often no shoes.

Poses are cute and clumsy, with legs

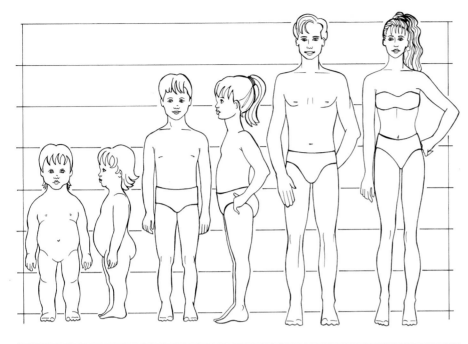

*10.36 (top) Stages of children's growth.*

*10.37 (bottom) Toddler's face, hands and feet.*

Eyebrows are also almost non-existent. The nose is usually shown as a little button tip with very small nostrils, and the mouth is a small, full rosebud. Hair is short, soft and fluffy, perhaps with a curl.

Hands, fingers, toes and feet are short, plump and well-rounded (Fig. 10.37).

## CHILDREN

In mid-childhood, between five and seven years of age, children have grown taller, their bones and muscles are more developed and they have lost a lot of their baby fat.

Although they are now around six heads tall, children's bodies have stayed about the same length, while their legs and arms have grown longer. The spine is straighter and the stomach flatter, but there is no waistline. Boys and girls are still similar in build.

Faces are slimmer and more defined. The facial features are still below the half way line of the head, but the eyes are now smaller, with one eye space between them. The nose is soft and upturned and the presence of teeth has made the mouth and jaw wider. Lips and cheeks are softly rounded (Fig. 10.38).

Hands and fingers are longer, but still plump. Hair is thicker, fuller and may be longer for girls than for boys.

## TEENAGERS

Teenagers are getting close to adulthood, and their six and a half or seven head-height proportions reflect this. Male and female differences are now obvious, with muscular development showing in the boy's shoulders and upper torso, and bust, waist and hip curves appearing in the girls. Legs are still a little shorter than for adults — the girl's torso finishes at level three and a half, while the boy's is a little lower at four.

The facial structure is now the same as an adult, but the features and contours still bear a little childish softness

askew with and plenty of movement. The neck is wide and short, the shoulders are narrow and rounded, and the weak spine throws the tummy forward.

The figure is only four heads tall. The head is full and round and the facial features are positioned in the lower third of the face. The eyes are large and round with one and a half eye widths separating them. When the eyes are wide open, there is hardly any eyelid.

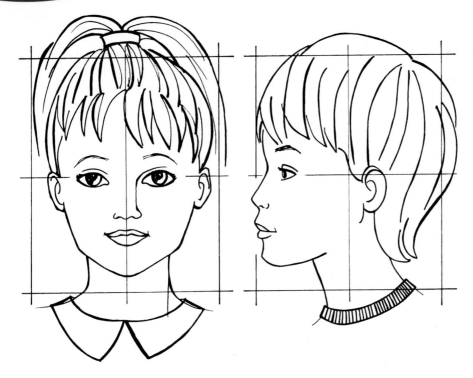

*10.38 Young children's faces*

and roundness. Smooth, light line-work and no expression lines looks youthful (Fig. 10.36).

# PRESENTATION AND LAYOUT

As well as being a design exercise, a drawing is a communication tool which reflects your approach to your work. You should always aim to present it as professionally as possible.

When planning a drawing, consider the following.

1. The subject matter.
2. The style.
3. The technique.
4. The media.
5. The pose and page layout.

Decisions about these will be based on the information to be communicated, on how the drawing will be used, and whether it is a production sketch or a fashion illustration.

Plan the layout before you commence drawing. Decide what you need to include on your page. This may or may not include title, figure with front and back views, fabric swatches and explanatory notes. Decide on the placement of the figure and mark this on the page. This will prevent you running out of room or having a tiny figure on a huge page. Consider the blank spaces on the page, because they are as important as the shapes.

Consider a border; it frames and anchors the figure to the page so that it is not floating in space. It also helps unite the different elements of your design. The page feels most balanced with a wider border at the bottom of the page than at the top. A border may be a continuous or broken outline, a cut-out frame, a decorative edging, or lettering arranged along one or more edges. A border can also be created by mounting your work onto cardboard.

When the planning is completed, refer to the elements and principles of design to see if it fulfils your requirements. Is the most important feature dominant on the page? Do the other details support the overall theme? Is there variety, harmony and unity? Is the page balanced? Is it interesting to look at? Is it easy to read? If the answer is 'yes' to all of these questions, you are well on the way to a successful illustration (see Fig. 10.18 on p. 118).

# EXERCISES FOR OBSERVATION SKILLS

- If your drawing gets tight from practising too hard, try some continuous line drawing to loosen you up. This involves drawing the figure without pausing or taking your pencil off the page. Your drawings will no doubt be quite distorted, but they usually have a quirky spontaneity about them which can be quite refreshing.

- Turn your photograph upside down and draw it upside down. This really helps your observation because it tricks your brain into thinking it hasn't seen the picture before, and that it had better have a really good look at it. The result … more accurate drawing!

- Similarly, if you get stuck on a pose or can't work out where you have gone wrong, stand your drawing up and look at it from a distance or hold it up to the mirror. From a different perspective you can analyse your work more objectively. Looking at your work afresh after leaving it for a couple of hours or overnight also helps your observation.

- If you are unsure about the next step to take in your drawing, make several photocopies and practise possible techniques on the copies to be sure of the right one before doing it on your original.

- Draw from top to bottom and left to right (if right-handed) so you don't smudge your work. If you have to lean on your work, place a piece of clean paper under your hand to keep your page clean.

CHAPTER 11

# INTRODUCTION

This chapter deals with the basic principles of drawing garments accurately.

Because other people will view your drawings, be aware that their interpretation may be different to your intention. In particular, if you use artistic licence to exaggerate proportions or to distort the figure or the clothing, the viewer may misinterpret the garments as having been designed that way.

In addition, because we work with a ten-head figure for fashion drawing and the standard figure is seven and a half heads, the proportions of the finished garment may vary from those in the sketch. The patternmaker must be able to adapt the drawing into a working pattern while still achieving the look wanted by the designer. Sometimes it helps to draw a quick seven and a half-head interpretation of the fashion sketch, to be sure that all the details can be fitted onto the normal, shorter figure.

For more information on garment parts and construction, refer to Chapters 12, 13 and 14. Chapter 10 also includes techniques for drawing shoes.

## THE ILLUSION OF THREE DIMENSIONS

Garments may be drawn flat, as if laid out on a surface, or three-dimensionally, as they appear when being worn. This chapter deals with garments as they look on the figure, but the basic principles also apply to flat drawings.

When drawing garments as they look when being worn, we need to create the illusion of three dimensions on a two-dimensional surface. To understand how this works, imagine a painting of a landscape. Following the rules of perspective, objects lowest on the page appear closest to the viewer, and objects higher up the page appear further away. The same principle applies to drawing garments. The front of a skirt, collar or trouser leg which is closest to the viewer is drawn lower down the page, and the sides which curve around the body and away from the viewer are placed higher up the page (Fig. 11.1).

## BASIC GARMENT SHAPES

In their simplest forms, most garments or parts of garments are cylinders. A sleeve is a cylinder which wraps around the arm, a collar is a cylinder which wraps around the neck, trousers are made up of three cylinders — one for each leg and one which encases the body. A skirt is also a cylinder.

The way a garment sits on a figure is determined by the shape and stance of the body beneath it, so draw a basic figure first as a guide for proportioning your garments. Even if you erase the figure after the garment is drawn, it will make your drawing more accurate.

To speed up your sketching, trace a well-proportioned fashion figure onto which you can draw the garments. The figure can then be erased or completed as you wish (see Chapter 10).

As with drawing figures, keep the garment shapes simple to start with. To

129

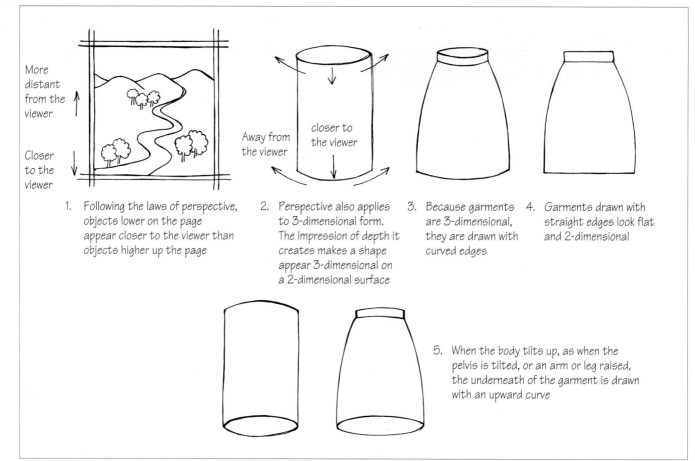

More distant from the viewer

Closer to the viewer

1. Following the laws of perspective, objects lower on the page appear closer to the viewer than objects higher up the page

Away from the viewer

closer to the viewer

2. Perspective also applies to 3-dimensional form. The impression of depth it creates makes a shape appear 3-dimensional on a 2-dimensional surface

3. Because garments are 3-dimensional, they are drawn with curved edges

4. Garments drawn with straight edges look flat and 2-dimensional

5. When the body tilts up, as when the pelvis is tilted, or an arm or leg raised, the underneath of the garment is drawn with an upward curve

*11.1  The illusion of three dimensions.*

begin your sketch, follow these four steps (Fig. 11.2).

1. Draw the basic figure in the pose which will best show the garment.

2. Over the figure, draw the garment silhouette, showing fullness and fit. Tilt shoulderline, waistline and hemline to follow body angles.

3. Add garment details (pockets, cuffs etc.), seams and fastenings. Show fabric folds and creases where the body and fabric moves and bends, using the body underneath as a guide.

4. Complete the drawing by erasing guidelines and adding finishing touches such as shading, detailed linework and fabric texture and pattern.

# THE FIT OF GARMENTS

Even though fitted garments show more of the body than do loose garments, they all have wearing ease which allows the body to move and turn with comfort. Only stretch fabrics are able to fit the body closely without wearing ease. Because garments sit on top of the body, there is a step where the garment edge finishes and the body emerges from beneath it. Showing this tiny detail, it may only be a millimetre, adds a lot of depth to your drawing (Fig. 11.3).

This 'step' can also be seen where garment pieces join or overlap. There is a step where a sleeve inserts into a cuff, or where a sleeve head inserts into an armhole. Drawing the garment as it is constructed — by drawing the sleeve and then the cuff as separate pieces, or

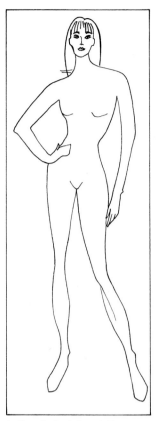

1. Draw the basic figure in the pose which will best show the garment

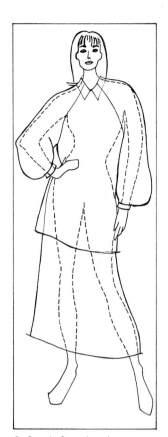

2. Over the figure draw the garment silhouette, showing fullness and fit. Tilt shoulderline, waistline and hemline to follow body angles

3. Add garment details (pockets, cuffs etc.), seams and fastenings. Show fabric folds and creases where the body and fabric move and bend, using the body underneath as a guide

4. Complete the drawing by erasing guidelines, and adding finishing touches such as shading, detailed line work and fabric texture and pattern

11.2 The basic steps to drawing a clothed figure.

the shoulder, armhole and side, and then adding the sleeve — makes a drawing look more realistic.

Garments do not stop at body edges; they wrap around the body. Therefore, as well as the raised step, be sure to show the slight curve as a neckline folds over the back of the shoulder, or as the cuff wraps around the back of the wrist.

The angle of the shoulders determines the set of the bodice, and the angle of the hips determines the swing of the hemline. Fabric creases and folds form at joints where the body bends, stretches or contracts, changes direction or where a part of the body protrudes. A fabric drape or fold begins at the point of support, and fans outwards until it is interrupted or fades away towards the garment edge. Drapes or creases usually begin at the shoulders, bust, underarms, elbows, waist, hips, buttocks, crotch and knees.

Be sensitive to slight changes in fit which occur with fashion trends. Shoulders may become broader or narrower, skirts become slimmer or more flared, blouses fuller or more fitted. These subtleties should be reflected in your drawings so they always look up-to-date.

Garment shoulderline, waistline and hemline are determined by the angles of the body

Drapes, creases and folds radiate away from the point of tension

Fabric gathers and folds follow the flow of the figure beneath, while stress lines such as at the knee radiate out towards the hem

Show the step between the garment and the body, and the curved edge which wraps around the body

Show the way the garment is put together . . .
Sleeve slots into armhole or . . .

. . . armhole slots into sleeve

. . . cuff slots into sleeve

Sleeve slots into cuff or . . .

11.3 The fit of garments.

## NECKLINES

Necklines curve around the cylinder of the neck and over the shoulders. Draw in the neckline shape as a whole to ensure a smooth flow from one side of the neck to the other, then erase where it passes behind the neck. The front view shows the front shaping only, while the three-quarter view shows the front and sides as they curve back over the shoulders (Fig. 11.4).

*11.4 Necklines.*

Garment shoulder line is raised slightly

Neckline curves over back neck and flows smoothly through to other side

NECKLINE: FRONT VIEW

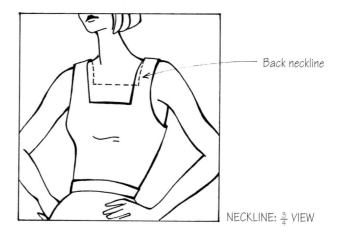

Back neckline

NECKLINE: ¾ VIEW

## COLLARS AND LAPELS

For drawing purposes, all collars have three basic features — the neck edge, the outer edge, and the connecting line between the two, known as the *fall*. Start drawing from the back of each collar, following the curve of the neckline.

Lapels are the same either side of the centre front line, although one side laps over the other (Fig. 11.5).

Buttons always sit on centre front on single breasted garments.

---

*11.5 Collars and lapels.*

TAILORED
COLLAR
AND LAPEL

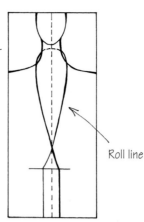
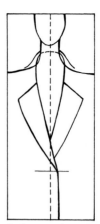
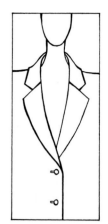

Roll line

1. Draw the roll line of the collar, crossing equally over the centre-front line, and curving smoothly around the back of the neck

2. Draw in the lapel shape and the fall to the shoulder line

3. Finish with the collar shape

Neckline forms a smooth curve around the back of the neck

STAND COLLAR

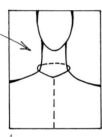
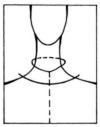
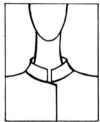

Draw the neck edge, the outer collar edge, and the fall line which links the two curves

1.

2.

3.

SHIRT COLLAR

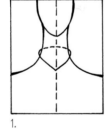
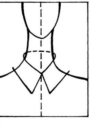
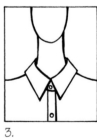

1.

2.

3.

OPEN COLLAR

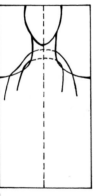

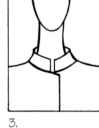

1.

2.

3.

## SLEEVES AND CUFFS

Because shoulders and sleeves form part of the silhouette, indicate the width and shape of the sleeve, the armhole shape, the fit of the underarm, and how the sleeve is attached to the garment. This may best be achieved by showing one arm raised or resting on the hip. If the sleeve end or cuff has no fastening, be sure to draw it big enough to fit over the hand (Fig. 11.6).

## SKIRTS AND PANTS

The waistlines and hemlines of skirts and pants usually curve down in front and up at the sides to create the three-dimensional effect of the garment moving back around the body. However, if the pelvis is tilted forwards, the waistline may shape down at the sides and up in the centre (Fig. 11.7).

The skirt or trouser silhouette is determined by the garment shape, its length and the fabric used. Indicate the drape of the fabric with the outline of the silhouette, and the amount of fullness by the number and depth of the folds through the length of the skirt or trouser leg, and at the hemline.

Take care with the position of the crotch on pants. The fabric folds at this point may be indicated with a simple squiggle. Movement folds may also be shown at the knees and across the hip if the leg is bent, and at the hem if the pants rest on the tops of the shoes.

To achieve correct leg shaping below the hem of short skirts and pants, draw the full leg first then erase above the hemline.

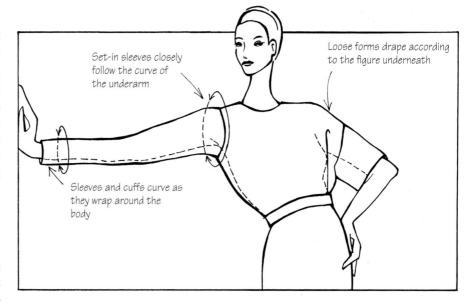

Set-in sleeves closely follow the curve of the underarm

Loose forms drape according to the figure underneath

Sleeves and cuffs curve as they wrap around the body

Waistband sits above narrowest part of waist

Fabric folds radiate out to follow shape of silhouette

1. Draw the silhouette of the skirt, tilting the hem and waist to follow the movement of the figure

2. Add the in–out undulations of the hemline, linking some up to the waistband

3. Fill in irregular gathers of different lengths, radiating out from the waistband

*11.6 (top) Sleeves and cuffs.*

*11.7 Skirts and pants.*

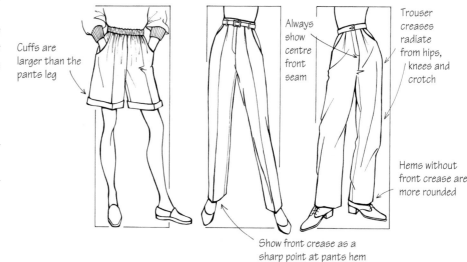

Cuffs are larger than the pants leg

Always show centre front seam

Trouser creases radiate from hips, knees and crotch

Hems without front crease are more rounded

Show front crease as a sharp point at pants hem

## GATHERS AND PLEATS

Gathers are shown by drawing the tiny folds and creases formed at the stitching line. These become fewer and more widespread as they fan out towards the outer hem edge. The hemline of a gathered skirt moves in and out in large columns and is drawn using an undulating up-and-down line. Some of the large hem folds link up with gathers at the top of the skirt, while others simply fade out to nothing. Regardless of the silhouette, the greater the depth and number of undulations shown in a hemline, the fuller the skirt appears (Fig. 11.8).

Pleats are similar to gathers but, instead of rounded folds, they are pressed flat and sharp, creating a zig-zag effect on the hemline. The in-out movement is still shown as up-down when drawn. Draw the basic skirt shape with a curved hemline, then add the vertical lines of the pleats. Link these with diagonal lines at the hem to represent the backward movement of the folded fabric.

Shading may be used with both pleats and gathers to indicate the underneath folds of fabrics.

*11.8 Gathers and pleats.*

Gathers

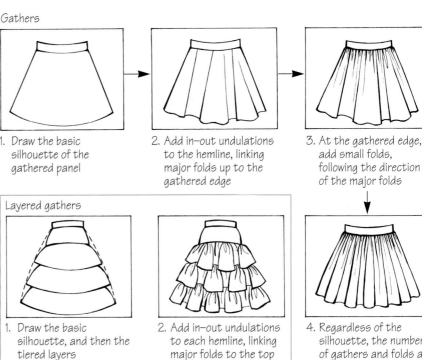

1. Draw the basic silhouette of the gathered panel

2. Add in-out undulations to the hemline, linking major folds up to the gathered edge

3. At the gathered edge, add small folds, following the direction of the major folds

Layered gathers

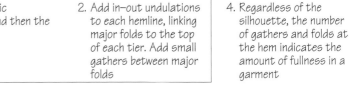

1. Draw the basic silhouette, and then the tiered layers

2. Add in-out undulations to each hemline, linking major folds to the top of each tier. Add small gathers between major folds

4. Regardless of the silhouette, the number of gathers and folds at the hem indicates the amount of fullness in a garment

Shirring

1. Draw the silhouette of the shirred area. Lightly apply closely spaced horizontal lines, following bodily contours

2. Apply short, irregular vertical strokes and gathers between the lines. Finish by reworking edges and stitching lines with a crinkly line

1.    2.    3.

Knife pleats
1. Draw the basic silhouette of the skirt, flaring the hemline where the pleats open out
2. Starting from the centre front and working to the sides, add the lines of the pleats as they flare from hip to hem. Width of the pleats may vary according to the swing of the skirt
3. Following the initial hemline shape, link the pleat edges with diagonal lines, to create the appearance of zig-zag folds

1.    2.    3.

Stitched-down box pleats
1. Draw the basic flared silhouette. Across the hips lightly draw a horizontal guideline, then vertical lines for the pleats
2. Below the hipline, redraw the pleats as two vertical lines spreading open as they move towards the hemline
3. Following the original hem shape draw the box pleats at the hem edge. The under-pleat is set higher, the front of the pleat is set lower, and the edges are sharp

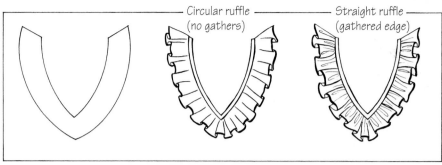

Circular ruffle
(no gathers)

Straight ruffle
(gathered edge)

1. Lightly draw the basic shape of the ruffle

2. Draw the undulating hemline, showing the fabric folding back on itself. Link the edges of the folds up to the seam edge

3. For ruffles with gathers at the seam edge, follow steps 1 and 2, then add short lines radiating out towards the hem

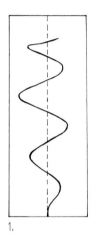

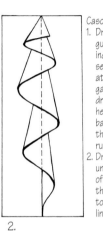

Cascade ruffles
1. Draw a dotted guideline to indicate the ruffle seam, where it attaches to the garment. Then draw the cascade hem as it flows back and forth, for the length of the ruffle
2. Draw the top and underneath edges of the folds, as they angle back towards the seam line

1.                2.

1.                2.

## RUFFLES AND FRILLS

Ruffles and frills may have gathers at the sewn edge or may sit flat. In either case, they are drawn in a similar way to gathers, with the folds spreading outwards towards the hem (Fig. 11.9).

## DRAPES, COWLS AND RUCHING

The folds of drapery fall from the point of support and fan outwards. Draw the outer edge of the folded fabric and the draped lines radiating to these folds. Allow your lines to taper off as the folds thin out.

Ruched seams are indicated with a wavy line. The folds of ruching drape from side to side, falling in the centre of the panel with the weight of the fabric. Show the outline of the folds on the edge of the garment (Fig. 11.10).

*11.9 (top & centre) Ruffles and frills.*

*11.10 Drapes, cowls and ruching.*

Draping

Drapes radiate out from the point of support

Cowl neck

1. Draw the basic neck shape and major folds as they drape from the shoulder and back neck

2. Fill in smaller folds between the major folds, following the same general direction

Ruching

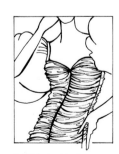

1. Draw the basic garment shape. Fill in the direction of major ruched lines, and the crinkled outline of the ruched section

2. Fill in horizontal gathers between the ruched folds, linking some to the crinkled outline

Connect brim to crown

1. Sketch the head, facial features and basic hair shape

2. Place the curved crown line across the forehead. Draw the wide outer edge of the brim, passing in a smooth curve over the face and behind the neck

3. Draw the full shape of the crown. Leave a slight gap at the top and sides of the head, depending on the fit of the hat

4. Complete the details, showing hat band and trimmings. Erase guidelines

5. For a downward brim, draw the outer brim edge and connect it up to the crown

1. Sketch the head, facial features and basic hair shape

2. Draw the band as a smooth curve around the head. Also draw the top shape of the hat, showing the curved seam

3. Connect the top shape to the hat band

4. Finish the hat, showing soft folds and details

Hats

Belts

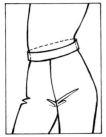

1. Draw the waistline, and place the circle of the belt above the narrowest part of the waist

2. Lightly sketch belt buckle and loops. Following the waist curve, show the belt strap passing through the buckle and loops. Complete details

Scarves

1. Draw the head and neck shape. Show the basic scarf shapes as they drape and wrap around the neck, and overlap each other

1. Complete by filling in the gathers and folds where the fabric forms loops and knots. Fabric folds will interrupt a pattern on the scarf

Gloves

1. Draw the hands accurately in the required pose. Following the contours of the hand and fingers, outline the glove shape. Thicken and round off the fingers, and simplify the shapes

2. Finish with cuffs, seams and decorative stitching

## ACCESSORIES: HATS, BELTS, SCARVES AND GLOVES

*11.11 Accessories: hats, belts, scarves and gloves.*

CHAPTER 12

# INTRODUCTION

Although fashion styles change from year to year, the basic components of fashion remain the same.

Fashion awareness involves knowing the terminology, the garments, garment parts and their variations. New designs can always be created

by putting garment parts together in different combinations. Similarly, historical styles can be recognised, understood and interpreted as they

are revived and modernised to become contemporary fashions.

The garments illustrated in this chapter are classic versions of each style, of which there are unlimited possibilities for variation and

adaptation.

# NECKLINES

A neckline is the outline or contour of the bodice around the neck or shoulders. It frames the face and directs the eye to, or away from, the face. A neckline must have an opening, or be large enough to pull over the head (Fig. 12.1).

The neckline may be finished by facing, piping, binding, ribbing or with a collar.

## COLLARS

A collar is a piece of fabric added to, or an extension of, the neckline of a garment. A collar may also be constructed separately and fastened to the garment so that it can be removed for laundering.

Like a neckline, the collar is a decorative feature which frames the face and

enhances the appearance of both the garment and the wearer. It is also functional because it provides warmth and protection for the neck (Fig. 12.2).

The three basic collar shapes (Figs. 12.3 & 12.4) are:

### 1. Flat
The flat collar is the same shape as the neckline and sits flat at the neck and over the shoulders. It is usually used in untailored garments.

### 2. Rolled
The rolled collar stands up at the neckline then folds over to sit on the shoulders.

### 3. Stand
The stand collar is a band which stands up from the neckline. It may sit close to the neck or stand away from it.

A lapel is the front facing of a coat or jacket which is joined to the collar and folded back. Depending on its shape and length, it is known as a *peak* or *notch* lapel. A wide lapel is known as a *revere*.

12.1 *Necklines.*

1. Round (necklace)  2. Scoop  3. U-shape  4. Horse-shoe  5. V Neck  6. Wide V Neck  7. Dickie  8. Slot  9. Florentine  10. Square  11. Mitred  12. Sweetheart
13. Camisole  14. Bateau (boat)  15. Off-shoulder  16. Asymmetric  17. Halter  18. Keyhole  19. Darted  20. Strap  21. Cross-over  22. Drawstring
23.(a)&(b) Draped  24. Tied  25. Stand-away  26. Built-up  27. Double  28. Bound  29. Cowl  30. Décolletage  31. Borded/piped  32. Inset  33. Ribbed
34. Plunge

12.2 (top)  Collar parts.

12.3  Basic collar shapes.

The construction of a basic collar

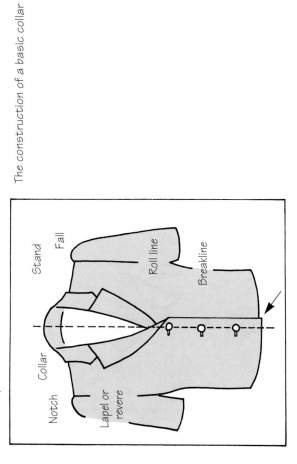

Stand
Fall
Roll line
Breakline
Collar
Notch
Lapel or revere

The three basic collar shapes

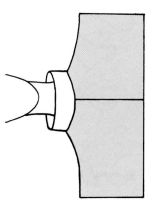
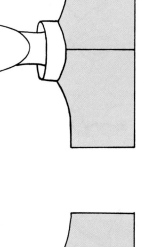

Leaf

Peak

1.  Flat collar

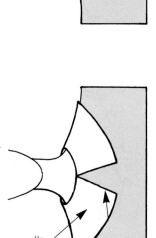
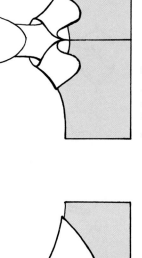

2.  Rolled collar

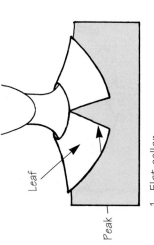

3.  Stand collar

12.4 Collars.

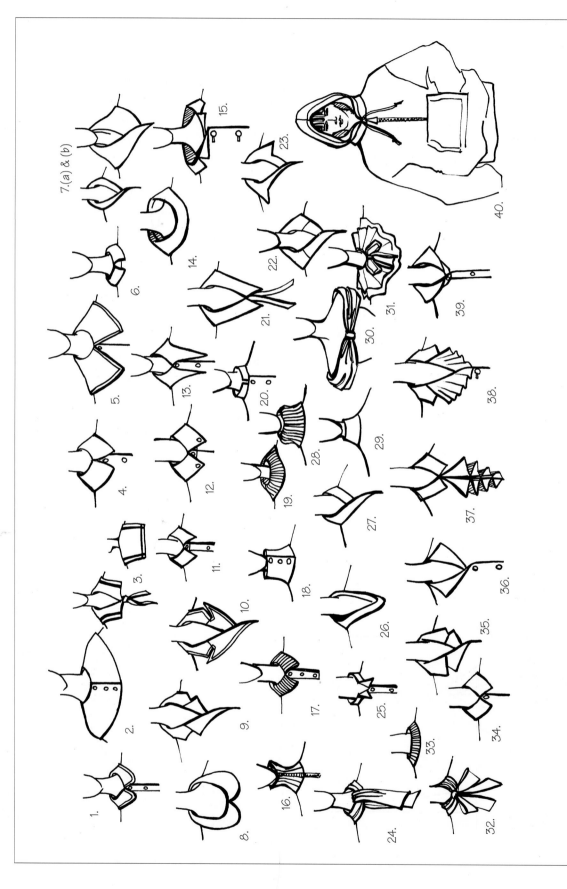

1. Peter Pan  2. Bertha  3. Sailor (Middy)  4. Eton  5. Puritan  6. Prussian  7.(a) & (b) Shawl  8. Horseshoe  9. Tailored  10. Peak lapel  11. Collar & stand  12. Button-down  13. Peaked  14. Picture  15. Stand-away  16. Funnel  17. Knit shirt  18. High  19. Turtle  20. Mandarin  21. Swallow  22. Strap  23. Milano  24. Ascot  25. Dandy wing  26. Stand-up  27. Cross-over  28. Polo  29. Draped  30. Choker  31. Pierrot  32. Bow tie  33. Crew  34. Convertible  35. Open convertible  36. Revere  37. Jabot  38. Frilled revere  39. Wing  40. Hooded

12.5 *Tops and bodices.*

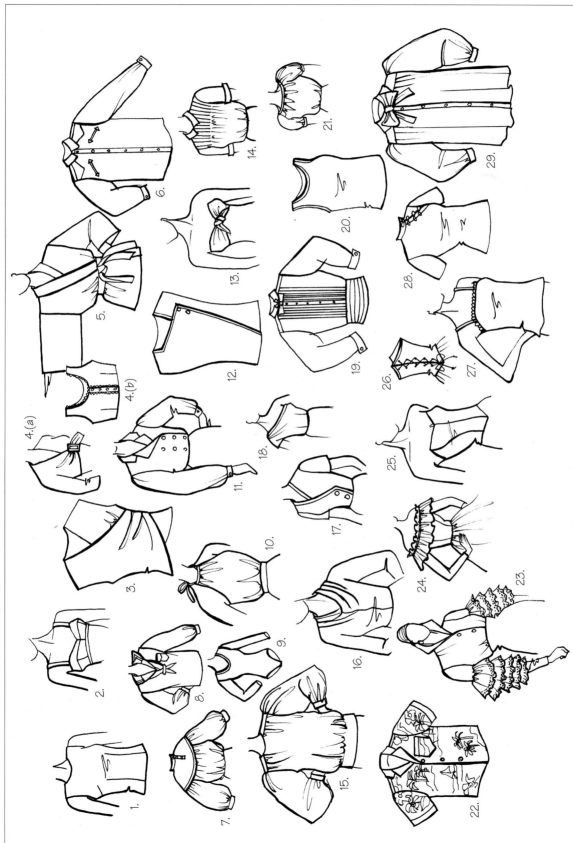

1. Fitted  2. Bra top  3. Wrap  4.(a) & (b) Midriff  5. Kimono  6. Western shirt  7. Cossack shirt  8. Middy blouse
9. Body suit  10. Halter  11. Double-breasted  12. Asymmetric  13. Bandeau  14. Pintucked blouse  15. Blouson
16. Draped  17. Cross-over  18. One shoulder  19. Tuxedo shirt  20. Tank top  21. Peasant blouse  22. Hawaiian shirt
25. Boned bustier  26. Corselet  27. Camisole  28. Chinese  29. Smock  23. Bettina blouse  24. Off-the-shoulder

# TOPS AND BODICES

A bodice is the upper part of a garment from the waist to the shoulders. It varies in length according to the placement of the shoulderline and waistline. A bodice may have no shoulders, be attached to a yoke at the shoulders, or attached to a skirt on the lower edge. It may be unfitted, fitted, darted or boned (Fig. 12.5).

# SLEEVES AND CUFFS

A sleeve is the garment component which covers all or part of the arm. The appearance of the sleeve is determined by the position of the armhole and underarm seams, fullness added to any part of the sleeve, and the sleeve hem or *cuff*. Because the arms are very mobile, the sleeve should allow enough room for movement. A *gusset* is a wedge-shaped piece of fabric inserted under the arm to give the sleeve more lift and movement. A *sleeveless* garment has a finished armhole without a sleeve.

There are two basic types of sleeve. The *set-in* sleeve is a separate piece of fabric attached to the armhole of the bodice (Fig. 12.7). The *unmounted* sleeve is cut in one piece as an extension of the bodice, with no connecting seams (Fig. 12.8).

Set-in sleeves may join the bodice in one of three ways.

### 1. Normal armhole
This is the best fit for most people because it follows the natural body–arm junction (Fig. 12.7(a)).

### 2. Raglan armhole
This has a shaped seam which curves diagonally from the armhole to the neckline or front of the garment (Fig. 12.7(b)).

### 3. Drop shoulder
In this instance, the shoulder is lengthened to extend past the body–arm junction (Fig. 12.7(c)).

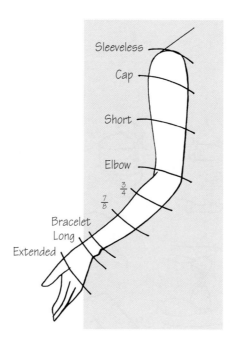

12.6 *Sleeve lengths*

BASIC TYPES OF SLEEVE

(a)

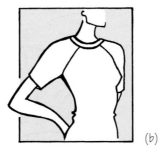

(b)

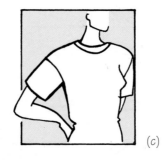

(c)

12.7 *Set-in sleeves.*

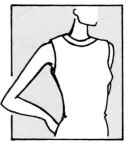

Sleeveless

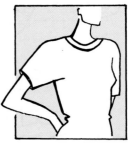

Unmounted sleeve

12.8 *Sleeveless and unmounted sleeve styles.*

12.9 Types of sleeve.

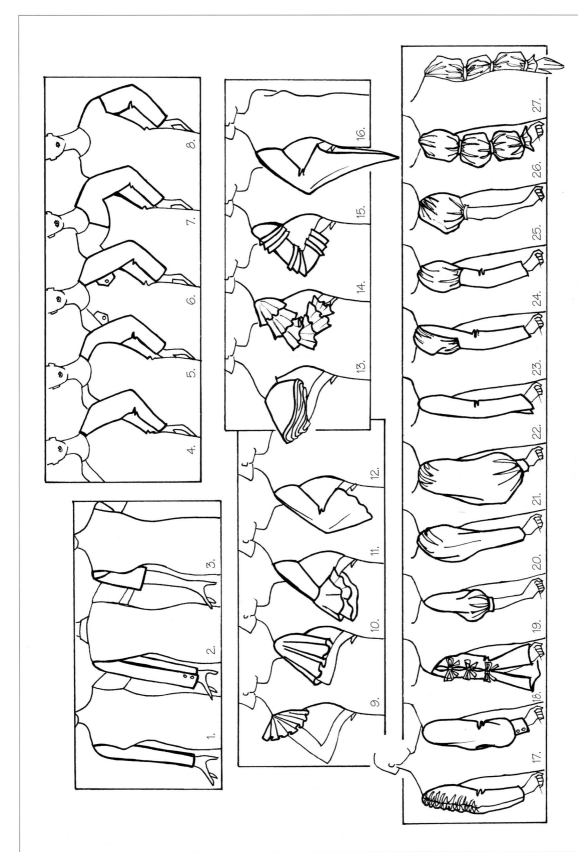

1. Set-in  2. 2 Piece tailored  3. Crescent head  4. Raglan  5. Saddle shoulder  6. Stylised raglan  7. Yoked raglan  8. Drop shoulder  9. Butterfly  10. Cape
11. Tiered  12. Bell  13. Layered  14. Frilled  15. Tucked  16. Angel or witch  17. Ruched  18. Cuffed  19. Split & tied  20. Bishop  21. Leg o' mutton  22. Balloon
23. Split  24. Inserted puff  25. Juliette  26. Puff  27. Bon-bon

## CUFFS AND SLEEVE FINISHES

Sleeves must be either wide enough at the bottom or have an opening to allow the arm and hand to pass through.

A cuff is a band at the bottom of the sleeve. It may be part of the sleeve turned back on itself, or a separate piece attached to the sleeve (Figs. 12.9, 12.10 & 12.11).

*12.10 Types of sleeve.*

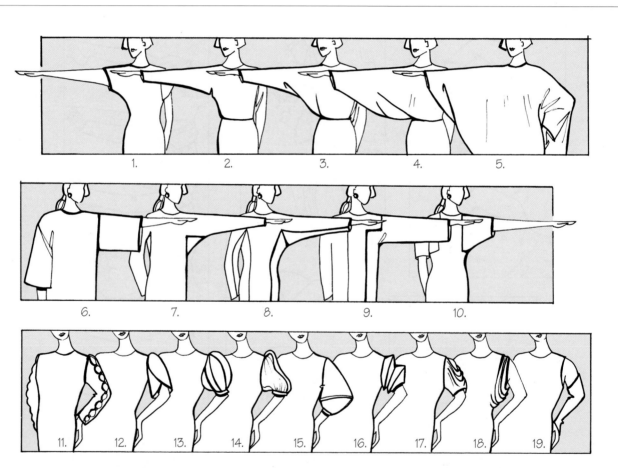

1. Cap  2. Magyar  3. Dolman  4. Batwing  5. Kite  6. Kimono  7. Gusset  8. Stylised gusset  9. Shaped armhole
10. Squared armhole  11. Edge-to-edge  12. Petal  13. Melon  14. Doubled  15. Lantern  16. Cartwheel  17. Draped  18. Underarm cowl
19. Sleevelet

12.11 *Cuffs and sleeve finishes.*

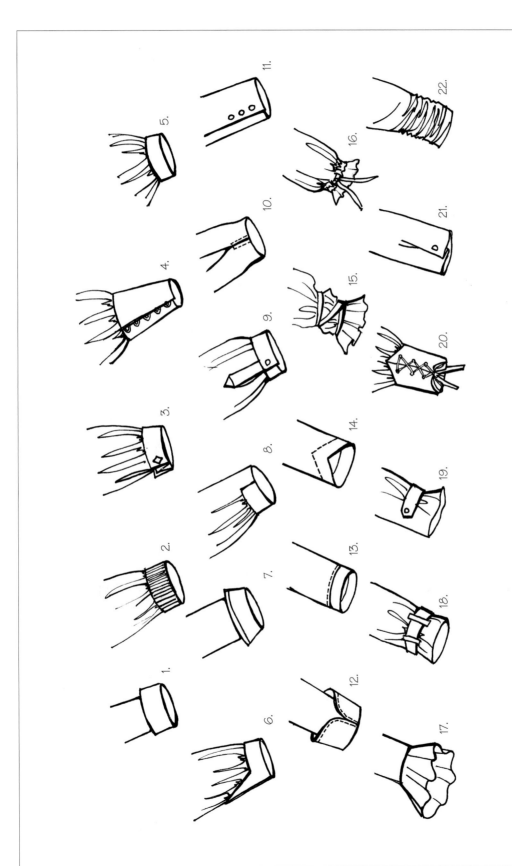

1. Turned up  2. Ribbed  3. French  4. Valentino  5. Closed  6. Shaped  7. Circular  8. Mock  9. Shirt cuff with vent & placket  10. Tucked  11. Tailored  12. Shaped
13. Bound  14. Faced  15. Wrapped  16. Drawstring  17. Ruffle  18. Belted  19. Tab  20. Laced  21. Folded  22. Ruched

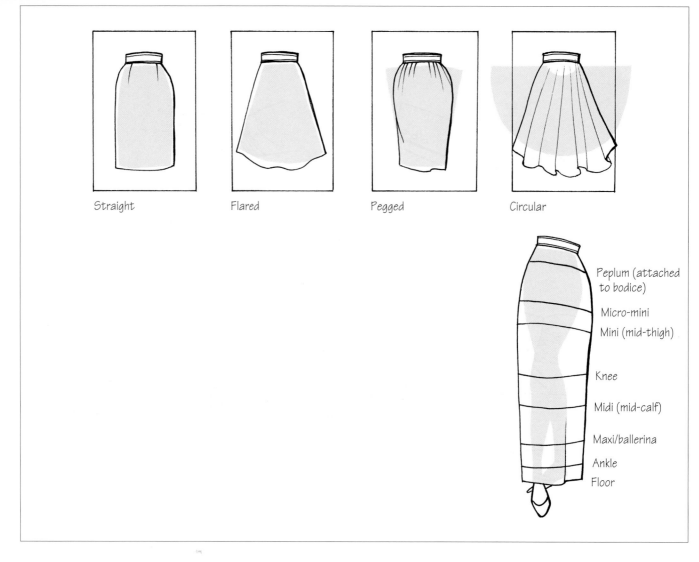

Straight   Flared   Pegged   Circular

Peplum (attached to bodice)

Micro-mini

Mini (mid-thigh)

Knee

Midi (mid-calf)

Maxi/ballerina

Ankle

Floor

# SKIRTS

A skirt is the lower part of a garment, or a separate garment, which sits on or below the waistline. Its shape is determined by the degree of width at the waist and the hem width. There are four basic skirt shapes (Fig. 12.12).

## 1. Straight
This shape has straight side seams which are shaped inwards with gathers, tucks or darts to fit the waist.

## 2. Flared
A flared skirt is a wedge-shaped skirt which increases in fullness from the hips to the hem. Gores are seamed panels which allow more fullness to be introduced to the hem area, while still fitting smoothly over the hip and thighs.

## 3. Pegged
The pegged shape is an inverted wedge which is wider at the waistline and tapered to the hemline. The excess fullness at the waist is drawn in with gathers, tucks or drapes. A skirt which is very tapered must be split or pleated at the hemline to allow movement.

## 4. Circular
A circular skirt is an extremely flared skirt which is slim at the waist and has a large amount of fullness at the hem. It may be cut from part of a circle, a full circle or several circles joined together.

A *peplum* is a short skirt sewn onto the bodice of a dress or jacket, or onto the waistband of a skirt.

Skirt hemlines change more than any other fashion feature and are an important part of the silhouette. Changes to the length of the skirt, even if only a couple of centimetres, will affect the balance of the entire garment (Figs. 12.13 & 12.14).

*12.12 (top) Basic skirt shapes.*

*12.13 Basic skirt lengths.*

GARMENTS AND GARMENT COMPONENTS

1. Dirndl  2. Pareo  3. A line  4.(a) & (b) Tiered  5. Button through  6. Pleated  7. Balloon  8. Trumpet  9. Pegged  10. Full circle  11. Flying panels  12. 4 gore  13. Half circle  14. Wrap  15. Godets  16. Back fullness  17. Kilt  18. Draped  19. Gathered  20. Peplum  21. Bias cut  22. Overskirt  23. Harem  24. Handkerchief  25. Back fullness  26. Circular with tucks  27. 6 gore  28. Yoked  29. Shaped hem  30. Train  31. Flared  32. Pegged  33. Flounced  34. Fish tail

# DRESSES

A dress is a one-piece garment having a bodice and skirt section. Dress shape is determined by the degree of width at the shoulders, waist and hemline (Figs. 12.15 & 12.16).

Dresses may be fitted, semi-fitted, unfitted, or a combination of these, and may be divided horizontally or vertically.

*12.15 Dresses.*

1. Sheath/tube  2. Shift/chemise  3. Princess fitted  4. Princess semi-fitted  5. Princess unfitted  6. A line  7. Yoked
8. Empire  9. Sundress  10. Drop waist  11. Blouson  12. Pinafore  13. Tunic

Horizontal divisions may occur at any point, but commonly follow natural body breaks at the shoulders, bust, waist and hips.

A *princess line* dress is fitted with long vertical seams which start above the bustline and end at the hem.

A dress may also be a two-piece garment consisting of matching bodice and skirt.

12.16 Dresses.

1. Jumper  2. Bias cut  3. Draped  4. Tent  5. Shirtmaker/shirtwaist  6. Rugby shirt  7. Two-piece  8. Coat-dress 9. Asymmetric  10. Caftan  11. Baby-doll  12. Cocktail  13. Gown

# JACKETS AND COATS

A coat is a warm and sometimes weather-proof outer garment worn over regular clothing (Figs. 12.17 & 12.18).

Coats tend to be classic garments with a long fashion cycle because they can be expensive and need to last for several seasons. Many coat styles are taken from men's clothing and modified for women's wear. Details such as length, colour, buttons, collar and trims may be changed to follow current trends, and a new silhouette can be created by changing the shoulderline and hemline.

Coats are often made from wool and worsted fabrics which are warm, long-wearing and attractive. They should be

*12.17 Jackets.*

1. Peplum   2. Bellboy   3. Cardigan   4. Loden   5. Battle/bomber   6. Sportscoat   7. Nehru   8. Bolero   9. Smoking   10. Mandarin
11. Shirt   12. Waistcoat/vest   13. Eton   14. Baseball   15. Chanel-style   16. Cropped   17. Single breasted blazer   18. Parka
19. Hacking/riding/hunting   20. Denim   21. Peacoat   22. Safari   23. Tuxedo   24. Ski   25. Box   26. Windbreaker   27. Edge-to-edge
28. Swingback/trapeze   29. Gilet   30. Norfolk   31. Double breasted blazer

lined so they can be easily slipped on and off. Wearing ease must be allowed for the bulk or stiffness of the fabric, and the extra garments usually worn underneath.

Raincoat fabrics should be water-resistant, and are usually light-weight for easy folding and carrying when not being worn. Plastics and vinyls repel water and often have eyelet- or air-holes under the arms to allow air to circulate because these fabrics do not breathe.

Hoods, zip-out liners and flaps are optional extras. A *shell* is a separate warm lining that can be fastened inside a coat.

A *jacket* is a short coat. A *cape* is a sleeveless, coat-like garment which encircles the neck and shoulders and covers the front, back and arms.

*12.18 Coats.*

1. Inverness/cape coat  2. Double breasted  3. Trench  4. Smock  5. Balmacaan  6. Wrap  7. Chesterfield  8. Princess/reefer
9. Reversible  10. Draped  11. Housecoat  12. Coachman  13. Tent  14. Box  15. Duffle  16. Cocoon  17. Redingote  18. Duster
19. Swagger/swingback  20. Kimono  21. Single breasted dress coat  22. Greatcote  23. Cutaway  24. Maxi  25. Stadium  26. Fur
27. Oilskin raincoat

# PANTS

A pair of pants (also known as trousers or slacks) is an outer garment which covers the hips and legs from the waist to the ankles, with each leg covered separately. The style of pants is determined by the length, the hem width and the hip-to-hem shaping. Shaping may be introduced at the waist, hips, knees or hem (Figs. 12.19, 12.20 & 12.21).

*Shorts* finish on or above knee length. *Jumpsuits* are pants attached to a bodice.

Pants are fitted to the waist with a waistband, elastic, drawstring, tie or belt. Fitted pants need an opening so they can be pulled on over the hips.

Pants have a centre front and centre back seam, and that part of the garment where the two legs join is known as the *crotch*. The length from crotch to waistband is called the *rise*. The inside seam from the crotch to the hem is known as the *inseam*, and is used to measure trouser length.

*Braces* are elastic shoulder straps which fasten to trousers by buttons or metal clips, and are worn to hold pants up.

---

*12.19 (top)* Basic pants shapes.

---

*12.20.* Basic pants lengths.

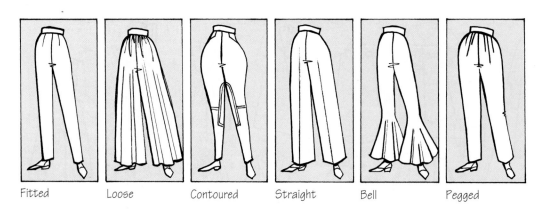

Fitted        Loose        Contoured        Straight        Bell        Pegged

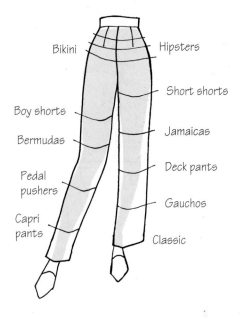

Bikini — Hipsters
Boy shorts — Short shorts
Bermudas — Jamaicas
Pedal pushers — Deck pants
Capri pants — Gauchos
Classic

12.21 Pants.

1. Bloomers  2. Jumpsuit  3. Rompers  4. Playsuit  5. Catsuit/unitard  6. Puff  7. Skort  8. Palazzo/patio  9. Oxford bags  10. Short shorts  11. Jamaica
12. Jodhpurs  13. High waisted  14. Jogging  15. Leggings  16. Stirrup/ski  17. Frilled  18. Knickerbockers  19. Toreador  20. Culottes/pantskirt  21. Bermuda
22. Capri  23. Stovepipe  24. Pedal pushers  25. Jeans  26. Wrap  27. Gauchos  28. Harem  29. Hipsters  30. Deck  31. Zouave  32. Dhoti  33. Boxers
34. Boy shorts  35. Hot pants  36. Overalls/dungarees  37. Yoked  38. Pareo/loin cloth  39. Track pants  40. Flares  41. Bike shorts  42. Pyjamas
43. Paper bag  44. Godet bell bottoms

# INTRODUCTION

Tailoring, draping and a combination of the two are, and have always been, the three main methods of constructing clothing.

*Tailored* garments are made by cutting flat fabric pieces and then sewing them together to fit the three dimensional body. Shirts, trousers, skirts, dresses and jackets are tailored.

*Draped* garments are hung on or wrapped around the body. The same piece of fabric can be used in different ways or for different purposes, and may be held in place with a belt or a sash, by tying or with pins, buttons or any fastening. A length of fabric may be draped over the shoulders as a shawl or wrapped around the waist as a skirt.

*Composite* garments combine both tailoring and draping. Some parts may be tailored and structured to fit closely, while others may be allowed to fall and fold softly from the shoulders, hips or waist.

Seams, darts, tucks, gathers, pleats, gores and drapes are used for shape, fit and decoration on all types of garment. They may be used alone, or in endless combinations and variations.

# SEAMS

Seams are formed when two garment parts are stitched together. They may be used to add shape to a garment or may add interest to a design as decorative panel lines. Seams are emphasised when outlined with decorative effects such as top-stitching, twin needle or contrasting stitching. Top-stitching also holds seams flat and gives a professional finish (Figs. 13.1 & 13.2).

## TYPES OF SEAM

### 1. Plain: pressed flat

### 2. Plain: pressed open
A plain seam is formed when the edges of the fabric are placed with right sides together and stitched near the edge on the wrong side of the garment.

### 3. Welt
A welt is a plain seam pressed flat to one side, and top-stitched.

### 4. Double top-stitched
This is a plain seam pressed open and top-stitched.

### 5. French
A french seam is sewn on the right side of the fabric then turned and stitched on the inside so that the raw edges are encased. Being a double seam, it is suitable for high quality garments and sheer fabrics where the seam will be seen.

### 6. Flat-fell

A flat-fell seam is a plain seam with one side of the seam allowance folded under and both edges top-stitched. Being triple stitched, it is very strong and used for sportswear and men's shirts.

### 7. Piped

A narrow, flat strip of bias fabric inserted into the seam so that it shows on the seam edge creates a piped seam.

### 8. Corded

This is a piped seam with cording inserted into the piping. It is often used for pyjamas, lounge suits and tailored jackets.

### 9. Slot

For a slot seam, the seam is pressed open, and top-stitched onto an underlay. It is often used with reversible fabrics.

### 10. Tucked

One fabric edge is folded under for a tucked seam, and top-stitched to the adjoining fabric piece.

### 11. Faggoted

Two folded fabric edges are caught together, with a row of zig-zag stitching, for a faggoted seam.

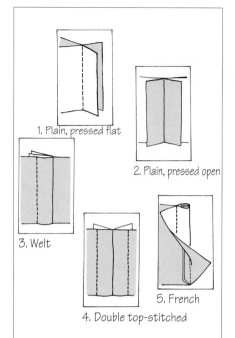

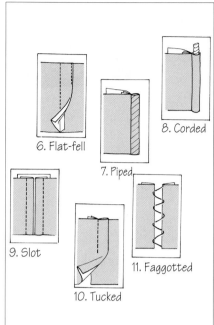

▲ 13.1 Types of seams.

▼ 13.2 Seams used for shaping.

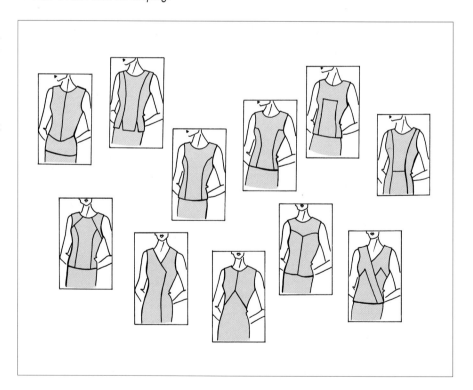

# DARTS

A dart is a V-shaped piece sewn out of a garment. It moulds the fabric to fit the curves of the body by removing excess fullness where it is not needed. Darts are used for bust and waist shaping on the front bodice, shaping over the shoulder blades and at the waist on the back bodice, over the elbow on fitted sleeves, and for the curve from waist to hips in trousers and skirts (Figs. 13.3 & 13.4).

*13.3 Basic darted garments.*

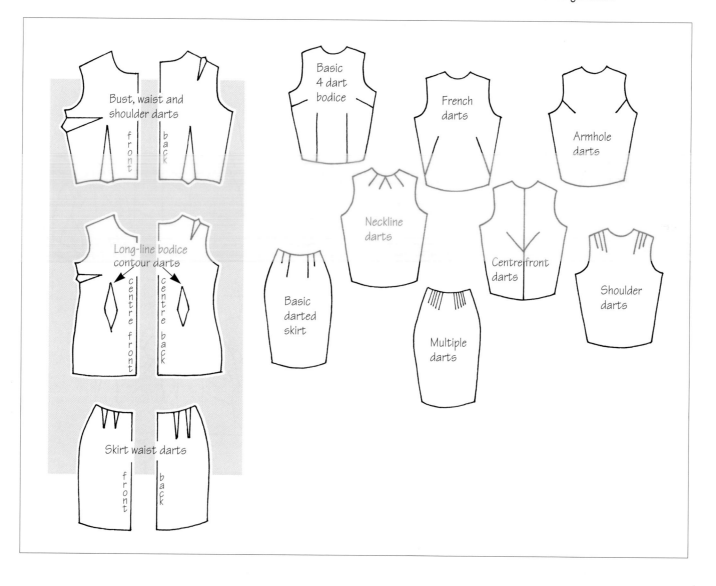

Darts taper gently and disappear to nothing at the point so that the shaping is smooth. Contour darts start and end in the centre of a garment whilst others may be placed to finish at the edge of a garment. Large darts can be split into several smaller ones and arranged decoratively to create a design feature in a fitted garment.

Darts may be avoided where panel lines or yokes are used because the excess fullness can be removed in the seams.

13.4 *Seams and darts used for shape and decoration.*

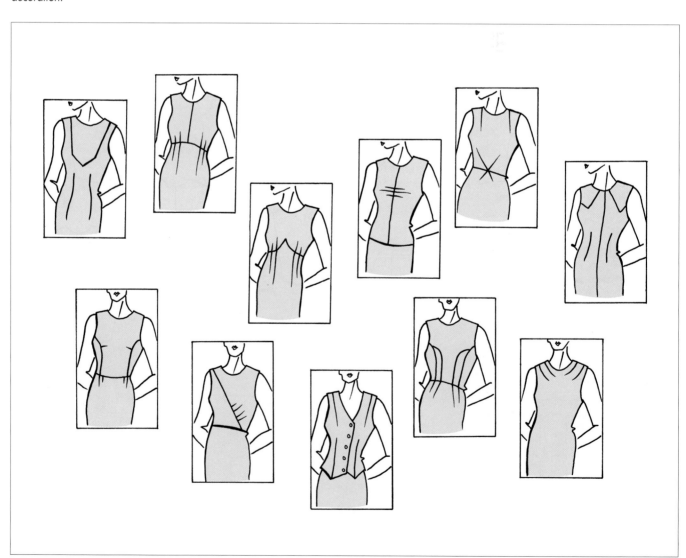

# TUCKS AND GATHERS

A *tuck* is a small fold of fabric stitched at the edge to hold it in place. Like a dart, it removes excess fullness from a garment. Tucks are usually used in straight lines, either horizontally, vertically or diagonally, and vary in width.

*Gathering* is the drawing together, with a thread, of excess fabric fullness. Gathering is especially suited to soft fabrics and the rounded, random folds create a soft look which is very flattering. Because light fabrics gather easily, much more fabric must be used to create the same impression of fullness as when heavier fabrics are used. Two or more rows of gathers are called *shirring* (Fig. 13.5).

*13.5 Tucks and gathers*

Shell tucks

Gathered straps

Corded tucks

Contour tucks

Released tucks

Action back

Contour gathers

Pin tucks

Diagonal tucks

Cross tucked yokes with gathered bodice and skirt

# PLEATS

Pleats are sharp folds of fabric which are pressed flat and stitched into place on the top edge (Figs. 13.6 & 13.7). Pleats are heat-set into the fabric so are most suited to thermo-plastic fibres like polyester and nylon. Natural fibres like wool, cotton and linen lose their pleats during laundering, but will hold pleats better if blended with a synthetic fibre.

Pleats are most commonly used in skirts. Excess fabric is taken out of each pleat at the waist, and tapered to nothing at the hip, so the skirt fits smoothly over the waist–hip curve. Pleats are crisp and smart and more slimming than gathers because they sit flat. They move with an elegant swing when the wearer walks.

Unpressed pleats are pressed flat at the top, with the rest of the length falling into soft folds. Pleats may also be stitched down to hip level for a yoke effect.

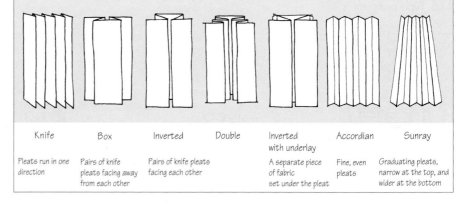

| Knife | Box | Inverted | Double | Inverted with underlay | Accordian | Sunray |
|---|---|---|---|---|---|---|
| Pleats run in one direction | Pairs of knife pleats facing away from each other | Pairs of knife pleats facing each other | | A separate piece of fabric set under the pleat | Fine, even pleats | Graduating pleats, narrow at the top, and wider at the bottom |

*13.6  Basic types of pleat.*

*13.7  A variety of pleats.*

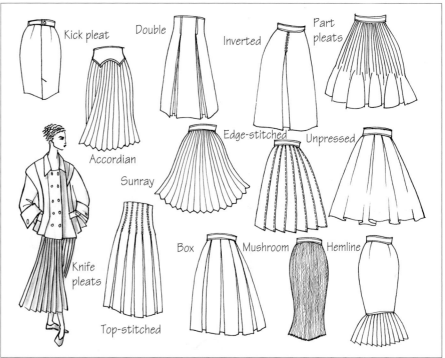

Kick pleat
Double
Inverted
Part pleats
Accordian
Sunray
Edge-stitched
Unpressed
Knife pleats
Box
Mushroom
Hemline
Top-stitched

# YOKES

The term yoke refers to the fitted upper part of a garment, usually on the shoulders or hips, to which the rest of the garment is sewn. A yoke may be used on the front or back of a garment and may be cut as part of the sleeves. It creates a smooth, horizontal line from which pleats, gathers, tucks or smocking may fall (Fig. 13.8).

*13.8 Yokes.*

# GORES AND GODETS

Gores are flared panels set into a bodice or skirt to increase width. Because they are vertical lines, they are slimming to the figure.

Godets are triangular fabric pieces sewn into the bottom of a garment to increase fullness or for decoration. They are usually used in skirts and sleeves (Fig. 13.9).

*13.9 Gores and godets.*

# DRAPING

A draped garment is one which hangs from or covers the body in loose folds of fabric (Fig. 13.10).

Drapes can be created with French drapery, unpressed pleats or simple folding. The drapes fall from the point or points supporting the fabric and can be controlled with invisible stitching which attaches the garment to the underlining. The flow of the folds can also be varied by shortening or lengthening, raising or lowering, tightening or loosening, adding or reducing fabric.

When cut on the bias grain, the fabric can be made to mould sensuously to the curves of the figure. The fabrics most suited to drapery are soft, light and flexible with enough body to fall into folds. Crepe, jersey, chiffon and silk satins are ideal. Stiff or thick fabrics are unsuitable because the folds sit out awkwardly from the body.

*13.10 Draping.*

# POCKETS

A pocket is a small bag inserted into or sewn onto a garment (Figs. 13.11 & 13.12). Although functional in origin, pockets are frequently used as ornaments. *Flaps* or *welts* may be false pockets which are unable to be used. Large pockets and multiple pockets make a garment look more casual and are used for putting hands in or for carrying things. Functional pockets should be placed within comfortable reach of the arm, at an easily accessible angle, and large enough to insert the hand.

*13.11 Basic pockets and their placement.*

1. Pocket shape should relate to the other garment design features

2. Pockets are often used symmetrically. Asymetry draws attention to one side

3. Pockets add bulk so care should be taken with their placement

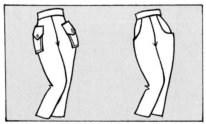

4. Pocket size should be in proportion to the rest of the garment

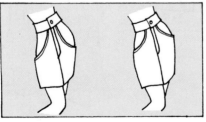

5. The drape of the fabric will distort pocket shape

Pockets are often used symmetrically in pairs. When only one pocket is used, attention is drawn to that side of the garment. The pocket shape should relate to the other design features of the garment, or it will confuse the design.

Pockets, especially those with flaps, add bulk so care should be taken with their placement in bust and hip areas.

Pocket size should be in proportion to the rest of the garment. Large pockets are best on loose-fitting garments whilst smaller pockets work better on more fitted clothing. The drape of soft fabric will distort the shape of a pocket.

*13.12 Variety in pockets.*

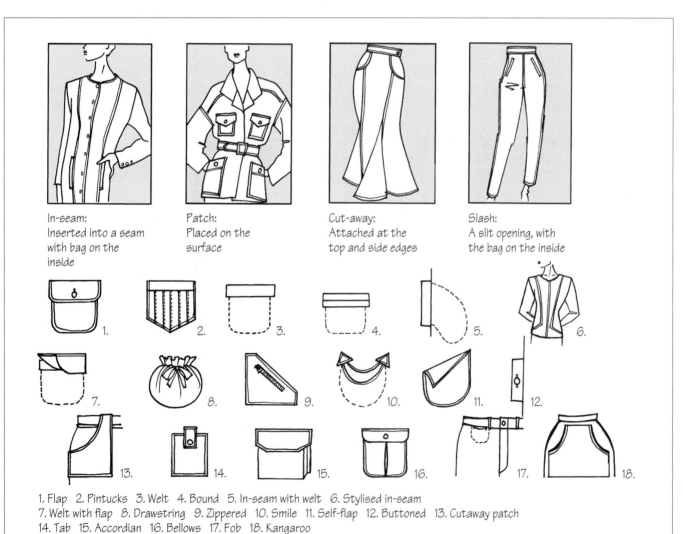

In-seam:
Inserted into a seam with bag on the inside

Patch:
Placed on the surface

Cut-away:
Attached at the top and side edges

Slash:
A slit opening, with the bag on the inside

1. Flap  2. Pintucks  3. Welt  4. Bound  5. In-seam with welt  6. Stylised in-seam
7. Welt with flap  8. Drawstring  9. Zippered  10. Smile  11. Self-flap  12. Buttoned  13. Cutaway patch
14. Tab  15. Accordian  16. Bellows  17. Fob  18. Kangaroo

# RUFFLES, FRILLS AND FLOUNCES

A ruffle is a fabric strip gathered or pleated and used as a trimming or finish, attached so as to leave one or both edges free. Ruffles are often used on skirts, sleeves and shirt fronts.

A frill is a narrow ruffle, usually used as a finish for the neck, armholes, sleeves or hem.

A flounce is a wide gathered or pleated strip sewn to a garment, with the lower edge left free. It is generally worn at the bottom of a garment, especially

*13.13 Types of ruffle*

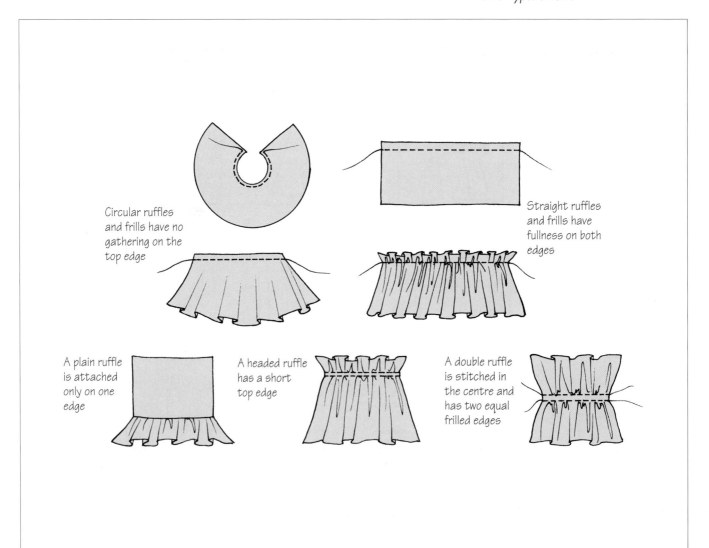

Circular ruffles and frills have no gathering on the top edge

Straight ruffles and frills have fullness on both edges

A plain ruffle is attached only on one edge

A headed ruffle has a short top edge

A double ruffle is stitched in the centre and has two equal frilled edges on skirts, and sleeve or cape hems, and is frequently used for evening wear.

Ruffles and flounces may be straight or circular. The straight ruffle has both edges the same length, and one edge is gathered or pleated to create folds. The circular ruffle is a curved strip with a shorter inner edge and longer outer edge. When the inner edge is stitched flat, the outer edge produces folds (Fig. 13.14).

As a general guide, the sheerer the fabric or the wider the ruffle or flounce, the fuller it should be. With gathered frills, fine textures use much more fabric than heavier textures. The hem of a flounce may be wired to exaggerate the folds (Fig. 13.14).

*13.14 Ruffles, frills and flounces*

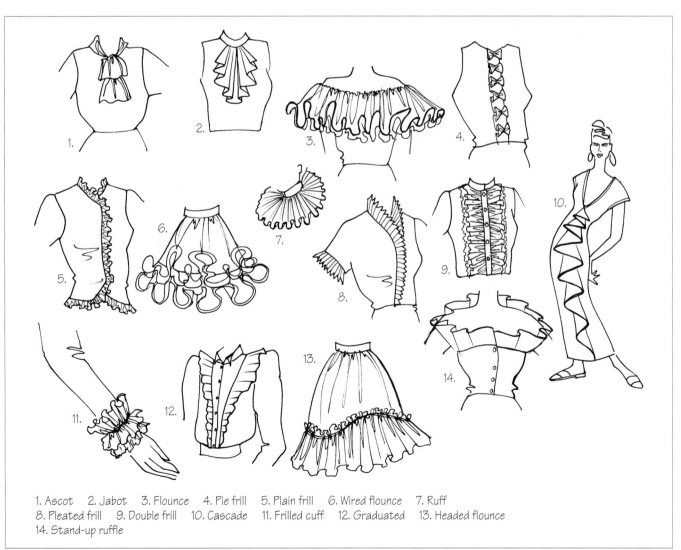

1. Ascot    2. Jabot    3. Flounce    4. Pie frill    5. Plain frill    6. Wired flounce    7. Ruff
8. Pleated frill    9. Double frill    10. Cascade    11. Frilled cuff    12. Graduated    13. Headed flounce
14. Stand-up ruffle

# EDGE FINISHES AND HEMS

A hem is the finished edge of fabric at the bottom or outer edge of garment or garment part (Fig. 13.15).

Fancy edges are mostly used on custom-made clothing, evening wear and up-market designer labels because they are expensive and not easily altered if hemlines need to be raised or lowered.

*13.15 Edge finishes and hems*

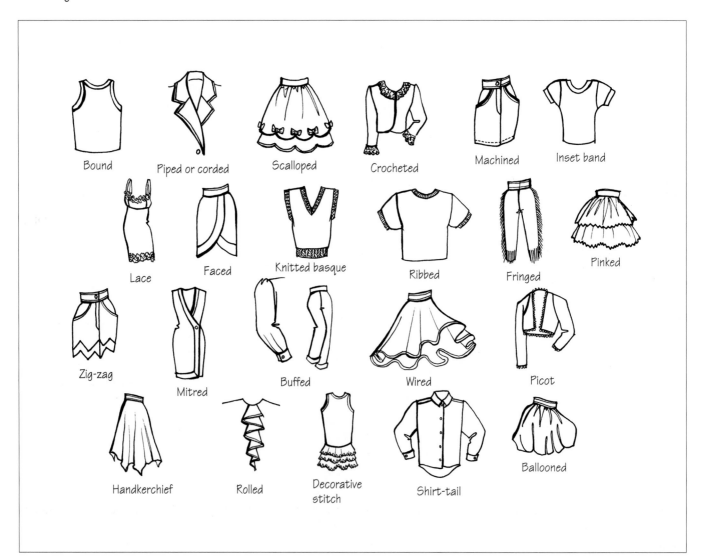

Bound

Piped or corded

Scalloped

Crocheted

Machined

Inset band

Lace

Faced

Knitted basque

Ribbed

Fringed

Pinked

Zig-zag

Mitred

Buffed

Wired

Picot

Handkerchief

Rolled

Decorative stitch

Shirt-tail

Ballooned

## CHAPTER 14

# TRIMMINGS AND TREATMENTS

# INTRODUCTION

Trimmings are details or accessories applied to the surface of a garment. They may be applied to uncut fabric, to cut garment pieces before machining, or once the garment has been made up.

Trimmings may be decorative or functional, or both. Those which may be removed without interfering with the basic structure of the garment, such as beading, appliqué and embroidery, are decorative and enhance the appearance of the design. Others, such as buttons and plackets, are functional because they are important to the fit and function of the garment and may also add interest to the design. Whether functional or decorative, trimmings should always be designed as part of the garment (Fig. 14.1). If applied carelessly or as an afterthought, they may compete with the visual structure of the garment instead of supporting it. A trimming should not be used unless it enhances the appearance of the design. The weight and size of any trimming should be compatible with the fabric weight. If the trim is too heavy or bulky it will drag and strain the fabric, and if too light may be overpowered by the fabric or the design.

## APPLYING TRIMS

Because of the skill required for their application, many trims must be hand-sewn or require specialised equipment, and this can add considerably to the cost of a garment. Most manufacturers send garment pieces out to specialist makers for this type of work.

In commercial garment production, hand-work is kept to a minimum because of the time and expense involved. Many decorative finishes such as beading, drawn thread work and smocking can be purchased by the metre as ready-made braids or fabric lengths and, when inserted, almost look like they have been hand done. The trimmings shown in this chapter are only a limited sample of the vast variety designers can choose from.

## TYPES OF TRIM

- *Appliqués* are decorative shapes sewn or glued onto a garment and include patches, embroidered shapes, flocking, stuffed and beaded shapes. Printed fabric may be cut up and the shapes appliquéd to plain fabric.

- *Badges* may be embroidered, flocked or metal. They are normally stitched onto the garment but some have a heat seal backing which may be ironed on.

- *Contrast fabrics* create interesting effects by combining fabric patterns, colours and textures on a single garment. Subtle treatments include lining or facing a garment in another fabric or, for a more obvious effect. Pockets, collars and cuffs may be contrasting.

- *Flowers* can be made from the fabric of the garment or purchased separately and applied. Their effect may be small, soft and delicate, or large, flamboyant and sophisticated. The stylised daisy was popular during the sixties and early nineties.

- *Elastics* come in varying colours and designs and can be attached directly to the garment as banding at waists, wrists and ankles, or used as accessories in belts and braces. Elastic eliminates the use of an opening and fastening, and is often concealed in a casing. Elastic thread can also be used for shirring.

- *Feathers and fur* add fun and sophistication to a garment. Skilful use of such trims is required because they

Spot trimming creates a centre of interest

Linear trimming accent the style lines of a design, including seam lines and garment edges

Areal trimming enriches and strengthens shapes

▲ 14.1 Trimmings affect the appearance of a garment in three ways.

▼ 14.2 Samples of trims.

1. (a) & (b) Embroidered badges   2. Metal trims   3. Flock badge
4. Embroidered appliqué   5. Beaded appliqué   6. Fur trimming
7. Flowered ribbon   8. Feathers   9. Ruffled elastic   10. Elastic casing

are bold and can easily overpower a garment. Most suppliers will dye feathers to match a fabric. They may be bought individually, as a motif (an arrangement of feathers on a backing) or by the length (these are priced by the piece, or per metre).

- *Passementerie* is a term which covers most embroideries, edgings, braids, cords and ribbons. They range from the plainest, simplest Russia braid or nylon ribbon to the most elaborate and expensive metallic braids and laces. Numerous fibres — wool, cotton, silk, rayon, nylon and raffia — and weaves — satin, faille, grosgrain, velvet, taffeta, knitting, plaiting and tubing — are used. Some braids must be used straight with mitred corners, while others are bias cut or flexible and can be shaped to follow garment edges or intricate patterns.

- *Ribbons* are strips of fabric of varying widths with selvedges on both edges. They may be threaded through buttonholes, lace or eyelets, or stitched flat onto a garment.

*14.3 (From top to bottom)*
*(a) Striped grosgrain ribbon*
*(b) Grosgrain ribbon*
*(c) Novelty printed ribbon*
*(d) Binding*
*(e) Metallic looped fringing.*

- *Binding* is a folded strip of bias cut fabric, ribbon or braid used as edging. It eliminates the need for facings.

- *Fringing* is a border of hanging threads, cords, tassels or beads which imparts a feeling of movement to a design. Self-fringe is made by pulling cross threads on the edge of a fabric and then hemstitching.

- *Piping* is a piece of folded fabric or cord sewn to the edge of a garment or inserted between two seams.

(Figs. 14.2, 14.3, 14.4, 14.5 & 14.6)

## BEADING

Beads may be purchased individually, strung by the metre, or in packs by weight. Like buttons, beads are made from a wide range of materials, ranging from metal to plastic to glass. They may be sewn, ironed, glued or studded onto a garment. The basic types of beading are:

- *Seed beads* are very small round beads.

- *Bugle beads* are tubular shaped beads in varying lengths.

- *Crystals* may be clear glass or plastic.

- *Stones*: Diamantes are very small glass stones, with a metal backing, often set into jewellery.

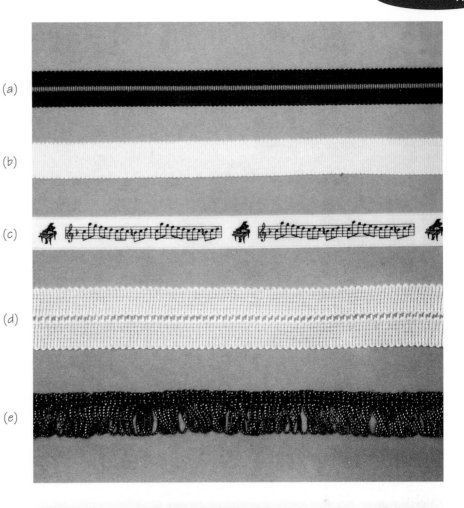

(a)
(b)
(c)
(d)
(e)

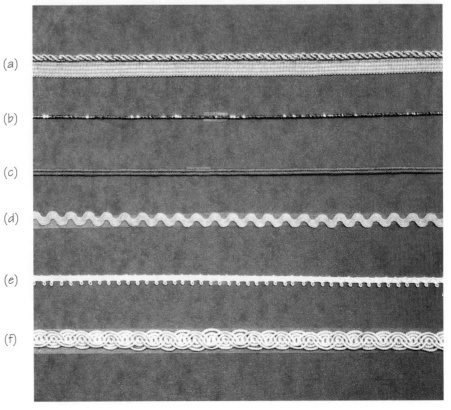

(a)
(b)
(c)
(d)
(e)
(f)

*14.4 (From top to bottom)*
*(a) Corded piping*
*(b) Metallic cord*
*(c) Russia (or soutache) braid*
*(d) Rick-rack braid*
*(e) Picot*
*(f) Gimp.*

(a)

(b)

(c)

(d)

14.5 *(From top to bottom)*
(a) *Tassled fringing*
(b) *Pom-pom braid*
(c) *Beaded fringing*
(d) *Ruffled ribbon*

Rhinestones are flat-back glass or plastic stones, with a mirror backing. They range in size from 4 mm to 30 mm, and shapes include round, diamond, oval and rectangular. They are often faceted.

Rondels are metal wheels studded with diamantes and used between beads.

- *Pearls* may be loose or strung, glass or plastic. They are usually cream, white or coloured. The most common shapes are round, tear-drop, rice or baroque which has surface indentations.

- *Sequins* (or *spangles*) are shiny metal or metallised plastic discs used to add sparkle and glitter to evening wear. A *paillette* is a large sequin, up to 20 mm diameter. A *cupped* sequin is a slightly concave sequin with a faceted surface. Sequins may also be *novelty* shapes.

- *Metal* such as caps, filler beads, chain and jewellery findings can be added to garments provided they are not too heavy.

## LACE

Lace is an openwork fabric composed of a network of threads which creates a pattern. Laces come in silk, cotton, linen, nylon or polyester. Different types of lace (Fig. 14.7) include:

- *All-over* This is a repeating pattern covering the fabric and available by the metre.

- *Edging* Edging comes in a variety of widths, straight on the sewn edge and scalloped or picot on the loose edge.

1. Teardrop pearls   2. Seed pearls   3. Rhinestones   4. Crystal beads
5. Seed beads   6. Bugle beads   7. Cupped sequins   8. Sequins
9. Novelty sequins   10. Metal trims and beads
11. Wood, ceramic and plastic beads

14.6 *Beads and sequins.*

All-over

Edging

Galloon

Insertion

Beading

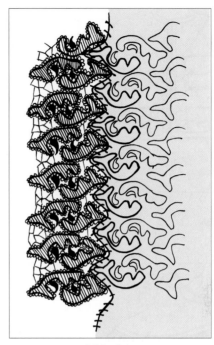

Joining lace

14.7 Lace.

- *Galloon*   This is a lace strip scalloped, picot or shaped on both edges.

- *Insertion*   This type of lace is a strip with straight edges, inserted between two pieces of fabric.

- *Beading*   Beading lace is a slotted lace through which ribbon, cording or braid can be threaded.

Lace may be used alone as a sheer, or with a lining for an opaque look. A very fine lace may be cut with a tulle lining for body and support. In couture garments lace is joined by overlapping the dominant shapes and appliquéing the edges to follow the design (Fig. 14.7). The seam allowance is then trimmed away so that the seam is almost invisible. This technique is known as mending stitch. Scalloped edging can also be applied using this technique.

14.8 (left)  Printing and painting.

14.9 (right)  Puffing.

Lace edging makes a useful finish for sheer fabrics which are not suited to a large hem or facing.

# MORE TRIMMINGS AND TREATMENTS

- *Printing and painting*   Airbrush, hand painting or silk screening create one-off designs with a subtle or commercial look as desired. Laser

14.10 Quilting.

14.11 Spaghetti.

14.12 Strapping.

14.13 Trapunto.

14.14 Arrowheads.

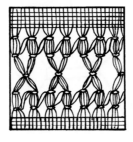

14.15 Drawn work.

copies of images or prints can be applied to fabrics via transfer printing which uses heat to fuse the print to the fabric (Fig. 14.8).

- *Puffing* Pleated or gathered fabric strips are inserted into a garment (Fig. 14.9).

- *Quilting* A design stitched onto two layers of fabric with light wadding sandwiched between is known as quilting. The stitching is usually done in straight lines, diamonds or a novelty pattern and is done before the garment is cut because the quilting process takes up both length and width. Fabric patterns can also be emphasised with quilting. Quilting gives texture, weight and warmth to a flat fabric and is used on garments such as parkas, ski jackets, dressing gowns and coat linings (Fig. 14.10).

- *Spaghetti* A bias strip of fabric that has been stitched and turned to form a finished tube is called spaghetti. It is used for belts, edging and openwork (Fig. 14.11).

- *Strapping* Strapping is spaghetti which has been pressed flat (Fig. 14.12).

- *Trapunto* Trapunto is a padded lining appliquéd to the underside of a garment, creating a relief effect for spot motifs. It can be done on garment sections such as yokes, cuffs, hems, pockets and lapels (Fig. 14.13).

# THREADS AND STITCHES

- *Arrowheads* Arrowheads are stays used on tailored garments at the joint of collars and lapels, pockets and pocket flaps and the ends of seams, tucks, pleats and vents. Bartacks are used on mass-produced garments but are not decorative (Fig. 14.14).

- *Drawn work* A decorative effect created by pulling out lines of threads in the fabric and embroidering the remaining threads is known as drawn work (Fig. 14.15).

- *Edging* Edging is decorative hand-stitching such as blanket stitch or hem stitch, or machine-stitching such as fine overlocking and scalloping. It is used to finish hems (Fig. 14.16).

- *Embroidery* Ornamental stitching done by hand or by machine over either the whole fabric or on selected parts is called embroidery. Silk, wool, cotton, rayon, raffia and metal threads are used in embroidery (Fig. 14.17 and see also Fig. 14.27).

- *Eyelet embroidery* In these instances, holes are cut or punched in the fabric and the raw edges overcast. Broderie Anglaise is a common example of eyelet embroidery (Fig. 14.18).

- *Corded embroidery* In this type of embroidery, the design is outlined with two rows of stitching and a soft cord is sewn in from underneath to form a raised line (Fig. 14.19).

- *Picot* Picot involves small loops used as edging on laces, ribbons or garment hems (Fig. 14.20).

- *Crochet* Crochet may be used as an edge trimming or as a fabric piece. It has a fairly heavy, slightly casual look, and is suitable mostly for daywear (Fig. 14.21).

- *Shirring* Shirring is when two or more rows of gathers are stitched in place to control fullness. Shirring is usually used on bodices, yokes and sleeves and elastic may be used in the stitching for stretch (Fig. 14.22).

- *Smocking* Smocking is when an ornamental shirred panel is decorated with embroidery to create a honeycomb pattern (Fig. 14.23).

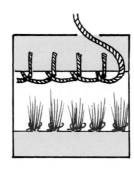

14.16 Edging.

14.17 Embroidery. (Courtesy of Arcade Badge.)

14.18 Eyelet embroidery.

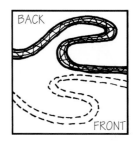

14.19 Corded embroidery.

14.20 Picot.

14.21 Crochet.

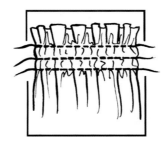

14.22 Shirring.

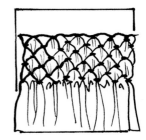

14.23 Smocking.

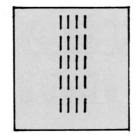

14.24 Top stitching.

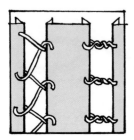

Faggotting

14.25 Open seams

- *Top-stitching* This is sewing on the right side of the garment which flattens seams as well as being decorative when used in contrasting coloured thread or in multiple rows. Pin-stitching is done right to the edge of a garment or seam. Twin-needle stitching is done by multiple-needle machines (Fig. 14.24).

- *Open seams* Threads can be used to join garment parts, leaving a gap between the edges. Faggoting is thread, ribbon or braid used straight or criss-crossed in an open seam (Fig. 14.25).

- *Open-work* This is when a cut-out design is inserted into a garment. Lace and sheer fabrics are often used and it may also include drawn or punch work (Fig. 14.26).

14.26 Open-work

14.27 Embroidery machines at work.
(Photographs courtesy of Arcade Badge.)

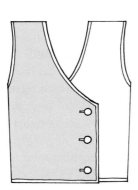

Women's garments wrap right over left

Buttons should be placed at stress points so the garment does not gape

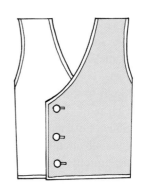

Men's garments wrap left over right

▲ 14.28 Openings.

▼ 14.29 Bows, ties and buckles.

# OPENINGS AND FASTENINGS

Openings are necessary in most garments so they can be put on and removed easily. Common placements for openings are at the neckline to go over the head; front, back or side seams to go over the shoulders, bust and hips; the wrist to go over the hand, and the ankle to go over the foot.

Fastenings should be placed close enough together and where most garment stress occurs to minimise gaping between them. Stress points occur at the neck, bust line, waist, and hip. Fastenings should also be placed where they are easily accessible and where they are unlikely to snag or cause friction or discomfort. They are generally not placed on the seat or back of the legs where they will be impractical, uncomfortable or not seen.

Traditionally, women's garments fasten right side over left, while men's fasten left over right. This means that women's buttonholes are on the right of the garment, men's are on the left (Fig. 14.28). Functional bits and pieces such as lining, elastic, zippers, buttons, hooks and eyes and shoulder pads are known as *findings*.

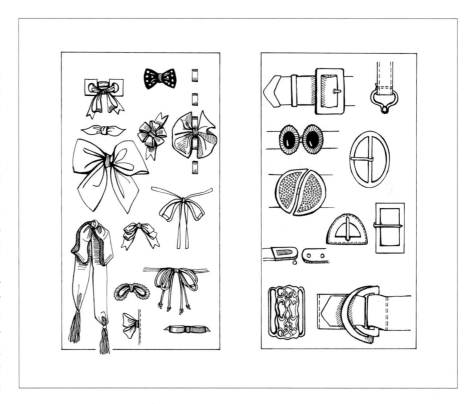

## BOWS AND TIES

These trims may be part of the garment, attached to the garment or a separate contrasting braid, ribbon or tie. A bow consists of two or more loops of fabric held in the centre by a tie or a knot. Bows can be stitched so they don't have to be tied each time or they may have flowing straps to be tied as the wearer chooses.

A tie is a scarf or band wrapped around something and tied in a knot. Buckles are used for fastening and decoration. They may be attached to a strap or tab on the garment, to a separate self-tie or belt or to a coordinating belt worn with the garment (Fig. 14.29).

## BUTTONS

Buttons are made from plastic (which may be dyed to match any colour), wood, mother-of-pearl or other shell, bone, horn, cloth (self-covered), metal, enamel, leather, glass, jewels and jet.

Buttons must be chosen to suit the style and fabric of the garment. Thick buttons are quite three-dimensional and, due to their bulk, are generally used in fewer numbers than fine buttons. Very heavy buttons will drag on light fabrics, and very delicate or expensive buttons may need to be removed before the garment is cleaned. The two basic types of button are:

### 1. Sew-through

Sew-through buttons have holes for attaching to the garment.

### 2. Shank

Shank buttons provide concealed attachment by means of a loop on the back of the button (Fig. 14.30).

Button sizing is designated by line which indicates the diameter of the button.

A buttonhole is an opening in a garment for a button to pass through. Loop buttonholes are usually used with half- or full-ball buttons. Because such buttons are relatively difficult to fasten, they are generally not used for daywear but are favoured for evening and bridal wear. *Frogging* is a cord or braid loop fastening used with a toggle or button (Fig. 14.31).

14.30 *Variety of button types and buttonholes.*

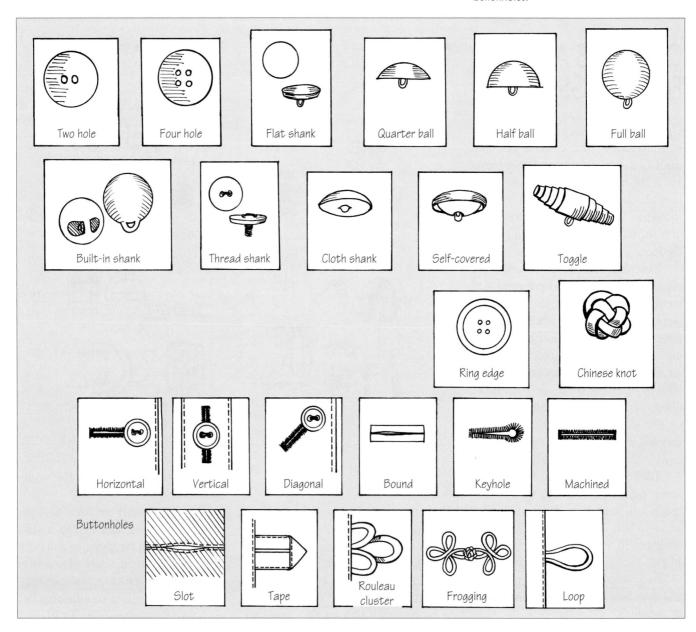

Two hole   Four hole   Flat shank   Quarter ball   Half ball   Full ball

Built-in shank   Thread shank   Cloth shank   Self-covered   Toggle

Ring edge   Chinese knot

Horizontal   Vertical   Diagonal   Bound   Keyhole   Machined

Buttonholes

Slot   Tape   Rouleau cluster   Frogging   Loop

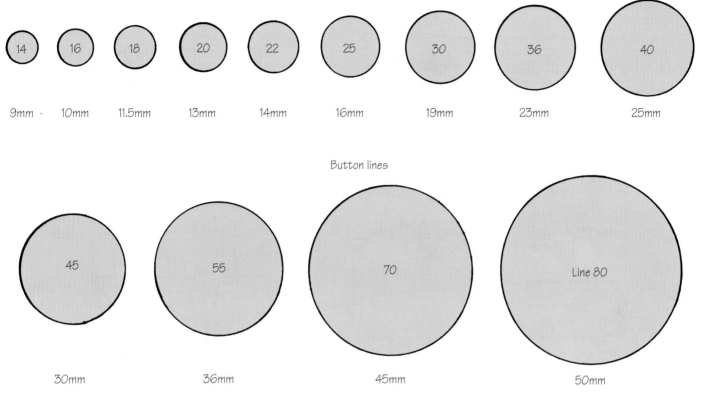

Button lines

14.31 *Button lines.*

## MORE TYPES OF FASTENING

(Fig. 14.32)

- *Hardware* Shiny metal or heavy-duty plastic clips, clasps, hinges, chains, ropes and cords can often be used to good effect on casual garments, denim and leather.

- *Hook and eye* A fastener with a metal hook and a metal or thread loop is called a hook and eye. They may be applied singly or continuously on a tape and may be covered with thread for a couture touch.

- *Lacing* The drawing together of garment parts or fabric with cording threaded through eyelets, hooks or loops is lacing. Lacing may create a drawstring effect or be criss-crossed for a tight fit as on a corset.

- *Studs, snaps, snap tape, rivets* A press stud is a functional snap of metal or plastic and is applied singly or continuously on a tape. Larger metal studs are decorative and used mostly on casual, sturdy fabrics such as denim and drill which are tough enough to support the pulling open of the stud. Lighter fabrics should be reinforced. Rivets are fixed studs used to strengthen seams and stress points such as pocket corners on jeans. Decorative rhinestone rivets are also available. Studs and rivets are sewn on or attached to the fabric with pointed prongs

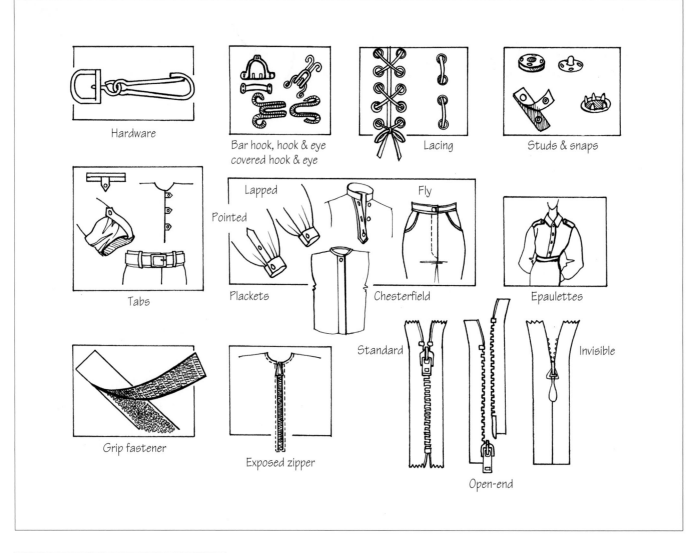

**14.32 Variety of fastenings.**

or a backing clip. Rhinestones may have a glue backing and can be ironed on.

- **Tabs** A small flap, sometimes a loop, used as part of a fastening or as decoration is a tab. Tabs used to hold a belt are known as belt-keepers.

- **Plackets** Sometimes known as tabs, plackets are finished slits or openings in a garment fastened with buttons, zippers, lacing or studs. A fly front is a placket with an overlapping flap of fabric which conceals a zipper or other fastening.

- **Epaulettes** An epaulette is a military style shoulder strap which gives width to the shoulder line.

- **Grip fasteners** Nylon and polyester fibres which stick to plastic hooks when pressed together and are easily peeled apart are known as grip fasteners.

- **Zippers** Zippers are available in plastic or metal with a variety of pulls and can be cut to any length and dyed to any colour. There are three basic types of zipper:

1. Standard — opening at the top and closed at the bottom
2. Open-ended — for jackets or completely open garments
3. Invisible — disappearing completely into the seam.

Zippers may be concealed in a seam or behind a placket or left exposed to accent seams, design lines or pockets. Garment parts may be zipped off for function or novelty. Better quality garments have a fabric shield behind the zipper so the teeth do not catch on the skin or clothing beneath.

## CHAPTER 15

# FIGURE TYPES: ACHIEVING PERFECT PROPORTION

# INTRODUCTION

Through a knowledge of figure types and the visual illusions created by dress, designers, couturiers and fashion retailers can help clients in selecting garments which suit them and enhance their appearance.

Fashion designers create coverings for the body, so they need to know how the body is constructed. They need to understand the skeletal and muscular structure of the moving and resting body frame in much the same way that furniture and interior designers use their knowledge of ergonomics to create comfortable surroundings.

When creating new styles, the designer works from a mental image of his or her body ideal. This figure is used as a prototype and the basis for proportioning designs and sizing patterns. In the designer's mind, the ideal body has perfect proportions and contours, correct posture and symmetrical features. However, each designer has his or her own version of perfection, and they often differ markedly. For this reason, the fit of clothes from different fashion labels can vary quite a bit. Your own figure is bound to differ in some way from the 'ideal', and you will find that some clothing brands suit your body type better than others.

# ALL BODIES ARE DIFFERENT

Our body design is determined by genetic heritage and nutritional and environmental influences.

The bone structure we are born with is influenced by our racial background and ancestral heritage and, except under rare circumstances, cannot be changed. Regardless of whether we are short or tall, small boned or large boned, our frame is a part of our individuality that we must all accept.

Different races have noticeably different body characteristics. Australian women, perhaps due to a warm climate and outdoor lifestyle, tend to be relatively tall and well-built, with broad shoulders, medium-sized busts and full hips. This figure type is similar to that of American women. Asian women are more petite, with a longer body, small bust, narrow hips, and proportionately shorter legs.

The designer for export markets should be fully aware of racial characteristics, including build and colouring, and the culture of the target customer to ensure that his or her designs are appropriate for the overseas consumer.

Body growth and development can be stunted or distorted if nutrition is inadequate in the early years of infancy and childhood. Growth patterns are also influenced by the environment. Lifestyle, exercise and cultural ideals of attractiveness and fashion correctness determine the parts of our bodies which receive most attention or which we strive to develop over others.

Our bodies also change as we go through the various stages of childhood, puberty, adulthood and old age. Garments designed for 18–25 year olds are usually more revealing and differently proportioned than those designed for the 45-plus age group, because changes in lifestyle, childbearing, weight gain or loss and the effects of gravity can drastically alter body shape and proportion.

Successful designers are those whose styles many people feel comfortable wearing, so the designer takes care to create garments which suit the average anatomies of his or her market sector.

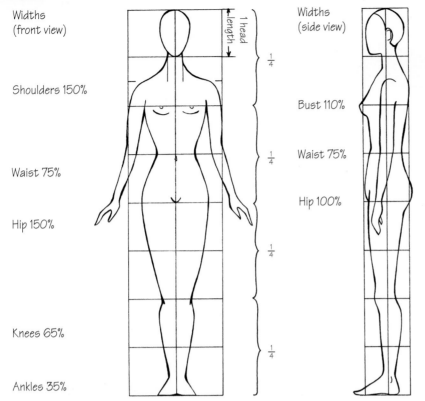

Widths (front view)

Shoulders 150%

Waist 75%

Hip 150%

Knees 65%

Ankles 35%

Widths (side view)

1 head length

¼

Bust 110%

¼

Waist 75%

Hip 100%

¼

¼

¼

Note: Although the classically proportioned figure (as discussed in Chapter 10 Sketching the Fashion Figure) measures 7½ head lengths, for convenience we work with an 8 head figure when discussing male and female average proportions.

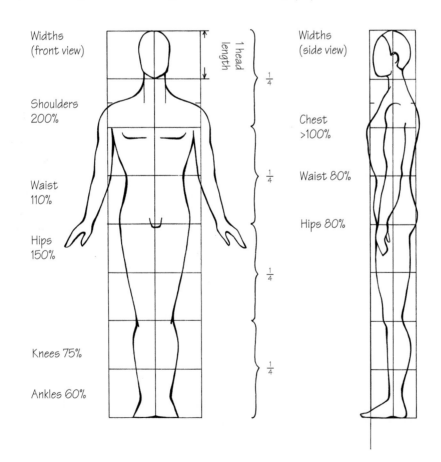

Widths (front view)

Shoulders 200%

Waist 110%

Hips 150%

Knees 75%

Ankles 60%

Widths (side view)

1 head length

¼

Chest >100%

¼

Waist 80%

Hips 80%

¼

¼

# BODY STRUCTURE

The structure and balance of the body is defined by proportion (height and weight), contour, posture and symmetry. Different combinations of these variables result in the endless variety of the human form.

## PROPORTION

Proportion is the relationship of each part of the body to the other parts, and the relationship of each part to the total body mass in terms of size, length and width (Figs. 15.1 & 15.2(b)).

Actual size, weight or measurement are not as important as these relationships, the sense of balance they create, and their combined total appearance.

## CONTOUR

Body contours are curves, bulges and hollows formed by muscles and fat deposits. Contours and weight distribution change with muscular condition, weight gain or loss, physical ageing, and the wearing of foundation garments.

Two people of the same weight and height may have quite different body shapes due to the different distribution of muscle and fat (Fig. 15.2(a)).

## SYMMETRY

The ideal figure is perfectly symmetrical, but most figures are slightly asymmetrical. Common irregularities to be found include one shoulder being higher than the other, one breast larger than the other, one leg or arm longer than the other, one hip higher than the other, and more curve on one side of the waist.

*15.1 Ideal female and male proportions, expressed as a percentage of the head length.*

These irregularities cause garments to hang unevenly or to wrinkle or strain on one side (Fig. 15.2(c)).

## POSTURE

Posture is the alignment of the limbs and the way the body is carried when walking, standing and sitting.

Fashionable postures have changed throughout history. Medieval ladies posed with their head and shoulders carried back and abdomen thrust forward to achieve a maternity look. The Gibson girl era of the early 20th century produced the S-shaped spine with bosom thrust forward and fully padded backside thrust out.

The modern ideal of good posture is achieved when the ear lobe, mid-shoulder, just behind mid-hips, just in front of mid-knee, and the outer ankle are aligned on a vertical line. Two commonly seen bad postures are the *slouch* — whereby the shoulders are rounded and the stomach protrudes — and the *upright* — whereby the back arches and the bust and abdomen are thrust forward (Fig. 15.2(d)).

Body movement is very much affected by fashions in shoes and skirts. Platform shoes produce a tottery walk, stilettos a mincing step, and clogs and slip-ons require a shuffle to keep them in place. The hobble skirt of the twenties allowed only tiny steps to be taken, whereas the loose, flowing patchwork skirts of the hippy era reflected the freedom culture of the times in the relaxed, casual stride it permitted.

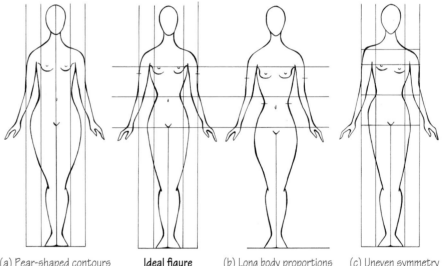

(a) Pear-shaped contours    **Ideal figure**    (b) Long body proportions    (c) Uneven symmetry

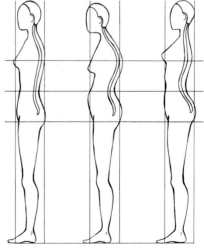

*15.2 Body features such as bust, waist, hips, arms and legs frequently vary from the ideal figure in proportion, contour, symmetry and posture.*

(d) Correct posture    The slouch    The upright

# BODY IDEALS

Although we are constantly bombarded with images of beauty and apparent perfection, body ideals exist more in our imaginations than in reality. Most people, even top models, have aspects of their build or appearance they would change if they were able. Nearly every person has physical features they consider to be assets and those they consider liabilities.

Every era idealises a different image. Even though our anatomy stays the same, it may be starved, fed, upholstered, supported, flattened, bound, implanted, surgically operated on or otherwise coerced into a variety of non-naturally occurring shapes and positions in an attempt to conform with prevailing body ideals.

Over the centuries, the figure most admired in women has ranged from the full, buxom figure to the flat-chested garçonne to the lithe and muscular athlete. Specific attention may be paid to either large or slender hips, long or short legs, flat or protruding bottoms, small hands, small feet, narrow and sloping or broad and square shoulders, and an endless combination of these features. At various stages in her life, a woman born at the start of the 20th century would have needed to look like Greta Garbo, Marilyn Monroe, Twiggy and Elle MacPherson just to stay in fashion!

Men are also required to change their physiques, but theirs is usually a more gradual process. Points of admiration for male bodies have been shapely legs, the large belly, wasp waist, barrel chest, genital bulge, small buttocks, broad shoulders and pronounced muscular development.

The body ideal for both men and women in this, the late 20th century, is a tall, well balanced, naturally curved, slender and physically fit form. Broad shoulders, slim hips and long legs are emphasised. Fashions are quite fitted and body-revealing, and there is strong emphasis on weight control.

Fashion models set the standard for the ideal figure. Because the camera makes them look up to five kilos heavier than they really are, and because the tall, slender figure makes the best clothes-hanger, models are taller and thinner than the average woman. They also have wide shoulders and slim hips, to allow garments to sit and drape well over a slender body.

According to the Australian Bureau of Statistics, from the 1989–90 National Health Survey, the average weight and height for Australian women over the age of 18 years, was 63 kilos and 163 centimetres (5' 4"). The 'short' figure is considered to be around 148 centimetres (4' 10"), and the 'tall' figure 170 centimetres (5' 7") and over.

Although agencies employ models who do not meet the following measurements, most specify the ideal build for a female model as 178 centimetres (5' 10") in height with the minimum being 173 centimetres (5' 8"), 89 centimetre (35") bust, 64 centimetre (25") waist and 89 centimetre (35") hips. From these measurements for the ideal female figure, it can be seen that the bust and hips measure the same, and the waist is approximately 25 centimetres (10") smaller. Any major variations from this indicate one of the figure types discussed later in the chapter.

The woman with a perfectly proportioned figure is the easiest body type to dress because she can wear almost all styles, including the more extreme fashions. Being balanced, both top and bottom are the same size. Weight gains or losses are distributed evenly so that the body still retains that balance.

A figure fault is a feature which deviates from our accepted standard of beauty at any point in time. Most people have at least one aspect which they consider to be a fault. Diet, exercise and correct posture can help modify the figure, but as we have already discussed, not a lot can be done about the basic body shape.

# ILLUSION DRESSING

When nature neglects to supply the right combination of body parts to produce a well proportioned figure, clothing can be used to correct the balance by drawing attention to assets and by camouflaging figure faults. This is done by adjusting the relative lengths and widths of the clothing being worn. Then, by using shape, line, colour, proportion and texture which are in slight contrast to the figure, the designer can further neutralise less-than-perfect features (Fig. 15.3).

There are four basic ways to balance out-of-proportion figures (Fig. 15.3(a)).

1. Redesign the problem area. For example, a dark skirt with vertical panel lines will create the illusion of a slimmer line for heavy hips.

2. Build up a too-small part so as to balance a normal or too-large part. For example, shoulder pads raise and widen thin, sloping shoulders to create a better balance with a heavier lower half.

3. Draw attention away from a figure fault by accentuating a good point. For example, a large collar which frames the face draws the eye up and away from heavy hips.

4. Conceal the figure fault. Large hips and legs are not as conspicuous under a full, long skirt as they are under a short, tight skirt.

Refer to Chapters 4, 5 and 6 for further information on using the Elements and Principles of Design to correct figure problems.

# FIGURE TYPES

There are seven basic body types — tall and thin, tall and heavy, short and thin, short and heavy, top heavy, bottom heavy, and thick waisted. The following charts

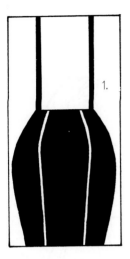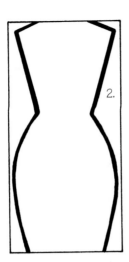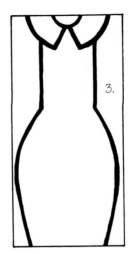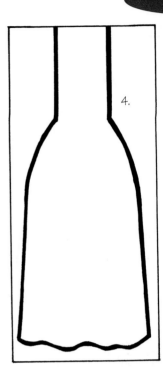

▲ 15.3(a) *Balancing out-of-proportion figures; for example, a bottom-heavy figure*

▼ 15.3(b) *Correcting figure faults with illusion dressing.*

(Figs. 15.4–15.10) analyse and provide specific information for these figure types, with further information given on lesser faults for fine tuning. If you are a combination figure, select the most appropriate guidelines for your overall figure type and modify them to correct the lesser problem areas.

It is important to remember that these are generalisations only, based on the visual appearance of the wearer. The two other important considerations which greatly affect a person's look are their personal colouring and their personality. A small, thin person with a boisterous personality and dark colouring may have the vitality to wear and not be over-powered by a bold print. On the other hand, a tall, thin person who should be able to wear bold colours and prints may look overwhelmed if they are fair in colouring and have a quiet personality.

| TO LENGTHEN AND NARROW | TO SHORTEN AND WIDEN |
|---|---|
| Straight silhouettes | Wide silhouettes |
| Long vertical lines | Horizontal lines |
| Lead eye up and in | Lead eye down and out |
| Vertical darts and seams | Gathers, pleats, yokes, wide collars |
| Smooth, flat textures | Bulky, heavy textures |
| Small, subtle prints | Large, bold prints |
| Single colour outfits | Contrasting colours |
| Cool, dull, dark colours | Warm, light, bright colours |
| Simplicity, no clutter | Plenty of detailing |
| Straight, slim sleeves | Full sleeves |
| Slim pants and skirts | Wide pants and skirts |
| Narrow, matching belt | Wide, contrasting belt |
| Body-skimming fit | Tight fit, blouson, layering |
| High heels | Flat heels |

| TO ATTRACT ATTENTION | TO DIVERT ATTENTION |
|---|---|
| Converging lines | Non-converging lines |
| Intricate structure | Minimal and simple structure |
| Applied decoration | No decoration |
| Warm, light and bright colours | Cool, dark and dull colours |
| Bright, bold, shiny textures | Flat, dull, matt textures |
| Large, busy prints | Plain colours or small, quiet prints |
| Clingy fabrics | Soft, non-clinging fabrics |
| Tight fit | Loose fit |

THE FASHION DESIGN MANUAL

*15.4 Tall and thin*

## FIGURE TYPE: TALL AND THIN

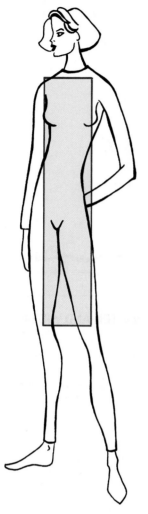

Closest to the ideal figure, this person can wear most styles, including exaggerated and high fashion garments.

If the figure is too thin, tall, angular or bony, minimise the appearance of height with horizontal lines and create the illusion of curves through the use of gentle fullness in pleats, tucks, soft frills, gathers and drapes.

Aim for a feminine look rather than severely cut or masculine, tailored garments. Accentuate curves by cinching the waist or hips with ties, belts, wide waistbands and hip yokes. Use softly rounded design lines to create the illusion of curves.

Layer various lengths in a shirt, vest and jacket, for example, to add bulk and fullness. Soften sharp shoulders, elbows, hips and knees through the use of soft fabrics. Avoid tightly fitted or clingy garments.

## AVOID

Vertical seams, sharp angles and points
Wide or low cut necklines or halter necks
Anything long, narrow, tapered or tight fitting
Sleeveless garments
Severe tailoring
Square or exaggerated shoulders
Short skirts, short trousers
Straight-through dresses
Solid colours
Small, dainty, fussy patterns
Clingy fabrics
Very high heels

## AIM FOR

| | |
|---|---|
| Tops: | Full; blouson; cinched waist; lots of detailing; high-cut necks; round necks; large collars |
| Sleeves: | Long and full, lots of detail; three-quarter or elbow length if not full |
| Jackets: | Rounded, raglan shoulders; double-breasted; waist length or longer |
| Skirts: | Long; full; tiered; A-line; bell silhouette; peplums |
| Trousers: | Wide; straight legs; flares; cuffs |
| Dresses: | Waisted; belted; draped; wide front panels |
| Coats: | Tunics; two-piece outfits; double breasted; details at hips and wrists |
| Colours: | Bright, light, warm, rich, contrasting |
| Patterns: | Big, bold prints; rounded motifs; plaids; tweeds; horizontal stripes |
| Textures: | Crisp; bulky; shiny; pile; nubby |
| Trims: | Rounded collars, cuffs, buttons, pockets |
| Accessories: | Large jewellery; wide belts; flat or low-heeled shoes with square or round toes; boots; scarves; bows; big squashy handbags; wide-brimmed hats or soft berets; elbow-length gloves; full hairstyle to balance head size |

*15.5 Tall and heavy*

| FIGURE TYPE: TALL AND HEAVY | AVOID | AIM FOR |
|---|---|---|

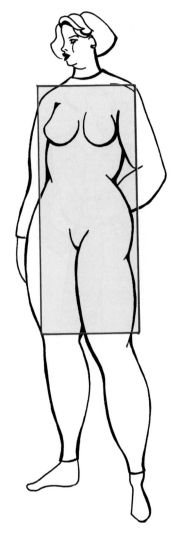  

This figure can look very dignified and powerful but, at times, overpowering.

Simplicity and subtlety is the key to creating a neat, clean look which slims without adding extra height. Use simple lines, minimal decoration and easy fitting garments which neither cling nor add fullness. Diagonal and asymmetrical lines and soft verticals will streamline and slenderise, whilst angular shapes will counteract the rounded forms of the body.

Anything fussy or delicate
Anything too tight or too bulky
Gathers; frills
Blousons; cropped tops; overblouses
Round pockets, collars or necklines
Sleeveless garments; cap or tight sleeves
Full gathered or very straight skirts
Horizontal lines; bold verticals; tent or princess lines
Loud, bold, bright colours and patterns
Heavy, stiff or clingy fabrics
Wide belts

| | |
|---|---|
| Tops: | 'V' necklines; pointed collars; neck detailing |
| Sleeves: | Set-in sleeves |
| Jackets: | Moderate length |
| Skirts: | A-line; pleats; centre pleat |
| Trousers: | Straight or slight flare; classic; solid colour |
| Dresses: | Full length; self belt; 'T', 'Y' and '↑' design lines |
| Coats: | Single breasted |
| Colours: | Single colours; subdued; cool, dark, dull |
| Patterns: | Subtle; muted |
| Textures: | Flat; firm; matt |
| Accessories: | Moderately sized belts, jewellery, handbags; clean, straight lines; medium height shoes |

THE FASHION DESIGN MANUAL

*15.6 Short and thin*

| FIGURE TYPE: SHORT AND THIN | AVOID | AIM FOR |
|---|---|---|

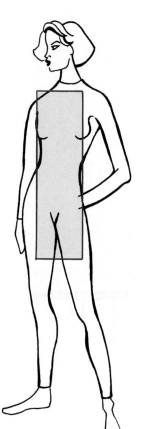

Being short and thin allows this type of figure to wear a variety of styles, as long as they do not overpower the delicate figure beneath. To achieve a soft, uncluttered look, use subtle design details and trims.

Because both height and width are required, verticals and soft horizontal lines may be used effectively, provided that the balance of the figure is correct; that is, neither too wide nor too tall. Diagonals also work well.

Avoid creating too much bulk, although a little fullness is necessary to fill out the figure. Tucks, gathers and shirring work well in semi-fitted or loose fitting garments.

Wide horizontals, including belts
Anything large, bold, bulky
Severe or exaggerated lines
Very wide shoulders
Layering
Anything tight fitting or clinging
Very long or pencil slim skirts
Long jackets
Capes; tent silhouettes
Strongly contrasting colours
Bold patterns
Heavy, bulky textures
Large, chunky jewellery and accessories

| | |
|---|---|
| Tops: | Blouson; round collars and necks; short 'V' neck |
| Jackets: | Soft tailoring; business suits; hip length; bolero; cropped |
| Skirts: | Pleated; full; flared; draped; bell; moderate length |
| Trousers: | All styles |
| Dresses: | Empire waist; shirtmaker; princess line |
| Coats: | 'T', 'Y' and '↑' design lines |
| Colours: | Bright; light; single colour |
| Patterns: | Small, subtle |
| Textures: | Shiny; firm; soft; fluid; smooth |
| Trims: | Delicate |
| Accessories: | Small, neat |

15.7 *Short and heavy*

| FIGURE TYPE: SHORT AND HEAVY | AVOID | AIM FOR |
|---|---|---|

Short, heavy people need to create the illusion of height with a long, narrow line. Clean, simple and strong lines are most flattering.

    Use straight, sharp lines to counteract rounded forms and flatten curves and bulges. Vertical lines are best, with horizontals to be avoided at all times. Diagonals and asymmetric lines are also flattering.

    Avoid anything which visually chops up the figure. Use single-colour outfits to create a longer line, and accessories such as scarves and jewellery to create interest. Beltless styles are best, or use narrow, half- or self-belts

**AVOID**

Horizontals
Rounded design lines
Anything chunky, heavy, bulky, sloppy, fussy
Anything tight, clingy, shiny, full, crisp
Princess line; tent silhouette
Gathers; frills; blousing
High necklines; turtlenecks
Yokes; wide panels
Bi-coloured or two-piece garments
Long skirts or jackets
Sleeveless garments
Double breasted styles
Warm, light, bright colours; strong contrasts; colour blocking
Large, bold prints
Heavy shoes; boots; wide belts

**AIM FOR**

| | |
|---|---|
| Tops: | 'V', 'U' necklines; open necks; collarless; low backs |
| Sleeves: | Long; straight; set-in |
| Jackets: | Finish just below widest point of hips |
| Skirts: | A-line; centre pleat; about knee-length |
| Trousers: | Narrow; straight leg; solid colour |
| Dresses: | Empire; A-line; sheath; chemise |
| Coats: | 'Y' design lines |
| Colours: | Single colour outfits; dark; dull; cool; subdued |
| Patterns: | Subtle, with vertical direction |
| Textures: | Matt; fine; firm |
| Accessories: | Medium or thin belts in matching colours; stockings and shoes colour related; medium heels; handbags, jewellery |

THE FASHION DESIGN MANUAL

15.8 Top heavy

## FIGURE TYPE: TOP HEAVY

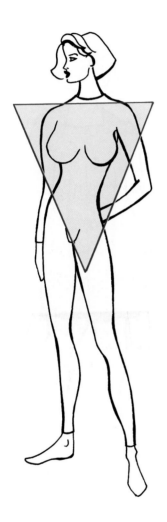

This figure has a large upper body in relation to the rest, usually due to a full bust. Use subtle colours and long vertical lines on top to down-play that part of the body. Avoid any detailingwhich draws attention to the upper part, or divert attention by using design detailing to draw the eye to the lower half of the body. A dark coloured top and light or bright bottom will helpcorrect the balance.

## AVOID

| Top: | Horizontal lines |
| --- | --- |
| | Yoke; gathers; tucks; trimmings |
| | Clingy, shiny, stiff fabrics |
| | Empire line |
| | High necklines; fussy or large collars |
| | Pockets; bows |
| | Tight fitting or short tops |
| | Short full sleeves |
| | |
| Bottom: | Tight skirt or pants |
| | Wide belts |

## AIM FOR

| Top: | Dull, dark, plain fabrics |
| --- | --- |
| | Smooth, soft textures |
| | Slim line, easy fitting shirts and jackets |
| | Shallow 'V' necklines; open collars with lapels |
| | Slim sleeves |
| | Vertical seams and darts |
| | A-line, shift and shirtwaist dresses |
| | |
| Bottom: | Light, bright, patterned fabrics |
| | Low waistline; hipline interest |
| | Flared or pleated pants |
| | Gathers; pleats |

| FIGURE TYPE: BOTTOM HEAVY | AVOID | AIM FOR |
|---|---|---|

This is a common figure type for women and features hips and thighs which are broad in comparison to the rest of the body.

    Being bottom heavy makes the figure look shorter because the width is close to the ground, so the emphasis here should be towards the top half and away from the lower half. A light, bright top and dark or dull bottom works well.

    Draw the eye to the face and neck and balance the figure with attractive collars, wide shoulders, yokes, gathers and decorative treatments. Trousers tend to make the hips look wider than skirts.

*Bottom:*    Tight fitting or very loose pants or skirts
                Horizontals at the hips or waist (e.g. shirt hems)
                Big pockets, yokes or trims
                Shiny or clingy fabrics
                Hipsters; flares

*Top:*    Long sleeves with big cuffs
                Tight, skimpy tops

*Bottom:*    Vertical lines
                Straight leg pants
                Flared skirts; A-line
                Matching belt
                Smooth, firm fabrics
                Solid colour or subtle print

*Top:*    Gathered sleeves tapering at wrist
                Shoulder pads
                Jackets end at hips or cover widest point
                Gathers; fullness
                Light, bright prints and colours
                Horizontals
                Neckline or collar interest

*15.10 Thick waisted*

| FIGURE TYPE: THICK WAISTED | AVOID | AIM FOR |
|---|---|---|

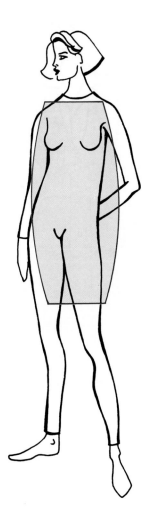

The waistline lacks definition when the waist measurement is similar to the shoulders and hips. Tubular silhouettes which hang from the shoulders to the hem are best for this figure. Avoid styles which are waisted or cling at the waist and which may add bulk or reveal bulges.

The best lines are verticals which lead the eye away from the middle and upwards to the face.

Horizontals
Clingy or bulky garments and textures
Wide, tight belts and waistlines
Trims or contrasts at the waist

Easy fitting garments; overblouses; empire lines; tunics
Dropped waist; hipsters
Neckline interest
Flared trousers and skirts; A-line
Smooth, firm, lightweight fabrics
Solid colours or subtle prints

# MORE HINTS FOR MINOR FIGURE PROBLEMS

## Long waist

If you are long-waisted, the length from waist to armpits is longer than the length from waist to hip/crotch. Opt for empire style or high-waisted dresses. Stockings and shoes that colour-match the skirt will elongate the legs. Wide belts, short jackets, vests, shifts and long, full skirts are suitable for this figure type.

## Short waist

Short-waisted is when the waist-to-armpit length is shorter than the waist-to-hip/crotch length. This makes the body look short and the legs too long. Princess line garments, beltless styles, dropped waistlines, hipster pants and low-slung belts create the illusion of more body length and shorter legs. A plain bodice and textured or patterned skirt makes the upper part seem relatively longer.

## Narrow shoulders

Extended or padded shoulders add width to narrow shoulders, as do cap or puff sleeves. Wide lapels, yokes, wide necklines, small collars, bateau necks and halter necks are also suitable.

## Broad/square shoulders

These make the figure look taller because the width is high on the body. Halter necks, narrow lapels, tent silhouettes and full skirts will correct this fault. Raglan sleeve seams give a downward slant which softens square shoulders, as do set-in or unmounted sleeves.

## Sloping shoulders

A V-line at the top of a vertical line gives shoulders a lift. Yokes, set-in sleeves and shoulder pads are other correctional devices.

## Long neck

Turtlenecks, high collars, scarves, ascots, cowls, ruffles, bows, and scarves at the neckline will modify this feature.

## Short neck

Uncluttered necklines, V- or U-necklines, long rope necklaces and open collars should be used in this instance.

## Flat chested

Bodice interest through gathers, shirring, tucks, yokes, cowls, bibs, pockets, scarves, bows and buttons will add fullness to this figure, as do vests, boleros and empire waistlines. Crisp fabrics are best.

## Straight hips

Add curves with pleated and gathered skirts, bold and bright pants and skirts. Avoid straight skirts.

## CHAPTER 16

# FITTING

# INTRODUCTION

The term 'fit' refers to the tightness, looseness and shape of clothing in relation to the person who is wearing it. A well-fitted garment is the right size and does not pull tightly or sag loosely when worn.

The importance of fit cannot be overstated. The designer checks every new style for the fit, and fashion retailers should know about fit to be able to correctly advise their customers. Fit determines the attractiveness, the appearance of quality, and the physical comfort of the garment. All of these factors influence the number of sales and the frequency with which a garment is worn or sits idle in the customer's wardrobe.

When talking about fit in this chapter, we are discussing classic styles and conventional standards of fit. Naturally, the guidelines as to what constitutes good or bad fit vary according to fashion trends, the individual design of every garment and personal taste.

If you require technical information on altering a pattern to achieve perfect fit, you will find the procedure explained in most patternmaking books.

# FITTING A GARMENT

The fitting of a garment is as much a part of the design process as the creation of the original design on paper. Once the first sample has been made up, it is fitted onto a model to confirm that the design is flattering and that the fit is correct. It is this fine-tuning of the original idea by the designer that determines the final look. Whether to take a little out or to add a little here or there can mean the difference between an average garment and an outstanding garment.

Fit depends on three factors — the design, the fabrics used, and the figure beneath the garment.

## THE DESIGN

The dimensions of a garment are determined by the prevailing fashion silhouette. By looking at past decades, you can see how fashions evolved from the tiny mini-skirts and skinny-rib tops of the 60s to the oversized non-fit of the Japanese designers in the early 1980s, to the clinging and revealing leggings and body-suits of the late 1980s.

The looseness or fullness a designer introduces into a garment in order to achieve the desired fashion look is known as *design ease*. A designer may intentionally make a garment oversized, or it may be loose, semi-fitted, fitted or a combination of these.

A *fitted* garment is quite tight and is shaped with seams and darts to closely follow the lines of the body. A *semi-fitted* garment still follows the shape of the body but may have tucks or gathers to introduce a little fullness. A *loose* garment is unfitted and, with gathers, tucks, pleats or inserts added for extra fullness, camouflages the body shape underneath. An *oversized* garment is a very large fit which is not sized or shaped to fit any particular figure and is often labelled as 'one-size-fits-all' (Fig. 16.1).

Clothing which is meant to be loose looks wrong if worn too tight, and clothing which is meant to be fitted looks too large if worn loose. Very snug fitting garments like those worn in the 1950s can be just as comfortable as looser

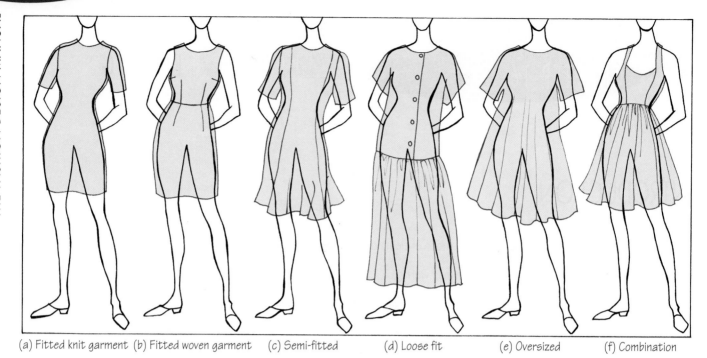

(a) Fitted knit garment  (b) Fitted woven garment  (c) Semi-fitted  (d) Loose fit  (e) Oversized  (f) Combination

▲ 16.1 (a) Knit fabrics with a lot of stretch require only shaped side-seams to give a tight, body-hugging fit.
(b) Woven fabrics require shaped seams and darts for a garment which fits well and shows the natural contours of the body.
(c) A softer line is created with panels, gathers or tucks which add fullness to a gently fitted garment.
(d) Bodily contours are concealed underneath soft, full, unfitted garments.
(e) Often made in knit fabrics, these garments are usually shapeless and designed to fit all shapes and sizes.
(f) Visual interest and figure flattery are created when the fit of a garment is close in some parts and loose in others.

◀ 16.2 Sufficient wearing ease must be allowed in all garments so that there is adequate comfort and room for movement.

styles, provided the snugness is even all over and the seams are placed so that they follow the natural body joints.

Regardless of the fashion, most garments are cut with *wearing ease* which should not be confused with design ease. Wearing ease is extra width over and above the actual body measurement which is added to a garment to provide comfort and allow movement (Fig. 16.2).

Fitted garments in woven fabrics require wearing ease, but knit fabrics may not because the stretch in the fabric permits mobility. Strapless garments require less wearing ease for a tighter fit, and larger figures look better in garments with more wearing ease, so that the garment doesn't wrinkle, gape or cut into the body.

Minimum wearing ease in a fitted garment is approximately 2.5 centimetres at the waistline (to allow for large lunches!), 5 centimetres over the hips to allow for sitting, 7.5 centimetres at the bust and 3.5 centimetres over the upper arm for arm and torso movement.

The amount of wearing ease designed into clothing is influenced by the intended use of the garment. Casual wear and sportswear require maximum movement allowance for athletic activity and comfortable relaxation and are therefore cut with more ease than other garments. Lingerie is designed to go under other clothing, so is cut close to the body with the minimum of ease, while outerwear, jackets and overcoats are cut with plenty of room to go over thick pullovers and other layers of clothing.

## THE FABRIC

The weight and texture of a fabric determines its performance while being worn and the types of silhouette for which it is suitable. Crisp fabrics such as taffeta stand away from the figure and look better if cut with some fullness to allow the silhouette to take shape. Flimsy fabrics such as voile also look better when generously cut because of their delicacy and their tendency to slip or tear at the seams if placed under strain due to tight fit.

Bulky or pile fabrics have a thickness when made up which makes them uncomfortable to wear if fitted too close to the body. The clinging nature of fabrics such as jersey or chiffon means that they sit closer to the body and are more revealing even if they are loose fitting. However, stretch fabrics such as Lycra® are intended for the closest of fit while still permitting maximum movement and comfort.

Lined garments wear and fit better than unlined garments. The soft, slippery texture of lining feels smooth against the skin, prevents the outer fabric stretching in areas which receive strain and does not grab on garments worn underneath. The fit of lined garments is smoother, movement is easier and putting on and taking off is more comfortable for the wearer.

## THE FIGURE

Even if the construction of a garment is perfect, badly fitting clothing may be caused by bad posture, an asymmetrical body, or by proportions or contours which differ from the ideal figure.

The way a person likes clothing to fit is a matter of personal preference. Some people like a lot of wearing ease, while others feel more comfortable in clothing which fits closely. However, clothing always affects the appearance of the body shape, especially with very tight or very loose garments. Drag lines, straining fabric, wrinkles and sagging folds can draw attention to figure faults and exaggerate less-than-perfect features.

Clothes which are too tight, especially on heavy people, make them look even heavier, as though they have outgrown their clothes. The opposite applies to baggy clothing on short, thin people, who can look smothered, as though they have shrunk or the clothes have stretched.

Although fashion retailers can assist their customers in selecting garments which fit well, they are not usually able to make alterations for individual requirements. Equally, commercial designers for the mass market cannot cater for the specific requirements of individual body types due to the endless variety they would have to try to accommodate. Mass produced apparel is constructed according to average measurements which the experienced designer has developed and knows will suit most people in a specific market sector.

*Standards Australia* publishes Size Coding Schemes for women's, men's and children's clothing. These are tables of anthropometric measurements which give the dimensions of various body types and were first collated in 1959 for use by Australian manufacturers as a guide for sizing garments to fit a large proportion of the Australian population. It is not compulsory to adhere to these standards. Copies of these measurement tables are available from the Standards Association of Australia.

Couturiers or designers who do made-to-measure garments for private clients are in an ideal position to design and fit styles to suit particular tastes, personalities, colouring and figure types of individuals. Unfortunately, this exclusive approach to clothing proves to be an expense not everyone can afford.

# WHAT IS GOOD FIT?

When a garment is being worn, the fabric interacts with the body in two ways — it hangs and it fits into the contours of the figure. The way it hangs is known as the *balance*, and the way it moulds against the body is known as the *set*.

## BALANCE

A balanced garment hangs or sits equally on each side of the figure and the vertical seams are perpendicular to the ground when viewed from the front, back or sides (Fig. 16.3). Bodices and skirts should be the same length front and back and level with the ground. Skirts and trousers should hang evenly on either side of the legs, and sleeves should sit equally on the front and the back of the arms.

Correct grain is essential for good balance. If the garment is slightly off grain it will not hang properly and may twist or sag after some wear. The lengthwise grain at a garment's centre front and centre back should be perpendicular to the floor and the crosswise grain over the chest, back and hip should lie parallel to the floor. The centre front grain in a bias cut garment should lie at true 45 degrees. See Chapter 17 for more information on grain.

Straight cut clothing is generally designed to hang in cylinders from the shoulders or the waist. If fitted onto the body, a garment should sit smoothly and evenly. Garments such as blouses, dresses or jackets, which are suspended from the shoulders, fit the body to the fullest part of the bust in front and shoulder-blade at back, then drape from

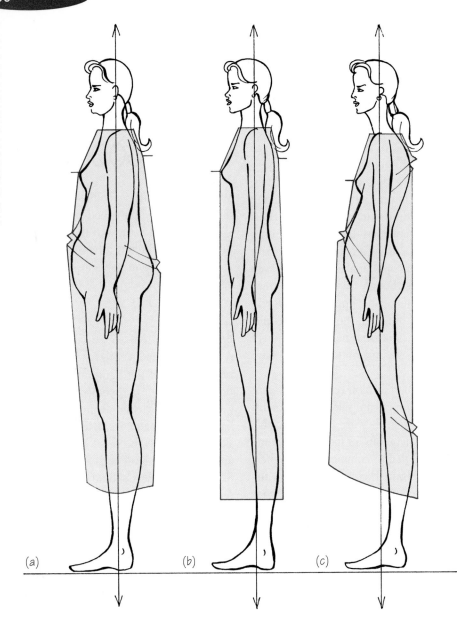

(a)  (b)  (c)

16.3 *Although balance should be perfect on non-perfect figures, it is often distorted when the garment rests or drags on a protruding part of the body.*
*(a) The bottom-heavy figure distorts the garment over the protruding tummy and buttocks.*
*(b) The well-balanced garment rests on the bust and shoulder-blades, and lightly skims over buttocks.*
*(c) The round-shouldered figure distorts the garment over protruding shoulders, tummy and calves.*

those points. The balance will be distorted by any area, for example the abdomen or buttocks, which protrudes beyond those high points because the garment will rest or drag on that fuller part of the body.

Garments designed to hang from the waist, such as skirts and trousers, are usually fitted to the fullest part of the stomach in front and the buttocks behind and will rest on any part of the body, for example the thighs or calves, which are more prominent than either of those two points.

## SET

Perfect set is when the fabric fits the body curves and hollows smoothly and without creases (Fig. 16.4). Creases, wrinkles or tension lines caused by bad fitting act like arrows pointing to a problem area and they should not be confused with the folds or drape lines caused by gathers and fullness which are an intended part of the design.

A garment which is too tight produces tight horizontal creases and can cause the garment to ride up on the body. Too much looseness results in loose vertical folds. Loose horizontals are caused by too much length and tight verticals and diagonals result from insufficient length and/or width.

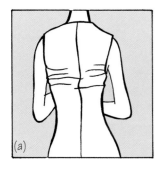
(a)

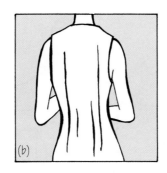
(b)

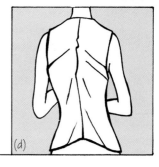
(c)

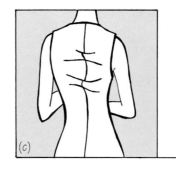
(d)

(e)

(f)

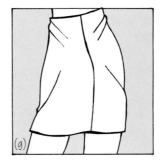
(g)

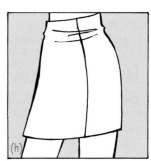
(h)

*16.4 The set of a garment may be perfect on one figure and faulty on another. Common faults are:*

*(a) Too tight. A broad shouldered or large busted figure may produce horizontal creases, showing that the garment fits too tightly.*

*(b) Too loose. Loose vertical folds indicate that the garment is too big across the shoulders and waist.*

*(c) Too long. Wrinkles across the shoulder-blades may be seen on very erect figures, indicating that the garment is too long in the body.*

*(d) Too short. This fault is often seen on round-shouldered figures, and is indicated by diagonal folds spreading out from the centre. It may also result in the hemline of the garment being pulled up at the centre.*

*(e) Too short. Tight diagonal lines pointing to the crotch indicate that the crotch seams are too short. This fault may be seen on a long-waisted figure.*

*(f) Too long. Loose, horizontal folds below the buttocks indicate that the pants are too long through the back body and thigh. This may be seen on short figures.*

*(g) Too tight. A prominent backside or tummy may produce diagonal lines where the garment is too tight.*

*(h) Too long. A hollow-backed or short-waisted figure may develop loose horizontal folds just below the back waist, where the garment does not fit the curve of the figure.*

## FITTING CHECK-LIST

The only way to check the fit of a garment is to try it on and move around in it, to see how it sits on the body when standing, sitting and in action. Study the front, back and side views. Do what you would normally do while wearing the garment: walk, sit, move, bend over, reach, bend and lift your arms (Fig. 16.5).

Clothes that fit properly, unless the style dictates otherwise, have the following features.

- Attractive appearance
- Comfort
- Allow freedom of movement without strain
- Follow the contours and joints of the body
- Are balanced
- Are cut on true grain
- Sit smoothly without grabbing, wrinkling or pulling over shoulders, bust, stomach, waist or hips
- Fastenings (zippers, buttons) and pocket openings do not gape or strain
- Curved edges (necklines and armholes) are smooth and continuous, follow the lines of the body and do not gape or cut into the flesh
- Vertical seams are perpendicular to the ground
- Horizontal seams are parallel to the ground (or dip slightly lower at the back waist as is more flattering)
- Hem is equidistant from the floor on all sides
- The neckline and shoulder seams sit straight on the shoulders and do not slip forward or back
- The shoulder pads and armholes are not too far in or out on the shoulder
- The armhole is deep enough for comfort, but not so deep that the hemline of the garment pulls up when the arm is raised
- There is enough width across the upper back to permit forward movement; for example, when driving a car or leaning the arms on a table
- Sleeve lengths are correct. Blouse sleeves should reach the wrist bone when the arm is bent, unless designed to accommodate a cuff or to be worn longer
- Darts point towards the fullest part of the figure, for example the bust point, and gently taper off a short distance from that point
- Shirts are long enough to stay tucked in

- The trouser crotch length is neither too short nor too long
- Front and back trouser creases hang in straight lines
- Coats and jackets are large enough to accommodate garments worn underneath.

*16.5 Checking the fit in a classically styled outfit. Fit requirements change according to the garment styling and amount of ease.*

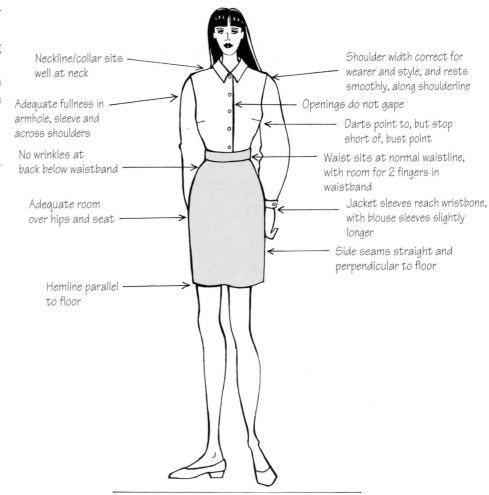

Neckline/collar sits well at neck

Adequate fullness in armhole, sleeve and across shoulders

No wrinkles at back below waistband

Adequate room over hips and seat

Hemline parallel to floor

Shoulder width correct for wearer and style, and rests smoothly, along shoulderline

Openings do not gape

Darts point to, but stop short of, bust point

Waist sits at normal waistline, with room for 2 fingers in waistband

Jacket sleeves reach wristbone, with blouse sleeves slightly longer

Side seams straight and perpendicular to floor

CHAPTER 17

# INTRODUCTION

This chapter covers the fundamentals of fabrics and the ways in which a designer uses them. The science or technology of textiles is a vast field and, for further information on fibres, construction, dyeing and finishing, you should consult specialised text books available on the subject.

The designer needs to be familiar with the characteristics of fibres and fibre blends to understand how they will perform during manufacture, when used in different styles and silhouettes, and when worn and laundered by the consumer. The designer must also identify and keep abreast of trends because fibres and textures move through fashion cycles just as silhouettes and colours do, and are influenced by changes in technology, lifestyle and consumer values. The process of selecting fabrics has already been covered briefly in Chapter 7.

# WHAT ARE TEXTILES?

The term 'textile' refers to any material which has been woven, knitted, bonded, felted, fused or otherwise manufactured, and may be used for a wide variety of purposes in fields as diverse as industry, sport and building.

A *fabric* is any textile from which garments are made. Fabrics are the raw materials of fashion, and the fabrication of a garment can improve a poor design or ruin a good design.

The appearance, feel and end use of a fabric is determined by the fibre content, the yarn structure, the fabric construction and the fabric finish.

# FIBRES

Fibres are raw threads or filaments which are made into fabric. Fibres are divided into three broad categories according to their origin.

## 1. NATURAL FIBRES

Natural fibres derive from natural sources. Cotton, linen, flax, jute and hemp are plant or *cellulosic* fibres. Wool, angora, mohair, cashmere and silk are animal or *protein* fibres.

Cotton, wool and linen have relatively short fibres, called *staples*, which range from about 2 centimetres to 50 centi-

metres in length. The silk moth larva produces silk in long strands known as *filaments*, which range from 300 to 600 metres in length. These filaments are cut to the right length for spinning into yarn.

Natural fibres often have irregularities known as *slubbing* which enhance the beauty of the fabric. A slub is a thickening or lump in the yarn.

## 2. MANUFACTURED FIBRES

Manufactured fibres, as the name suggests, include all fibres which do not occur naturally. They are produced as a chemical solution and extruded through a die with tiny holes known as spinnerets

COTTON AUSTRALIA

COTTON BLEND AUSTRALIA

The Woolmark
PURE NEW WOOL

The Woolblendmark
WOOL RICH BLEND

*17.1 The Australian Cottonmark and Cottonblend mark are registered trade marks which are controlled by the Australian Cotton Foundation. These marks help consumers recognise quality Australian cotton products. The Cottonmark is used with quality goods which are manufactured wholly of cotton, and the Cottonblend mark is used with quality goods which have a minimum cotton content of 50 per cent. The Woolmark and Woolblendmark are registered trade marks of the International Wool Secretariat and indicate high quality woollen products. The Woolmark is an assurance by the manufacturer that a product is made of pure new wool and the Woolblendmark is an assurance that a garment comprises a minimum new wool content of 60 per cent.*

*17.2 The beauty, comfort and versatility of wool make it a perennial fashion favourite. (Photograph courtesy of the International Wool Secretariat, Australia Branch.)*

to create long thread-like filaments which are then spun. The solution may have colour added before being extruded. This is known as solution dyeing and gives a high degree of colour-fastness (Fig. 17.3).

The two sources of manufactured fibres are:

**(a) Regenerated cellulose fibres**

Rayon, acetate and viscose are made from plant cellulose, usually wood pulp or cotton waste, and are blended with a chemical solution

**(b) Synthetic fibres**

These are manufactured entirely from chemicals such as acetylene, acetic acid, hydrogen cyanide, petroleum, coal and

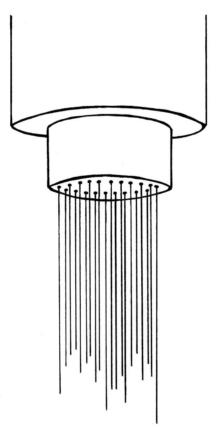

*17.3 Manufactured fibres are created in different shapes — round, octagonal, three-sided, according to the shape of the extrusion holes in the spinneret.*

*17.4 Manufactured elastomeric fibres are used in many garments such as lingerie and swimwear, which require stretch for comfort or close fit. (Photograph courtesy of Berlei.)*

oil. Nylon, polyester, microfibre, polyurethane, elastomer, acrylic and polyvinyl chloride (PVC) are synthetic.

Manufactured fibres are *thermoplastic*; that is, they become pliant when heated and retain the shape they are set in once they have cooled. This enables them to be permanently crinkled, pressed or pleated.

## 3. INORGANIC FIBRES

Inorganic fibres are made from glass, minerals and metals, and include fibreglass, asbestos and metallic yarns. Fibreglass is only suitable for industrial use, and clothing use for asbestos is limited to fire-proof suits. Although aluminium coated with polyester or cellulose film is the most commonly used metal for clothing and accessories, pure gold and silver are also occasionally used. Lamé, brocades and embroidery use metallic fibres.

| APPAREL FIBRES AND SOURCES | FIBRE PROPERTIES<br>Advantages | Disadvantages | FABRICS AND USES |
|---|---|---|---|
| **Natural fibres** | | | |
| Cotton: seed bolls of cotton plant | Strong, durable<br>Absorbent, cool<br>Soft or crisp handle<br>Comfortable<br>Dyes and prints well<br>Withstands high heat<br>Versatile<br>No static<br>Washes well<br>Not expensive | Poor drape<br>Wrinkles unless treated or blended<br>Weakened by sun, mildew, and perspiration<br>Shrinks<br>Burns easily<br>Inelastic | Versatile, trans-seasonal fabrics in knits and wovens. In summer, light fabrics for smart casual, semi-dressy and workwear. In winter soft, bulky cottons for warmth and comfort.<br><br>Underwear, hosiery, jeans, sportswear, workwear, outerwear, shirts/blouses, dresses, skirts, trousers.<br><br>Batiste, calico, cheese cloth, chiffon, chintz, corduroy, damask, denim, drill, flannelette, gabardine, gingham, knits, lawn, moleskin, muslin, organdie, percale, pique, poplin, sateen, seersucker, terry towelling, ticking, velvet, voile. |
| Linen: fibrous stalks of flax plant | Tough, durable<br>Absorbent, cool<br>Medium to hard handle<br>Lustrous, smooth<br>Crisp, comfortable<br>Lint free<br>Withstands high heat | Poor drape<br>Wrinkles easily and retains wrinkles<br>Affected by mildew and perspiration<br>Poor dyeing<br>May shrink or stretch<br>Pressing can cause shine<br>Burns easily<br>Best if drycleaned<br>Can be expensive | Light to heavy weight linens are crisp and smart for spring and summer skirts blouses, dresses, suits.<br><br>Also used for handkerchiefs and household items. |
| Wool: fleece of sheep | Durable, light<br>Very absorbent<br>Soft to medium handle<br>Easy to tailor<br>Very good drape<br>Warm in winter, cool in summer<br>Comfortable<br>Dyes well<br>Resilient<br>Resists wrinkles<br>No static<br>Flame resistant<br>Re-useable | Weak when wet<br>Shrinks/mats with heat, moisture and agitation<br>Pills<br>Can be scratchy<br>Attacked by moths<br>Damaged by bleach and perspiration<br>Best if drycleaned | Versatile, trans-seasonal knitted and woven fabrics.<br><br>Outerwear, suitings, skirts, dresses, coats, jackets, knitwear, hosiery, underwear.<br><br>Barathea, bouclé, challis, crêpe, faille, felt, flannel, gabardine, jersey, serge, tartan, tweed, twill, velour, voile, woollen, worsted. |
| Silk: silk worm cocoons | Very strong/durable<br>Absorbent<br>Medium to soft handle<br>Lustrous, smooth<br>Drapes well, light<br>Comfortable<br>Wrinkle resistant<br>Moth/soil resistant<br>Dyes well<br>Flame resistant | Holds body heat<br>Weakened by sun, perspiration and soap<br>Attacked by insects and silverfish<br>Best if drycleaned<br>Shows water marks<br>Yellows with age<br>Expensive | A luxurious fabric, silk is used in evening wear, bridal wear, lingerie, blouses/shirts,. and dresses, suits, scarves and neckties.<br><br>Brocade, chiffon, crêpe-de-chine, dupion, faille, georgette, grosgrain, habutae, organdza, ottoman, pongee satin, shantung, shot silk, taffeta, tussore, velvet. |
| **Manufactured fibres** | | | |
| Viscose/Rayon: wood pulp cellulose | Very absorbent<br>Medium to soft handle<br>Drapes well<br>Comfortable<br>Dyes/prints well<br>Colourfast<br>No static/pilling<br>Inexpensive | Relatively weak<br>Low durability<br>Holds body heat<br>Wrinkles unless treated or blended<br>Low resilience<br>Weakened by water and mildew<br>Shrinks/stretches<br>Heat sensitive | Linings, blouses/shirts, dresses, lingerie, sportswear, jackets, neckties. |
| Elastomeric: polyurethane | Strong, durable<br>Soft, smooth handle<br>Very elastic<br>Lightweight<br>Easy-care | Non-absorbent<br>Heat sensitive<br>Yellows with age | Always blended with other fibres, both natural and manufactured, for woven and knitted fabrics.<br><br>Foundation garments, exercise and dancewear, swimwear, ski wear, hosiery. |

| APPAREL FIBRES AND SOURCES | FIBRE PROPERTIES | | FABRICS AND USES |
| --- | --- | --- | --- |
| | Advantages | Disadvantages | |
| Acetate: wood pulp cellulose | Silk-like finish<br>Fair absorbency<br>Soft handle, lustre<br>Fair drape<br>No shrinkage<br>Dyes well but fades<br>Insect and mildew resistant<br>No pilling<br>Inexpensive | Relatively weak<br>Poor durability<br>Creases<br>Heat sensitive<br>Low abrasion resistance<br>Attracts static electricity<br>Not easy-care | Linings, swimsuits, dresses, shirts/blouses, lingerie, scarves and neckties. |
| Triacetate: wood pulp cellulose | Crisp, silk handle<br>Lustrous<br>Fair drape<br>Easy-care<br>Wrinkle resistant<br>Resilient<br>Dyes well<br>Resists fading<br>Dries quickly<br>No shrinkage<br>Thermoplastic | Relatively weak<br>Non-absorbent<br>Poor durability<br>Attracts static electricity<br>Low abrasion resistance | Used for blouses, dresses, bonded fabrics, pleated garments, rain-wear, light knits. |
| Acrylic/Modacrylic: oil and coal | Wool-like finish<br>Strong, durable<br>Soft to medium handle<br>Bulky/fluffy/warm<br>Lightweight<br>Good drape<br>Resilient<br>Retains shape<br>Crease/flame resistant<br>Dyes well, colourfast<br>Easy-care | Low absorbency<br>Heat sensitive<br>Pills<br>Attracts static electricity | A good wool and fur substitute, used for fluffy and pile fabrics, knitwear, dresses, outerwear, sportswear, babywear, jackets, skirts, trousers, bathrobes, socks. |
| Polyester: petroleum products | Strong, durable<br>Medium to hard handle<br>Good drape<br>Wrinkle resistant<br>Dyes well<br>Colourfast<br>Resilient<br>Easy-care<br>No stretch/shrinkage<br>Versatile<br>Thermoplastic | Low absorbency<br>Holds body heat<br>Spun yarns pill<br>Absorbs oil stains<br>Attracts static electricity | Sewing thread, linings, lingerie, dresses, blouses/shirts, skirts, suits, sportswear, childrenswear, permanent press garments. |
| Nylon: coal, air and water | Very strong<br>Durable<br>Medium to hard handle<br>Lustrous<br>Good drape<br>Lightweight<br>Quick drying<br>Elastic<br>Resilient<br>Colourfast<br>Wrinkle/soil resistant<br>Thermoplastic | Low absorbency<br>Holds body heat<br>Heat sensitive<br>Attracts static electricity<br>Pills<br>Absorbs dyes and oil stains<br>Damaged by sun | Used for linings, hosiery, lingerie, swimwear, raincoats, windbreakers, slacks, dresses, blouses. |
| Metallic: metals | High sheen<br>No shrinkage<br>Luxurious<br>Insect and mildew resistant | Weak<br>Tarnishes unless coated<br>Non-absorbent<br>Heat sensitive if plastic coated<br>No stretch | Eveningwear, dancewear, trimmings, decorative effects. |

# IDENTIFICATION OF FIBRES

An experienced designer can often identify fabrics simply by sight and feel. However, to positively identify an unknown fibre, a number of chemical and microscopic tests can be conducted.

The burn test is the most convenient test to perform in the design studio. This procedure involves carefully and briefly igniting a cluster of fibres, or a small piece of the fabric, and observing the burning process before extinguishing the flame. The results you should look for are:

- Protein fibres — wool, hair and silk — burn with the smell of burned hair and leave an easily crushable, solid ash bead. Wool should extinguish once the source of the flame is removed.
- Cellulose fibres — cotton, linen, flax and rayon — ignite readily, burn rapidly, and smell like burned paper. Any ash left is soft and powdery.
- Acetates and synthetics melt away from the flame before burning and leave a solid ash bead which is hard to crush. In burn victim cases, the molten fibre melts onto the skin and can cause more severe burns than the actual flame.

Another test for acetate is nail polish remover. Acetone is the solvent for acetate and dissolves the fibres when applied to the fabric.

Inorganic fibres do not burn, although the polyester coatings used on metallics will.

Fabrics composed of blended fibres can be identified by separating and testing the individual types of fibre. Unknown materials can be sent to testing laboratories for specific identification.

All garments must carry a label identifying their fibre content. See Chapter 18 for more information on labelling.

# YARNS

Spinning is the process of twisting fibres into continuous strands, or yarns, which are then woven, knitted or otherwise made into fabric (Fig. 17.5).

In preparation for spinning, fibres are sorted into long and short lengths. Long staples are used in more expensive, high quality yarns because they are smoother, more supple, have a slight sheen and are very durable. Yarns with short staples are rougher and have a shorter life span.

*Tex* is the international yarn counting system, and describes yarn thicknesses by weight in grams per thousand metres. Therefore, the tex of a fine yarn could be 10, while a 50-Tex yarn is much coarser.

The term 'denier' is used to describe the thickness or diameter of a filament, with a higher number indicating a thicker filament. Therefore, 15-denier stockings are made from a much finer filament than 30-denier stockings. Vehicle tyres use 840-denier yarns for strength.

## BLENDED YARNS

Different fibres may be used together to create a blended yarn which minimises the undesirable qualities of both yarns and maximises the desirable qualities. For example, a natural fibre such as wool is often successfully combined with a synthetic fibre such as polyester to create a fabric which looks and feels like wool, but has increased durability, is more insect proof, can be permanently pleated, is crease resistant, has little static electricity, is washable and comfortable to wear. Other frequently blended fibres are polyester and cotton, polyester and viscose, and wool and nylon.

Blended fibres are labelled with the highest fibre content listed first as a percentage of the total. So, a blend of 65 per cent cotton and 35 per cent polyester is labelled cotton/ polyester. Blends of equal quantities may be listed in any order.

# CONSTRUCTION

The construction of a fabric determines its weight, drape, durability and texture. There are three basic methods of fabric construction — woven, knitted and non-woven.

## 1. WOVEN FABRICS

Woven fabrics are created by interlacing vertical yarns, known as *warp*, with horizontal filling yarns, known as *weft* (Fig. 17.6). The warp yarns are stretched lengthways onto the weaving loom, and the weft yarns are inserted alternately over and under the warp, in a back and forth movement. The openness or tightness of a weave depends on the number of warp and weft yarns per centimetre. Fabrics with a high thread count, that is, yarns per square centimetre, are the most durable.

The *selvedge* runs down the sides and is usually a slightly different weave from the body of the fabric. Its purpose is to strengthen the cloth and prevent the yarns from unravelling.

Plain, twill and satin are the basic weaves and most other weaves are variations of these. The structure of a weave is changed by altering the arrangement of the warp and weft threads. *Dobby* and *jacquard* weaves are more intricate designs which are woven with special attachments which raise and lower the warp yarns to allow the weft yarns to pass through. Damask, brocade and tapestry are jacquard weaves, and small geometric-patterned structures are known as dobby weaves.

Patterns can be created by using different coloured yarns in the warp, the weft or both. These are known as *yarn dyes*, and the pattern and colour are the same on both sides of the cloth.

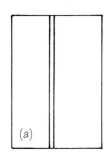
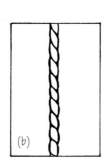
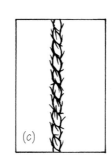
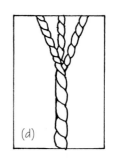
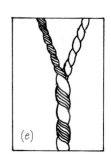

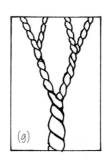
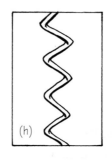
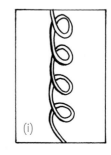
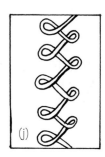

17.5  *Types of yarn.*

*(a) Monofilaments are single strands, such as those used in hosiery and sewing threads.*

*(b) Multifilaments are multiple strands twisted together as they extrude through the spinneret. They tend to be smooth and lustrous.*

*(c) Spun yarns are created by mechanical spinning which twists shorter staples together. Spun yarns are more irregular and fuzzier because of their fibre ends, and are inclined to pill.*

*(d) Ply yarns consist of several yarns twisted together to create extra bullk, strength or unusual effects.*

*(d) Combination yarns occur when yarns of different fibre, composition or twist are placed side by side and then spun together.*

*(f) Blended yarns combine different fibres at the un-spun (or staple) stage so that the fibres are evenly mixed when the yarn is spun.*

*(g) A cord yarn is produced by twisting two or more ply yarns together.*

*(h) Crimped, (i) coiled or (j) looped yarns are textured yarns which are made by treating straight manufactured filaments with chemicals, heat or machinery so that their shape is changed.*

## 2.  KNITTED FABRICS

Knits are created by looped yarns linked together to form a flexible fabric which is used for everything from bulky pullovers to sheer lingerie (Fig. 17.7).

The horizontal rows of loops running across a fabric are called *courses*, and the vertical rows running down are called *wales*.

A fabric is knitted flat or as a tube, and may be knitted widthways by weft knitting or lengthways by warp knitting. The *gauge* is the number of stitches per centimetre or per inch, and the greater the number of stitches, the finer the fabric.

The basic weft knits are plain (single jersey), rib, purl and double knit (Fig. 17.8). Because the method is basically the same as hand knitting, weft knits have a similar appearance to hand-knits, are inclined to run if a loop is broken, and tend to curl at the edges, making them difficult to cut and sew.

Warp knits stretch more horizontally than vertically, do not unravel or run and include tricots and raschel knits (Fig. 17.9).

*Fully fashioned* garments are knitted to the finished garment shape so there is no off-cut waste. Shaped collars, shirts, cardigans and pullovers are made in this way (Fig. 17.10).

Knitted fabrics are comfortable to wear because the knitted structure enables them to breath and move with the body. Their elasticity allows them to drape well and not crease as much as woven fabrics, but they are inclined to lose their shape with wear and laundering.

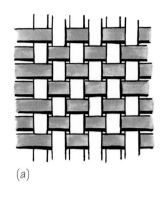

(a)

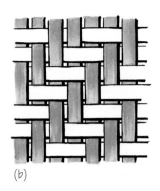

(b)

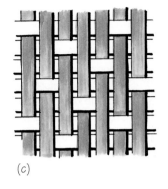

(c)

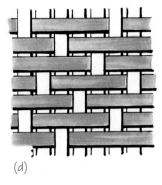

(d)

(e)

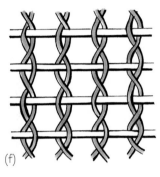

(f)

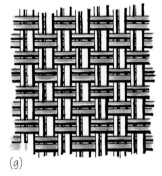

(g)

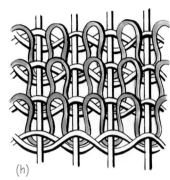

(h)

**17.6 Types of weave.**

(a) Plain weave is the simplest and most common of all weaves structures. It has a one-over-one-under pattern and is strong and durable.

(b) Twill has a two (or three or four) -over-two-under weave which creates a very strong fabric. The diagonal rib pattern known as a wale may move from left to right or right to left. Twill is a tight, firm weave and produces durable, strong fabrics. Herringbone is a variation of twill weave.

(c) Satin weave creates a smooth, high drape fabric with a lustrous sheen. The surface reflects light because it is made up of long warp floats which run in one direction and extend over four to eight weft yarns. Satin tends to be the weakest of the three basic weaves.

(d) Sateen is a variation of the satin weave, in which the weft floats extend horizontally over the warp yarns. It is generally less lustrous than satin.

(e) Rib weave is a variation of plain weave, with alternating thick and thin yarns which create a ribbed effect. The different thicknesses may be placed in a parallel or perpendicular arrangement.

(f) Leno weave is an open, lace-like construction. The warp yarns are twisted together and the weft yarn is inserted between them. Although it looks fragile, the twisting of the yarns provides strength and stability.

(g) Basket weave is another variation of the plain weave, created by treating two or more yarns as one. Because the yarns are not twisted together, the weave tends to be more open and less stable than plain weave.

(h) Pile fabrics have an extra filling or warp thread which is drawn into loops on the surface of the fabric. The pile may be looped for towelling, clipped for corduroy, or sheared for velvet and fake furs.

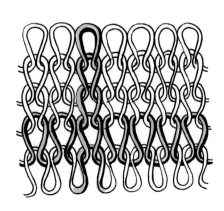

**17.7** Wales are the rows of loops which run down the length of a knitted fabric and courses are the loops which run across the fabric.

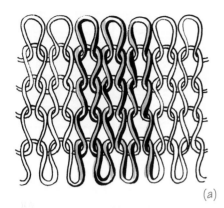

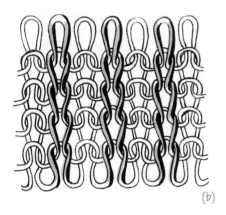

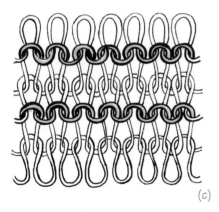

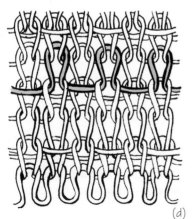

(a)

(b)

(c)

(d)

◀ 17.8 (a) Plain (single jersey) knits are recognisable by the vertical V-shaped patterns on the face of the fabric, and horizontal rows of half-circles on the back. They stretch more horizontally than vertically.
(b) Rib knits are used for knitted garments, cuffs and waistbands. They feature strong vertical ridges of alternating plain and purl stitches, and have considerable horizontal stretch and recovery. Back and front sides are the same.
(c) Purl knits feature horizontal rows of half-circles on both sides of the fabric. The knit stretches both horizontally and vertically, and the fabric is usually reversible.
(d) Double knits are knitted with two needles and two yarns simultaneously, so that two fabrics are knitted as one. Front and back sides look the same. The knit is stable and firm, with considerable give which will not stretch or sag.

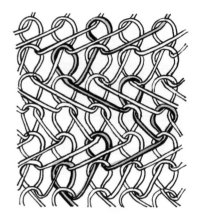

▲ 17.9 Tricot knit. Warp knits include tricot and raschel knits. Tricot has a fine ribbed texture and soft drape, and is often used for linings, casual- wear and lingerie. Although the nature of the raschel stitch varies according to the design of the fabric, it usually has an open, textural and web-like structure and is used for lace, net, crochet effects and a variety of patterns.

▲ 17.10 The change in pattern can be seen on fully-fashioned garments, where garment pieces are shaped by increasing and decreasing stitches so that no cutting is required.

## 3. NON-WOVEN FABRICS

Non-woven methods are the simplest ways of making fabrics. Non-wovens are formed from fibres which are intermeshed, fused or bonded together by chemical, thermal or mechanical means, thereby eliminating spinning, weaving or knitting. They have limited use in fashion because they lack drape and strength, and are usually too bulky for clothing (Fig. 17.11).

Felts, nets, braids and bonded fabrics are examples of non-woven fabrics. Felts are made from wool, hair or man-made fibres and are used for millinery, slippers, furnishings and floor coverings. Fused fabrics are used in garment construction as interfacings. Netting and braiding are used in lace-making.

---

*17.11 Fusing is a non-woven interfacing fabric used to reinforce other fabrics. The criss-cross web of fibres is chemically bonded together.*

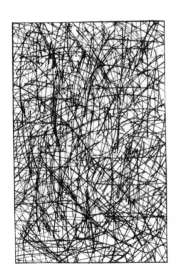

# FINISH

Finishing treatments are applied to fabrics for functional or decorative purposes. *Grey (greige) goods* are unfinished goods straight off the loom, and most undergo finishing to perfect their appearance. Removal of imperfections, discolouration and loose fibres, and stabilisation to minimise stretching and shrinkage are routine procedures which enhance performance and often also improve the fabric's appearance.

Further functional treatments affect the performance of the fabric, and are used to improve the suitability of the fabric for its end use. *End use* is the function for which a fabric is intended. For example, anti-static, crease-resistance, stain-resistance, waterproofing and flame-resistance are finishes that might be applied to a fabric intended for use in protective industrial clothing.

Decorative finishes affect the appearance or handle of a fabric and include flocking, dyeing, printing, bleaching, starching, mercerising, glazing and crêping.

When production is completed, the fabric is rolled onto a flat cardboard core or tube. The finished bolt or roll, known as a piece, may have from 40 to 100 metres on it, depending on the weight of the goods.

# DESIGNING WITH FABRICS

Fabrication is the process of matching a design to a fabric. To do this, the designer must know how a fabric will behave and whether it will be suitable for a particular style. A fabric may be selected for a design already planned, or a garment may be designed specifically to suit the nature of an available fabric. Whichever comes first, the fabric cannot be forced into a design or silhouette which is not compatible with its character. The designer must consider both physical and visual qualities when fabricating a style.

## PHYSICAL QUALITIES OF FABRICS

Physical qualities determine the silhouette capabilities of a fabric and therefore dictate the types of styling for which a fabric can be successfully used. Firm fabrics such as worsted wools, gabardine and linen are used for a tailored look because they are heavy enough to support tailored details and strong shapes. Soft fabrics such as crêpe, jersey, chiffon and challis are suitable for draped garments which show the body contours (Fig. 17.12).

Fibre, yarn, construction and finish are physical qualities which determine the hand and weight of a fabric. *Hand* is the texture, body, drape or feel of a fabric. A fabric with a good hand is one with quality that can be felt or will suit the intended design.

*Weight* is the lightness or heaviness, thinness or thickness of a fabric. Fabric weight is discussed in terms of grams per metre (gsm) — or ounces per yard with, for example, five ounce shirting — of flat, unstretched fabric. A light weight cotton might be 100 gsm, while a heavy cotton would be 248 gsm.

The fabric weight should vary with the type of garment and the season. Blouse weight fabrics are lighter than dress and bottom weights. Bottom weight fabrics are used for jackets, skirts and trousers. Winter weight fabrics are usually very heavy for added warmth.

### Supporting fabrics

Supporting fabrics such as underlining, interfacing and lining are used in a garment's inner construction and provide a means of adjusting the weight and hand of a fabric to suit the garment or parts of the garment which require reinforcement (Fig. 17.13).

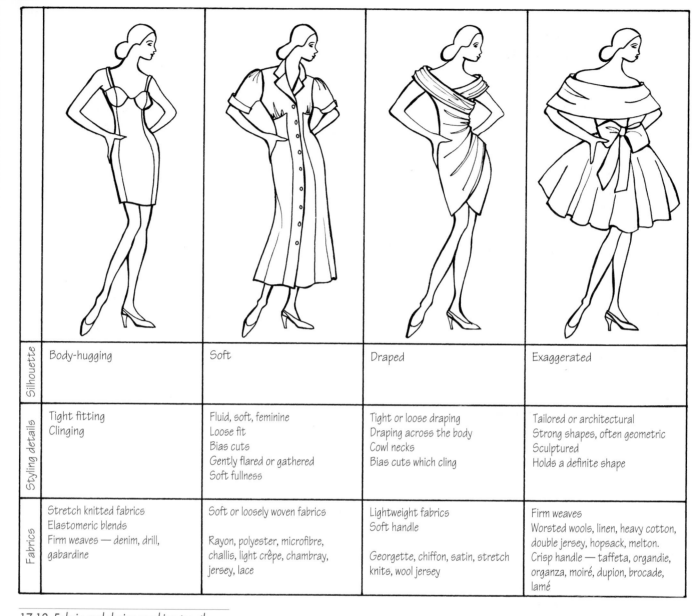

| | | | | |
|---|---|---|---|---|
| **Silhouette** | Body-hugging | Soft | Draped | Exaggerated |
| **Styling details** | Tight fitting<br>Clinging | Fluid, soft, feminine<br>Loose fit<br>Bias cuts<br>Gently flared or gathered<br>Soft fullness | Tight or loose draping<br>Draping across the body<br>Cowl necks<br>Bias cuts which cling | Tailored or architectural<br>Strong shapes, often geometric<br>Sculptured<br>Holds a definite shape |
| **Fabrics** | Stretch knitted fabrics<br>Elastomeric blends<br>Firm weaves — denim, drill,<br>gabardine | Soft or loosely woven fabrics<br><br>Rayon, polyester, microfibre,<br>challis, light crêpe, chambray,<br>jersey, lace | Lightweight fabrics<br>Soft handle<br><br>Georgette, chiffon, satin, stretch<br>knits, wool jersey | Firm weaves<br>Worsted wools, linen, heavy cotton,<br>double jersey, hopsack, melton.<br>Crisp handle — taffeta, organdie,<br>organza, moiré, dupion, brocade,<br>lamé |

*17.12 Fabric and design working together.*

Underlining is a light weight fabric cut and sewn as one with the garment. It provides crispness, body and support, and helps retain the shape of, and reduce wrinkling in the outer fabric. It preserves the shape and grain of a loosely woven or limp fabric, and protects and prolongs the life of the outer fabric. It also provides an opaque quality for sheer fabrics.

Interfacing is usually bonded or sewn to the wrong side of the outer fabric and gives body, substance, smoothness and shape retention to such parts as collars, cuffs, lapels, necklines, plackets, armholes and hemlines. Interfacing also prevents unwanted stretching.

Lining is an inner garment which is assembled separately and sewn to the inside of the outer garment. It provides a smooth inner finish, comfort and warmth for the wearer, helps retains the garment shape and prevents stretching and wrinkling in the outer garment. Light, transparent fabrics or rough prickly fabrics are usually lined.

The amount of stiffness required in a garment changes with fashion styling, but supporting fabrics must always be compatible with the weight of the outer garment fabric.

### Grain

Grain is the direction of the threads in a cloth. Lengthwise grain follows the direction of the warp, and crosswise grain follows the direction of the weft. Bias grain is when either of the two grainlines are placed diagonally for cutting.

The comfort and drape of a garment is affected by the grain. Most garments are cut with the crosswise grain which

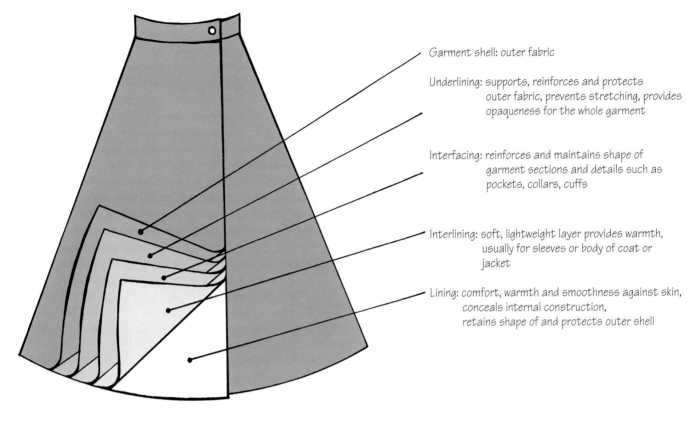

Garment shell: outer fabric

Underlining: supports, reinforces and protects
outer fabric, prevents stretching, provides
opaqueness for the whole garment

Interfacing: reinforces and maintains shape of
garment sections and details such as
pockets, collars, cuffs

Interlining: soft, lightweight layer provides warmth,
usually for sleeves or body of coat or
jacket

Lining: comfort, warmth and smoothness against skin,
conceals internal construction,
retains shape of and protects outer shell

17.13 Supporting fabrics.

has more elasticity, running horizontally around the body. This provides wearing ease across the shoulders, torso and over the hips and legs. Crosswise grain is normally only used vertically as a border effect; it drapes a little stiffly and gives a fuller look to a garment. Lengthwise grain drapes more softly than crosswise grain but has very little give and normally runs vertically from shoulder to hemline (Fig. 17.14).

The bias grain has the most stretch and drapes very softly. It tends to sag at the hemline and usually requires levelling. Bias cut garments allow subtle fitting because the fabric moulds to the

17.14 Fabric grain. Most garments are cut with the crosswise grain going around the body and the lengthwise grain running from the shoulder to hem.

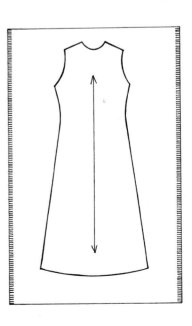

Weft yarns
Crosswise grain

Selvedge

Warp yarns
Lengthwise grain

True bias

body by stretching or contracting to give a smooth easy fit. Madelaine Vionnet was the originator of the bias cut in the 1920s.

## VISUAL QUALITIES OF FABRICS

The visual quality of a fabric is created through the colours, textures and patterns visible on its surface (Fig. 17.15). Also known as 'surface interest', visual quality determines the way a fabric is used by a designer. A bold fabric often works best with a simple design so that the textures or patterns are allowed to dominate. On the other hand, a plain fabric either requires excellence of cut to achieve beauty and the appearance of quality, or needs trimmings and design details which add interest to the garment.

A *pattern* is an overall design achieved through the interplay of values and colours. It is introduced mainly through printing and weaving to relieve the monotony of plain fabric, and to create interest in or camouflage less expensive cloth. A *motif* is a single unit of a pattern which is usually repeated.

Fabric patterns fall into the following five basic categories:

### 1. Geometrics

These are straight-line non-representational patterns consisting of textures, stripes, checks and plaids.

### 2. Dots and spots

These are simplified curved forms arranged in geometric or random formation, such as foulard and polka dot.

### 3. Abstract patterns

These patterns are simplified, abstracted or stylised motifs inspired by natural sources and organized into a recognisable pattern. They include paisley, tie-dyes, ethnic designs and ikat.

### 4. Naturalistic patterns

These are realistic or recognisable representations of flora and fauna such as florals and animal prints, as well as natural motifs such as nuts, shells and insects.

### 5. Conversational patterns

These are designs using recognisable motifs based on manufactured motifs such a food, tools and equipment, cars and buildings, or activities and scenic views such as sporting activities, village scenes, domestic life and cartoons.

# USING PATTERN

To be suitable for apparel design, a two-dimensional pattern must retain its effectiveness when used three-dimensionally, when seamed, darted, gathered, draped and moulded around the body.

The stronger the fabric pattern, the more difficult it is to style. Large shapes, bold colours and hard, definite outlines can easily overpower both the design and the wearer, or may cause undesirable visual illusions. Bold patterns require little or no trimming and are best with simple, direct styling which does not interfere with the fabric design.

Softer or blurred outlines and small textured patterns are more versatile and easier to use because they are not so dominant. Very fine patterns often appear as a solid colour from a distance, and may be styled as such.

The following technical considerations are important when designing with patterned fabrics.

### 1. Matching patterns

This involves designing and cutting a garment so that the pattern matches when the seams are sewn together. Bold checks, stripes and plaids look clumsy if not matched. However, a lot of fabric can be wasted when trying to match large repeats.

### 2. The repeat

The repeat is the amount of fabric required for a pattern to duplicate itself. A large repeat is unsuitable for trims or small garments and looks best in simple styles with few seams. Large repeats need to be placed carefully on the garment so that one part of the pattern is not used more than others.

### 3. Pattern scale

The size of the pattern must complement the proportions of the garment. Small patterns are suitable for most garments, but bold patterns need to be selected to specifically suit a particular design. An all-over bold pattern always enlarges the figure.

### 4. One-way patterns

These patterns have all motifs facing in one direction, or look quite different when inverted. One-way prints often use extra metreage because the garment pieces have to be cut facing the same way and do not lock in as efficiently as two-way prints which can be cut either way.

### 5. Placement of pattern

Care should be taken to ensure that a bold part of a print does not land at the bust, tummy, derrière or crotch and draw the eye straight to an undesirable focal point.

### 6. Directional effects

Some patterns may appear patchy or uneven, or have a strong vertical, horizontal or diagonal visual pull when viewed from a distance. A good rule of thumb is that patterns which carry the eye up to the wearer's face suit most people.

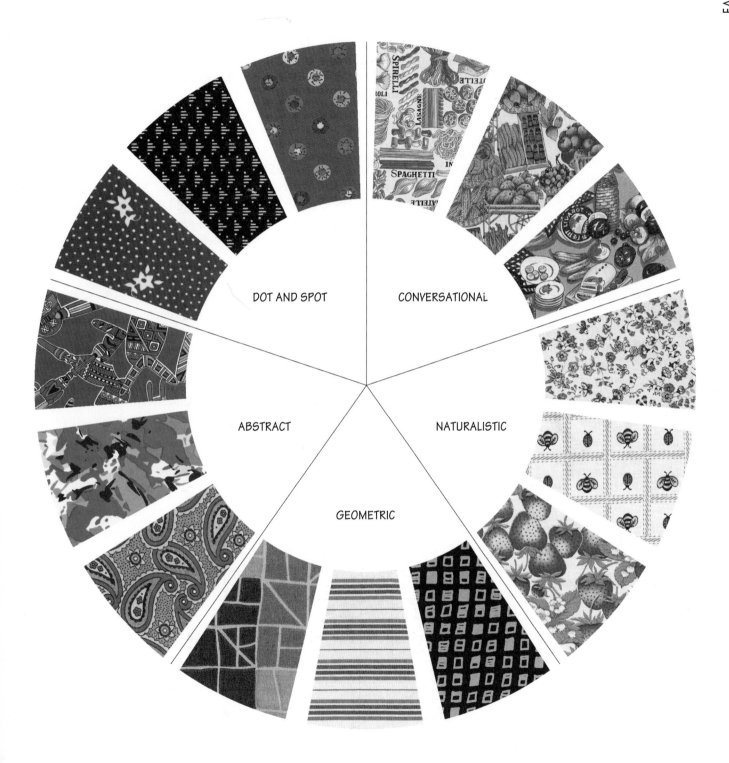

17.15 Types of pattern. (Fabrics courtesy of Lincraft Fabrics.)

DOT AND SPOT

CONVERSATIONAL

ABSTRACT

NATURALISTIC

GEOMETRIC

# DETERMINING FABRIC QUALITY

Look for the following as indicators of the quality of a fabric.

## 1. Straight grain

The weft (or filler) yarns should meet the selvedge at right angles. If they are oblique to the edge, the fabric is off grain and will not hang correctly.

## 2. Regular weave

Weaving irregularities such as knots, weak spots and thick or thin areas which cause the fabric to wear unevenly, can be detected by holding the cloth up to the light.

## 3. Slippage

Pull the cloth between your two thumbs and two forefingers, both cross-wise and lengthwise. If the threads move apart easily, the fabric may pull away from the seams when sewn, or form holes (Fig. 17.16).

## 4. Length of fibres

Fold the fabric and examine the folded edge. Surface fuzz on a firm weave may indicate the use of short, low-grade fibres which cause problems due to pilling or fabric weakness.

## 5. Pilling

Rub the cloth surface briskly. Look for fibres rubbing up into balls, or the surface nap rubbing off. This is pilling and it spoils the look of a fabric.

## 6. Even print and/or dye colour

Look for colour which has rubbed off, white or undyed spots and bad alignment of print motifs as indicators of faults or poor quality. Dye which rubs off is known as *crocking*.

## 7. Print alignment

Geometrics, stripes, or checks should line up at right angles to the selvedge. An off-grain print makes fabric look crooked even if cut correctly.

## 8. Sizing

Over-use of sizing (frequently used to give body to a poor quality fabric) can be detected if visible powder appears when the surface is lightly rubbed.

## 9. Fabric resilience

This can be tested by lightly crushing the fabric in the hand. If the cloth does not recover quickly, the fabric will always look wrinkled.

## 10. Workability

Drape or fold the fabric in the way it will be used to see if it will perform well in the design.

## 11. Wash testing

Whenever possible, wash and dry or dryclean a sample of the fabric according to the care instructions to test for colour-fastness and shrinkage.

The following glossary of fabric names, patterns and treatments encompasses many fabrics commonly used by designers.

*17.16 Slippage of threads under pressure is undesirable.*

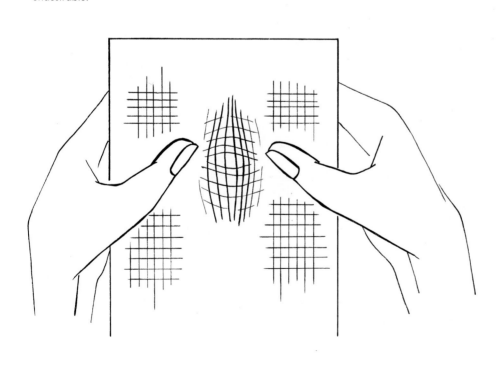

# Glossary

## Plain Weaves

| | |
|---|---|
| **Calico** | A smooth, tightly woven, lightweight cotton. Features some slubbing or irregularities and may show specks of trash. Often printed for dresses and used for toiles. |
| **Canvas** | A strong, heavyweight fabric in cotton or cotton blends. Used for upholstery, blinds, tents. |
| **Cheesecloth** | A loosely woven plain weave, similar to but heavier than muslin. Usually cotton. |
| **Challis** | A soft dress and blouse weight fabric, in wool or other fibres. Often printed with delicate florals and paisleys. |
| **Chiffon** | A light, soft, transparent fabric with good drape; silk or manufactured fibres. Used for eveningwear. |
| **Georgette** | Soft, slightly sheer fabric with good drape. Matt, crêpey texture; used mostly for blouses and eveningwear. |
| **Hessian** | Otherwise known as burlap, a coarse, strong fabric made from jute, hemp or cotton. Used for furnishing and floor coverings. |
| **Linen-look** | A fabric made from a manufactured yarn which features the characteristics of linen yarn. Used for suits, dresses and blouses. |
| **Microfibre** | A polyester fabric available in a variety of weaves. Good drape is due to ultra-fine yarns which give a silk-like handle. |
| **Muslin** | Inexpensive cotton or cotton blend with soft, fine, gauzy texture. Often made with low grade fibre, and may feature slubbing and dark specks. |
| **Organza** | A sheer, crisp, fine weave fabric with a slight sheen; silk or manufactured fibres. Cotton fibres are known as organdie. Used for bridal and eveningwear. |
| **Poplin** | Light to medium weight cotton or cotton blend with fine crosswise rib. Used for childrenswear and dresses. |
| **Taffeta** | A crisp, smooth eveningwear fabric with pronounced scroop (rustling sound). Silk or manufactured fibres. |
| **Voile** | Crisp, light, transparent fabric, usually in cotton or cotton blends. |

## Twill Weaves

| | |
|---|---|
| **Denim** | Strong cotton fabric with coloured warp and white weft yarns. Traditionally coloured blue. Used for workwear, casual wear, jeans and jackets. |
| **Flannel** | Soft cloth in twill or plain weave with slightly brushed surface. Comes in many fibres and weights. Used for suiting and winter shirts. |
| **Gabardine** | Medium to heavy fabric made in natural or manufactured fibres. Strong, smooth weave with low lustre used for trousers, jackets, suits. |
| **Herringbone** | Traditionally a woollen fabric, now available in different fibres. The weave is a variation of twill in which the broken diagonal ridges form a zig-zag pattern. |
| **Twill** | Strong, smooth fabrics with pronounced diagonal rib. Made in natural and manufactured fibres, in various weights. |

## Satin Weaves

| | |
|---|---|
| **Crêpe-backed satin** | A reversible fabric with shiny satin on one side and dull crêpe on the other. |
| **Sateen** | Appears similar to satin, with slightly less lustre. Often made from cotton. Used for furnishings and eveningwear. |
| **Satin** | With a slippery, lustrous surface and dull reverse side, this fabric drapes well and is used for eveningwear, blouses and lingerie. Made from silk or synthetic fibres. |

## Knits

| | |
|---|---|
| **Double-knit jersey** | A weft knit fabric knitted on two sets of needles to create a firm hand with limited crosswise stretch. Identical on both sides. |
| **Fleecy** | Knitted fabric brushed on the wrong side to create a soft nap. Used for tracksuits, sweatshirts and sportswear. |
| **Honeycomb** | A textured knit with limited stretch used almost exclusively for polo shirts. |
| **Raschel** | A coarse or open knit, typically used for novelty knits, laces and net. |
| **Rib** | Used for pullovers, cuffs and waistbands, this knit has strong ridges running vertically. |
| **Single-knit jersey** | A plain weft knit with limited crosswise and no lengthwise elasticity. Closely knit, smooth, firm handle, used for casual tops and dresses. V-shaped texture on front and half-circle on back. |
| **Tricot** | A warp knit fabric in synthetic fibre with vertical face wales. Smooth, silky surface and mainly horizontal stretch, suitable for lingerie, linings and casual wear. |

## Textured and Patterned Weaves

| | |
|---|---|
| **Clipped spot** | Extra filling yarn is added to the weave to form a raised spot on the fabric surface. May also be printed. |
| **Cloqué** | Any fabric with a raised or embossed design. |
| **Crinkle chiffon** | Chiffon with a crinkle finish for textural interest. |

| | |
|---|---|
| **Dobby** | A fabric with a small, regularly spaced geometric motif. Often cotton or cotton blend and used for blouses. |
| **Dupion** | Plain weave silk fabric with strong horizontal slubbing effect. Crisp hand, suitable for eveningwear and suiting. Also made in synthetic fibres. |
| **Embossed brocade** | Similar to cloqué, with a metallic or synthetic yarn for a glittery effect. |
| **Jacquard** | A patterned texture, sometimes expensive because of the complex weaving process. |
| **Lamé** | Fabrics using metallic yarns for a dressy, glittery look. May be woven or knitted. Used for evening and formal wear. |
| **Moiré** | A woven taffeta-type fabric with water-mark effect embossed on the surface. Suitable for eveningwear. |
| **Shot crinkle taffeta** | Taffeta with a shot effect created with different coloured warp and weft threads so that the colour changes as the fabric moves. The crinkle is a textural finishing treatment. |
| **Yor Yu** | A woven fabric with a pronounced crinkle texture. Frequently available in polyester, cotton or blends. |

## DOTS AND SPOTS

| | |
|---|---|
| **Coin spot** | Large dots approximately the size of a coin. |
| **Pin spot** | The smallest dot used, spaced at regular intervals over the fabric. |
| **Polka dot** | Medium-sized dots, between pin and coin. |
| **Random spot** | Spots of any size irregularly spaced over the fabric. |

## STRIPES AND LINEAR TEXTURES

| | |
|---|---|
| **Candy stripe** | Printed or woven stripes of varying widths which imitate striped candy. |
| **Corduroy** | Pile fabric created by cutting the extra filling thread to produce lengthwise ribs of different widths. Usually in cotton and blended fibres. |
| **Faille** | Tightly woven fabric with a fine, crosswise rib. Made from cotton, silk, wool or manufactured fibres, and used for formal wear. |
| **Pinstripe** | A narrow, coloured, woven or printed stripe up to two millimetres wide. May be called chalkstripe when the stripe is white on a dark background. |
| **Rib pique** | Heavier warp yarns used with regular weft yarns to create a vertical ridge in this cotton or cotton blend fabric. |
| **Yarn-dyed chambray** | A fine, shirting-weight cotton with alternating white dyed warp yarns and white weft yarns. |

## CHECKS AND PLAIDS

| | |
|---|---|
| **End-on-end shirting** | A plain weave with combined coloured and white warp yarns and white weft. Used for men's shirts. |
| **Gingham** | Firm, light or medium-weight cotton or other fabric, with two different coloured warp and weft threads, woven to produce an even check. Used for dresses, shirts, aprons, children's wear. May also be printed and is usually white and another colour. |
| **Houndstooth** | Traditionally woven in wool, a small regular check which resembles a four-pointed star. Commonly done in white and a strong contrasting colour. |
| **Madras** | Fine cotton or other fibre, woven in multiple coloured checks. |
| **Tartan** | Twill weave plain design which may be woven or printed. Originally woven in wool in traditional Scottish designs, now woven in a variety of colours, patterns and fibres. |
| **Windowpane check** | A wide, printed or woven check. |

## FLORALS

| | |
|---|---|
| **Naturalistic floral** | A realistic floral representation, available in numerous designs and printed on most types of base cloth. |
| **Stylised floral** | Stylised florals are abstracted motifs and appear in many variations on all types of fibre and weave. |

## PRINTS

| | |
|---|---|
| **Ikat** | A technique where the warp yarns are printed before weaving so that the design is broken when the weft threads are woven in. |
| **One-way print** | The motif faces one direction so that, if the fabric is cut the other way, the print appears upside-down. |
| **Patchwork print** | Combinations of several prints placed adjacent to each other on the one fabric. |

## STITCHED AND EMBROIDERED SURFACES

| | |
|---|---|
| **Broderie Anglaise** | Embroidery of floral or other designs punched or cut and then overcast. Otherwise known as eyelet embroidery. Made in dress width and narrow widths for trimmings. |
| **Cut-work** | Cut-work holes provide textural contrast to sheer fabrics, embroidery and satin floral appliqué. |
| **Embroidered and corded net** | Net may be embroidered, corded, beaded and sequined to create a rich and varied surface texture. |

| **Embroidered base cloths** | Most plain base cloths can be embroidered; for example, net, organza and dupion silk. |
| **Quilting** | Quilting is formed by stitching together two or more layers of lightweight fabric with wadding between the layers. The stitching forms a definite pattern on the surface. Because of its warmth, it is suitable for winter jackets and dressing gowns. |

## LACES

| **Corded lace** | Cording is stitched to the face of the lace to enhance the motifs. |
| **Guipure** | A rich lace with large motifs held together by cords or coarse net. Creates a strong relief effect. |
| **Printed lace** | As with any other base cloth, lace may be printed over to achieve a multi-coloured sheer fabric. |
| **Raschel** | Knitted on a raschel machine, this lace is quite fine and is similar to, although cheaper than, Chantilly lace. |
| **Ribbon lace** | Motifs in the lace design are reinforced with ribbon sewn on top. |

## PILE AND NAP FABRICS

| **Knit fake fur** | A knitted fabric with deep, lofty pile. Frequently acrylic or other manufactured fibre. |
| **Panne velvet** | The velvet pile is pressed flat in one direction to give a lustrous finish. It is sometimes printed and may be stretch, woven or knitted. Pile pressed in several directions is known as crushed velvet. |
| **Printed fake fur** | This is pile fabric which imitates real animal fur. The pile is woven and the animal spot is printed onto the pile. |
| **Terry towelling** | This fabric is very absorbent because of the uncut pile on both sides of the fabric. Uncut pile on one side only is known as terry cloth. It may be woven, knitted or stretch and is usually cotton or cotton blends. Terry is good for towels, casual wear and bathrobes. |
| **Velvet** | Fabric with short, soft, thick pile made from cut loop warp yarns with a rich, lustrous texture. Made from silk or manufactured fibres. |

## NON-WOVENS

| **Interfacing** | The fibres in interfacing are bonded together with heat, pressure or a chemical agent. This fabric is not very strong but, when fused to another fabric with an adhesive backing, adds strength and body to a garment. |
| **Leather-look vinyl** | A plastic PVC (polyvinyl chloride) material, backed with a woven or knitted fabric. An extremely strong, durable and waterproof fabric, available in a variety of textures. |
| **Net** | An open, knotted fabric used for bridal wear, eveningwear and sometimes as a supporting fabric. Available in a variety of weights and in natural or manufactured fibres. Very soft, fine net is known as tulle. Although traditionally knotted, today many nets are raschel knitted. |
| **Wadding** | Otherwise known as fibre-fill, wadding is used in quilted fabrics and as an interlining for warmth in garments. Similar to felt and available in different thicknesses, the fibres form a loose web which can be easily pulled apart. |

## CHAPTER 18

# INTRODUCTION

For many designers with the entrepreneurial spirit, going into business for themselves is the only way to fulfil ambition. Unfortunately, talent and creativity as a designer only make up a small part of the skills required to build a successful fashion label. The other major ingredient in the success formula is good business management, an area which many designers treat as secondary in importance.

Much of the work a designer does has already been covered in previous chapters, particularly Chapter 7, The Role of the Designer. For someone starting a new enterprise it is important that sound business practices be put into place from the outset. Be sure to contact the small business agency operated by your state government, or the trade association most appropriate to your business for advice and information. (See Chapter 23).

## ESTABLISHING THE IMAGE OF YOUR LABEL

The fashion industry is primarily about selling image, so the designer of a fashion label must be clear about exactly what image he or she wishes to present. The characteristic look of a designer's product is known as *house image*. House image is defined by styling, quality of materials and make, price and the way the product is marketed (Fig. 18.1).

Once a label is well established in a particular market, it is usually impossible to move successfully into another area with the same name and product. To overcome this, a designer may introduce a *diffusion* range which is a new label aimed at a different market, thereby allowing expansion into a different area without affecting the established label.

The market positioning and image of a label largely determine the way the garments are produced. There are two basic approaches to garment design and production. The first is *couture*, where the garments are individually cut and custom-made for each client. This is the most prestigious, although smallest, sector of the fashion market. The second is *ready-to-wear* (or *prêt-à-porter*), whereby the garments are cut and manufactured in bulk for a targeted segment of the population. Most of the fashion sold at retail level fits into the latter category.

### HAUTE COUTURE

Haute couture translates literally from the French as 'high dressmaking'. Although couture exists in other fashion centres around the world, Paris is considered to be the home of haute couture.

The Fédération Française de la Couture du Pret a Porter des Couturiers et des Créateurs de Mode is couture's representative organisation in Paris. It has three 'chambres syndicales' representing the different aspects of the French fashion industry. These are:

1.  Chambre Syndicale de la Couture Parisienne.
2.  Chambre Syndicale du Prêt-à-Porter, des Couturiers et des Créateurs de Mode.
3.  Chambre Syndicale de la Mode Masculine.

The Fédération was founded by designers in Paris in 1868 to protect their designs from plagiarism. To qualify for membership, a fashion house must employ at least 20 staff, operate an *atelier* or workshop in Paris, and stage two collection showings of at least 75 garments twice yearly. The designer at this level is known as the couturier (male) or couturière (female). Couturiers create individually designed and produced garments. Because they are in the privileged position of designing according to the dictates of their own inspiration, their garments are characterised by a high degree of creativity, originality and mastery of execution.

Garments may be custom-designed for a client, or custom-made. Every aspect of a custom-designed garment, from the original design to the selection of fabric and trims and the final fit, is created exclusively for a particular client. Custom-made, or made-to-order, garments are ordered from a sketch, photograph or sample of an existing model and made up for the client. In both cases, several fittings are required and much of the sewing and decoration is done by hand.

Haute couture is highly valued because it provides a constant source of ideas unrestrained by financial considerations. It acts as a stimulus to other designers and the industry as a whole. However, the high quality of materials and workmanship means that the garments are extremely costly to produce. In the realm of Parisian haute couture, a suit may carry a price tag of up to $A30 000, and an evening dress up to $A60 000. This, combined with the enormous cost of the collection showings, means that most houses actually lose money on the couture side of their operations.

However, the couture establishes the designer's name, image and prestige. This in turn stimulates millions of dollars of sales through *licensing*. Licensing is an arrangement whereby a designer is paid a royalty by a manufacturer in exchange for the use of the designer's name on a particular product. Most design houses have licensing arrangements for everything from perfume and cosmetics to jewellery, hosiery, eyewear, homewares and chocolates. Perfumes in particular have proven very lucrative for many European and American designers while in Australia accessories, eyewear and homewares have been successfully licensed (see Chapter 20). Couture houses rely on their prêt-à-porter or ready-to-wear collections to provide profitable access to larger markets.

## READY-TO-WEAR

This is the part of the clothing industry which provides fashion for the majority

18.1 Australian fashion labels. (Courtesy of TMG.)

of the population. As the name suggests, ready-to-wear enables a customer to try a garment on, purchase it and wear it or take it home immediately. Retail outlets carry a selection of colours and sizes in a variety of styles for the customer to choose from, and the fit is standardised to suit the average figure, thereby eliminating the need for fittings. Ready-to-wear garments are mass-produced and cover all levels of price and quality. Up-market and designer label ready-to-wear is produced in limited quantities, uses high quality materials and making, and carries correspondingly high price tags. Larger quantities and lower grade materials generally go hand in hand with lower prices.

The international ready-to-wear collections are presented twice yearly in February/March and September/October, but the garments on the run-way are not automatically mass-produced for retail selling. Although ready-to-wear is more commercial than couture and often absorbs influences from street fashions, many garments in a designer's collection are still quite experimental and innovative, and have to be modified for volume production and made more affordable for the general public.

Most fashion in Australia, whether it be designer label or chain store merchandise, is manufactured along ready-to-wear lines. Australia does not have a haute couture industry to compare with the likes of Paris and Milan, although there are quite a few couturiers who run small workrooms producing creative and original designs for select clients.

# GARMENT PRODUCTION

Garment production may be done by a design house itself using in-house cutters and machinists or, more frequently, by hiring outside contractors known as *makers*.

The production of couture garments is generally done in-house. Couturiers often work from small premises with a shop or showroom at the front and a work-room out the back. Because of the close working relationship the couturier develops with his or her clients, and the fact that these garments are one-off or cut in small quantities and require careful fitting, it is appropriate that the work be carried out in an atelier or studio type environment where the designer can work closely with the patternmakers, machinist and hand-sewer (Fig. 18.2).

The creation of a couture garment follows the processes of patternmaking, toile construction, fitting, alteration, refitting and finishing already discussed in Chapter 7. The fabric may be sent outside for treatments such as machine embroidery, pleating or dyeing, but all other tasks are completed in-house.

*18.2 Couturier Johnathan Ward does several fittings to ensure that the design and fit of his garments is perfect.*

Although the creativity, superb finishing, attention to detail and delicate hand-work that characterise couture work means that a wedding dress may take more than 40 hours to complete, the production process for couture or made-to-measure is relatively straightforward when compared to the planning, organisation and handling required for the production of thousands of garments for a ready-to-wear range. The next section will therefore deal with the more complex manufacturing tasks involved in the mass-production of garments.

## MASS PRODUCTION

The size of a company and the number and type of garments produced determines the production system a design house uses. Very large manufacturers such as Bonds and King Gee who are able to invest in sophisticated technology, plants and equipment, frequently choose to manufacture in their own factories because they benefit from economies of scale, the elimination of the middleman, and greater control over their own product.

Fashion houses who choose not to carry the large overheads of factories and employees, use outside contractors. An outside contractor, or maker, may work either exclusively for one design house or for several, and may carry out one step in the production cycle or the entire process. For example, the fabric, patterns and samples may go to a cutter, then the cut pieces go to a maker, then the sewn garments go to a presser who sends the finished goods back to the fashion house.

Alternatively, the maker may do all the manufacturing. She or he is supplied fabric and patterns, samples and making specifications and, for a price negotiated beforehand, the maker will cut, machine, press and deliver the finished garments to the fashion house by a specified date. This process is known as Cut, Make and Trim or CMT. In some instances the maker may even order materials, manufacture, pack the garments and dispatch them direct to the retailer.

Makers may operate a factory or farm the work out to *outworkers*, who are machinists working from their own

| INSIDE MANUFACTURING | |
|---|---|
| ADVANTAGES | DISADVANTAGES |
| • Maximum control over cutting accuracy, fabric yields, machining techniques and product quality.<br>• More control over lead times and deliveries and the ability to schedule in special orders or small runs.<br>• Less time spent in moving goods and people.<br>• Depreciation of machinery and equipment is tax deductable. | • Large capital investment and higher overheads in setting up and maintaining factory.<br>• Costs of under-utilisation of facilities and staff during quiet times, as well as down time suffered through repairs and maintenance.<br>• Staff costs for holidays, sick leave, overtime rates, hiring and training. |
| OUTSIDE MANUFACTURING | |
| ADVANTAGES | DISADVANTAGES |
| • Flexibility of planning production schedules and quantities to suit seasonal cycles.<br>• No pressure of plant utilisation during quiet periods.<br>• Access to the latest technology without the capital investment and associated costs.<br>• Access to a wider range of skills and specialised machinery than otherwise possible.<br>• Lower personnel problems and costs because they are borne by the contractor.<br>• Enables a small company with limited capital to get established. | • Reduced control over quality of workmanship and reliability of deliveries.<br>• Longer lead times.<br>• Increased risk of errors through misunderstandings.<br>• Allowance must be made for return and repair of sub-standard garments.<br>• Greater costs and risk of damage or loss of goods through increased movement of materials and garments. |

### RISKS OF OFF-SHORE PRODUCTION

• Quality and security against theft and copying is difficult to control.
• Lead times are longer due to shipping schedules and customs clearances.
• Deliveries may be delayed due to such factors as unavailability of materials, bad weather, political instability and strikes.
• Communication difficulties arise from language and cultural differences.
• Currency rate fluctuations cause difficulties in price negotiations.
• Overseas factories will often only handle larger quantities, with minimums usually starting at 500 units.

premises, often at home. Makers have different production capabilities according to the skills of their employees and their equipment and machinery, so the right maker must be chosen to ensure that the quality, quantity and type of garment able to be manufactured matches the requirements of the designer. Some makers specialise in tailored jackets, some do skirts and trousers, others shirts, and some do only stretchwear. Reliability is absolutely essential as retailers may cancel an order if the goods are faulty or delivered late.

Both inside and outside manufacturing arrangements have advantages and disadvantages.

## OFF-SHORE PRODUCTION

To minimise production costs, Australian companies are increasingly manufacturing overseas. The high cost of wages in Australia, compared with those in certain Asian and underdeveloped countries, means that, even with freight costs and government duties and restrictions, garments can be brought into Australia at a price lower than if they were manufactured here.

The type of work done off-shore varies. It may be as simple as embroidery done on a pre-cut panel, or it may be total production from the provision of all materials to the making, finishing, labelling, packaging and shipping back to Australia. Treatments and materials which cannot be obtained in Australia are often available overseas.

The problems associated with off-shore production are similar to those experienced with local contractors, but magnified because the distances and turn-round times are greater. The design house may hire an agent to supervise the operations, or station an employee overseas to represent it and protect its interests. Importers of goods fully or partly manufactured overseas must be aware of the duties and restrictions applied by the Australian government.

For assistance in this area contact the Australian Customs Service office in your state.

# PRODUCTION PROCESSES

While the previous season's garments are still being manufactured, and styles for the new ready-to-wear range are being developed, the production manager starts planning a production schedule for the new season. Production commences once the new styles have been designed, patternmade, sampled, approved and graded.

Production planning determines when and how the garments in a range are to be manufactured. The production manager prepares a flow chart of every activity, such as cutting, sewing and finishing, and distributes the work load over the allotted time to ensure that production flows smoothly and there are no bottle-necks or delays. This work is scheduled to fit in with fabric and trim deliveries, production capacity and lead times, and delivery schedules.

*18.3 Marker preparation. The cutter lays out the various pieces and sizes of the pattern so that no fabric is wasted, and traces them onto paper. (Photograph courtesy of Table Eight.)*

The cutters and machinists, or outside makers, are issued with production sheets and make specifications for all the styles for the coming season, so that cutting markers and fabric can be prepared (See Figs. 7.14–7.16). Actual manufacturing procedures are as follows:

## 1. MARKER PREPARATION

Traditionally, the cutter lays out all the pattern pieces, placing them closely to minimise wastage, and matching stripes, checks, patterns and one-way naps. The pattern pieces are then traced out onto a length of paper or light card, known as a *marker* (Fig. 18.3).

Markers can now be prepared and printed by computer. The most recent technology enables the pattern layout to be held in the memory of the computerised cutter and no paper marker is required at all (Fig. 18.4).

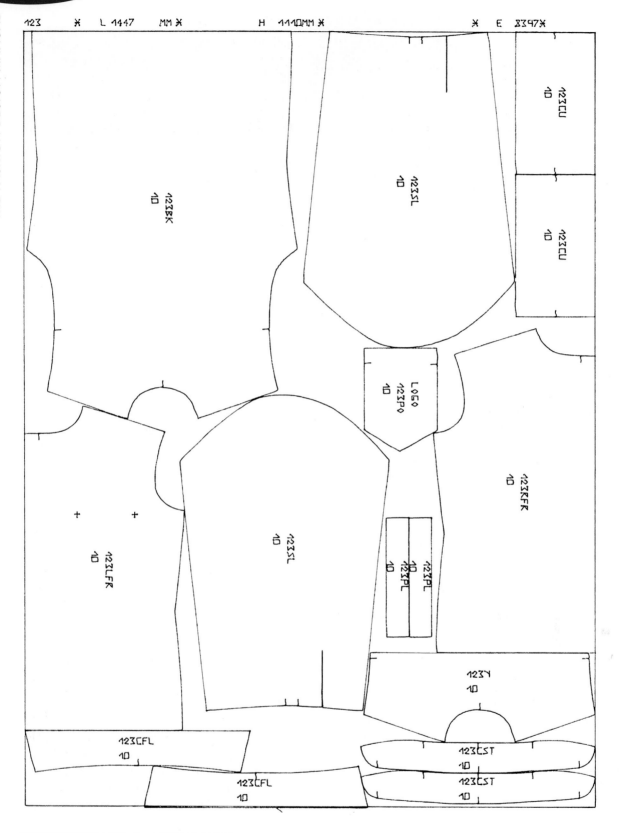

18.4 Computer marker. This finished marker for a size 10 shirt has been prepared by computer. (Marker courtesy of Lectra Systems ™.)

## 2. LAY PREPARATION

A *lay* is the number of fabric thicknesses spread out on a table ready for cutting. A spreading machine holding the roll of fabric moves back and forth over the length required for the marker, unrolling layer upon layer of smooth, straight fabric. A lay may be one thickness or up to 300 thicknesses deep, depending on the fabric. The paper marker is then placed on top, ready for cutting (Fig. 18.5).

## 3. CUTTING

The cutter uses an electric saw with either a round or straight blade to cut around the pattern pieces. Straight knife cutters can cut lays to a depth of 25 centimetres (Fig. 18.6). Drills which pierce the fabric or cut out a small hole are used for internal markings such as dart points or pocket holes. Modern cutting devices use jets of water or laser beams for faster and more accurate cutting. Garment parts may also be cut with a metal die, a sharp tool which cuts like a biscuit-cutter when pressed against the fabric.

18.6 The hand-held straight-knife cutter is guided around the pattern shapes on the marker, to cut single or multiple fabric layers. (Photograph courtesy of Table Eight.)

18.7 Finished cut. The cut pieces are tied together and labelled ready for trimming and sorting for the machinists or makers. (Photograph courtesy of Creative Cutting.)

## 4. BUNDLING

Cut work is bundled, tied and ticketed to indicate the style, size and quantity. Then, together with all the trims required for making such as buttons, labels and shoulder pads, the work is placed in cut work bins in the order in which they are to be sewn, ready for distribution to the machinist. If being done outside, the maker collects the cut work with the make specifications, production sheet and correct production sample. Computerised factories by-pass the bundling or sorting operation with overhead carriers which transport garment parts to the appropriate work station (Fig. 18.7).

## 5. MAKING

Garment production generally follows one of two systems.

### (a) Make through

This method is used in small factories and for high-class work whereby one machinist makes the entire garment.

### (b) Progressive bundle (or piecework)

With this method, each machinist makes up only one section of a garment. These sections are then assembled by other machinists into the whole garment. The work is rotated to alleviate boredom. It

18.5 Lay preparation. A spreading machine is used to unroll the fabric in smooth, straight layers. (Photograph courtesy of Bonds.)

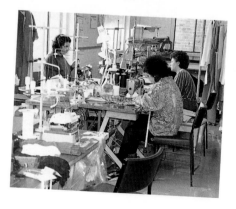

18.8 The production room must be well organised to ensure that the machinists can work as quickly and efficiently as possible. (Photograph courtesy of Table Eight.)

ensures a more consistent and higher quality of work and is faster. Piece workers are paid according to how much work they produce.

All the information necessary for the assembly of the garment, including thread, needle type, stitch type and length, is evident from the sample and is stated on the specifications sheet (Fig. 18.8).

## 6. FINISHING

This includes special tasks, overlocking, hemming, buttons and buttonholes completed away from the production machinist. Most ready-to-wear has no hand-finishing but better quality garments may have details such as belt and button loops, buttons, linings secured and hems levelled by hand (Fig. 18.9).

## 7. PRESSING

Pressing is only done during construction on better garments and is known as *under-pressing*. Open seams and facings

18.10 Quality control. Garments are cleaned and checked for quality, and ticketed ready for packing. (Photograph courtesy of Bonds.)

may be pressed during making and the garment moulded with steam presses. Once completed, all garments are given a final pressing in-house or are sent to a pressing service and hung on hangers ready for checking.

## 8. QUALITY CONTROL

Garments are cleaned inside and out of loose threads, lint and spots and are checked for sewing quality, accuracy, flaws and imperfections (Fig. 18.10). They are also checked against the order to ensure that quantities, colours and sizes are correct. Imperfect garments are sent back to the machinist for repairs, or sold off as seconds. When outside makers do not produce acceptable quality, repairs should be at their own cost, and where extra fabric is required as a result of mistakes or poor quality, the cost should be deducted from their payment.

## 9. DISPATCH

Garments may be kept as stock or to await the rest of the order destined for a particular retailer. If the order is complete, swing tags are attached, the

garments are packed into garment bags or cartons and dispatched to the stores (Fig. 18.11). Upon receipt, the store counts and quality controls the garments to ensure that the order is correct, complete and meets the specified standard.

# COSTING

The production cost of a garment must be calculated so that the wholesale price, which is the price retailers pay for goods they purchase from a manufacturer, can be determined.

As discussed in Chapter 7, the design department fills in a costing sheet for each completed sample, detailing materials and approximate labour costs. The costings are then reworked by the production department, because fabric yields and labour costs invariably alter when the garments go into mass production.

18.11 Dispatch. Garments ready for shipping are packed carefully to minimise damage and soiling in transit. (Photograph courtesy of Table Eight.)

18.9 Although hand-finishing is kept to a minimum in mass-production, occasionally small details need to be hand-worked. (Photograph courtesy of Table Eight.)

If the wholesale price is likely to meet buyer resistance because it is perceived as being too high for the garment or does not fit into the price structure of the store selling the merchandise, the designer may collaborate with the production department to work out cheaper ways to make the garment, either by modifying the design, simplifying the manufacturing or cutting back on quality or quantity of materials.

## COSTING SHEET ANALYSIS

Costing methods are as varied as the companies that do them, but the general process is outlined below. The costing sheet in Figure 18.12 has been completed for a fashion house which uses outside makers for production.

## STYLE

The garment is given a code number or name, plus a couple of words and a production sketch which describes the style. The code number may be developed according to the pattern number, fabric and colour as follows.

*Fabric story* (drill) — 87000
*Pattern number* — 147
*Garment code* — 87147

The same garment in a different fabric might be:

*Fabric story* (rugby knit) — 52000
*Pattern number* — 147
*Garment code* — 52147

## FABRIC

The total metreage or yardage (otherwise known as *yield*) of each fabric in the garment is multiplied by its cost per metre/yard. Some manufacturers allow around 5 per cent extra for wastage and errors. Lining and interfacing fabrics are costed in the same way.

## ACCESSORIES

These include all extras such as trimmings, treatments and packaging costs, and cover everything from buttons, zippers and shoulder pads, to pleating and embroidery, to labels and swing tags. A description of the item may be included here. The cost per unit is multiplied by the number of trimmings used on each garment.

## CUTTING

If cutting is done by an outside contractor, there will be a set price per garment cut. Prices are always lower for larger quantities. If the cutting is done in-house, the cost is based on the cutter's gross wage (including on-costs such as sick-leave and holiday pay), divided by the number of garments cut. So, for example if the cutter earns $25.00 per hour and cuts 40 dresses per hour, the cutting cost is 63 cents per garment.

## MAKE PRICE

Making covers the cost of sewing, trimming and finishing the garment, including hemming and pressing. The procedure for calculating the making cost is the same as for cutting and, once again, the more garments made in a particular style, the lower the cost per unit.

## OVERHEADS

These are the costs of running a business and include designing, pattern-making and sampling, employing staff and owning or leasing and running equipment, premises and machinery. Overheads are covered by a set dollar value, or a percentage added to the cost of materials and CMT. Overhead costs are determined by the size of the company and the structure of the business. The percentage is calculated by dividing the annual costs of running the business by the number of garments sold over, say, a 12 month period to give the average amount to be added to each garment.

## FREIGHT

The cost of shipping each garment from the maker to the manufacturer and/or on to the retailer must also be added. Freight costs are higher for imported garments, and may also include import duties and agents' fees.

## TOTAL COST

This is the final cost of the garment, resulting from the addition of all of the costs outlined above.

## WHOLESALE PRICE

The wholesale price is determined by adding a mark-up to the total cost. The mark-up covers additional expenses, such as discounts, sales commission and other overheads not included in the total cost, plus a margin for profit.

As a general guide, most manufacturers aim for a 100 per cent mark-up on the total cost to achieve the wholesale price, and retailers add another 100 per cent to the wholesale price to achieve the retail price. That is, the selling price of the garment from a retail outlet is approximately four times the cost of manufacturing that garment. For example, a dress costing $50 to manufacture would wholesale for $100, and would retail for $200. However, some companies work on a mark-up as low as 40 per cent.

The percentage mark-up is arrived at by dividing the profit (wholesale selling price minus cost price) by the cost price.

*Example 1*
$$\frac{\text{Profit } \$74.39}{\text{Cost } \$74.39} \times \frac{100}{1} = \begin{array}{l}100 \text{ per cent}\\ \text{mark-up.}\end{array}$$

*Example 2*
$$\frac{\text{Profit } \$29.76}{\text{Cost } \$74.39} \times \frac{100}{1} = \begin{array}{l}40 \text{ per cent}\\ \text{mark-up.}\end{array}$$

| | FABRIC | COST | YDGE | WIDTH | TOTAL | STYLE |
|---|---|---|---|---|---|---|
| 1. | PASTE FLORAL BEMBURG PRINT | $9·50 | 3·8 M | 115 | 36·10 | 87147 |
| 2. | | | | | | |
| 3. | | | | | | |
| 4. | | | | | | |
| 5. | | | | | | |
| 6. | | | | | | |
| 7. | | | | | | |
| 8. | | | | | | |

### INTERFACING

| Pieces: Fusing Service 2 | Cost: ·14c | Total: ·28c |
|---|---|---|
| Ydge: 1·2 M cuts 2 | Cost: 2·25 | Total: $2·70 |

### BUTTONS

| | Amount | Size | Type | Cost | Total |
|---|---|---|---|---|---|
| 1. | 11 | 15mm | JAKOYA SHELL | 42c | $4·62 |
| 2. | | | | | |
| 3. | | | | | |
| 4. | | | | | |
| 5. | | | | | |
| 6. | | | | | |
| 7. | | | | | |
| 8. | | | | | |

| MAKE | $20 -50 | |
|---|---|---|
| Fabric | 38·80 | |
| Access | 6·40 | |
| O/heads +10% | 6·69 | |
| Cut | 1·50 | |
| Disc. | — | |
| Freight | 50c | |
| Our Cost | 74·39 | |
| W/sale | 148·78 | |
| Percentage | M/U 100% | |
| Price No 2 | | |
| Price No 3 | | |

### OTHER ACCESSORIES

| Shoulder Pads: | |
|---|---|
| Elastic: | |
| Zip: | |
| Belt: | |
| | |
| Pleating: | |
| Trims: | |
| LABELS etc. $1·50 . | |

*18.12 Costing sheet. (See also Figs. 7.14 & 7.15 for the design and make specification sheets that accompany this sheet.)*

## COST MERCHANDISING

The actual mark-up, and therefore the final wholesale price, of a garment is finally determined by the question 'Does it look worth the price?' If not, the price may be lowered to make it more acceptable. Sometimes the garment may look more expensive and the price can be raised. These pricing adjustments definitely affect the sales potential of a garment, so much so that occasionally a manufacturer will offer a garment with a very low mark-up, known as a *loss leader*, to attract buyers who may then buy from the other garments in the range.

Price number 2 and Price number 3 on this cost sheet are alternative prices prepared for different clients, which might have a different percentage mark-up.

# LABELLING

Labelling is the fashion industry's identification system and serves two primary functions. Firstly, the label brands a garment as the product of a particular manufacturer, designer or store. Consumer loyalty can be built up through label familiarity, and customers may purchase a garment because of the status, fit, quality or styling they associate with a particular label. The identification label reflects the company's image, and is usually sewn at the centre back neck, waistband or inside jacket facing. Some labels are attached to the outside, and become a design feature and status symbol. Printed labels are cheapest to produce and are generally used on less expensive garments, while woven twill or satin labels with folded edges are used in better quality garments.

The second function of labelling is to inform customers about the goods they are buying (Figs. 18.13 & 18.14). The Trade Practices Act, which is administered by the Federal Bureau of Consumer Affairs, requires that textile articles be labelled with the following information:

- textile fibre content
- care instructions
- size coding
- country of origin (if imported)
- brand name
- fire hazard for children's night wear.

This information should be supplied on one label where possible, but several labels are acceptable. The label must be permanent and remain legible and attached throughout the useful life of the garment. It should be clearly visible and easily accessible and placed so as not to irritate the wearer. These labels are often tucked under the designer label or inserted into a side-seam. Items to which a permanent label cannot be attached must be supplied with a removable ticket, an information pamphlet or printed instructions on the packet.

---

*18.13 International Care symbols and meanings.*

Fibre content labels show the predominant fibre first, with the other fibres following in order of decreasing content, sometimes listed as a percentage. With this system, a Polyester/Wool label indicates higher polyester content, while a Wool/Polyester label indicates a higher wool content. Information regarding labelling standards for textiles and clothing is available from the Standards Association of Australia.

There is a wide range of Australian standards applying to textiles and clothing, but those of particular interest are:

AS 2392–1990  Labelling of Clothing, Household Textiles and Furnishings

AS 1957–1987  Care Labelling of Clothing, Household Textiles, Furnishings, Piece Goods and Yarns

AS 2622–1987  Textile Products — Fibre Content Labelling

AS 1182–1980  Size Coding Scheme for Infants' and Children's Clothing

AS 1344–1975  Size Coding Scheme for Women's Clothing

| CARE SYMBOLS AND MEANINGS | | |
|---|---|---|
| WASHING | 〰60° | Can be washed |
| | | Number inside indicates temperature in degrees centigrade |
| | ⊠ | Do not wash |
| BLEACHING | △ | Can be bleached |
| | ⊠ | Do not bleach |
| PRESSING | 🔲 | Can be ironed. Dots inside iron symbol indicate temperature |
| | | • Up to 120°C – Cool |
| | | •• Up to 150°C – Medium |
| | | ••• Up to 200°C – Hot |
| | ⊠ | Do not iron |
| DRY CLEANING | Ⓐ | Can be dry cleaned with any solvent |
| | Ⓟ | Can be dry cleaned with terchorethylene or white spirit |
| | Ⓕ | Can be dry cleaned with white spirit only |
| | ⊗ | Do not dry clean |

18.14 Content and care instruction labels.
(Labels courtesy of Pont and Co.)

**C1**

| ALL COTTON | POLYESTER & RAYON |
| ALL NYLON | POLYESTER & VISCOSE |
| ALL RAYON | POLYESTER & WOOL |
| ALL WOOL | COTTON & NYLON |
| PURE LINEN | COTTON & RAYON |
| PURE SILK | |
| PURE WOOL | ONE SIZE FIT MOST |

**C1**

| ACETATE | SMALL |
| ACRYLIC | MEDIUM |
| POLYESTER | LARGE |
| TRI-ACETATE | |
| VISCOSE | |

**C7**

MADE IN AUSTRALIA — OS, XOS, SSM, SM, S, M, L, XL, XXL, XS

POLYESTER & ACETATE
POLYESTER & ACRYLIC
POLYESTER & COTTON
POLYESTER & NYLON

**SIZING**

C2 — Women 8 to 26
SIZE 8 — To fit cm — BUST 75 — WAIST 55 — HIP 80

C2 — Baby 00 to 1
SIZE 00 — Weight 8 kg — Length 68 cm

C2 — Children 2 to 16
SIZE 2 — Height 92 cm — Waist 54 cm

C7 — NUMBERS FROM 1 TO 46

**WORK LABELS**

C3 — No. _____  Size _____  M. _____  F. _____

**FIRE WARNING**

C6 — WARNING — HIGH FIRE DANGER KEEP AWAY FROM FIRE

C4 — STYLED TO REDUCE FIRE DANGER

C3 — LOW FIRE DANGER

PRICES:
C1 _____
C2 _____
C3 _____
C4 _____
C5 _____
C6 _____
C7 _____
C8 _____
C9 _____

**Care instructions**

C3 — CARE INSTRUCTIONS — HAND WASH, DRIP DRY, WARM IRON

C3 — CARE INSTRUCTIONS — HAND WASH, DRIP DRY, COOL IRON

C4 — CARE INSTRUCTIONS — HAND WASH, DRIP DRY, WARM IRON / POLYESTER

C4 — CARE INSTRUCTIONS — HAND WASH, DRIP DRY, WARM IRON / COTTON

C4 — CARE INSTRUCTIONS — HAND WASH, DRIP DRY, WARM IRON / POLYESTER & COTTON

C4 — CARE INSTRUCTIONS — HAND WASH, DRIP DRY, WARM IRON / POLYESTER & VISCOSE

C4 — CARE INSTRUCTIONS — HAND WASH, DRIP DRY, WARM IRON / ACRYLIC

C2 — DRY CLEAN ONLY (A) — WARM IRON

C4 — CARE INSTRUCTIONS — WARM MACHINE WASH, DO NOT BLEACH, TUMBLE DRY, WARM IRON

C4 — CARE INSTRUCTIONS — HOT MACHINE WASH, SPIN DRY, HOT IRON / COTTON

C5 — POLYESTER COTTON — WARM MACHINE WASH, WARM RINSE WELL, DO NOT BLEACH, REDUCED SPIN, MAY BE TUMBLE DRIED — WARM, WARM IRON, DRY CLEANABLE (P) (50)

C5 — CARE INSTRUCTIONS — HAND WASH IN WARM WATER, DO NOT SOAK BLEACH OR WRING, DRY DRY OR DRY WITHOUT DELAY AWAY FROM DIRECT HEAT, WARM IRON ONLY, DRY CLEANABLE (P) (30)

**C8**

C8 — WASHING INSTRUCTIONS — HAND WASH, DRIP DRY, WARM IRON / POLYESTER & VISCOSE / ONE SIZE FIT MOST / MADE IN AUSTRALIA

C8 — WASHING INSTRUCTIONS — HAND WASH, DRIP DRY, WARM IRON / COTTON / ONE SIZE FIT MOST / MADE IN AUSTRALIA

C8 — WASHING INSTRUCTIONS — HAND WASH, DRIP DRY, WARM IRON / POLYESTER COTTON / ONE SIZE FIT MOST / MADE IN AUSTRALIA

C8 — WASHING INSTRUCTIONS — HAND WASH, DRIP DRY, WARM IRON / POLYESTER & COTTON / ONE SIZE FIT MOST / MADE IN AUSTRALIA

C8 — CONTENT: POLYESTER, COTTON, POLYESTER & COTTON, POLYESTER & VISCOSE / SIZES FROM 8 TO 16: SMALL, MEDIUM, LARGE, X LARGE, XX LARGE

**SELF ADHESIVE SIZES**

C9

|  |  |
|--------|------|
| S | 6 |
| | 8 |
| M | 10 |
| L | 12 |
| XL | 14 |
| | 16 |
| | 18 |
| XXL | 20 |
| | 22 |
| | 24 |
| | 26 |

AS 1954–1976  Size Designation Scheme for Men's Clothing

AS 1249–1990  Children's Nightclothes having Reduced Fire Hazard

AS HB11–1988  Handbook of Textile Standards for Students

Swing tags are non-compulsory tickets attached to the outside of a garment where they are clearly visible when hanging on a rack. Useful as another form of advertising, they also provide easy identification for the retailer and shopper, with information on the brand, style number, size and price.

# COMPUTERS IN GARMENT PRODUCTION

As well as being indispensable for standard business application, computers are now used in virtually every area of apparel planning and production, and increasingly in apparel design.

## COMPUTERS IN RANGE PLANNING

Computer technology can be used by management, marketing, merchandising and design staff to:
(a) cost and price garments, using fabric and trim estimates,
(b) record styles,
(c) analyse sales in terms of colours, sizes and styles,
(d) record fabrics and trims in stock and on order,
(e) calculate fabric and trim requirements with automatic updates for new or completed orders,
(f) coordinate fabric deliveries, production and stock deliveries, and
(g) compile and print cutting sheets.

The sales team may use computers to:
(a) collate customer details, account information and orders,
(b) produce progress reports for budget and sales forecasts,
(c) check stock availability for re-orders,
(d) prepare correspondence and promotional material; for example, memos, newsletters, mailing lists,
(e) analyse orders by delivery date, style, fabric, size, range, story, season, customer, agent, sales level, and
(f) analyse sales territories and competing outlets.

## COMPUTER AIDED DESIGN (CAD)

Computer Aided Design (CAD), the use of colour graphic computers and design software for the design and production of professional quality images, has made rapid developments in the last few years (Fig. 18.15).

CAD assists designers by relieving them of the tedious, repetitive aspects of their work and allows them to concentrate on more creative areas. CAD can be used for the following functions:
(a) photographs of models can be scanned in so the garments look like they are being worn,
(b) silhouettes and details can be erased and modified, and garment parts interchanged,
(c) 16.7 million colours can be chosen for shade variations or completely new colours. These colours can be identified using international colour coding systems such as Pantone®,
(d) fabric swatches showing accurate colours and textures can be applied directly to the design on the screen. A textile swatch file, colour palette file and design library is stored in the computer's memory,

*18.15 Computer Aided Design (CAD) opens up a wide range of creative possibilities for the designer. (Computer images courtesy of Lectra Systems ™.)*

(e) completed designs can be shown to merchandisers, buyers and customers, who can see exactly what the finished product will look like. This reduces the number of samples needed, shortens the design cycle and reduces design and workroom costs, and

(f) new routes of communication and networking are opened up. Finished designs, complete with measurements, textures and coded colours, can be sent via modem on a telephone line to manufacturers interstate or overseas, enabling separate functions to be carried out in different locations.

## TEXTILE DESIGN USING CAD

(a) Textile patterns, prints, weaves, knits and textures can be scanned in from pictures or from the actual cloth, or a video camera linked to the computer can take the textile image into the system and onto the screen,

(b) patterns can be used life-size, scaled down to fit the illustrated garment design, or scaled up for detailed design modification,

*18.16 Digitising the pattern. The pattern pieces are put into the computer by digitising, or marking, each point. (Photograph courtesy of Bonds.)*

(c) modifications include size and colour changes, motifs added or changed, repeats changed,

(d) a library of garment shapes is held in memory and can be used to try out new prints, textures and weaves,

(e) colour separations of the design can be made, ready for printing, and

(f) costings can be done for prints and knits using several colours. The computer calculates what colours are used in the design and in what percentages (the cost of the dyeing depends on the colour).

## DESIGNER'S SKETCHING SYSTEMS USING CAD

(a) Quick, accurate sketches can be drawn on the VDU,

(b) existing illustrations in the computer's memory can be used as a starting point and modified as required,

(c) there is a choice of illustrating media, from basic line drawing with varied line thicknesses, to airbrush, solid colour, water colour or oils effects, even brush strokes and shading to represent folds and draping. Freehand sketching is possible with a stylus and tablet,

(d) photographic images of faces and bodies can be input and 'clothed' for a very realistic image, and

(e) full colour, finished sketches, drawings or glossy photographs can be generated.

## COMPUTER AIDED MANUFACTURING (CAM)

Computer technology in apparel production has been available since the 1960s. Computerisation and automation streamline every stage of the production process. It minimises costs, increases the rate of throughput, increases productivity and improves product quality. Com-

puter technology also allows quick responses to changing conditions, more flexibility and a competitive edge.

## PATTERNS AND GRADING USING CAD (Figs. 18.16 & 18.17)

(a) Pattern design systems enable the patternmaker to prepare new patterns from basic blocks or existing production patterns by manipulating them on the VDU screen,

(b) every point and line of a pattern can be moved to separate parts, introduce seams, add seam allowances, or add darts, pleats and fullness,

(c) once size grading rules are input by the operator, grading can be performed automatically, and

(d) a stack grade is shown on the screen so that the coordinates for each size can be checked.

## MARKERS AND CUTTING USING CAD/CAM (Figs. 18.18 & 18.19)

(a) Once patterns are correct and graded, the computer plots the cutting lay. Alternatively, the layout is planned on the VDU screen and transferred directly to the computerised cutter, eliminating the

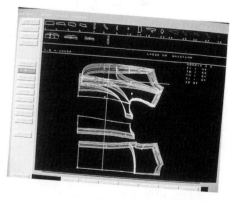

*18.17 Computer grading. The graded nest created by the computer shows several sizes stacked together. (Computer image courtesy of Lectra Systems ™.)*

need for paper patterns and markers,

(b) the cutting efficiency of a lay is shown as a percentage and the pattern pieces can be arranged to achieve considerable savings through reduced fabric wasteage,

(c) fabric spreading systems are automated, and

(d) a high speed automatic cutter can cut up to eight times faster than a human and twice as accurately.

## PRODUCTION PROCESSES USING COMPUTER MOVER SYSTEMS (CMS)

(a) Workstations are fully automated to reduce handling. A computer controlled arm brings the garment right to the sewing machine, maximising comfort and efficiency for the operator. Some operations can

even be completed without removing the garment from the carrier, and

(b) some machinery is semi-automated, so that the stitching follows a pre-programmed path which is electronically controlled.

As well as actual garment manufacturing capabilities, computer software systems can be used to plan production schedules and forecasts, and to monitor and evaluate production progress. With the use of modems, any part of the design and production process can now be controlled from anywhere in the world.

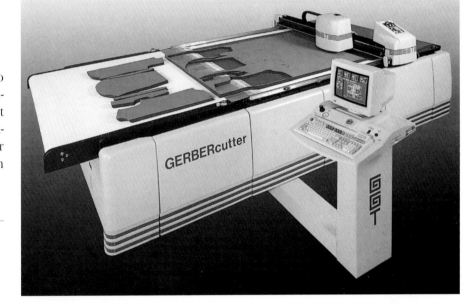

▲ 18.19 Computerised cutting. This medium-ply cutter used for Computer Aided Manufacturing (CAM) has a vacuum system which holds the fabric to the table. (Photograph courtesy of Gerber Garment Technology Inc.)

▼ 18.18 Marker making. The cutting lay is prepared by the computer operator, and drawn onto large sheets of paper by a high-speed plotter. (Photograph courtesy of Lectra Systems ™.)

CHAPTER 19

# INTRODUCTION

Apparel manufacturers sell their finished garments to fashion retailers who in turn sell to consumers. Sales are either done directly from manufacturer to retailer or through a wholesale distributor or agent.

Selling and production commence once the garments for the new range have been designed, patternmade and sampled. The manufacturer may start production before the range is sold to retailers, thereby permitting rapid delivery because the styles are already in stock. However this can be risky for the supplier because large inventories may accumulate if a style does not sell as well as anticipated. Also, profits may be lost if orders on a best seller exceed supply.

Alternatively, and more commonly, production commences once the range has been shown to the retail buyers and orders have been placed. Apparel ordered before production commences is said to be ordered *on indent*.

# FROM THE MANUFACTURER TO THE RETAILER — WHOLESALE SALES

Wholesale sales describes the selling of merchandise to others who will then retail it. Every year the manufacturer presents from two to six ranges to the retail buyers. These include First Summer, Second Summer (including Holiday and Resort), First Winter and Second Winter. In addition to this, some companies continually release new styles throughout the year. In Australia, holiday and resort ranges are usually incorporated into second summer because the seasons coincide. However, in the northern hemisphere holiday and resort ranges have a special significance because many people holiday in warmer climates and require summer clothing during their winter season. Also, end of year formals and Christmas parties are an ideal opportunity to brighten up store windows with glamorous evening wear.

The timing of range showings and deliveries varies considerably, but is approximately as shown below.

| SEASON | SHOWING | FOR DELIVERY |
|---|---|---|
| 1st Summer (Spring/transeason) | mid-March to end April | July/August/September |
| 2nd (High) Summer, including | mid-July to mid-August | October/November/December |
|    Holiday (formals/Christmas/New Year) | | |
|    Resort (for travelling and holidays) | | |
| 1st Winter (Autumn/transeason) | mid-September to end October | February/March/April |
| 2nd Winter (optional) | mid-February to end February | May |

Garment deliveries are usually grouped into fabric and coordinate stories, and staggered so the retailers have a steady supply of new stock.

## LAUNCHING THE RANGE

The method of launching the range depends on the image of the company and the type of garments being sold. High profile fashion houses stage professionally modelled, highly publicised fashion shows in prominent venues to attract attention to their new season's designs. Members of the media, social columnists, fashion editors and notable clients are invited to ensure maximum publicity.

For smaller or less up-market manufacturers, showings may take place at their own showrooms, with garments simply hanging on racks or demonstrated by a house model and salesperson.

## SELLING THE RANGE

The selling period lasts for two to four months. Sales staff make appointments with clients to view the range at the manufacturer's showrooms, where the client is free to inspect garments at close range and to consult the style book made available for this purpose (Fig. 19.1).

The style book is like a catalogue which shows illustrations of the garments grouped into stories with style numbers and descriptions, fabric swatches of all colourways, alternative fabrics, prices and delivery dates (Fig. 19.2).

Fashion houses with interstate and country clients may send their samples out on the road with travelling sales representatives who call into the buyer's office or make presentations from temporary premises such as an hotel room.

Alternatively, an agent may be engaged to sell on behalf of the manufacturer for a commission, usually 10 per cent of the total sales. The agent maintains a showroom, sometimes carries stock, and may represent several non-competing labels which can be carried

19.1 The range is shown in the manufacturer's showroom where there is room for the buyer to view the garments in comfort. (Photograph courtesy of Table Eight.)

by the same customer. For example, an agent may carry eveningwear from one manufacturer, skirts and blouses from another, knitwear from another and belts from an accessories supplier. This selection of ranges offers the retail buyer a variety of styles and garments. It also allows the agent the flexibility of dropping a line which is not selling well while still receiving income from the others.

## MANUFACTURER'S DISTRIBUTION POLICY

Distribution is the process of getting the apparel from the manufacturer to each retail outlet in the correct quantities, styles, colours and sizes, and at the proper time.

The distribution of merchandise is planned so that it is sold through the most appropriate outlets in the best geo-

graphical locations whilst not creating unfair competition between retailers, and to maximise sales.

Although new customers are constantly sought, distribution policies must exist to look after the interests of existing clients. Many manufacturers opt for *selective distribution*, which restricts the selling of a particular brand to only one retailer within a trading area. This sometimes acts in the interests of the supplier by creating competition between the retailers who want to carry the label.

Manufacturers of high profile, well-known national or international brands, such as jeans, often have a policy of *open distribution* and will sell to any outlet regardless of location. An open distribution policy does not suit a retailer wanting to offer exclusive merchandise to his or her customers.

A company may manufacture fabrics and/or apparel as well as sell the merchandise through its own stores. This is known as a *vertical operation* and allows the company to grow by expanding into different levels of the fashion industry.

A company may also grow *horizontally* by staying at the same level within the industry. For example, a company

19.2 Style books are used by manufacturers or wholesalers when selling to retailers. This example serves a dual purpose as style sheet and order form. (Style sheet courtesy of Palmer Corporation.)

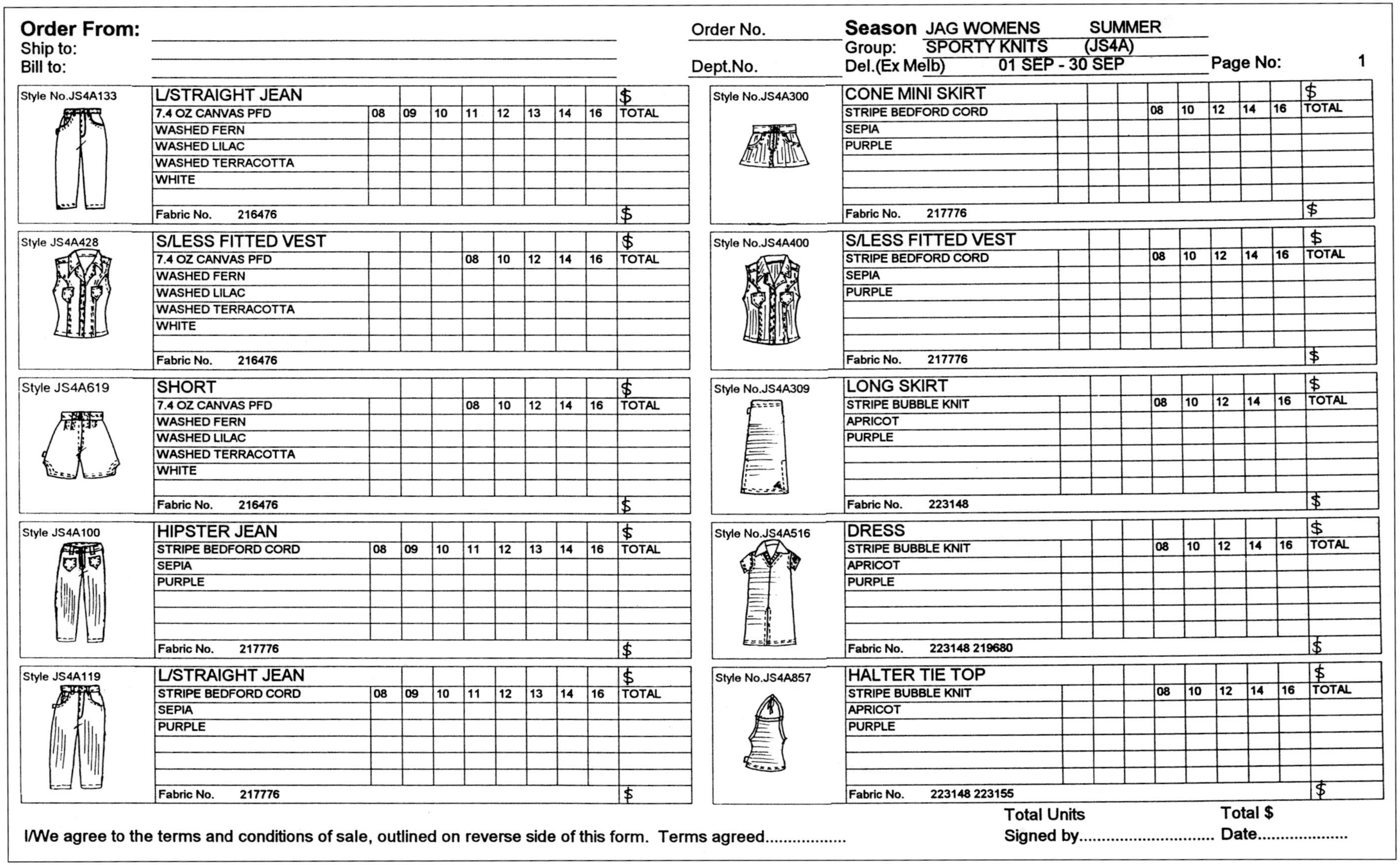

**Order From:**
Ship to:
Bill to:

Order No. _____
Dept.No. _____

**Season** JAG WOMENS    SUMMER
Group: SPORTY KNITS (JS4A)
Del.(Ex Melb)   01 SEP - 30 SEP    Page No:   1

### Left panel items

| Style | Description / Colours | 08 | 09 | 10 | 11 | 12 | 13 | 14 | 16 | $ TOTAL |
|---|---|---|---|---|---|---|---|---|---|---|
| JS4A133 | **L/STRAIGHT JEAN** — 7.4 OZ CANVAS PFD / WASHED FERN / WASHED LILAC / WASHED TERRACOTTA / WHITE — Fabric No. 216476 | | | | | | | | | $ |
| JS4A428 | **S/LESS FITTED VEST** — 7.4 OZ CANVAS PFD / WASHED FERN / WASHED LILAC / WASHED TERRACOTTA / WHITE — Fabric No. 216476 | | | | | | | | | $ |
| JS4A619 | **SHORT** — 7.4 OZ CANVAS PFD / WASHED FERN / WASHED LILAC / WASHED TERRACOTTA / WHITE — Fabric No. 216476 | | | | | | | | | $ |
| JS4A100 | **HIPSTER JEAN** — STRIPE BEDFORD CORD / SEPIA / PURPLE — Fabric No. 217776 | | | | | | | | | $ |
| JS4A119 | **L/STRAIGHT JEAN** — STRIPE BEDFORD CORD / SEPIA / PURPLE — Fabric No. 217776 | | | | | | | | | $ |

### Right panel items

| Style | Description / Colours | 08 | 10 | 12 | 14 | 16 | $ TOTAL |
|---|---|---|---|---|---|---|---|
| JS4A300 | **CONE MINI SKIRT** — STRIPE BEDFORD CORD / SEPIA / PURPLE — Fabric No. 217776 | | | | | | $ |
| JS4A400 | **S/LESS FITTED VEST** — STRIPE BEDFORD CORD / SEPIA / PURPLE — Fabric No. 217776 | | | | | | $ |
| JS4A309 | **LONG SKIRT** — STRIPE BUBBLE KNIT / APRICOT / PURPLE — Fabric No. 223148 | | | | | | $ |
| JS4A516 | **DRESS** — STRIPE BUBBLE KNIT / APRICOT / PURPLE — Fabric No. 223148 219680 | | | | | | $ |
| JS4A857 | **HALTER TIE TOP** — STRIPE BUBBLE KNIT / APRICOT / PURPLE — Fabric No. 223148 223155 | | | | | | $ |

Total Units _____    Total $ _____
Signed by ..................    Date ..............

I/We agree to the terms and conditions of sale, outlined on reverse side of this form.   Terms agreed..............

RETAIL: BUYING AND SELLING FASHION

may remain totally retail but introduce new labels to diversify products, or even open new branches.

## THE BUYER

Buyers are representatives from retail outlets who view the latest ranges and make purchases for the coming season based on the budget allocated to their department or store.

Although some designers have little contact with the sales side of business, apparel manufacturers, designers, sales staff and buyers are all in the business of satisfying the needs and wants of the retail consumer, so liaison between them can be very useful. The sales staff can play an important role by acting as intermediary between designer and buyer, and by relaying back to the designer comments about the range itself and information about possible future directions. A buyer can also provide valuable feedback which will assist the designer's timing in presenting the right garment at the right time. By suggesting certain directions that experience has led him or her to anticipate, the buyer can bring the designer closer to actual market needs.

When viewing the range, a buyer has to consider the age, economic bracket and lifestyle of his or her clientele, and to decide, up to six months in advance, what they will be looking for and when they will want it. If the garments shown are not right for the target customer, the buyer should not order, regardless of his or her personal preferences.

Buyers making purchases for different retail locations will be looking for different things from the same range. A buyer from Queensland will require very different garments for his or her clients than will a buyer from Tasmania. Ideally, the range will have garments which appeal to both.

Although the ability to predict which garments will and won't sell is vital to the survival of the company, every range

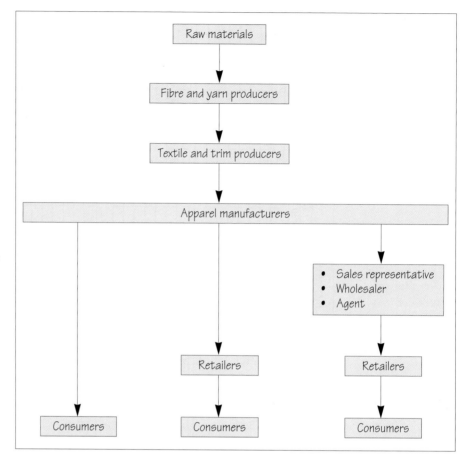

has its surprises. A garment which sells only moderately in the showroom may be a hot seller when it reaches the shop-floor and generate many reorders.

## RETAIL SALES

The dynamics of the fashion retail market have a major impact on the Australian economy as a whole, as can be seen from a report released by MINTEL which states that overall sales for clothing in Australia in 1992 reached $10 billion in retail dollars.[1]

Retailing is the direct selling of merchandise to individual consumers in exchange for money or credit. Success at retail level is one way to measure a designer's success because it is an indicator of consumer acceptance. Retailing is the last step in the channel of distribution which takes a garment from raw materials stage via the designer, manu-

*19.3 Fashion distribution channels. Retailers are the last step in the distribution of fashion before it reaches the consumer.*

facturing process and sales people to the consumer (Fig. 19.3).

### TYPE OF OUTLET

There are approximately 2822 men's and boys' and 9673 women's and girls' fashion retail outlets in Australia.[2] The basic types of retailer are:

#### 1. Department stores

Department stores are so called because stock is displayed in separate sections,

1. This data is drawn from MINTEL's study of the market for casual wear in Australia.

2. Unpublished figures from the Australian Bureau of Statistics, August 1992. These figures only include those retailers who employ staff.

or departments, within the store. These stores carry a wide range of fashion and general household merchandise across a range of price levels. Department stores offer many services such as credit facilities, lay-bys, delivery and mail or phone orders. In Australia, the two largest department stores are David Jones and Myer/Grace Bros. Others include John Martins in Adelaide and Aherns in Western Australia.

## 2. Branch stores

A branch store is an offshoot of an already well-established store which is opened in another location. The original store is known as the *flagship store* and is usually the leading store representing a retailer or designer.

Although the buying, merchandising, advertising and management of branch stores usually conforms to a centralised policy set by the parent store, different locations may adapt their decor, fittings, merchandise and displays to suit the local market. Branch store merchandise may also be available through other retailers, with the parent company acting as the wholesale supplier. Jag and Country Road are examples of branch stores around Australia.

## 3. Chain stores

These are a series of identical stores in different locations, operated from a central buying office. They sell own-brand merchandise which is only available at these stores, and the merchandise and layout is essentially uniform throughout all the stores. Cue, Sportsgirl, Katies and Sussan are well-known fashion retail chains.

## 4. Variety Stores and Discount Department Stores

These stores carry a wide variety of merchandise in the lower price bracket ranging from grocery items to sporting goods and clothing. Kmart, Target, Coles and Big W fall into this category.

## 5. Specialty stores

These offer only apparel or one type of apparel, and are often known as boutiques. Bridal wear, maternity wear, uniforms, accessories, shoes and menswear are frequently sold in specialty stores.

Because these stores tend to be small and operate independently, their prices are usually higher than chain stores in order to cover their lower sales volumes and higher overheads.

## 6. Mail-order (direct-mail marketing)

Mail-order houses offer merchandise to their customers through catalogues. They enable customers to shop at home, order by mail or telephone, and pay by cheque or credit card with a money-back guarantee if the purchaser is not satisfied with the goods. Some mail-order houses have catalogue showrooms or retail outlets and even some retailers find that catalogue phone and mail orders bring them increased business.

Telecommunication shopping, done from home via television or computer, is set to become more important in the future as technology advances.

## 7. Franchise

A franchise is an independent store which pays to use the name and market the product of an established company. The parent company, or *franchisor*, may offer assistance in organisation, training, advertising and management, and carefully monitors the progress of the franchisee. Fashion franchise operations are not very common.

## 8. Concession store

This is a store within a store; for example, the Covers and Carla Zampatti stores in Grace Bros' Sydney store. Concessions are let out to fashion houses for a rental per square foot of space occupied, and/or a percentage of turnover. Overheads are minimised for the concessionaire who only provides fixtures, fittings, point of sale merchandise and staff, while the concession giver is able to offer increased product variety without the risk of carrying the stock themselves.

Concept Shops are similar to concession stores in that they may be a store within a store, or an area which is dedicated to carrying one particular label. However, with a concept shop the merchandise is owned by the retailer, not the fashion house.

## 9. Party-plan selling

This type of retailing is done without a store by selling directly to customers through parties held in private homes. The sales person presents the apparel, takes orders, schedules delivery dates and makes bookings for further parties. The host or hostess receives a gift for holding the party. Lingerie, children's wear and knit fashions are often sold in this way.

## 10. Factory outlets

Factory outlets are owned by apparel manufacturers who sell samples, seconds, ends of lines, overruns and out-of-season goods direct to the public at reduced prices. These stores are usually located near the factory or away from their regular retail accounts.

## LOCATION OF OUTLET

A store has more chance of success if the location is convenient for customers. Because many fashion purchases are impulse buys, more passing traffic usually means a higher volume of sales, and the retailer can then operate on smaller mark-ups and lower prices while still making good profits.

Before opening a new store, market research is done to determine the clothes shopping patterns of the local population. The retailer needs to know the amount of passing pedestrian traffic, how, when and where these people shop, their ages, income and fashion style, the busy and quiet times, what competition is in the area, and how well other businesses are doing.

## STORE IMAGE AND POSITIONING

A store cannot be all things to all people, and a certain degree of specialisation is necessary if a store is to project a strong fashion image to the consumer. In the same way that the fashion designer understands the requirements of the people who will wear his or her designs, the fashion retailer must focus on satisfying the needs and wants of the targeted customer by creating a certain environment, and by supplying a specific type of merchandise within a set price range.

*Image* is the personality or character presented to the public, and is determined by the store's merchandise, interior decor, window display, promotion and customer services. The aim of the retailer is to provide an inviting atmosphere which the customer relates to and

*19.4 The polished and spacious decor in Bracewell's Sydney boutique reflects the up-market and fashion-forward merchandise the store carries. (Photograph courtesy of Michael Bracewell.)*

feels comfortable in, and which creates excitement and a desire to purchase.

Regardless of whether a store carries its own label, a single label or a mix of labels, it positions itself in the market according to its level of *fashion leadership*.

There are three levels of fashion leadership.

### 1. Strong fashion leadership

There are relatively few of these stores because only a small section of the population requires or can afford the latest styles the moment they first appear. They carry 'better-end' designer fashions which rate highly in the areas of innovation, originality, quality and price. Such stores include Carla Zampatti, Trent Nathan, George Gross and Harry Who, Read's of Woollahra, Bracewell and Riada in Sydney, and Saba in Melbourne (Fig. 19.4).

### 2. Mainstream fashion

Stores in this category are most numerous. They offer fashions which are part-way through their life-cycle and rising in popularity. They suit the majority of the population by offering moderate styling and prices. Most department stores are positioned at this level, even though they may have departments dedicated to forward fashions. Such stores include David Jones, Country Road, Sportsgirl, General Pants, Just Jeans and Cue.

### 3. Mass market

These volume retailers offer their versions of well established, successful styles to fashion followers, at lower prices. Target, Katies and Kmart fit this category.

# FASHION RETAIL ORGANISATION

As well as the day-to-day management activities of customer service, financial record-keeping, stock-taking and staff

supervision, important functions for a fashion retailer are *merchandising* and *fashion promotion*.

## MERCHANDISING

Merchandising is the planning, buying and selling of fashion goods to a target group of consumers. Merchandise planning ensures that garments that will sell the best are in the store at the right time and at the right price for the customers, and keeps stock turning over steadily and profitably. Knowing in advance what stock is coming in means that promotions can be planned accordingly.

When working out the merchandise plan for the coming season, they buyer prepares the following:

### 1. The dollar merchandise plan

This is how much money can be spent for the coming season, with a budget based on last year's turnover and anticipated future selling conditions. The buyer must consider profit objectives, expected sales, stock levels and rate of turnover, operating expenses, population, employment and demographic changes and economic conditions.

### 2. The buying plan

The buying plan is a general outline of the types and quantities of merchandise to be purchased, manufacturers' delivery times, and the budget allocated to each purchase.

Although this plan cannot be finalised until the manufacturers' ranges have been viewed, it ensures that the planned assortments are in line with customer demand and frees the buyer to concentrate on the fashion styling when selecting merchandise.

### 3. Assortment planning

This is a comprehensive and detailed break-up of the various styles, quantities, sizes, colours and prices of merchandise to be stocked in a coming season. For example:

40 × Pure Wool Pullovers
Size Breakup — 10 × S, 20 × M, 10 × L
Colours — Red, Yellow, Navy, Black
Wholesale Price —$50.00 per unit

To stock *in depth*, the buyer purchases large quantities of one or a couple of styles across a range of sizes. Basic items such as jeans and T-shirts are stocked in depth because the buyer can be sure they will sell well.

To stock *in breadth*, the buyer orders smaller quantities of a wide range of styles, fabrics, colours, prices and sizes to tempt the customer into multiple purchases.

When planning the assortment, a buyer must keep up with fashion trends yet still maintain the established store image. While there is usually some basic stock which is in constant demand year after year, there should also be enough variety in new styles to appeal to the different requirements of customers who fall within the target market.

Timing is an important factor in assortment planning. Deliveries from manufacturers should coincide with consumer demand cycles so that there is sufficient quantity and variety of stock for times of peak demand. For example, party dresses will be much more in demand before Christmas and New Year than they will be in late January.

Quantities are also important because stock shortages and excesses both mean lost dollars. A buyer who orders insufficient numbers of a style which sells out quickly may not be able to reorder if the manufacturer is out of stock or is already working on next season's range. Equally, the retailer does not want to be left with excess stock which must be marked down at the end of the season. A *markdown* is a price reduction on a garment in an attempt to move the stock. Even worse is *terminal stock*, which is unsaleable.

## OPEN-TO-BUY

Buyers always leave some leeway in their budgeting to top up on goods which are selling well and to add new merchandise as market opportunities present themselves. The Open-To-Buy (OTB) is the amount of money a buyer has available for this purpose at a particular point in time. The OTB works to a short time frame, usually two weeks or a month, and is determined by deducting the cost of goods already purchased from the total of planned purchases as indicated by the Dollar Merchandise Plan.

## SOURCES OF SUPPLY

Once the merchandise planning is completed, the buyer sets out to shop the market. Although suppliers already known to the buyer will satisfy many requirements, new ideas, better merchandise, higher margins, and therefore new suppliers, are constantly sought. The buyer will visit manufacturers, wholesalers, importers, agents and brokers, both locally and overseas, in the quest for better products to offer his or her customers.

Some Australian retail buyers make buying trips to international collections and trade fairs. Those who do may, in addition to ordering directly from overseas manufacturers, purchase samples at retail level and have them developed by local or overseas manufacturers to a specific price point. Expensive items sourced in Europe or the US can often be manufactured more cheaply in countries such as India, Brazil and China.

Alternatively, retailers stocking imported fashion may buy from an importer who is locally based and carries sample ranges for the buyer to view. Or they choose to operate through an overseas-based buying office which provides member retailers with market information and will buy from designers and manufacturers on their clients' behalf. Importers and buying agencies minimise buying trips and language difficul-ties by acting as intermediaries between buyers and suppliers, and carry out legal procedures in regard to importing, duties and quotas.

At the local level, the buyer goes to manufacturers' or agents' showrooms to view the sample ranges, or makes appointments for their representatives to call on him or her. Buying from manufacturers can involve long lead times if orders are placed before production commences. If merchandise is made to order, the manufacturer usually sets minimum order quantities.

Wholesalers, on the other hand, often carry stock and can therefore offer short lead times of a couple of weeks or less. Some even offer a cash and carry service from the showroom. Wholesalers will usually supply small, mixed quantities for small retailers, but don't carry enough stock for volume orders.

Local and international fashion centres regularly hold apparel markets or trade shows which house displays of fashion designers and manufacturers in one location for a limited time. These shows allow buyers to get an overview of general trends, source new suppliers and make comparisons between the available merchandise.

The buyer usually places orders three to six months in advance of the time that the garments will be in the store, with locally made products often as close as six weeks prior. Although consumer tastes change according to fashion cycles, and the buyer must anticipate what those changes will be for the next season, the needs and wants of a target market are assessed according to past and current sales evaluations. This means that the buyer is always operating in two time zones, the past and the future.

Buyers themselves exert an influence on fashion trends because they pre-select items from the designer's range. This selection is based on the buyers' knowledge of customer preferences, irrespective of what the designer's recom-

THE FASHION DESIGN MANUAL

mendations or their personal choices may be. Buyers' choices can affect the public perception of a particular designer because they determine the styles, colours and quantities that are available to the consumer.

## COMMON BUYING STRATEGIES

### 1. Regular buying

This is the standard procedure for purchasing merchandise from a manufacturer. The buyer views the sample range and places an order according to style, colour, size and price.

### 2. Sampling and reordering

In this instance small quantities in a selection of styles or colours are ordered to test consumer reaction. The styles which sell well are then reordered in larger quantities.

### 3. Specification buying

The buyer, in collaboration with the manufacturer, develops a style to be produced exclusively for his or her retail outlet. All aspects of styling, fabrics, trims, colours and quality are specified by the buyer. Such garments may be produced with the store's own label, and are known as a *private label brand* or *own brand*. Alternatively, the buyer may request that minor garment details, for example buttons, colour combinations or fabric, used for existing styles be altered to avoid direct competition with other retailers. Specification buying ensures exclusivity of stock and can enhance the store's image and create customer loyalty if the stock cannot be obtained elsewhere.

### 4. Job lot buying (or odd lots)

This type of buying is the bulk purchase of leftover stock, made up of an assortment of styles, colours and sizes, at a flat reduced price.

## ORDERING

The buyer places a purchase order with the apparel manufacturer, who writes up the order form detailing the goods to be delivered, the price and the delivery date, the terms of sale and shipping instructions (Fig. 19.5). Any goods which have not left the manufacturer's premises by the completion date may be subject to cancellation because retailers cannot afford to carry stock which is delivered late in the season.

New season's merchandise is put out on the retail floor well before the wearing season. Spring clothes are in the stores mid-winter, and winter clothes start appearing in February, after the New Year sales. Stores try to sell out of stock before the actual wearing time so that, if the weather is unseasonal, the consumers have already made their purchases and sales are not affected.

Garments being delivered interstate or overseas must coincide with the selling and wearing seasons for those locations.

## PRICING

The prices a fashion retailer charges are based on the store's pricing policy, the cost of overheads and the wholesale cost of the garments. Price is not entirely set on what the product costs to make or buy — this is used as a guide, but the retailer must judge what the consumer will pay for the product in question. Pricing policy must be low enough to attract customers yet high enough to make a profit.

*Mark-up* is the difference between the wholesale cost of a garment and the retail price. The mark-up may be calculated as a percentage of the wholesale cost or the retail price but, either way, there is no set mark-up rate. Ideally retailers aim for 100 per cent on top of the wholesale cost, but this is not always realisable. Some of the mark-up is profit, but the rest covers operating expenses and overheads, plus losses from damaged

▶ *19.5 The order form is completed by the sales person representing the wholesaler and a copy is given to the buyer. (Order form blank courtesy of Michael Bracewell.)*

goods, shoplifting, markdowns and unsold items.

Other factors which influence pricing are competitors' prices for the same or comparable merchandise, manufacturers' recommended retail prices, and supply and demand.

## RETAIL PROMOTION

Promotion is the publicising and selling of a product to a target group of consumers. Promotional activities should be planned well in advance to coordinate with current fashion themes, seasonal displays and stock in the stores. Promotion of a product is carried out by means of visual merchandising, advertising and publicity (including special publicity events).

### 1. Visual merchandising

Visual merchandising is the attractive presentation of goods and services for the purpose of creating a distinctive store image. It is the combined effect of store layout, store design, lighting, fixtures, signage, mannequins, and window and interior displays.

Because much of the merchandise in competing stores is similar, if not identical, the way the garments are placed on view can directly affect customer acceptance and the level of sales. Displays are changed regularly to allow customers to see the fashions easily, to give greater visibility to slow moving stock, and to show new stock to the best advantage.

Fashion displays in windows and inside the store may be used to:

(a) convey a fashion story by featuring the newest trends,

## VEGAN HOLDINGS PTY. LTD.

264 Oxford St, Paddington 2021
Phone: 61-2-360 6192  Fax: 61-2-360 3490

1277

SALES ORDER **FASHION LEADERS PTY LTD**   Dept. No. ___   Season: **WINTER**

Ship To: **Head office – 721 Cooper St, Surry Hills.**   Group: ___

Bill To: **"          "**   Delivery (Ex Syd): **20th March**

| STYLE NUMBER | DESCRIPTION | COLOUR | ONE SIZE | 1 8 | 2 10 | 3 12 | 4 14 | 5 16 | QTY | UNIT PRICE | TOTAL |
|---|---|---|---|---|---|---|---|---|---|---|---|
| 006Z | Long Sleeved Blouse | White | | 2 | 4 | 4 | 2 | | 12 | 75-00 | 900-00 |
| | | Cream | | | 1 | 2 | 1 | | 4 | | 300-00 |
| | | | | | | | | | | | |
| 0023 | Lined Vest | Black | | 1 | 2 | 2 | 1 | 1 | 7 | 48-50 | 339-50 |
| | | Olive | | 1 | 2 | 2 | 1 | 1 | 7 | | 339-50 |
| | | Grape | | 1 | 2 | 2 | 1 | 1 | 7 | | 339-50 |
| | | | | | | | | | | | |
| 1045 | Lined Jacket | Black | | 1 | 2 | 2 | 1 | | 6 | 138-00 | 828-00 |
| 1046 | Lined Wrap Skirt | Black | | 1 | 2 | 2 | 1 | | 6 | 69-00 | 414-00 |
| 1047 | 2-Pleat Trousers | Black | | 1 | 2 | 2 | 1 | | 6 | 81-00 | 486-00 |
| | | | | | | | | | | $ | 3,945-00 |

PLEASE NOTE
These garments cannot be cancelled as they are manufactured against your order.  Adjustments will not be accepted after 7 days of order placement.

AGENT ___

Date **29th September.**

Terms Agreed
**Payment 7 days – 5% Disc.**

Signed By ___

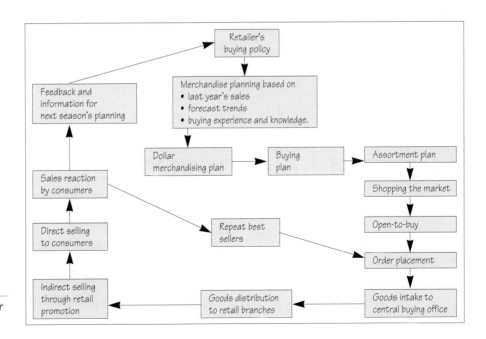

▶ 19.6 Merchandising and buying cycle for a fashion retailer.

(b) demonstrate how fashions should be worn, coordinated and accessorised,

(c) create a mood by highlighting the spirit of a season; for example, gift giving for Mother's Day or Christmas, and

(d) direct-sell to customers by tempting them with merchandise, prices and possible bargains.

## 2. Advertising

Advertising is a paid announcement designed to bring the attention of the customer to the retailer's name and product. This may be done through:

(a) print (newspapers, magazines) and broadcast (radio, television) media,

(b) direct mail — brochures, postcards and newsletters which are sent personally to each customer,

(c) catalogue — in-store and mail order,

(d) in-store announcements and videos,

(e) packaging — printed with the retailer's name, and

(f) outdoor and transit advertising — signs on billboards, in railway stations, on buses and taxis.

## 3. Publicity

Publicity is the free and voluntary giving of information to promote a company, brand, product, person or event, mainly through newspapers, magazines, television and radio. Because publicity is directly under the control of media editors, the retailer has little, if any, control over the selection of merchandise, the way it is styled, and the context in which it is used. Publicity can be gained through:

(a) special events such as fashion parades, charity fund-raisers, awards, ceremonies, sporting events, rural shows, celebrity appearances,

(b) sponsorship — sport, the arts, education,

(c) sample giveaways,

(d) press releases and telephone contact — to alert the media to newsworthy events,

(e) editorial — television, magazine and newspaper articles, garments in fashion features, listings in stockists columns, and

(f) promotional clothing; for example, garments being conspicuously labelled.

## SELLING FOR NEW DESIGNERS

New designers wanting to break into the market sometimes have to try less conventional methods to get a foot in the retail door. The following approaches can be good starting points for a new designer.

### 1. Consignment

Garments sold on consignment are 'lent' to a retailer who pays for them only when they are sold. After an agreed length of time, any unsold merchandise can be returned to the supplier who may then try to sell it elsewhere.

This arrangement benefits a retailer who wants to introduce more expensive or avant-garde fashions into the store without any financial commitment. It also benefits the supplier who wants to test the market response to his or her designs before entering into mass production. However, the new designer selling on consignment must be sure to establish clear policies with the retailer in case the goods become shop-soiled or are shop-lifted.

### 2. Retail cooperatives

These often suit beginning designers with limited finances. By sharing premises, facilities and personnel, outlay on overheads can be kept to a minimum and available funds can be spent on production of garments. The shop rental is split between members, and each person is allocated time as sales consultant in the shop as well as space to display their merchandise.

### 3. New designers' centres

These are retailers who appeal to a specific market wanting forward-looking and individual designs by stocking only new designer labels. Each designer rents a space within the store to display their own label. The store supplies the sales staff and takes a small percentage of the goods sold on consignment basis.

### 4. Markets

Many burgeoning designers gain experience by selling their merchandise at local markets. Direct contact with customers provides the opportunity to respond quickly to their wants and needs. Overheads are low and the one or two days per week selling means the rest of the week can be spent on production.

PART

3

## CHAPTER 20

# AUSTRALIAN STYLE: INFLUENTIAL AUSTRALIAN DESIGNERS

# INTRODUCTION

The nature of the fashion industry is one of constant change. As trends come and go, so do the people who create those trends — the designers.

Some designers make a big splash for a short time and then fade away. Others work quietly and steadily, gradually building up a loyal clientele, but without ever creating headlines. Very few do both; that is, create headlines and manage to keep on creating headlines season in, season out, year after year. This is because the fashion industry requires apparently conflicting skills. The ability to create and innovate must be tempered with an exacting technical knowledge of fabric, garment construction and manufacturing techniques. Add to this the necessity of maintaining a high profile, constantly marketing one's product and remaining abreast of, if not slightly ahead of, consumer tastes and trends.

Not to mention running a business! Few people are able to maintain the high level of output required in all of these areas, especially when the designing process is repeated for four to six ranges a year, with around 100 garments per range. This chapter provides a brief profile of prominent designers who have contributed something unique which has changed or made a strong contribution to Australian fashion.

# CREATORS AND CREATIONS

Some outstanding fashion labels result from the fruitful merging of two talented people — one the creator, the other the marketer or business manager. Other labels, inspired by necessity or function, have seen years of development and because of their history are now part of our Australian culture. They reflect our way of life, our attitudes, and the things we value. Still others have sprung from the sheer creative force of a single individual. These individuals are very often artists at heart who have chosen the medium of clothing as their means of expression.

There is constant debate as to whether Australians should look overseas for fashion inspiration, or gaze deeper into the Australian psyche to find a style uniquely their own.

From the selection of designers profiled in this chapter, it can be seen that, regardless of one's viewpoint, Australia offers the best of both worlds. There are designers such as R. M. Williams and Ken Done who create undeniably Australian clothing. There are also extremely talented designers such as Trent Nathan and Inge Fonagy who take their lead from international trends and adapt ideas to suit Australia's climate and lifestyle.

## PRUE ACTON (1943-)

The textile design course at Melbourne's RMIT was the training ground for one of Australia's best known designers whose fashion design career spanned a period of 30 years.

Prue Acton commenced designing in 1963 when, with a modest loan from her parents, she set up business in Flinders Lane. The business took six months to become established and, by 1982, had expanded to an annual worldwide turnover of $11 million.

Prue Acton designs are distinctly Australian and her use of colour and texture is inspired by local urban and rural environments. High quality fabrics and finishes, femininity, comfort, and harmony with the wearer are important to her designs. Natural fibres — silk, pure cotton, wool, leather and suede — are predominant in Prue Acton garments.

Prue has dressed many Australians with the uniforms she has designed for such organisations and events as the State Bank of Victoria, the 1976, 1984 and 1988 Olympics, and World Expo '88. Her controversial Australian flora and fauna designs for the 1984 Los Angeles Olympics won the award for the best-dressed female athletes.

Prue's list of credits is considerable. She has won numerous Wool Fashion Awards, was made a member of the FIA Hall of Fame in 1973 and was awarded an OBE in 1982.

Prue Acton closed the doors of her fashion house in 1990 to concentrate on other design interests — colour consulting for Dulux and Shell, designing homeware, bed linen, greeting cards and calendars, and painting.

20.1 Prue Acton.

## COUNTRY ROAD AUSTRALIA: STEPHEN BENNETT AND JANE PARKER

Country Road was founded in 1974 by Stephen Bennett. His original concept was to produce women's shirts to complement the strong growth in jeans experienced in the 1970s. This ability to recognise and go with a market opportunity is one of the factors that has made Country Road so successful in the Australian fashion scene for over two decades.

In the early 1970s Stephen Bennett was working in sales for Thomas Wardle and Trent Nathan. With a small family loan he set up a workroom and retail shop in a two-storey terrace in Hawthorn, Melbourne. His sister, Jane Parker, having completed a degree in design, cutting and patternmaking at Emily Macpherson College, joined the company as designer 18 months after Country Road's inception.

When Country Road first started production, the garments were made by menswear manufacturers, giving the classic styles a masculine quality. The first shirts were distributed widely through department stores, including Myer and Georges, and were so successful that the apparel range was immediately expanded.

Only six years after its formation, Country Road had ten retail stores throughout Australia. A period of rapid expansion followed the buy–out of Country Road by Myer Emporium Ltd (now Coles-Myer) in 1981. By 1987, 37 additional retail stores had been opened. The menswear range was introduced in 1984. Many of these inaugural products are still part of Country Road's core business.

In 1987, the company was purchased back by its founders, and subsequently listed on the Australian Stock Exchange. Rapid expansion continued, with the opening of four stores in the USA in 1988, the introduction of the Home-

20.2 Jane Parker and Stephen Bennett.

wear collection in 1989, and the opening of the International Concept Store on 43rd and Madison Avenue, New York, in May 1992.

Country Road currently has over 70 retail stores in Australia and New Zealand, and 19 stores in the USA. It has a string of awards to its credit, including induction to the FIA Hall of Fame, The Fashion Group International's 1992 Award for Excellence and the FIA's 1994 Grand Award for Excellence.

Stephen Bennett and Jane Parker make clothing for the Australian way of life. The Country Road style is versatile, easily coordinated, urban contemporary dressing. The garments are relaxed and subtly sophisticated for Casual Career, Urban Weekend and Rugged Weekend wear. Natural fabrics predominate.

Country Road customers are defined more by lifestyle and attitude than by age and socio-economic factors. They are people who enjoy the contemporary shopping experience, appreciate quality, fabric and good design, and who understand value for money.

20.3 Ken and Judy Done.

## DONE ART AND DESIGN: KEN DONE (1940–), JUDY DONE (1943–)

Although the origins of Done Art and Design were not fashion related, clothing and accessories are now the biggest sellers in a business which retails through 300 outlets in Australia, Japan, Singapore, Europe and the USA, and has a $50 million a year turnover.

Judy Done creates fabric designs from entire works or small sections of paintings by her husband, Ken Done. The combination of these two talents has resulted in a style which is both recognisably Australian and internationally popular. The secret of Done Art and Design's fashion success is the concept of art to wear. It turns clothing into an easily understandable work of art that many people feel comfortable wearing.

Done Art and Design had its origins in 1979 when Ken Done left a successful career as an art director in the advertising industry to concentrate on painting. To launch the opening of his own gallery, Ken printed up 12 T-shirts with a sketchy design of Sydney Harbour. They were an instant sell-out and soon he was selling T-shirts as well as paintings. In 1982 the first store was opened in Sydney's Rocks area, a move which exposed Ken Done to the tourist, and

especially Japanese, market where he has attained cult status.

Judy entered the business in 1986. Her background as a fashion model and designer in her own businesses enabled her to steer the clothing arm of the company from simple T-shirts and leisure-wear to a fully-fledged fashion range which offers swimwear, resortwear, sports-wear and accessories.

There are two distinct ranges. The all-seasons range is an across the board trans-seasonal collection designed around Australiana. The prolific images of Sydney Harbour and the Barrier Reef are central themes.

The Judy Done resort range introduced in 1988 releases two collections each year with up to ten stories. Judy emphasises an approach to design that reflects our lifestyle as dictated by our climate. Garments focus on ease and simplicity of styling to complement the strength of the prints, and are made from Australian-made pure wools, cottons and cotton blends. Market appeal is based on an image of relaxed and confident dressing. Australian beach, floral and bird motifs, all exuberantly and optimistically coloured, typify the Done Art and Design style.

Done Art and Design licenses Oroton to make accessories and the Ink Group to produce cards, calendars and related stationery.

In 1993 the FIA awarded Judy Done the Grand Award for Excellence, for Outstanding Achievement in Original Design and Export.

## GEORGE GROSS AND HARRY WHO DESIGN COMPANY: GEORGE GROSS (1943–), HARRY WATT (1937–)

George Gross settled in Adelaide after emigrating from Hungary with his family in 1957. He studied dentistry but he made his first move into fashion while still a teenager by designing some glitzy outfits which were immediately snapped up by a local dancer and boutique owner. He has remained in the fashion industry ever since, gaining experience as a fashion merchandising executive with Myer and the Ann Harding chain of boutiques. Although he has no formal training apart from a short pattern-making course, George Gross does his own sketching and patternmaking. His garments feature beautiful fabrics, simplicity and ease of line, and convey a feeling of sensuous vitality.

Harry Watt was born in Adelaide and worked in the travel industry before moving into fashion. He joined forces with George Gross and in 1973 they opened their first store in Rundle Street, Adelaide.

The first Harry Who range was released in 1978. The range has always presented a younger, more relaxed and casual approach to dressing. Knitwear features strongly. Harry has won two FIA awards for menswear.

George Gross and Harry Watt produce 11 ranges annually, including the diffusion line G2. They now have five signature retail stores as well as supplying 150 up-market retailers and in-store boutiques. In 1994 they were chosen as

20.4 *George Gross (top) and Harry Watt.*

the designers of the new Qantas uniform, and George Gross was elected to the FIA Hall of Fame after winning FIA awards for four consecutive years.

## JAG

In 1968 Adele Palmer opened her first boutique, Artemis, in Chapel Street, Melbourne. Although she had only nine months of patternmaking training and funded the venture herself, her talent for colour, texture and commercial design ensured that her designs were a huge success.

Adele married Rob Palmer, a marketing executive, in 1972, and together they launched the Jag label, which featured superbly cut denim jeans and casual weekend wear.

In 1974 the Palmers set up production and retail headquarters in the United States. They opened a Jag boutique in Beverly Hills and were soon supplying top fashion stores such as Neiman Marcus, Saks and Bloomingdales. By 1978 their annual turnover was $30 million.

In 1980 they returned to Australia and launched Adele Palmer DBA (Doing Business Again), a range of better and evening sportswear in silks and crisp cottons. This label is now known as Adele Palmer and is city-dressing focused. 1982 saw the re-emergence of the more casual Jag label.

Adele Palmer was elected to the FIA Hall of Fame in 1985 and 1988, the only designer to be elected twice.

Palmer Corporation went public in 1987. In 1988 Palmer participated in the Bicentennial Wool Corporation Parade, and in 1989, 1990 and 1992 Jag was awarded a Gown of the Year Award for the label most popular with shop assistants throughout Australia. In 1989 the 'Rob Palmer Award for Design Excellence' was introduced to honour Rob Palmer who had passed away that year, and to encourage young Australian design talent.

The Jag style is most well known for its sportswear and casual daywear, and the addition of Jagmen and Jag Junior has considerably broadened the appeal of Jag designs.

Jag garments are characterised by their versatility, comfort, innovative use of decorative trims and rich textural and colour combinations. They fit into the upper-middle market sector, and

20.5 *Adele Palmer.*

retail through Jag's 21 company-owned stores, as well as department stores and selected boutiques. Watches and lingerie are manufactured under licence for Jag.

Adele Palmer is no longer involved in the company, having resigned from her position in 1995 to pursue her own interests.

## LINDA JACKSON (1950–)

'I have always been fascinated by legends and myths, colour and light, rainbows and lightning, music and dance, theatre and costumes, the art of colour healing, the history of textiles, weaving and embroidery and dyes, the Australian Aborigines, Africans, American Indians, Chinese, Japanese — their tribal and ethnic costumes — and photography, painting and travel. Somehow all of these things are a part of what I do.'

Linda Jackson is an artist who works in the field of fashion. She chooses not to conform to the trends of mainstream fashion, preferring instead to offer a unique vision of her environment, a vision which is constantly enriched through travel, research, music, art and photography.

*20.6 Linda Jackson.*

Linda studied fashion design at Emily Macpherson College, and photography at Prahran Technical College in Melbourne. From 1969 she travelled and lived in New Guinea, Asia, Paris and London, before settling back in Sydney in 1973 where she established Linda Jackson Couture.

Her collaboration with Jenny Kee commenced at this time and lasted ten years, during which time they delighted the local and international fashion media with their exuberant Australiana collections and parades.

Then, as now, Linda derives much of her imagery from Australia. Many of her garments are one-off creations, often exclusively hand-painted or printed. She designs not on paper but in her mind, then drapes fabric directly onto the body, using the human form as the frame on which she arranges her colours and shapes.

The construction of Linda's designs may be based on the simple forms of traditional clothing which interrelate with the body when tied, draped, swathed or wrapped. Or it may draw on the more sophisticated haute couture techniques of designers like Vionnet, Fortuny, Dior and Charles James, whose work Linda studied while in Paris.

Linda continues to paint and print her own fabrics, and designs exclusive clothing for her coterie of clients. She works from her studio in Bronte, Sydney, and also designs furnishing fabrics, rugs, cards and wrapping paper.

Much of Linda Jackson's work is exhibited in the Australian Collection of the National Gallery in Canberra, the Powerhouse Museum in Sydney, and the Victorian National Gallery.

## JENNY KEE (1947–)

Jenny Kee first came to the attention of the Australian public in 1973 when she opened the Flamingo Park Salon in Sydney's Strand Arcade with partner Linda Jackson.

Prior to this, Jenny had lived in London where, during the mid-sixties, she had worked at the markets selling antique clothing. When she came back to Australia she was inspired by the beauty of her country, the native flora and fauna, opals, and the culture and traditions of the Aborigines.

From these constant sources of inspiration she designs the hand-knits and textiles for which she is renowned here and overseas. Jenny Kee garments are built around her printed fabrics. They are usually loose and can be layered or draped to suit the wearer. Favoured fibres are silk, cotton and pure wool. Colours are strong and bold, like the Australian earth, sky and ocean.

Although Jenny grew up in Sydney, she has an exotic appearance which hails from her Chinese father and English/Italian mother. She uses a stylised self-portrait as the distinctive trade-mark for her Jenny Kee label.

In 1977 Jenny Kee and Linda Jackson won the Lyrebird Award for Fashion Innovation. In 1983 Jenny's Opal Oz fabric was used by Karl Lagerfeld for Chanel, and in 1986 she designed a rug for the new Parliament House in Canberra. Jenny Kee's work has been exhibited in Tokyo, London and all over

*20.7 Jenny Kee.*

Australia. A licensing programme launched in 1988 now sees her talents applied to the design of rugs, scarves, fabrics, bed-linen, murals, ceramics, knitting books, placemats, coasters, and swimwear.

## 100% MAMBO: DARE JENNINGS (1951–)

Dare Jennings' passions are surfing, rock and roll, and art. So what else could he do but establish a clothing label which unites and gives free expression to these aspects of popular Australian culture?

The label was born in 1984 with the launch of a range of surfwear which broke away from the traditional surfing icons of 'babes, boards and tubes'. Instead, it offered prints and graphic designs which were irreverent, satirical and eclectic, yet at the same time very Australian in content. The name '100% Mambo' was found on a 1950s jazz record cover.

20.8 Dare Jennings.

Allan and artist David McKay, plus anyone else who can come up with a good idea.

At the 1990 Sydney Design Show, Mambo launched a range of upholstery fabrics. They have also produced a book, held a major art exhibition, and in 1992 launched a record label whose recordings will retail where Mambo products are sold.

The 1992 Powerhouse Fashion of the Year award selected Mambo clothing for inclusion in the museum's collection of decorative arts and design. Mambo exports T-shirts and board shorts to 15 countries, including Japan, the USA, France, Italy, England and New Zealand.

The clothing range is broad and encompasses everything in mens- and womenswear from boardies, swimwear, shoes and accessories to ski-wear.

The intelligence, attitude and quirky sense of humour of the Mambo product is evident in everything Dare Jennings puts his hand to. The often used motif of the farting dog seems to symbolise Mambo's willingness to blow a raspberry at surfing, fashion, and product and marketing traditions, and to thrive on doing just that.

Mambo design is Australiana of a different sort — it expresses our deprecating sense of humour through the use of motifs such as the Hills Hoist, sprinklers, Bogong moths, fibro houses, and scenes of suburbia being invaded by aliens. The colours are suitably bold and brash.

Mambo has avoided the limitations of an identifiable house style by employing the talents of a number of artists, including Adelaide ceramicist Gerry Wedd, Mental as Anything guitarist Reg Mombassa, Martin Plaza, Crowded House musician Nick Seymour, cartoonist Matthew Martin, illustrator Richard

## MERIVALE AND MR JOHN: JOHN HEMMES (1931–), MERIVALE HEMMES (1931–)

John Hemmes emigrated to Sydney from Amsterdam in the early 1950s. He married Merivale in 1954 and they went to London together in the late 1950s. There they witnessed first-hand the youth-quake starting to shake the international fashion scene and immediately saw the possibility of supplying these latest fashions to the youth market in Australia.

Once back in Australia, they lived in Merivale's mother's garage, and Merivale started making hats. John sold the hats to department stores during the day and worked as a drinks waiter at night.

In 1961 they opened a small boutique called the House of Merivale, in Castlereagh Street, Sydney. This boutique epitomised the swinging sixties scene, stocking the fashions of Acton, Nathan and Norma Tullo, and the latest imports flown in from overseas.

In order to get exactly the image she wanted, Merivale started designing her own gold lamé mini-dresses and the animal prints which became part of her signature look. The Mr John label for menswear followed soon after, and the

20.9 Merivale and John Hemmes.

frilly, brightly coloured shirts and tight fit-and-flare trousers outraged those with more traditional tastes. The crowds trying to pack into the store got bigger and overflowed onto the street and, in 1963, Merivale set up a factory to cater to the ever-growing demand.

A self-taught designer, Merivale is acknowledged as an innovator of young fashion in Australia. She was one of the first to recognise that fashion was a part of music, a part of the booming 60s scene, and gave the kids exactly what they wanted and couldn't get enough of.

With John Hemmes at the business helm, Merivale and Mr John have now moved out of fashion and continue to diversify into restaurants, cafés, bars and property.

## TRENT NATHAN (1940–)

The Trent Nathan label supplies quality fashion to the top end of the Australian market. The company was started in 1961 as a young, high fashion label. At that time Trent Nathan's innovative styles were at the forefront of the swinging sixties youth movement in Australian fashion. He now no longer aims to set trends but is more a mainstream designer, creating fashion which is strong and modern, classic and contemporary, and which has appeal across several age groups.

Trent Nathan has never undertaken any formal fashion training, but was virtually born into the industry. His mother's company, White Collar Girl, manufactured clothing for Myer, and Trent's earliest recollections are of being in her workroom and factory, surrounded by fabrics and garments. He learned about garment construction as he grew up in this environment and through hands-on experience.

After leaving school, Trent started as a retail cadet with Myer and worked in visual merchandising. Before long he was working in the family business which was renamed Trent Nathan Pty Ltd in 1961. Growth during the 1960s and 70s was steady. The company was a partnership until 1984, when Trent purchased the total shares to become sole owner and Chairman. A period of expansion during the 1980s and into the 1990s brought sales, including licensed products, to in excess of $40 million annually.

Trent Nathan ranges display his flair for colour, fabrication and coordination. The garments range from denim jeans to knitwear to silk eveningwear and are

20.10 Trent Nathan.

aimed at consumers aged 25 plus with a middle to high income who demand quality, prestige and versatility, and are socially or career active. The high quality of the fabrics and make reinforces the attention to detail and striving for a product which suits the specific requirements of this market.

Approximately 50 per cent of the garments are manufactured locally. They are distributed through the company's 11 retail outlets, through concept stores within department stores, and department stores and selected boutiques across Australia. The company handles its own sales of womenswear, and the Trent Nathan name is licensed for the production of homewares, menswear, resortwear, sleepwear, lingerie, ties, scarves, jewellery, sunglasses and leather goods.

To add to his string of FIA Awards, in 1992 Trent Nathan was awarded the FIA Grand Award for Fashion Excellence for 30 years' service to the industry.

## BRIAN ROCHFORD (1936–)

Working with his family in the millinery trade provided Brian Rochford with experience in the fashion industry from an early age. He worked in the family business for 17 years and built it into one of the largest millinery suppliers in Australia.

In 1969, when the local industry was dying due to competition from cheaper imported hats, Brian switched his attention to swimwear, active wear and fashion. He conducted his own market research on the swimwear market (by visiting Sydney's beaches and seeing what the girls were wearing!).

Brian has always concentrated on giving consumers what they want — garments which not only fit well and perform well, but are high quality and look good at the same time. His innovations have contributed greatly to Australian swimwear design — the soft-bra swimsuit top, the roll-down one-piece swimsuit, and bikini separates which enable women to buy a different size top to the bottom, are three of his ideas.

In the 1980s, Brian Rochford was one of the first to see the possibilities in the active and gym wear market, and understood the potential for gym wear

20.11 Brian Rochford.

as street wear. The release of the body-suit as an essential wardrobe item was a contributing factor to his 100 per cent increase in turnover in 1988.

Brian Rochford has 33 concept stores throughout Australia, all decorated in his distinctive black and gold colour scheme and carrying swimwear, resort, weekend, active, career and after five collections. His stores carry everything from midriff T-tops and easywear shorts to casually elegant halter tops and sarong style skirts. The concept stores enable him to merchandise his products in the best way and, through tempting window displays, fully-trained staff and regular fashion parades, he introduces customers to each Rochford Collection.

Brian Rochford develops new colours and fabrics with Australian mills and, whenever possible, sources his materials locally. His Australian made garments are now being sold in New Zealand, the Philippines, the USA and Japan.

Brian Rochford has won 15 FIA Awards for Fashion Excellence, and is a member of the Fashion Industry's Hall of Fame.

## SIMONA:
## INGE FONAGY (1929–)

Inge Fonagy is the creative force behind the Simona Group. In 1950 she emigrated from Switzerland and settled in Melbourne. She moved to Sydney in 1960 where she worked as a buyer for Chatterton, and her husband George Fonagy worked for Ralex.

Inge, trained in patternmaking, cutting and fashion illustration, knew that she could produce better fashions than she was buying so she started working from home, making her own samples and selling them to boutiques. She named her new label after her own maiden name, Simona.

Once the business had become established, Inge set up premises and a factory in Market Street, Sydney. This

20.12 Inge Fonagy.

enabled her to ensure the quality of workmanship essential for her up-market label. She started importing the best fabrics direct from Italy and Switzerland, sourcing from the same suppliers as Yves Saint Laurent, Dior, Givenchy and Ungaro.

In the early days, her retail outlets included the major department stores and selected boutiques. Simona now operates retail concept stores in Mosman, Sydney, and in David Jones and Myer stores Australiawide.

Inge Fonagy's timing was perfect for the birth of the Simona label in 1961. Australian fashion was set to boom, and the public was ready for the career oriented, sharp, chic and classic fashions she produced with her manager-husband. She designed for the 60s woman, offering her evening, business and casual wear to suit her modern lifestyle.

Simona clothing is designed for Australian women who seek quality and superior workmanship. It is classical with a modern twist. To cater for the 1990s, Simona has diversified into new labels like Shiman Maghazey, Simona Studio (which is imported knitwear) and the larger-size label, Simona Plus. There is

also a Corporate Uniform Division.

Most Simona garments are manufactured locally and of those most are produced in-house. Simona is still family owned, with the second generation fully involved in the management, business, and retail decisions and operations.

## SPEEDO

The MacRae Knitting Mills commenced operations in Sydney in 1914, but the name 'Speedo' did not come into being until 1928 as the result of a competition to find a brand name for the company's swimming costumes. The winning entry was 'Speed on in your Speedo'. Production of Speedo swimwear commenced in 1929.

In the late 1920s, Speedo introduced the racer back style of swimsuit for men, with narrow straps which cut away from the shoulders, and a front modesty skirt. It was made from knitted silk, wool or cotton and became the standard racing gear for swimming champions.

In the 1956 Melbourne Olympic Games, the popularity of Speedos was greatly boosted by the fact that nearly all the Australian swimmers wore them. The change from cotton to nylon swimwear in the late 1950s meant that new prints and colours and form-fitting shapes became possible.

In 1959 Speedo commenced exporting to the USA and soon after found markets in New Zealand, England, Europe, Japan and South Africa. In 1972, Speedo supplied swimwear to the fifty-two nations competing at the Munich Olympic Games and, in 1976, was the official swimwear licensee for the Montreal Olympic Games. By 1977, Speedo was selling in Canada, eastern Europe and South America.

In 1986, the MacRae family sold Speedo to the Linter Group of Companies and, in 1991, Speedo was taken over by the English-based company Pentland. Gloria Smythe was the designer

20.13 Speedo logo — 'Speed on in your Speedos.'

at Speedo for 28 years and retired when the company was taken over in 1991.

The evolution of Speedo swimwear reflects the changes in Australian society. At the turn of the 20th century the standard attire for swimming was the two piece tunic and drawers for women, and the one piece woollen neck-to-knee for men. The development of new fabrics, first nylon, terylene and then Lycra®, have gone hand-in-hand with changes in styling so that progressively briefer and lighter coverings have become like a second skin and allow complete freedom of action in the water.

Speedo now produces a fashion range of beach and active leisurewear, including men's, women's and children's swimwear, bathing caps, goggles, bags and towels, men's and ladies woven and knitted beachwear, shirts, shorts, dresses, tights and gymwear.

## SPORTSGIRL/SPORTSCRAFT

Sportscraft and Sportsgirl are important in Australian fashion because they have been in the business for over three-quarters of a century and because of the wide range of fashion labels they offer the Australian consumer.

Electra French Pleating was founded in 1914 by Wolf Bardas who had just emigrated to Australia from London where he had been a womenswear tailor. He set up a small factory in Carlton with his three sons and son-in-law, and was soon producing quality ladies slacks, blouses and skirts. Their pleated skirts

soon became bestsellers and formed the foundation of a successful sportswear coordinates range known as Sportscraft.

The first Sportsgirl store was opened in Swanston Street, Melbourne in 1947 as a retail outlet for the Sportscraft label. Sportsgirl expanded during the 1940s and 1950s under the management of Morris Bardas. In 1959, David Bardas took over the reins and created the active, young and fun Sportsgirl image that we know today.

Sportsgirl has two flagship stores — the Sportsgirl Centre in Collins Street, Melbourne and in the Skygarden Centre, Sydney. Other retail outlets include 144 Sportsgirl stores, major department stores, selected boutiques, and Sportscraft's own boutiques.

Through its wide range of exclusive house labels, Sportsgirl stores serve a large market ranging in age from 15 to 40 plus.

Sportsgirl labels include David Lawrence, Design Collection by Carolyn Taylor and Elle B. Other labels under the Sportscraft banner include Sportscraft and Sportscraft Mens.

The Sportsgirl/Sportscraft group of retail and manufacturing companies was

20.14 David Bardas.

bought by Truworth Pty Ltd, a South African based retailer, in 1994. Annual turnover in the mid-1990s was over $250 million, and future plans for expansion include marketing products overseas.

## WEISS:
## PETER WEISS

Adele and Peter Weiss produced their first collection in 1975 and from that time quickly established a reputation for the quality design and astute marketing of their up-market fashions.

Peter Weiss is the business and marketing talent behind the label. He initially trained as a cellist at the Conservatorium of Music in Sydney, but ended up working for twelve years in his father's budget dress manufacturing business. Adele migrated to Sydney from Dublin, Ireland, and found work first at Mark Foy's, then at the quality fabric house of Sekers. She is the creative and innovative talent.

Weiss's first big success was in designer sportswear, with a range of mix-and-match separates which gave customers the opportunity to coordinate their own look from the selection of classics. They stayed with this philosophy of providing a total concept through versatile multi-piece collections which reflected the way of life of the Australian woman, and covered everything from daywear to eveningwear.

In 1981, Weiss started designing and manufacturing corporate wardrobes for large organisations, including Ansett Airlines and Westpac. In the same year the first Weiss boutique was opened. By 1990, there were eight Weiss and Weiss Pringle shops in Sydney and Melbourne, plus Weiss Pringle corners in most David Jones stores around Australia. These feature Pringle of Scotland knitwear which colour-coordinates with Weiss bottoms and shirts.

Another successful concept, Weiss Art, was launched in 1986. Weiss Art products are instantly recognisable by

*20.15 Peter Weiss.*

the distinctive black and white graphic designs which are displayed on merchandise ranging from apparel to bed linen to golfing items. Weiss Art is sold through duty free stores and franchise stores around Australia.

Weiss has won the FIA Award, the David Jones Supreme Award and the Helena Rubinstein Silk Fashion Award.

Adele Weiss is now working on a new venture to design and promote a range of totally Australian-produced woollen garments. The wool is grown, processed, spun, dyed and knitted locally, and sold under the Boonoke Great Australian Jumper Company label. She is also pursuing her interest in painting.

## R.M. WILLIAMS (1907–)

Reg Williams grew up on a farm in the mid-north of South Australia. From an early age he took on a variety of work to earn a living. He was a lime-burner in the mallee country of Victoria, spent time in the West Australian goldfields, was camel boy on a survey expedition

through the heart of Australia, and worked as a mounted stockman on pastoral stations where he learned bush-lore from the local Aborigines and bushmen of the cattle camps.

During the Great Depression he set up camp with his young family in the Flinders Ranges, eking out a living sinking wells and crafting bush saddlery and station equipment.

Williams then moved to Adelaide to work from an old woodshed at the rear of his father's house in Prospect. Although he started with no capital and meagre means, R.M. Williams gradually assembled a team of talented craftspeople to help him make his bushman's items. His reputation was spread by word of mouth and, by the end of the 1930s, he was receiving orders for his elastic sided boots and other wares from all over Australia.

Although his diverse range of high quality, specialised products were sought after in bush towns and local retailers were stocking the goods, it wasn't until 1978 that R.M. Williams opened its first retail outlet outside of Prospect. This was in Toowoomba, Queensland. There are now nine stores around Australia,

*20.16 R.M. Williams.*

two in London, and another in New Zealand, as well as agents who distribute the product in Europe, United Arab Emirates and Japan.

Initially a functional product created to meet the specialised requirements of our rural inhabitants, many of the R.M. Williams apparel and footwear items have become Australian classics which are happily worn by city dwellers and fashion followers both locally and overseas. In spite of this, R.M. Williams has been careful to stay with their market niche by avoiding mainstream fashion and by preserving the unique character of the product.

The extensive range of clothing and accessories, as recognised by the Longhorn brand, includes men's and women's boots, hats, belts, coats in oilskin and wool, vests, trousers, jodhpurs, skirts and shirts.

As well as running his business, Reg Williams has for many years been very active in organising riding and equestrian events around Australia, and working on 'Hoofs and Horns', the magazine he founded in 1944. He also assisted the establishment of the Stockman's Hall of Fame at Longreach, Queensland. Reg is still involved with R.M. Williams Pty Ltd, which is now owned by R.M. Williams Holdings and is controlled by a partnership of his friends.

## CARLA ZAMPATTI

Carla Zampatti is a Sydney-based designer who, as her name suggests, was born in Loverno, Italy. She came to Australia in 1950 with her parents and settled in the West Australian mining town of Bullfinch.

Carla started designing and making clothes while still at school in Perth, then moved to Sydney in 1963. She had no formal training but gained experience in the fashion industry by working for a manufacturer. Using her own savings and working from home, she started her business by making and selling samples

20.17 Carla Zampatti.

works mainly with natural fabrics, and prefers classic colours.

Carla Zampatti has 28 of her own retail outlets around Australia, including boutiques in the major department stores. She contributes much to business and fashion through her participation on numerous boards and councils, and regularly judges business and fashion awards. Since 1988 she has been a Trustee to the Board of the Art Gallery of NSW. In 1979 Carla Zampatti won the FIA Lyrebird Award, in 1980 she was named the Bulletin/Qantas Business-woman of the Year and, in 1994, she was voted Designer of the Year in the FIA awards. In 1985, and again in 1987, she collaborated with Ford Australia to design the Carla Zampatti Edition Laser and Meteor. Since 1986 she has design-ed the Commonwealth Bank Corporate Wardrobe.

to boutiques. Zampatti Pty Ltd was launched when she presented her first small collection in 1965.

In 1967 Carla showed her first collection nationally and, in 1970, she renamed her company Carla Zampatti Pty Ltd. 1972 saw the opening of her first Carla Zampatti boutique.

Carla's success has resulted from her ability to design garments which are many things to many women. She takes into consideration the needs of office workers and busy career women who have families to look after, as well as the young woman who requires a special dinner dress.

The Zampatti style is recognisable by the simple, uncluttered sophistication which combines her Italian and Australian sensibilities. She believes that simple garments, beautiful fabrics, and beautiful making is the best fashion image a woman can present.

By designing as many as six hundred pieces a year, she is able to offer her clients a seemingly endless range of co-ordinating suits, dresses, blouses, trousers, skirts, jackets and even lingerie. She

# AND MANY MORE ...

There are many talented Australian de-signers, past and present who, for various reasons, have not been included in this profile. Their talents and contributions to Australian fashion should be noted and their names warrant a mention. They are: Geoff Bade, Adam Bennet, Robert Burton, Vivien Chan Shaw, Covers (Marilyn Said and Barry Taffs), Keri Craig, Robbie Cranfield, Anthea Crawford, Leon Cutler, Perri Cutten, Jill Fitzsimon, Stephen Galloway, Robyn Garland, Wendy Heather, Chris Jacovides, John Kaldor, Jane Lamerton, Daniel Lightfoot, Stuart Membery, Morrissey and Edmiston, Kenneth Pirrie and Norma Tullo.

**CHAPTER 21**

# INTRODUCTION

The career path you follow once you have completed your training is determined by a number of factors. There can be a degree of luck involved in finding the job of your dreams — that is, by being in the right place at the right time — but 'luck' tends to be brought about more often by careful planning than by chance.

To ensure you end up in the position you want, doing the work you really enjoy, there are several steps you can follow.

# GETTING STARTED

## GOALSETTING

The first step in goalsetting is to find out what you really want out of your job, your career . . . . . your life! Analyse what is important to you, what your needs are, what you are good at, not good at, what you enjoy doing and what you don't want to do.

Think about what you might want in the future as well as the present. Once you know what you want, you can set your goals to make sure you are headed in the right direction.

## NETWORKING

The best jobs often come about by word of mouth, so keep in touch with anyone you know in the industry. These industry contacts are also handy sources of information once you are working. Membership in trade organisations and groups, and attending fashion functions

also helps you meet influential and knowledgeable people.

## READING

Subscribe or borrow from the library trade journals, newspapers, fashion magazines and anything that keeps you in touch with who is doing what and where.

Advertisements in the employment section of newspapers can help you get the job you are looking for, as well as give you an indication of what you might expect to earn in the fashion industry.

## EDUCATION

The fashion industry and related technologies are changing so rapidly that you need to constantly upgrade your skills. Regular study, part-time or night courses, and attendance at seminars and conferences will help keep you up to date.

Computer literacy is essential since

the local fashion industry is rapidly updating with the latest technology in order to compete with imports from overseas. CAD/CAM (Computer Aided Design and Computer Aided Manufacturing) is becoming increasingly important to all areas of fashion — don't get left behind.

# CHOOSING YOUR CAREER

The following list of fashion-oriented careers will make you aware of the many career paths open to you in the fashion industry. Although it only covers apparel-related careers, there are further opportunities to design, produce, promote or sell fashion accessories including shoes, hosiery, millinery, bags, belts and jewellery. There are also non-fashion positions which are essential to the running of a fashion business such as management, finance, administration, warehousing and distribution, engineering and maintenance. Finally, there are associated industries which service the fashion industry. These include advertising agencies, textile and apparel care (dry cleaners, laundries), employment agencies and education.

If you have skills in these latter fields, don't overlook them as a means of getting into fashion 'through the back door'.

Many of the occupations listed are not accessible to fashion graduates because most require some degree of on-the-job training or experience. Graduates usually start off as assistants or trainees in the area of their choice, or they take on any job they can to get started in the industry and gradually work their way around to where they want to be.

The qualifications mentioned here are an indication of what is generally required, but are not essential in all cases. Previous experience is also a significant qualification.

The main areas of employment are in Textiles, Apparel Manufacturing, Retail and Fashion Promotion. The home sewing industry has employment opportunities in the areas of marketing, management and retail sales of patterns, fabrics and trims but, because the pattern companies are based either in the USA or Europe, there are no employment opportunities in the design or merchandising fields in Australia.

# THE TEXTILE INDUSTRY

Only five per cent of fashion textiles are produced in Australia, with most of those being manufactured in Victoria. Although many fabrics designed in Australia are printed overseas, textile designers, dyers, printers and agents operate in the manufacturing centres of major Australian cities.

Major textile industry employers are fibre manufacturers, textile mills, testing laboratories and textile agents. Other sources of employment are converting houses, textile design studios and garment manufacturers who design their own fabrics.

## TEXTILE RESEARCH SCIENTIST

### Job description

These scientists research different textile constructions and finishes to improve their performance and to create new fashion fabrics.

### Training/Skills

Tertiary qualifications in textile technology, chemistry, chemical engineering or physics are required. Good organisational, analytical and problem solving skills; enjoyment in working with technical equipment and chemicals, attention to detail and the ability to write test reports are also prerequisites to this type of employment. A worker in this field may also need to operate machinery.

## TEXTILE LABORATORY TECHNICIAN (DYE TECHNICIAN)

### Job description

Dye technicians are involved in textile design, production and quality control. They set quality standards for fibres, yarns, textiles and finishes, obtain and analyse test data, interpret designs and prepare specifications for textile production, as well as establishing suitable dyes and finishes.

### Training/Skills

Tertiary training in Textiles is required (see Textile Research Scientist).

## TEXTILE DESIGNER

### Job description

A textile designer creates designs for application to the surface of a fabric through printing or dyeing, or creates designs woven or knitted into the structure of the fabric.

### Training/Skills

Textile design training is necessary, as are the ability to anticipate trends in fibres, colours, prints, weaves and knits; plenty of creative ideas for new fabric ranges each season; good drawing skills; the ability to plan repeats; and knowledge of yarns, dyes, finishes, technical processes, manufacturing and machinery.

## TEXTILE COLOURIST

### Job description

A colourist prepares colour combinations and stories for each textile design.

### Training/Skills

Tertiary textile design training, along with good colour sense and awareness of colour trends; technical knowledge of dyes and fabrics, and fast, accurate painting and drawing skills are required for this job.

## TEXTILE STYLIST

### Job description

The textile stylist is responsible for a textile manufacturer's long-range planning of colours, weights and textures. He/she also guides textile designers during the development of a fabric range — from initial concept to completion.

### Training/Skills

Training in textile science and fine arts plus considerable industry experience are essential. Skills in every aspect of textile design, production, marketing and sales; an understanding of garment manufacturers' and consumers' desires;

extensive industry contacts and resources, and a strong fashion sense are also necessary attributes.

## TEXTILE PRINTER

### Job description

The textile printer prints a colour, pattern or design onto a fabric surface, and prints yardage, which is repeated all over the fabric or single placement prints on cut panels.

### Training/Skills

Commercial printing training plus on-the-job experience are needed. Knowledge of stencil cutting, art work, machine and hand printing techniques, screen making, colour mixing, textile designs and repeats, inks and dyes, the set-up, operation and mainteinance of automatic and manual printing machinery and basic mechanical skills as well as an understanding of curing procedures are all needed for this position.

## TEXTILE SALES

### Job description

This job involves marketing a textile product to the next level of the apparel production process. Fibre producers market their product to yarn or fabric manufacturers, greige goods producers sell to converters, and finished yard goods are sold to apparel manufacturers and fabric retailers.

### Training/Skills

Textiles, marketing or business qualifications are necessary, combined with on-the-job-training. Sound knowledge of the product and the industry; an understanding of merchandising; good people and communication skills; the ability to give informed advice to the customer when required, and a willingness to compete and strive to meet sales targets are further requirements for this job.

# APPAREL MANUFACTURING

Apparel manufacturers operate all over Australia. From the home dressmaker to high technology manufacturing giants, the processes of designing, patternmaking and garment construction remain essentially the same.

Career opportunities are numerous and varied within this field, because people with good creative, technical and organisational skills are always in demand. In the past, much of fashion production was learned on the job but, with the use of modern computerised technology (CAD and CAM), vocational training is increasingly necessary.

Certain personal attributes are common amongst those involved in fashion production. They need to be well organised, fast workers and able to work under the constant pressure of producing frequent ranges of garments within short time frames. Most employment is to be found with fashion manufacturers.

## FASHION MERCHANDISER

### Job description

A fashion merchandiser determines the current and long-range direction of a manufacturer's range and works with the designer during the development of the range to ensure that both management objectives and the needs of the market are met each season.

### Training/Skills

Fashion merchandising or design qualifications plus industry experience are needed. This job requires skills in every aspect of fashion design, production, marketing and sales. A merchandiser must understand the image and style of the label; have an awareness of current fashion trends; be able to evaluate the market, competitors' products and prices, analyse sales figures, and interpret market

research; have good industry contacts and a strong fashion sense.

## FASHION DESIGNER

### Job description

A fashion designer creates original ideas or adapts existing styles into new designs for saleable garments, sketches designs, coordinates fabrics and trims, and may patternmake and fit sample garments. Designers tend to specialise in one area, for example menswear, childrenswear, knitwear, swimwear or lingerie.

### Training/Skills

Fashion design or fashion technology training and a knowledge of patternmaking, fit, fabrics, trims and garment production are prerequisites. Creative flair and the ability to adapt current trends to suit the market place; a constant flow of ideas; sketching ability; a good understanding of design and trends in fabric, colour, line, and proportion; the ability to supervise sample room activities and an understanding of costing, selling and marketing are also necessary attributes for this career.

## PATTERNMAKER/GRADER

### Job description

A patternmaker makes the pattern from the design sketch and then grades it into different sizes ready for production.

### Training/Skills

A patternmaking course which teaches flat pattern making, draping onto a dress form, grading, garment construction and some CAM, plus on the job training are required. Employees in this position must understand fit; have a trained eye for line and proportion; be accurate with measurements and calculations and be able to interpret designer sketches.

## SAMPLE HAND

### Job description

A skilled machinist who works as part of the design team is the sample hand who sews the prototype of a new style from the designer's sketch to test the pattern, and advises on times, costs and methods for mass production.

### Training/Skills

Machinist training along with a good knowledge of garment construction techniques, to work out the best way to make up the new garment without a sample to follow, are necessary. Also required of this position is a basic understanding of patterns, manual dexterity and the ability to work quickly, neatly and accurately.

## GARMENT CUTTER

### Job description

The garment cutter prepares fabric lays, traces the patterns and cuts the fabric.

### Training/Skills

Garment cutting qualification and on-the-job training are needed. Accuracy with measurements and calculations; skill when handling cutting equipment; manual dexterity, physical fitness and good eyesight are added qualifications for this position.

## PRODUCTION MACHINIST

### Job description

A machinist who operates various types of industrial sewing machines to assemble and finish garments is the production machinist. This person may assemble garment parts or an entire garment.

### Training/Skills

Qualifications for this position include garment assembly training; knowledge of apparel construction techniques; operational knowledge of different in-dustrial machinery; neat, steady, fast and accurate work standards; good eye-sight and manual dexterity.

## PRODUCTION MANAGER

### Job description

The production manager plans and monitors the production of garments either in-house or outside to ensure that delivery dates and quality standards are met.

### Training/Skills

Training is often by entry-level position as assistant in the sampling or production departments of a clothing manufacturer. The job requires technical and organisa-tional skills; knowledge of garment assembly methods and quality control; mathematical ability for record keeping, ordering materials, inventory control and costing estimates and the ability to manage and motivate people.

## SHOWROOM SALES

### Job description

The salesperson presents the apparel range to buyers from retail outlets, writes orders, keeps records and provides follow-up service to retail accounts.

### Training/Skills

Fashion, merchandising, marketing or business training, combined with on-the-job experience are needed. A sound knowledge of the product and the in-dustry; an understanding of and ability to demonstrate current styling and design trends, fabrics and colours; an awareness of customers' needs; a willing-ness to compete and strive to meet sales targets; a personal sense of style; an out-going personality and good communica-tion skills are further requirements of the sales position.

## SALES REPRESENTATIVE

### Job description

The sales representative takes a sample range 'on the road' to sell to existing clients and to open new accounts. Travel-ling sales reps attend sales meetings before each new range is launched to learn about new fabrics, colours, detail-ing, how garments are worn, and selling points. Sales reps also give feedback on customers' needs and wants to the manufacturer.

### Training/Skills

Refer to Showroom Sales. Further attri-butes include good organisational skills; the ability to work independently and a willingness to travel and be away from home.

## FASHION AGENT

### Job description

A fashion agent is an independent sales agent who sells apparel and accessory ranges to retail customers on behalf of one or several manufacturers. This job include may fashion importing and exporting.

### Training/Skills

Refer to Showroom Sales. Business management skills are also required for this position.

# RETAILING

The retail industry offers many fashion career opportunities. Those who are most likely to succeed usually combine an interest in fashion with an enjoyment for working with people.

Retail outlets are numerous and staff turnover tends to be fairly high, so there are good entry-level opportunities for those who do not have or who are undertaking relevant training. The experience of working directly with customers is valuable for advancement into management, merchandising, buying or designing positions.

## FASHION COORDINATOR (FASHION DIRECTOR)
### Job description
Responsibility for the on-going fashion image and long-range market planning of an entire retail store or chain of stores rests with the fashion coordinator. This person also oversees and coordinates all fashion buyers, fashion departments and fashion promotions, and travels overseas regularly to monitor the international scene.

### Training/Skills
Refer to Fashion Buyer.

## FASHION BUYER
### Job description
A fashion buyer plans, buys and determines the price of fashion stock for a fashion department or store, and is responsible for the budget, sales and profits of that department or store.

### Training/Skills
Requirements include fashion, business or merchandising training. Some stores provide in-house training for floor sales staff. Retail experience; an awareness of fashion cycles, consumer needs and latest trends; an understanding of social and lifestyle trends; technical knowledge of apparel; a good head for business, details and figures; the ability to interpret trends from sales figures and to keep to a budget; confidence in making decisions; the ability to deal with suppliers and a willingness to travel are further prerequisites.

## STORE MANAGER
### Job description
The store manager oversees every aspect of a store's day-to-day operations, including buying and selling, personnel, promotional activities, inventories and finances.

### Training/Skills
This position is usually an advancement from sales or buying, with training in fashion, merchandising or business. Skills are as for sales and buying positions. Good merchandising skills, management skills and people skills are also necessary.

## FASHION SALES
### Job description
A person in this position sells fashion garments and accessories to the public.

### Training/Skills
Required training includes fashion, merchandising or retail. Some stores, particularly the larger department stores, conduct in-store training programmes. A knowledge of store merchandise and image; an awareness of current trends, coordination and fit; personal style; knowledge of store procedures, from handling cash and credit cards to packaging purchases, counting stock, re-ordering and maintaining displays; good communication skills and enjoyment in dealing with people are also needed.

## VISUAL MERCHANDISER (DISPLAY ARTIST)
### Job description
The visual merchandiser devises and executes imaginative displays in store windows and within the store and arranges merchandise to promote new fashions and attract customers.

### Training/Skills
Visual merchandising qualifications; an understanding of the use of lighting, signage, mannequins and display props; lettering, painting, drawing, basic carpentry and sewing skills; knowledge of design elements and principles, fashion trends, accessorising and merchandising and a good imagination for creative and original effects are required.

# FASHION PROMOTION

## FASHION PUBLIC RELATIONS
### Job description
A fashion public relations person communicates fashion ideas and trends to the public and develops a company's image or profile with the aim of creating demand and increasing sales for that company's product or services. This person also organises magazine editorial, media exposure, press releases, product launches, displays or exhibitions, fashion parades, advertising, educational kits and photography. Major employers of this position include fabric houses, fashion designers and manufacturers, pattern companies, fashion retailers or agents, department stores, chain stores and shopping centres, trade associations, advertising agencies, graphic design studios and in-house art departments.

### Training/Skills
Training is required in communications or journalism, along with fashion, advertising, graphic or commercial art qualifications. Also sought after is a familiarity with electronic and print media; an understanding of fashion and advertising trends; the ability to communicate ideas; good writing and people skills; an abundance of creative and original ideas; personal style, confidence, drive and selling skills.

## FASHION DIRECTOR/EDITOR

### Job description

A person in this position determines the fashion image and content of a publication by ensuring that the stories, photography, advertising and editorials are appropriate for the readership. The fashion director/editor also coordinates and plans the material, interprets trends, supervises staff, monitors the local and international industry and maintains contacts with leading designers and manufacturers. Major employers include magazines, newspapers, trade and commercial publications. Opportunities are limited.

### Training/Skills

Training is needed in fashion or journalism, along with a sharp eye for fashion and social trends; an overview of the international and local fashion scene; good administrative skills; a willingness to travel; the ability to make decisions, plan and manage staff; personal flair and sophistication.

## FASHION WRITER

### Job description

This person writes articles for trade and commercial fashion publications and general magazines and newspapers.

### Training/Skills

Fashion design or journalism training, along with the ability to write well, creatively, clearly and for the readership are needed. The writer must be good at research, analysis and the observation of fashion and society; understand the fashion industry and fashion trends and meet deadlines.

## FASHION ILLUSTRATOR

### Job description

Artistic layouts for advertising, publicity and store displays, sketches for trade publications, and technical garment drawings for manufacturers' style books are done by the fashion illustrator. Major employers include apparel manufacturers, fabric houses, retailers, advertising and promotional agencies, magazines, pattern companies. Illustrators tend to work freelance and often employ an agent to attract work. Opportunities are limited.

### Training/Skills

Commercial art, fine art or fashion training; excellent fashion illustration and rendering skills; an understanding of how clothing and fabrics perform when worn; flair with drawing figures and faces; the ability to work quickly and accurately in a variety of styles and media; an eye for detail; the ability to capture an image or mood; an understanding of fashion trends and styling for accessories, make-up and hairstyles and up-to-date knowledge of advertising styles, media and techniques are necessary requirements of this position.

## FASHION PHOTOGRAPHER

### Job description

This person photographs or films garments and accessories for advertising, promotional or educational purposes and may use fashion models or still shots, props and backgrounds to create artistic effects or strong moods, or simple catalogue style photographs which show the product clearly. Major employers include advertising agencies, retail stores, fashion publications, photographic studios and fashion houses.

### Training/Skills

Training in photography and film processing; an interest in art, visual composition, design, fashion and people; knowledge of advertising and fashion trends; the ability to interpret a style and create the appropriate mood; sound technical skills in lighting, cameras, film and darkroom procedures; knowledge of set, backdrop and prop preparation and good communication skills are needed.

## FASHION STYLIST

### Job description

A fashion stylist sources, coordinates and styles fashion apparel, accessories, props and models for photographic sessions or fashion parades and promotions. Major employers include photographers, advertising agencies, publicists, magazines, large retailers and shopping centres, fashion designers and manufacturers and film companies.

### Training/Skills

The fashion stylist needs to have fashion, photographic, journalism or advertising training or experience; good organisational skills; an awareness of fashion trends and fashion history; extensive industry contacts for products and suppliers; a creative sense of style and colour; some understanding of photography and good communication skills.

## FASHION MODEL

### Job description

A model wears garments and accessories to demonstrate how they look, fit and perform on the body, with the aim of inspiring the viewer to purchase. Major employers incude apparel manufacturers, advertising agencies, photographers, fashion or modelling agencies.

### Training/Skills

Model school training in posture, speech, hair and make-up are required of the fashion model. Fashion or sales training is useful for a post-modelling career. The ability to pose, stand, move, turn and walk well; confidence when working in a showroom in front of clients, on a runway in front of audiences, or in front of the camera; good appearance and posture, perfect grooming and health;

fashion consciousness and an outgoing personality are added requirements. A fashion model is ideally tall and slim because photographs add visual weight.

# OTHER CAREERS

## COURIER

### Job description

A couturier designs and makes original garments to order for private clients and usually employs patternmakers and machinists for garment production. Couturiers are employed by exclusive boutiques or are self-employed.

### Training/Skills

Fashion design and garment production training; a knowledge of design, colour and fabrics; couture methods of garment assembly, including tailoring, bridal work, decorative finishes, beading, embroidery and millinery; patternmaking, sewing and fitting skills; small business acumen (costing, quoting) and good communication and people skills.

## DRESSMAKER

### Job description

A dressmaker drafts patterns and makes garments to order for clients, as well as doing repairs and alterations. Major employers include boutiques, couturiers and theatre companies. Many dressmakers are self-employed.

### Training/Skills

Patternmaking and garment construction training are necessary along with skills similar to a couturier.

## FASHION FORECASTER

### Job description

A market analyst who predicts fashion directions by studying consumer tastes, local and overseas trends and shifts in supply and demand is known as a fashion forecaster. Major employers include textile producers, apparel and accessories manufacturers and major fashion retailers.

### Training/Skills

Experience and knowledge of the fashion industry, business, marketing, economics, psychology and statistics and extensive industry contacts are requirements for this position.

## FASHION OR COSTUME CURATOR

### Job description

This type of curator locates, identifies, gathers information on and stores textiles, apparel and accessories from the past, from other cultures and from contemporary designers. The curator also cleans and restores old or damaged textiles and garments, prepares exhibits and lectures for the public. Major employers of fashion curators include museums, libraries, art galleries and occasionally film and television wardrobe departments.

### Training/Skills

University training in fine arts, science, textiles, history or fashion; research skills; knowledge of clothing and fashion history; a wide range of contacts and resources; ideas for exhibitions and displays and the ability to work independently are necessary.

## COSTUME OR WARDROBE DESIGNER

### Job description

This type of designer designs costumes and accessories for a character in accordance with the historical period, culture and personality being portrayed. Many costume designers also do set and properties design. Theatres, opera and dance companies, film or television production companies, costume shops or hire companies are the major employers of these designers.

### Training/Skills

Fashion or costume training; on-the-job experience; a knowledge of lighting, trompe-l'oeil, stage and screen effects; an interest in art and design; awareness of current costuming techniques and styles; garment construction, drawing, patternmaking, draping and sewing skills; the ability to work within a budget; good materials and service resources; historical research skills; ability to work with temperamental and artistic personalities and an adaptable, innovative and resourceful nature are prerequisites for the designer.

## CHAPTER 22

# INTRODUCTION

There is no specific path to follow for a career in the fashion industry. When planning future studies, you need to decide:

- which field you want to work in,

- the qualification that will help you get there,

- the range of subjects the course covers,

- the length of the course and location of the institution.

This chapter outlines the fashion courses offered at various institutions around Australia. It is not possible to present the full list of courses and subjects offered at each institution because these change continually according to curriculum requirements, availability of resources and funding, and student demand. In most cases the highest qualification is listed, but many institutions offer summer schools, shorter or part-time courses and some also offer post-graduate courses.

All details are as accurate as possible at the time of printing, but it is advisable to contact the appropriate college or university early in the preceding year to confirm such things as availability, application dates and entry requirements.

# QUALIFICATIONS

The three main categories of qualification in fashion education are government degree courses, government non-degree (diploma or certificate) courses, and private non-degree courses.

Degree courses are offered by universities and run for three or four years. Entry requirements include the successful completion of an accredited Year 12 course of study, or equivalent, plus an interview and a portfolio of work. As well as fashion design courses, general design degrees are offered by many art courses and could be considered as an alternative path of study.

Government non-degree courses are offered by the Department of Technical and Further Education (TAFE). Diploma courses offer three-year professional vocational training covering a range of related areas and may require Year 12 qualifications for entry. An interview and portfolio may also be necessary. Associate Diploma courses are two years full-time or four years part-time, may also require Year 12 for entry and offer vocational training in specialised areas.

Advanced Certificate courses are 18 months to two years full-time, and three to four years part-time. These train in supervisory and managerial skills and usually require Year 10 qualifications. Certificate courses teach practical skills for specific trades or crafts as part of traineeships or in preparation for further training.

Short or part-time courses may also be undertaken with a Statement of Attainment presented on completion. These often require no previous experience.

Private colleges offer independent diploma, certificate and part-time courses. The courses are set by the individual colleges and, because the standards, qualifications, length of courses and fees are self-governed, they do not necessarily correspond to standards in other institutions. The private courses listed in this chapter have not been classified according to quality or suitability of tuition, so the intending student should carefully investigate the credentials and reputation of each school as well as the course content.

# SUBJECTS

As discussed in Chapter 21, the areas of expertise required by the fashion industry are design, technology, marketing, retailing and management. When selecting a course of study, you should decide which of these areas you wish to pursue and shop around to find the course with the most appropriate range of subjects. Chapter 21 gives you an idea of the skills needed for various occupations, although these vary widely depending on the specific nature of the job, the company concerned and the particular skills and preferences of the individual.

The following charts give a general listing of the courses and their subjects offered at various tertiary institutions in Australia. In these charts, G = government institution, P = private institution, C = correspondence course, and P/T = part-time course.

## NEW SOUTH WALES

| INSTITUTION | COURSE | Fashion (F)/ Textile (T) Design | Garment Technology/ Prod'n | Textile Technology | Fashion Marketing/ Retail | Fashion Management |
|---|---|---|---|---|---|---|
| **SYDNEY INSTITUTE OF TECHNOLOGY (TAFE)** | G | | | | | |
| East Sydney Campus | | | | | | |
| Arts and Media Training Division Tel. (02) 9339 8617 | | | | | | |
| Diploma of Arts, Fashion Design | | ● F | ● | | | |
| Fashion Design Certificate (P/T) | | ● F | | | | |
| Certificate of Fabric Design and Printing | | ● T | | | | |
| Fashion and Manufacturing Training Division Tel. (02) 9339 8617 | | | | | | |
| Offers a number of fashion technology courses, see below | | | ● | | | |
| Ultimo Campus Tel. (02) 9217 4300 | | | | | | |
| Certificate in Textile Products | | | | | | ● |
| Certificate in Dyeing | | | | | | ● |
| Certificate in Fabric Care | | | | | | ● |
| **SOUTHERN SYDNEY INSTITUTE (TAFE)** | G | | | | | |
| Lidcombe College Tel. (02) 9749 3300 | | | | | | |
| Advanced Certificate in Designer Knitwear | | ● T | ● | ● | | |
| Advanced Certificate in Designer Textiles | | ● T | ● | ● | | |
| Apparel Management Computer Systems | | ● F | ● | | | ● |
| CAD Apparel Operations | | | ● | | | |
| CAD Apparel Pattern Modification | | | ● | | | |

# NEW SOUTH WALES CONT'D

| INSTITUTION | COURSE | Fashion (F)/ Textile (T) Design | Garment Technology/ Prod'n | Textile Technology | Fashion Marketing/ Retail | Fashion Management |
|---|---|---|---|---|---|---|
| THE NATIONAL INSTITUTE OF DRAMATIC ART (NIDA)<br>Tel . (02) 9697 7600 | G | | | | | |
| Diploma Dramatic Art in Design (Costume,Scenery, Props) | | ● | | | | |
| Associate Diploma in Theatre Crafts (Costume) | | | ● | | | |
| OPEN COLLEGE OF TAFE<br>Tel. (02) 9318 7617 | C | | | | | |
| Advanced Certificate Commercial Needlecraft | | | | | ● | ● |
| Fashion Technology (Grading) | | | ● | | | |
| UNIVERSITY OF TECHNOLOGY, SYDNEY<br>Ultimo Campus 6<br>Tel. (02) 9330 8923 | G | | | | | |
| Bachelor of Design, Fashion and Textiles | | ● F, T | ● | | ● | ● |
| UNIVERSITY OF NEW SOUTH WALES<br>School of Fibre, Science and Technology<br>Tel. (02) 9385 4452 | G | | | | | |
| Bachelor of Science in Textile Technology | | | | ● | | |
| Bachelor of Science in Textile Management | | | | ● | ● | ● |
| CHARLES STURT UNIVERSITY<br>Tel. (069) 332 589 | G | | | | | |
| Bachelor of Visual Arts in Textiles | | ● T | | | | |
| KVB COLLEGE OF VISUAL COMMUNICATION<br>Tel. (02) 9922 4278 | P | | | | | |
| Assoc. Diploma in Fashion Design Assoc.<br>Short, Day and Evening Courses | | ● F | ● | | | |
| THE WHITEHOUSE SCHOOL<br>Tel. (02) 9267 8799 | P | | | | | |
| Diploma of Design, Fashion<br>Short and Evening Courses | | ● F | ● | | ● | ● |
| SCHOOL OF VISUAL ART PTY LTD<br>Tel. (02) 9360 4655 | P | | | | | |
| Diploma of Fashion Design | | ● F | ● | | | |

# FOR FURTHER INFORMATION

# VICTORIA

| INSTITUTION / COURSE | | Fashion (F)/ Textile (T) Design | Garment Technology/ Prod'n | Textile Technology | Fashion Marketing/ Retail | Fashion Management |
|---|---|---|---|---|---|---|
| ROYAL MELBOURNE INSTITUTE OF TECHNOLOGY (RMIT)<br>Faculty of Art and Design<br>Tel. (03) 9660 2173 | G | | | | | |
| Bachelor of Arts in Fashion (Design) | | ● F | ● | | ● | |
| Bachelor of Arts in Fashion (Design with Merchandising) | | ● F | | | ● | |
| Bachelor of Arts in Textile Design | | ● T | | ● | ● | |
| School of Design<br>Department of Visual Merchandising<br>Tel. (03) 9606 2423 | | | | | | |
| Associate Diploma of Arts in Visual Merchandising | | | | | ● | |
| MELBOURNE COLLEGE OF TEXTILES (TAFE)<br>Tel. (03) 9389 9111 | G | | | | | |
| Assoc. Diploma in Fashion Design and Production | | ● F | ● | ● | ● | ● |
| Assoc. Diploma of Arts (Australian Art Fashion) | | ● F, T | ● | | ● | |
| Advanced Certificate in Clothing Manufacture | | ● F | ● | | ● | |
| Advanced Certificate in Designer Dressmaking (Small Business) | | ● F | ● | | ● | |
| Apprenticeship in Garment Cutting | | | ● | | | |
| Assoc. Diploma of Arts (Screen Printing Design) | | ● T | | ● | | |
| Assoc. Diploma of Arts (Tapestry) | | ● T | | ● | | |
| Assoc. Diploma of Arts (Studio Textiles) | | ● T | | ● | | |
| Assoc. Diploma of Marketing and Merchandising (TCF) | | | | | ● | ● |
| Assoc. Diploma Applied Science (Textile Technology) | | | | ● | | |
| Assoc. Diploma Applied Science (Dye Chemistry) | | | | ● | | |
| M^CCABE ACADEMY OF DRESSMAKING AND DESIGN<br>Tel. (03) 9650 2737 | P | | | | | |
| Student Diploma Courses | | ● F | ● | | | |
| Professional Cutting, Designing and Patternmaking | | | ● | | | |

## FOR FURTHER INFORMATION

TAFE colleges which offer specialist courses have been listed above. Other Victorian TAFE colleges throughout metropolitan and country areas offer further Fashion Technology courses.

ACT

| INSTITUTION | COURSE | Fashion (F)/ Textile (T) Design | Garment Technology/ Prod'n | Textile Technology | Fashion Marketing/ Retail | Fashion Management |
|---|---|---|---|---|---|---|
| CANBERRA INSTITUTE OF TECHNOLOGY<br>School of Applied Arts and Design<br>TEL. (06) 207 3744 | G | | | | | |
| Diploma of Applied Arts in Fashion | | ● F | | | | |
| Advanced Certificate in Garment Production | | | ● | | | |
| Certificate Courses in Design Studies, Millinery and Aboriginal Art and Fashion | | ● F | ● | | | |
| AUSTRALIAN NATIONAL UNIVERSITY<br>Institute of the Arts, Canberra School of Art<br>Tel. (06) 249 5833 | G | | | | | |
| Master of Arts (Visual) in Textiles | | ● T | | ● | | |
| Graduate Diploma of Art (Visual) in Textiles | | ● T | | ● | | |
| Degree in Textiles | | ● T | | ● | | |
| Associate Diploma in Textiles | | ● T | | ● | | |
| UNIVERSITY OF CANBERRA<br>Faculty of Applied Science<br>National Centre for Cultural Heritage Science Studies<br>Tel. (06) 201 2369 | G | | | | | |
| Bachelor of Applied Science,<br>specialisation in Conservation of Cultural Materials | | | | ● | | |
| CANBERRA TEXTILE TRAINING CENTRE<br>Tel. (06) 281 3487 | P | | | | | |
| Pattermaking, Dressmaking, Fibre Arts<br>Creative Clothing and Tailoring | | | ● | | | |

## FOR FURTHER INFORMATION

TAFE colleges which offer specialist courses have been listed above. Other TAFE colleges throughout the ACT metropolitan and country areas offer further Fashion Technology courses.

## WESTERN AUSTRALIA

| INSTITUTION / COURSE | | Fashion (F)/ Textile (T) Design | Garment Technology/ Prod'n | Textile Technology | Fashion Marketing/ Retail | Fashion Management |
|---|---|---|---|---|---|---|
| **SOUTH EAST METROPOLITAN COLLEGE OF TAFE**<br>Bentley Campus<br>Tel. (09) 470 0660 | G | | | | | |
| Certificate of Small Business, Apparel | | | • | | | |
| Certificate of TCF (Textile, Clothing, Footwear) Retail Sales | | | | | • | |
| Certificate of TCF Retailing | | | | | • | |
| Certificate of Garment Production | | | • | | | |
| **CENTRAL METROPOLITAN COLLEGE OF TAFE**<br>West Australian School of Art and Design<br>Tel. (09) 427 2533 | G | | | | | |
| Diploma of Arts, (Fashion and Textiles Art and Design) | | • F, T | | | | |
| **CURTIN UNIVERSITY OF TECHNOLOGY**<br>School of Art<br>Tel. (09) 351 2282 | G | | | | | |
| Bachelor of Art, Major in Fibre Textiles | | • F, T | | • | | |
| **EDITH COWAN UNIVERSITY**<br>Western Australian School of Visual Art<br>Tel. (09) 370 6819 | G | | | | | |
| Bachelor of Visual Arts | | • T ,F | | | | |
| Western Australian Academy of Performing Arts<br>Tel. (09) 370 6400 | | | | | | |
| Diploma of Production and Design | | | | | | |

## FOR FURTHER INFORMATION

Western Australian TAFE colleges throughout metropolitan and country areas offer further Fashion Technology courses.

## SOUTH AUSTRALIA

| INSTITUTION | COURSE | Fashion (F)/ Textile (T) Design | Garment Technology/ Prod'n | Textile Technology | Fashion Marketing/ Retail | Fashion Management |
|---|---|---|---|---|---|---|
| DOUGLAS MAWSON INSTITUTE OF TAFE<br>Marleston Campus<br>Tel. (08) 416 6465 | G | | | | | |
| Certificate in Apparel (Small Business)<br>Advanced Certificate in Textile, Clothing & Footwear Studies<br>Advanced Certificate in Custom-made Footwear | | ●<br>●<br>● | ●<br>●<br>● | | | |

## FOR FURTHER INFORMATION

Douglas Mawson Institute of TAFE is the focus college for the Fashion Programme offered by the DETAFE in South Australia. Vocational training for the Clothing and Fashion industry is offered and linked with programmes in feeder colleges.

## QUEENSLAND

| INSTITUTION | COURSE | Fashion (F)/ Textile (T) Design | Garment Technology/ Prod'n | Textile Technology | Fashion Marketing/ Retail | Fashion Management |
|---|---|---|---|---|---|---|
| MT GRAVATT COLLEGE OF TAFE<br>Tel. (07) 3215 1300 | G | | | | | |
| Diploma of Arts (Fashion)<br>Associate Diploma of Arts (Fashion) | | ● F | ●<br>● | | ● | |
| QUEENSLAND UNIVERSITY OF TECHNOLOGY<br>School of Public Health<br>Tel. (07) 3864 3368 | G | | | | | |
| Bachelor of Applied Science, Home Economics | | ● F | | | ● | ● |
| UNIVERSITY OF SOUTHERN QUEENSLAND (USQ)<br>Tel. (076) 31 2107 | G | | | | | |
| Bachelor of Visual Arts, Major in Textiles | | ● T | | ● | | |

## FOR FURTHER INFORMATION

Queensland TAFE colleges throughout metropolitan and country areas offer further Fashion Technology courses.

## TASMANIA

| INSTITUTION / COURSE | | Fashion (F)/ Textile (T) Design | Garment Technology/ Prod'n | Textile Technology | Fashion Marketing/ Retail | Fashion Management |
|---|---|---|---|---|---|---|
| LAUNCESTON COLLEGE OF TAFE<br>Tel. (003) 36 2725<br><br>Certificate in Fashion Industry Studies<br>Certificate in Fashion Enterprise Skills<br>Professional Clothing Construction<br>Pattern-making, Garment Fitting | G | ● F | ●<br>●<br>●<br>● | ● | ● | ● |
| UNIVERSITY OF TASMANIA<br><br><br>Launceston School of Art<br>Tel. (003) 243 601<br><br>Bachelor of Fine Arts, Textiles<br>Associate Diploma in Fine Arts, Textiles | G | | | ●<br>● | | |

## FOR FURTHER INFORMATION

TAFE also offers Certificate courses in Fashion Vocational Skills. For information on courses offered at Hobart Technical College of TAFE and the North West Regional College of TAFE, contact Launceston College.

## NORTHERN TERRITORY

| INSTITUTION / COURSE | | Fashion (F)/ Textile (T) Design | Garment Technology/ Prod'n | Textile Technology | Fashion Marketing/ Retail | Fashion Management |
|---|---|---|---|---|---|---|
| NORTHERN TERRITORY UNIVERSITY<br>Tel. (08) 89 466 315<br><br>Associate Diploma of Arts (Fashion Technology)<br>Certificate in Fashion Technology | G | ● F | ●<br>● | | | |

## FOR FURTHER INFORMATION

There is no tertiary admissions centre for the NT.

NATIONAL

| INSTITUTION / COURSE | | Fashion (F)/ Textile (T) Design | Garment Technology/ Prod'n | Textile Technology | Fashion Marketing/ Retail | Fashion Management |
|---|---|---|---|---|---|---|
| STOTT'S CORRESPONDENCE COLLEGE<br>Tel. (03) 9654 6211 (and offices in each state) | P/C | | | | | |
| Dressmaking, Pattern Drafting and Fashion Design | | ● F | ● | | | |
| ICS CORRESPONDENCE SCHOOLS A/ASIA PTY LTD<br>Tel. (02) 9201 4511 or (1800) 67 4411 (Australiawide) | P/C | | | | | |
| Dressmaking | | | ● | | | |
| Patterncutting | | | ● | | | |

**CHAPTER 23**

# INTRODUCTION

Many of the organisations listed have branches or affiliated organisations in other states. In most cases, only the head or federal office has been listed and may be contacted for interstate and membership enquiries.

These details were confirmed prior to publishing, but it is possible that names, addresses or contact numbers have since changed.

# TRADE ASSOCIATIONS

ANTI-COUNTERFEIT ACTION
GROUP
John Ramsden
PO Box 268
Mooroolbark, Vic 3138
Tel. (0418) 354 430

This group was formed by local fashion manufacturers and franchise agents and works with federal authorities to eliminate the manufacturing and retailing of counterfeit clothing.

AUSTRALIAN CONFEDERATION OF
APPAREL MANUFACTURERS
65 Berry Street
North Sydney, NSW 2060
Tel. (02) 9963 7500

A federally registered body, this confederation represents the wearing apparel industry in NSW.

AUSTRALIAN COTTON
FOUNDATION LTD
729 Elizabeth Street
Waterloo, NSW 2017
Tel. (02) 9319 3677

The ACF represents all agricultural sectors of the cotton industry and provides support to growers, processors, local designers and textile and clothing manufacturers. The 'Cottonmark' and 'Cottonblend' marks symbolise quality cotton goods.

AUSTRALIAN PRODUCTION DESIGN
ASSOCIATION
PO Box 92
Paddington, NSW 2021

This association represents costume, scenery and lighting designers working in theatre, film, television and special events.

THE INTERNATIONAL WOOL
SECRETARIAT AUSTRALIA BRANCH
Wool House
369 Royal Parade
Parkville, Vic 3052
Tel. (03) 9341 9111

The IWS Australia Branch provides technical and marketing services to textile and garment manufacturers, and campaigns for the increased use of wool and the Woolmark. The Australia Branch works with the head office and inter-

national branches of the IWS to promote the qualities of wool locally and internationally. It assists in the development of new woollen products, sets standards and establishes testing procedures. On the fashion level, the IWS offers forecasting services, trade workshops, fabric sourcing, advertising, consumer publications, publicity and market research. The 'Woolmark' and 'Woolblendmark' are internationally recognised symbols of high quality woollen or woolblend products.

DESIGN INSTITUTE OF AUSTRALIA
The Design Institute of Australia promotes excellence in design and public awareness of the role of designers. The Institute assists the professional development of members through newsletters, lectures and seminars, and is involved in design education. It also represents the views of Australian designers to governments, and internationally. The Design Institute can be contacted at:

Employers House
50 Burwood Road
Hawthorn, Vic 3122
Tel.   (03) 9819 6837
       (1800) 331 477

## THE FASHION GROUP
INTERNATIONAL INC

The Fashion Group International® of
Sydney Inc
PO Box A2068
Sydney South
NSW 2000
Tel. (02) 9281 3601

The Fashion Group International of
Melbourne
PO Box 372
Richmond, Vic 3121

Founded in New York in 1930 to serve
the need of executive women in fashion
and related industries to exchange ideas
and resources in the fashion business,
the Fashion Group International Inc. is
one of the largest fashion networking
organisations in the world, with 7000
members in ten countries. The Group
provides information and assistance to
members through the FG Fashion Group
Bulletin from New York, the local newsletter, industry reports, slide presentations
of European designer collections, conferences, and overseas contacts for
business travellers. It also offers career
advice, workshops and scholarships to
fashion students. Membership is open
to women in management positions
with a record of achievement in the
fashion industry.

## FASHION INDUSTRIES OF
AUSTRALIA

Merged with the Textile Clothing and
Footwear Council of Australia in 1995.
Refer to the entry for the Council of
Textiles and Fashion Industries of
Australia Ltd.

## NATIONAL RETAIL AND
WHOLESALE INDUSTRY TRAINING
COUNCIL LTD

This training council co-ordinates training in sales, merchandising and management for people working in retail, including fashion retail, and is located at:

PO Box 405
Suite 2E, Level 2, 9 Burwood Rd
Burwood, NSW 2134
Tel. (02) 745 3122

## RETAILERS COUNCIL OF
AUSTRALIA

The Retailers Council of Australia represents non-food retailers (including
fashion retailers). It initiates and influences policies which protect, promote and advance the profitability and
competitiveness of the retailing industry.
State associations are represented on
the Council's Board. The Council can
be found at:

Level 2, 20 York Street
Sydney, NSW 2000
Tel. (02) 290 3766

## SILK CORPORATION OF AUSTRALIA

The Silk Corporation provides technical
advice and information and promotes
the use of Chinese silk.

8 Little Queen Street
Chippendale, NSW 2008
Tel. (02) 9319 2266

## SOCIETY FOR RESPONSIBLE DESIGN

The aim of the SRD is to work towards a
sustainable future through environ-
mentally and socially responsible design
practices in all industries, including
fashion. The society holds regular meetings, conducts lectures, organises exhibitions and issues a newsletter entitled
'Loose Leaves'. Membership is open
to all, particularly designers interested
in assuming responsibility for the
environment.

PO Box 73
Rozelle, NSW 2039
Tel. (02) 9564 0721

## STANDARDS ASSOCIATION OF
AUSTRALIA

The Standards Association prepares,
publishes and maintains Australian standards for Australian industry and the

public. A list of Australian Standards
which relate specifically to Textiles and
Clothing is available from Standards
Australia offices. Contact:

1 The Crescent
Homebush, NSW 2140
Tel. (02) 9746 4600

## COUNCIL OF TEXTILES AND
FASHION INDUSTRIES OF
AUSTRALIA LTD

Formerly the Textile Clothing and Footwear Council of Australia, the name was
changed in 1995 following a merger
with Fashion Industries of Australia Ltd.
The Council specialises in liaison with
government for the development and
delivery of industry policies and
programmes. The Australian Fashion
Awards are a major promotional event.
A range of membership services are
available. Membership includes TCF
manufacturers from every state, and
other industry associations.

Level 4, 380 St Kilda Road
Melbourne, Vic 3004
Tel. (03) 9698 4460

## AUSTRALIAN LIGHT
MANUFACTURING INDUSTRY
TRAINING ADVISORY BOARD

(Formerly Australian Textile Clothing and
Footwear Industry Training Board.) With
employer and union representatives, the
main function of the Industry Training
Advisory Board is to advise state and
federal governments on the training
needs of TCF industries, and to develop
and accredit training resources and
programmes to competency standards.
Each state has a representative training
board or council.

First Floor, 132–138 Leicester Street
Carlton, Vic 3053
Tel. (03) 9348 1311

## TEXTILE CLOTHING AND
FOOTWEAR UNION OF AUSTRALIA

Formerly Amalgamated Footwear and
Textile Workers' Union and Clothing and

Allied Trades Union of Australia, this Union protects and advances the interests of TCF industry workers through constant contact with members and employers. It also lobbies government on matters of concern to members.

132 Leicester Street
Carlton, Vic 3053
Tel. (03) 9347 2766

## TEXTILE DISTRIBUTORS ASSOCIATION

This national body represents distributors who supply textiles to clothing, soft furnishing, upholstery and other manufacturers and/or retailers.

GPO Box 1429
Canberra, ACT 2601
Tel. (06) 247 0582

## THE TEXTILE INSTITUTE

The Textile Institute is an international association covering some 100 countries. It spans every sector and occupation relating to fibres and their uses, including fashion. Its mission is to promote professionalism and provide a global network for the long-term development of the industry. Contact:

Mike Hyland (NSW Section)
Tel. (02) 832 1666

## TEXTILE PRINTERS ASSOCIATION (VICTORIA)

The Treasurer
2–12 St Phillip Street
Brunswick, Vic 3057
Tel. (03) 9388 0322

The TPA (Vic) is a common-interest body able to set industry standards for its members. It provides a communication link between suppliers and printers, and acts as a forum for industry discussion, problem-solving and opportunity-seeking.

## TEXTILE SCREEN PRINTING ORGANISATION INC.

Addresses the needs of textile screen printers, including printers of T-shirts and garments, continuous fabrics, non-wearable textiles, piece printers, students, teachers and others.

PO Box 566
Ashmore City, Qld 4214
Tel. (07) 5591 3977

# CHAMBERS OF MANUFACTURERS/ CONFEDERATIONS OF INDUSTRIES

## CHAMBER OF MANUFACTURERS OF NSW

65 Berry Street
North Sydney, NSW 2060
Tel. (02) 9957 5792

## AUSTRALIAN CHAMBER OF MANUFACTURERS

380 St Kilda Road
Melbourne, Vic 3004
Tel. (03) 9698 4111

## TASMANIAN CHAMBER OF COMMERCE AND INDUSTRY

30 Burnett Street
North Hobart, Tas 7000
Tel. (002) 34 5933

## SOUTH AUSTRALIAN EMPLOYERS CHAMBER OF COMMERCE AND INDUSTRY INC.

136 Greenhill Road
Unley, SA 5061
Tel. (08) 8373 1422

## CHAMBER OF COMMERCE AND INDUSTRY OF WESTERN AUSTRALIA

190 Hay Street
East Perth, WA 6004
Tel. (09) 365 7555

## QUEENSLAND CHAMBER OF COMMERCE AND INDUSTRY

Industry House
375 Wickham Terrace
Brisbane, Qld 4000
Tel. (07) 3831 1699

## NORTHERN TERRITORY CHAMBER OF COMMERCE AND INDUSTRY INC.

5/2 Shepherd Street
Darwin, NT 0800
Tel. (089) 89 81 5755

These independent state bodies provide assistance to manufacturers (including apparel manufacturers) on industrial relations matters, including pay rates, award conditions, leave entitlements etc.

# CRAFT ORGANISATIONS, GUILDS, GALLERIES AND COLLECTIONS

## ART GALLERY OF SOUTH AUSTRALIA

North Terrace
Adelaide, SA 5000
Tel. (08) 8207 7000

This gallery houses a collection of approximately 300 items, featuring Australian, European and Asian costume, textiles and fashion accessories.

## AUSTRALIAN COSTUME AND TEXTILE SOCIETY INC.

PO Box 277
Woollahra, NSW 2025
Tel. (02) 9712 1752 (Ms Rosalind Rennie)

Meetings and lectures held by this Society cover the historical, contemporary, ethnic and creative aspects of costume and textiles.

## AUSTRALIAN LACE GUILD

The Australian Lace Guild was founded in 1979 to exchange information and promote lace and lace-making as a craft throughout Australia. Activities include the co-ordination of proficiency tests, production of a national quarterly maga-

THE FASHION DESIGN MANUAL

zine, state newsletters for local activities and regular meetings and classes. Contacts are listed in the telephone directory in capital cities under Lace Guild or Crafts Council.

## NATIONAL GALLERY OF AUSTRALIA
GPO Box 1150
Canberra, ACT 2601
Tel. (06) 240 6411

The NGA has several costume and textile collections. The Australian Decorative Arts collection includes 'art clothes' and textiles including work by Jenny Kee, Linda Jackson and Peter Tully, as well as a comprehensive collection of theatre designs. The International Decorative Arts collection includes both Fashion and Theatre Arts. The Asian Art collection has extensive holdings of textiles, mainly of Indian and South-east Asian origin.

## AUSTRALIAN WAR MEMORIAL
Curator of Military Heraldry
GPO Box 345
Canberra, ACT 2601
Tel. (06) 243 4211

The Military Heraldry Collection contains an extensive selection of military uniforms, clothing, craft and textiles.

## AUSTRALIAN BATIK AND SURFACE DESIGN ASSOCIATION INC.
The Secretary
PO Box 43
Gladesville, NSW 2111

This association exists for artists who work with dyes, pigments and other forms of fabric and fibre decoration.

## THE COLOUR SOCIETY OF AUSTRALIA INC.
PO Box 272
Artarmon, NSW 2064
Tel. (02) 9950 4530

The Colour Society provides a forum for the discussion of colour in all fields, promotes interest and research into all

aspects of colour, and advises on colour education. A national conference is held every two years with guest speakers from Australia and overseas. State divisions also hold regular meetings. The Society provides a Colour Information Network which lists member expertise and publishes 'Spectrum', a journal covering colour-related events and developments. The membership is drawn from people whose work and interests involve colour.

## CRAFTS AUSTRALIA
Level 5, 414–418 Elizabeth Street
Surry Hills, NSW 2010
Tel. (02) 9211 1445

Crafts Australia represents, develops and promotes the crafts industry nationally and internationally. A national computerised database of craft information, known as Craftline, provides information about any aspect of the crafts in Australia. Each state has its own Crafts Council dealing with local matters.

## THE EMBROIDERERS GUILD OF NSW INC.
76 Queen Street
Concord West, NSW 2138
Tel. (02) 9743 2501

The Guild holds regular meetings, conducts classes and workshops, and has extensive resources including a library, a collection of costume, lace and embroidery items and a slide collection. Guilds exist in all Australian states.

## THE KNITTERS GUILD OF NSW INC.
The Secretary
PO Box 70
Bexley South, NSW 2207
Tel. (02) 9570 3026

## HANDKNITTERS GUILD INC.
The Secretary
40 Story Street
Parkville, Vic 3052
Tel. (03) 9347 6037

The knitters' guilds foster and promote the craft of hand-knitting. They hold regular meetings, exhibitions and workshops and have resources including libraries and collections of modern and antique knitting.

## HAND WEAVERS AND SPINNERS GUILD OF NSW INC.
PO Box 653
Burwood, NSW 2134
Tel. (02) 9747 2083

## HAND WEAVERS AND SPINNERS GUILD OF VICTORIA
3 Blackwood Street
North Melbourne, Vic 3051

These guilds bring together people who are interested in handweaving, spinning, dyeing and associated textile crafts.

## NATIONAL GALLERY OF VICTORIA
180 St Kilda Road
Melbourne, Vic 3004
Tel. (03) 9208 0222

The Costume and Textile Collection contains an estimated 20 000 pieces and represents international and Australian items from antiquity to the present day.

## THE NATIONAL TRUST
Costume collections are held by most state branches of the National Trust. Refer to your local telephone directory for contact addresses and telephone numbers.

## THE POWERHOUSE MUSEUM
PO Box K346
Haymarket, NSW 2000
Tel. (02) 9217 0111

The Clothing and Textiles Collections have around 14 000 clothing accessories and textile articles from around the world, dating from the 4th century to the present day.

TECHNOLOGY EDUCATORS
ASSOCIATION
PO Box 71
Gordon, NSW 2072
Tel. (02) 9499 2259

The Technology Educators Association provides support, information and resources mainly for those involved in secondary school textiles education nationally. The 'TEA News', a journal covering textiles, design and technology, is issued ten times per year.

Australian fashion magazines readily available to the public from newsagents or through subscription include: *Mode, Vogue, Elle, Studio* and *Marie Claire.*

## INDUSTRY PUBLICATIONS

### APPAREL INDUSTRY
Yaffa Publishing Group Pty Ltd
17 Bellevue Street
Surry Hills, NSW 2010
Tel. (02) 9281 2333

This is a national magazine for fashion manufacturers which covers recent events, updates, new technology, trade fairs and issues concerning the industry. One issue per year includes a retail apparel buyers' guide.

### AUSTRALASIAN SCREENPRINTER
Cygnet Publications Pty Ltd
PO Box 1389
West Perth, WA 6872
Tel. (08) 9322 1168

This industry journal is available by subscription and is published six times per year. Its readers are screen printers and screen makers throughout Australasia, 65 per cent of whom are directly concerned with fabric and textile screen printing.

### AUSTRALASIAN TEXTILES
PO Box 286
Belmont, Vic 3216
Tel. (03) 52 55 2699

This is the official journal of the Society of Dyers and Colourists and several other textile societies. Services all aspects of

the Australian and New Zealand textile industries. Six issues per annum, by subscription, it includes the Australasian Textiles Index.

### AUSTRALASIAN TEXTILES INDEX
(See above address)

Updated annually, this lists Australian textile manufacturers and suppliers to the industry. It can be purchased separately or with the Australian Textiles subscription.

### AUSTRALIAN FASHION DIRECTORY
Nicholson Media Group
PO Box 206
Hawksburn, Vic. 3142
Tel. (03) 9826 8448

A NSW and Victorian based buying guide to fashion labels. Updated editions released annually in June/July. $10.

### AUSTRALIAN STANDARDS FOR TEXTILES AND CLOTHING
1 The Crescent
Homebush, NSW 2140
Tel. (02) 746 4700

Lists of standards are available from Standards Australia offices. (See Chapter 23.)

### AUSTRALIAN TEXTILE, FOOTWEAR AND APPAREL
Morescope Publishing Pty Ltd
PO Box 93
Camberwell, Vic 3124
Tel. (03) 9882 9922 or (008) 801 952

Australian Textile, Footwear and Apparel (formerly Textile and Apparel Index) is compiled in association with the TCF Council and is a complete reference to all aspects of the Australian textiles and apparel industries.

### AUSTRALIAN TEXTILE RESOURCES
25 Baxter Street
Fortitude Valley, Qld 4006
Tel. (07) 3854 1664

A database service providing information on fabric sources Australiawide and overseas, this system links subscribers wishing to locate fabric with suppliers who hold required stocks, and vice versa.

### CARE LABELLING
Available from offices of Federal Bureau of Consumer Affairs in each state, as listed in local telephone directories. This free booklet provides information about textile care labelling requirements and usage.

### MANAGEMENT MANUAL FOR THE AUSTRALIAN CLOTHING INDUSTRY
University Partnerships
University of New England
Armidale, NSW 2351
Tel. (067) 711 097

Written by Harold Scruby and Ray Day and produced by University Partnerships, this is an 'industry specific' manual which covers the major areas involved in managing a small to medium sized clothing company in Australia today. Topics include business planning, finance, marketing, operating and sources of assistance.

## RAGTRADER
Thomson's Business Publications
47 Chippen Street
Chippendale, NSW 2008
Tel. (02) 9699 2411

This is a national fashion industry magazine. One issue each year contains the Ragtrader Label Directory.

## SELLERS AND SOURCES
275 Coppin Street
Richmond, Vic 3121
Tel. (03) 9428 5729

An illustrated monthly fashion merchandise report which reviews Australian, European and American fashion market trends in apparel and accessories, this magazine is available by subscription only.

## AUSTRALIAN SUPPLIERS OF LOCAL AND OVERSEAS PUBLICATIONS

### EUROPRESS DISTRIBUTORS
Head Office
123 McEvoy Street
Alexandria, NSW 2015
Tel. (02) 9698 4922

Distributes international fashion magazines and publications Australiawide.

### FASHION FORECAST SERVICES
6/93 Victoria Road
Hawthorne, Vic 3122
(03) 9813 3111

Fashion forecast reports and international magazines.

### PUBLISHING AND PRODUCTION PROJECTS
Edgecliff Mews
19/201 New South Head Road
Edgecliff, NSW 2027
Tel. (02) 9326 2501

Producers of local material and importers of overseas publications relating to the garment industry, 'Publishing and Production Projects' produces the following books:

### TRIED AND TESTED
(Written by David Jerram and Ronnie Hoffman)
A basic guide to quality control for the apparel industry.

### HANGING BY A THREAD
(Written by David Jerram and Ronnie Hoffman)
A basic guide to apparel sewing threads.

### A CUT ABOVE THE REST
(Written by Rose Samuels and Ronnie Hoffman)
A basic guide to apparel marker-making and cutting.

## RAGTRADE RESOURCES PTY LTD
Resource House
36 The Avenue
Newport, NSW 2106
Tel. (02) 9907 9474
Melbourne Office (03) 9886 1165

Services to the textile, apparel and fashion industries, including fashion videos, magazines, mail order catalogues, retail and prediction reports, overseas sample shopping services and computerised design systems.

## TOWER BOOKS
PO Box 213
Brookvale, NSW 2100

Tower Books are importers and Australia-wide distributors for the following Japanese fashion magazines:
Gap Women's Collections
Gap Men's Collections
Gap Haute Couture
Gap Fashion Show
Fashion News
Prêt-à-Porter Collections

## AUDIO-VISUAL MATERIAL

### VIDEO EDUCATION AUSTRALASIA
111a Mitchell Street
Bendigo, Vic 3550
Tel. (03) 54 42 2433 or (1800) 034282

Local and overseas videos produced and distributed by Video Education Australasia. Australian-produced titles include:
Manufacturing Clothing in Australia
Young Australian Designers
Wool, A Fabulous Fibre
Designing Retail Fashion in Australia
Marketing Sportsgirl
Mambo — Wearing the Image
The Art of Ken Done
Computers in Fashion
Designing to Please

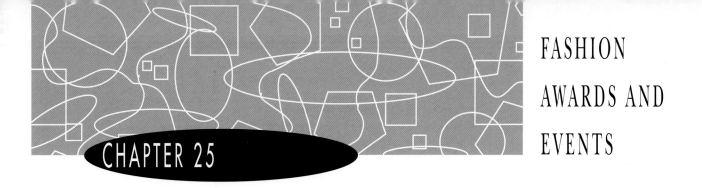

CHAPTER 25

# INTRODUCTION

This chapter covers the awards currently being offered to students and others in the fashion industry. Some of the awards mentioned here are new, and may not continue year after year. Others, like the Gown of the Year and the Australian Fashion Awards, have been running for decades. So keep your eyes and ears open for opportunities to promote yourself and your talents by becoming involved in as many of these as you can.

This information was accurate at the time of printing, but dates, places, conditions and prizes may change, and should be confirmed if you intend applying. Names and addresses of organisations not listed here can be found in Chapter 23.

# INDUSTRY AND GENERAL AWARDS

## AUSTRALIAN FASHION AWARDS

Presented by the Fashion Industries of Australia, the Australian Fashion Awards aim to promote Australian fashion and the fashion industry to consumers, retailers, the government and internationally.

Professional designers and design houses are eligible to enter. The categories are set each year, and the selection of finalists is done by panels of experts from fashion media and independent consultants. The awards presentation and parade is held annually.

The Australian Fashion Awards Statue, (commonly known as the 'Oscars' of the fashion industry) is awarded. To apply, contact the FIA.

## AUSTRALIAN INDUSTRY'S HALL OF FAME

Presented by the FIA. Upon winning five Australian Fashion Awards, a designer becomes a member of the Hall of Fame. In 20 years, over 200 Awards have been presented and there are 18 Hall of Fame members. They include:

| | |
|---|---|
| Sportscraft | 1976 |
| Prue Acton | 1978 |
| Trent Nathan | 1979 |
| George Gross | 1979 |
| Brian Rochford | 1980 |
| Covers | 1982 |
| Country Road | 1982 |
| Jag | 1984 |
| Sally Browne | 1985 |
| Perri Cutten | 1988 |
| Adele Palmer | 1988 |
| Weiss | 1988 |
| Seekers Australia | 1994 |

## THE AUSTRALIAN GOWN OF THE YEAR

Launched in 1953 and presented by The Mannequins and Models Guild, a division of the Shop, Distributive and Allied Employees' Association, the competition aims to discover and promote Australian fashion design talent at all levels.

Established designers, students and amateur designers are eligible to enter. There are eight sections, covering all categories of women's outerwear. The designer of The Gown of the Year is awarded a prize of $5000 and a trophy. Cash, goods and/or trips are also awarded for each section.

Entries close in June, and a Gala Presentation Evening is held in July. A selection of 60 entries goes on tour and is shown in over 100 parades around Australia, to the benefit of many charities.

For further information, contact:

The Mannequins and Models Division
of the SDA
5th Floor, 53 Queen Street
Melbourne, Vic 3000
Tel. (03) 9629 2299

## DESIGN FX — THE AUSTRALIAN T-SHIRT AND FABRIC SCREEN PRINTING AWARDS

Administered by the Textile Screen Printing Organisation, this award aims to encourage and reward original designs and to promote textile screen printing.

The awards are open to screen printers and artists. Categories are T-Shirt/Individual Prints, and Fabric Designs, each with a variety of sub-groups, including student work. Entries close in September and the presentation of $5000 worth of prizes is made at a gala event in November.

## FASHION OF THE YEAR — THE POWERHOUSE MUSEUM SYDNEY MORNING HERALD

Inaugurated in 1991 by the Powerhouse Museum and The Sydney Morning Herald, the Fashion of the Year project is an annual selection of contemporary fashion to be acquired for the museum's collection of Decorative Arts and Design. The selection represents significant fashion themes chosen from Australian and international designers.

Applications from designers are not accepted. Selection is made by a panel of fashion editors and museum staff. The garments and accessories of mainstream, as well as small independent designers, are considered.

There are two categories — fashions designed and made in Australia, and those purchased from an international fashion house. The winners are displayed in the 'Style' exhibition at the Powerhouse Museum for a year.

## GOLDEN GOWN AWARDS

Open to all dressmakers and designers, these awards show-case the work of rising professional and amateur designers and dressmakers.

Categories include bridal, daywear and formal evening wear. Total prizes include cash, scholarships and goods valued at over $15 000. Applications close late March/early April and the presentation evening is held late May. Contact:

The Secretary, Golden Gown Awards Inc.
PO Box 15
Wagga Wagga, NSW 2650
Tel. (069) 212 444

## 'NESCAFÉ BIG BREAK' AWARDS

Sponsored by NESCAFÉ, this award provides backing for young Australians to fulfill their ambitions and to contribute to Australian business, culture and community life.

Awards are open to applicants aged 16 to 21 years, and any idea or project can be submitted. Although not aimed exclusively at fashion, past winning ideas have included a skiwear label, a fashion label and a sewing engineering business.

Eight grants of $20 000 each are awarded to young Australians. The awards are heavily promoted, and applicants should telephone 008 630 630 for information.

## NORTHERN TERRITORY FASHION AWARDS

These awards are open to all designers, Australiawide, and are sponsored by the Northern Territory Government, Department of Industries and Development and local business. Their aim is to promote fashion and fashion designers in the Northern Territory. The categories

are set each year. Prizes are cash awards totalling approximately $10 000. Contact:

The President
PO Box 155
Parap, NT 0820

## RAQ FASHION DESIGN AWARDS

These awards are sponsored by the Retailers Association of Queensland to promote Queensland fashion design, manufacture and fashion retail industry. All Queensland fashion designers are eligible.

Categories include Swimwear, Resort, Designer Day Dressing, Active Sportswear, Menswear, Bridal, PM Wear, Childrenswear, Innovative and Student. The winner is awarded an overseas study tour.

The awards are staged in October and applications must be forwarded by August to:

RAQ Fashion Design Awards
PO Box 191
Red Hill, Qld 4059
Tel. (07) 3367 1716

## TOP OF THE CLASS AWARD

This award is presented by the FIA. Entry is open to students from universities, technical colleges and government-accredited private fashion design schools. The Australian Fashion Awards Statue is presented, plus two months' experience with each of six of Australia's leading fashion companies, totalling one year's salaried work.

## WEARABLE WOOL AWARDS

Held in Armidale, these awards are open to all designers and dressmakers with the aim of promoting the use of woollen fabrics and fibres.

The categories are Handcrafted Fibres, Dressmaking, Secondary School and Open Design, plus Student Encouragement Award and a Special Award of $4000 and trophy. Total prizes value over $21 000. Entries close March, and the presentation night is in late April/May. Contact:

Wearable Wool Awards
PO Box 812
Armidale, NSW 2350
Tel. (067) 728 974

## WESTERN AUSTRALIAN FASHION AWARDS

These awards are presented by the WA Fashion Manufacturers Association Inc., with the aim of broadening consumer awareness of the excellence of the Western Australian fashion industry.

The awards are open to all Western Australian designers, and the garments must be produced and retail in WA. The winning designers are awarded a trophy. The awards are staged in October and applications must be forwarded by September to the Western Australian Fashion Manufacturers Association Inc.

# STUDENT AWARDS

These awards are offered to students Australiawide, statewide, or to a group of selected colleges. The smaller awards offered to individual colleges are too numerous to list.

## ANNITA KEATING FASHION SCHOLARSHIP

This scholarship was launched in 1994 as a joint initiative of the FIA, The Whitehouse School and the KLM Royal Dutch Airlines. It is open to Australian students between the ages of 17 and 25 who have successfully completed Year 12, or who have relevant work experience in the industry. Entrants must analyse current

fashion trends and design a range of outfits around a fashion theme.

The scholarship provides a two-year full time Associate Diploma of Design in Fashion at The Whitehouse School, Sydney, and an overseas study tour of the European fashion capitals with KLM Royal Dutch Airlines. It is valued in excess of $40 000.

Entries close in August, semi-finalists are notified by mail in October, and the winner is announced at The Whitehouse School graduation parade in October. Application forms are available from The Whitehouse School or the FIA.

## DU PONT LYCRA® STUDENT FASHION DESIGN AWARDS

Held by Du Pont Australia Ltd since 1981 to provide an opportunity for students to show their work to the fashion industry, these awards are open to third and final year full-time fashion design students from invited colleges nationally. Prize money and certificates are awarded to the winning designers.

Entry forms and details are sent to the competing colleges in February and judging is held in September. An awards evening and parade is held in Sydney in October.

## SMIRNOFF INTERNATIONAL FASHION AWARDS

The Smirnoff International Fashion Awards were held for the first time in Australia in 1991, although they have been held overseas for eight years. They provide an opportunity for Australian students to compete against fashion students from around the world. Final year students studying at approved fashion design colleges around Australia are eligible.

Several themes are set by Smirnoff. The national winner wins a trip overseas for the international judging. The international winner is awarded the Smirnoff

statuette plus a sizeable cash grant ($US10 000 in 1994).

National judging is in August, and the international parade and judging is held in October. For further enquiries contact the college where you are studying or:

Smirnoff Brand Manager
Swift and Moore Pty Ltd
10–28 Biloela Street
Villawood, NSW 2163
Tel. (02) 724 6222

## THE YOUNG ITALO-AUSTRALIAN FASHION SCHOLARSHIP AWARDS

These awards are held in November and are organised by The Young Italo-Australians. They are open to final year students, or those who have completed a recognised fashion course, with the aim of promoting Italian culture and fashion and to benefit young Australians.

A new theme is set each year. Thirty finalists are selected from the initial entries and the winner is awarded $6000 fashion tuition at the Accademia Italiana della Moda in Florence and a return flight to Italy. Contact:

The Young Italo-Australians
6/4 Montrose Road
Abbotsford, NSW 2046
Tel. (02) 569 4522

# FASHION EVENTS

Locations and dates are correct at the time of printing but, because they may change from year to year, contact names and numbers are given for confirmation.

## AUSTEX

The Australian International Textiles Clothing and Footwear Machinery and Services Exhibition is a trade exhibition of machinery, accessories, fabrics and threads, plus conferences and seminars. It is held in Melbourne every two years during July. Contact:

Exhibitor Services Pty Ltd
Tel. (02) 872 6255

## AUSTRALIAN CRAFT SHOW

This show presents the work of Australian craftspeople. Textile crafts, hand-made fashion items, painted, dyed, printed and woven garments and other craft items are shown. Annual events are scheduled for November in Sydney and Canberra. Contact:

June Bibby
Tel. (02) 427 6120

## AUSTRALIAN FASHION FRAMEWORK

The Australian Fashion Framework team undertakes a world tour each year, putting on shows that promote Australian design and fashion. This is a non-government, non-profit, self-funded organisation, operating since 1987. All proceeds from the overseas Fashion Shows are given to recognised charities in the countries where the shows are held. Contact:

John Scriven, Director
10 Royalist Road
Mosman, NSW 2090
Tel. (02) 9953 1598

## FASHION FORECAST

These are audio-visual presentations of the European and American Collections held by the Fashion Group in February and June each year. Showings are in Melbourne and Sydney, and members and non-members of the Fashion Group may attend.

## FRONTLINE TRADE FAIR AND NATIONAL MERCHANDISE CONFERENCE

Frontline Stores Australia Ltd is a national retail buying group based in Melbourne. Their product range includes men's, women's and children's apparel, homewares, footwear, manchester, outdoor apparel and equipment, dress fabrics and soft furnishings.

In April and September each year, a national trade fair and promotional merchandise conference is held in Melbourne. These shows are closed to the public and admission is permitted only to member retailers and preferred suppliers. Contact:

Frontline
PO Box 404
Canterbury, Vic 3126
Tel. (03) 9888 5766

## GARMENT TECH

Embroidery, Screen Printing and Machinery Trade Fair. Held in the AJC Function Centre, Randwick Racecourse, Sydney, annually in July. Contact:

Exhibitor Services Pty Ltd
Tel. (02) 872 6255

## INTERNATIONAL FASHION JEWELLERY AND ACCESSORIES FAIR

Held annually in Sydney (February and September), Melbourne (February and August) and Brisbane (July), entry is restricted to trade buyers only. Contact:

Thomson World Trade Exhibitions
Level 9, 140 William Street
East Sydney, NSW 2011
Tel. (02) 357 7555

## MENSLAND TRADE FAIR AND CONVENTION

The trade fair for this national retail buying group is held in Moonee Valley (Melbourne) each year in March and September. This convention is closed to the public and admission is only for member retailers and preferred suppliers. Contact:

Mensland
Tel. (03) 9429 8266

## POWERHOUSE STUDENT FASHION AWARDS EXHIBITION

The Student Fashion Awards is an annual exhibition which showcases the work of some of Australia's most lively and innovative young fashion design students. The work on show includes garments created for some of the major fashion industry awards, as well as outfits from the Student Designer of the Year from the fashion design courses at the University of Technology, Sydney, the Sydney Institute of Technology Fashion Design Studio and The Whitehouse School. The exhibition is held annually at the Powerhouse Museum.

## STITCHES AND CRAFT SHOW

The latest techniques in home sewing, needlecraft, hand knitting, and handcrafts are displayed at annual events scheduled throughout the year in Sydney, Melbourne and Brisbane, featuring technical workshops and open to trade and the public. Contact Thomson World Trade Exhibitions (see above).

## SYDNEY BRIDAL EXPO

Held at the Sydney Convention and Exhibition Centre, Darling Harbour, in April, the expo features the latest bridal fashions and covers all aspects of the wedding day. Contact:

Graham Stroud Events and Marketing Pty Ltd
Tel. (02) 583 1137

# INDEX